W9-AGA-221

Rethinking Nationalism and Ethnicity

Nationalism and Internationalism

General Editor

Mortimer Sellers
(University of Baltimore)

Editorial Board

This series discusses issues of cultural identity, and the proper role of national and ethnic affiliations in the world's structures of legal and political power.

ISSN: 1360-9335

Rethinking Nationalism and Ethnicity

The Struggle for Meaning and Order in Europe

Edited by
Hans-Rudolf Wicker

Oxford • New York

First published in 1997 by
Berg
Editorial offices:
150 Cowley Road, Oxford, OX4 1JJ, UK
70 Washington Square South, New York, NY 10012, USA

Berg is an imprint of Oxford International Publishers Ltd.

Library of Congress Cataloging-in-Publication Data

A catalogue record for this book is available from the Library of Congress.

British Library Cataloguing-in-Publication Data

A catalogue record for this book is available from the British Library.

ISBN 1 85973 926 1 (Cloth)
       1 85973 931 8 (Paper)

Typeset by JS Typesetting, Wellingborough, Northants.
Printed in the United Kingdom by WBC Book Manufacturers, Bridgend, Mid Glamorgan.

Contents

Contents

Acknowledgements

Conducted between 1992 and 1995, COST-A2, a research project dedicated to 'Migration: Europe's Integration and the Labour Force', was part of the European Commission's programme for 'European Co-Operation in the Field of Scientific and Technical Research (COST)'. With twenty European countries participating, COST-A2 was one of the first social sciences projects ever to be carried out in the context of the COST programme, which is otherwise dominated by issues of technology and the natural sciences. The project's pioneering role was reflected in the difficulties faced by the Management Committee of COST-A2 – of which the editor himself was a member – in its efforts to conceive, design, co-ordinate, and implement the project. Concepts, channels of information, and trans-national research networks had to be developed from scratch before the actual project could be launched successfully.

Despite certain difficulties of implementation, the research policy impulse provided by the European Commission eventually produced a considerable range of interesting results. The most visible sign of the success of COST-A2 were the various interdisciplinary workshops and conferences organized in many European countries, during which a wide range of research findings were exchanged, discussed, and finalized for publication. One of these conferences took place from 2–4 March 1995, at the University of Berne. The very broad theme of the conference – 'Nationalism and Ethnicity' – was broken down into the following three sub-topics: 'Ethnicity and the Construction of Identity', 'Ethnicity and the Nation-State', and 'Ethnicity and Nationalism in Eastern Europe'. Thirty speakers presented their papers, and their findings were deepened in the lively discussions that ensued. With the publication of the present volume, some of these papers are now available to a wider audience. Considering the highly topical nature of the articles in this collection with respect to both politics and the social sciences, we feel quite certain that this book will contribute to a more informed discussion of the issues surrounding nationalism, ethnicity and multiculturalism.

We want to express our gratitude to all those individuals and institutions who, in one way or another, helped to bring about the Berne conference and the present publication. In particular, we thank the Commission of the European Union, the Swiss National Science Foundation, the Office Fédéral de l'Education (Berne), and the Max and Elsa Beer-Brawand Foundation (Berne) for the financial support of the Berne conference. Special thanks go to the Office Fédéral de l'Education for its generous financial support of pre-publication work and for its substantial contribution towards the cost of printing. Last but not least, I am very grateful to Dr Ueli Hostettler of the Institute of Ethnology at the University of Berne, who took upon himself the less than easy task of preparing the present volume.

Introduction: Theorizing Ethnicity and Nationalism

Hans-Rudolf Wicker

Postmodernism, Production of Meaning and Hidden Agendas

There is a broad consensus among social scientists today about the theoretical status of ethnic, cultural and national categories. Indeed, one is even inclined to say that a canon has developed around these concepts – a canon that now fairly dominates the discussion, the gist of which can be summarized as follows: there is no such thing as an ethnic, cultural, or national essence; formations which appear as ethnic groups, as cultures, or as nations should no longer be considered as suprasubjective wholes that generate and determine human action. Instead, they should be interpreted as the products of history, therefore as resulting from concrete acts that are motivated by people's interests. Such formations are constructions naturalized by social actors in the interest of their own social standing; only then are they equipped with a coherent history and a homogenous, territorial character. What social scientists are expected to do according to this theoretical canon, then, is to examine which social actors participate in generating such concepts of ethnicity, culture and nation, and to locate the strategies and processes of construction that are used to make such totalities become real. Thus, like social classes, ethnic groups, cultures and nations are thought to exist not *in* themselves but only *for* themselves.

Accelerated by the crisis of representation in the social sciences that took place during the 1980s and swept away the last vestiges of classical representation, the paradigm shift from suprasubjective wholes, structuralism and functionalism to interest-guided social actors is now complete; this is what Alain Touraine (1988: 10) has referred to as 'bringing the social actor back in'. This change has become evident as a growing number of manifestos by social scientists implicitly or

– 1 –

explicitly renounce all future use of 'essentialism' in favour of a renewed interest in 'constructivism' (Keesing, 1994; Vayda, 1994; Friedman, 1994: 67–77). In recent years, anti-essentialism has become a prominent academic attitude and considerable scientific energy has been spent to prove the 'poverty of primordialism' (Eller and Coughlan, 1993) – although much of this activity produced no more than yet another critique of certain well-known passages from Shils (1957) and Geertz (1963: 109), the two social scientists credited with being the first to use the concept of primordialism. The anti-essentialist and anti-primordialist fervour spreading through academic institutions is not primarily the result of an extraordinary leap of knowledge, even though such a leap could be inferred from the emergence of post-structural and postmodern thinking. Instead, it should be seen as an attempt to create a moral distance between the social sciences and the powerful fundamentalisms that are currently shaking the world and could – according to Huntington's analysis (1993) – lead to a 'clash of civilizations'. To be sure, the scientific community, alarmed by the recent rise of essentialist and primordialist thinking, is trying to take a definite stand against a social development which is gaining in strength despite of, and in contradiction to, the warnings sounded by social scientists. Whether in the garb of religious sectarianism and cultural puritanism or under the guise of nationalism, racism, ethnic cleansing, or political tribalism, all current essentialisms are forms of social, political and symbolic action used to dogmatize and ruthlessly implement processes of inclusion and exclusion; as such they are in fundamental opposition to the principles of an open society as defined by Popper (1945). The current anti-essentialism, notably prevalent in North American and European academic circles, is therefore far more than just an expression of a new scientific insight. It forms part of a larger discussion about the values and norms that will determine the future development of humanity. It is worthwhile, therefore, to take a closer look at (1) how this anti-essentialist discourse is being conducted in the social sciences, (2) to examine what answers the social sciences have been finding with the 'fundamental epistemologies', as Byron Good (1994: 7) has aptly termed them, and (3) to illuminate the background that provides the framework for the new 'anti-essentialist conceptions'. It is in dealing with this last point that my critique of an excessive use of the poststructuralist approach in the social sciences will first be sketched out. By answering these questions we will provide a general context for the discussions collected in the present volume.

(1) The scientific examination of primordialism and essentialism from a poststructuralist point of view involves two tasks. It is necessary to demonstrate, firstly, that the primordial and the essential are not given but constructed by human beings for specific purposes, and secondly, to show how the social sciences of the classical period contributed to the construction of complex wholes (Tylor, 1958 (1871): 1) such as nations, cultures, and ethnic groups, that is, to concepts that proved very congenial to the essentialist spirit of the modern age. In the hands of social scientists, constructivism is transformed into an instrument of deconstruction, of the very strategy, in other words, which has become the defining characteristic of scientific postmodernism (Denzin, 1994). Revealing the constructed nature of social reality entails the deconstruction of the underlying forms of knowledge which serve to legitimize this process. The methodological leaps required to launch the deconstructivist enterprise have involved a radically different approach to the classical writings of science: they are no longer read as descriptions of reality but as autonomous texts that generate reality and, in so doing, reflect the intentions of the author, as well as the ideologies and the relationships of power in their time. Edward Said's (1978) book, *Orientalism*, and the collection of essays published by Clifford and Marcus (1986) under the title *Writing Culture* are among the better known works that have demonstrated through detailed analysis how ethnographers of the classical period have presented and described the 'other' in terms of 'race' 'culture', and 'ethnic group' – how, in other words, reality has been (co-) generated by science. In much the same way, historians have deconstructed the totalizing concept of the nation, thereby revealing its true nature as an imagined community (Anderson, 1991 (1983)); that means they have described how the idea of the nation has been used to generate precisely those national and civic realities needed to carry out the project of modernity. Myths of national origin have been shown to be as much part of the construction as national languages, national emotions, national rituals, national institutions and national economies (Hobsbawm, 1990; Noiriel, 1991; Greenfeld, 1992; Calhoun, 1993).

The deconstructivist approach has undoubtedly generated a vast number of new and valuable insights into the mechanisms underlying the production of history and reality. In particular, it has liberated us from all the philosophies and teleologies that proclaimed the primacy of the 'naturally given' and saw no need to talk of social actors except as passive bearers of history, religion, culture, functionality, or structure. Some of the new scientific writing – best described as 'invention literature' – particularly underscores the radical shift from the 'given' to the 'constructed'. Since social, institutional and psychological practices are now viewed as products of human action, it follows that they can be analysed under the sign of invention. Indeed, invention has become one of the leading metaphors for the social sciences in recent years. In this light, tradition is as much an invention of the human mind (Hobsbawm and Ranger, 1983) as culture (Wagner, 1981), kinship (Trautmann, 1987), heterosexuality (Murray, 1995), demography (Lenoir, 1995), politics (Neckel, 1994), primitive society (Kuper, 1988), or the nation-state (Bauman, 1992). Already, the list of publications and articles in the inventionist mode is almost endless. Other subjects deconstructed by means of the inventionist approach include the everyday, pornography, the working class, illness, death, ritual, the environment, responsibility, poverty and solidarity.

Yet regardless of the new and no doubt interesting subject matter brought to light by these studies, one question obviously remains: what kind of 'new reality' is actually being created by the inventionist approach? The sheer number of 'inventionist' publications would require that this new genre of scientific writing be subjected to the same deconstructivist mode of investigation as the classics of the social sciences. According to the deconstructivists' own argumentation such an analysis would not yield a picture of the real world but would demonstrate how the social sciences are investing the world with meaning and, thus, co-generating it. This brings us to our second point.

(2) As poststructuralists have shown, cultures, ethnic groups, nations, and identities were elements of the 'fundamental epistemologies'. My concern is of course not to determine whether or not such totalities ever existed, nor whether they were shaped by divine or merely human intervention. Instead, I am interested in focusing on the new patterns of meaning generated by the critique of modernity's totalizing modes of thinking. These patterns are so easily discernible that no profound analysis is required to bring them to light. The new, magic terms are reflexivity, flexibility, negotiability, situativity, transitionality, hybridity, and process. A few examples should be suffice to indicate the relevance of this new thinking, which defines itself to no small degree by its opposition to the modern habit of thinking in totalities. According to Sanjek culture is

> under continuous creation – fluid, interconnected, diffusing, interpene-
> trating, homogenizing, diverging, hegemonizing, resisting, reformulating,
> creolizing, open rather than closed, partial rather than total, crossing its
> own boundaries, persisting where we don't expect it to, and changing where
> we do. (1991: 622)

What Sanjek is saying here in one concise sentence has been repeated in so many variations over the past years (Swidler, 1986; Hannerz,

1992; Friedman, 1994: 78–90; Keesing, 1974; 1987; 1994; Vayda, 1994; Borofsky, 1994) that no further quotes are necessary. According to this new mode of reading, culture has ceased to be a suprasubjective totality that determines human action and forms identities. Instead, it has become an implicit part of intersubjective communication and social action, and includes, in the form of rules, strategies, contradictions, and restrictions, all the proper characteristics of such communication and action. Since human action is dynamic by nature, culture, also, is forever changing. The resulting 'cultural flow' (Hannerz, 1992: 32) is part of a 'semantic praxeology' (Vervaeck, 1984) and of a 'signifying practice' (Lury, 1992: 368) accessible only through an 'open-ended interpretative process' (Barth, 1989).

In much the same manner, other totalizing concepts such as ethnic group, identity, and nation were rid of the problematic connotation of statism and rendered flexible. As luck would have it, a term already existed to replace the concept of the 'ethnic group': on a purely semantic level, 'ethnicity' (Glazer and Moynihan, 1975: 5) incorporates all the dynamic elements required for a new idea to be embraced today. The quick and universal acceptance of 'ethnicity' seems to owe less to the strong world-wide increase of 'ethnically inspired dissonance' (Connor, 1973) or 'ethnic revival' (Smith, 1981; Huntington 1993) than to the fact that the term itself implies 'change' and 'flow'. Redundant phrases such as *creating ethnicity* (Roosens, 1989), *ethnicity as process* (Staiano, 1980), *ethnicity as action* (Wieviorka, 1994), and *ethnicity at work* (Wallman, 1979) seem primarily intended to underline the irreversibility of the decline of the static and the continued ascendancy of process.

Even the once powerful concept of the nation (static), stripped by poststructuralist critiques of all its essentialist elements, now just barely survives in its one dynamic aspect – nationalism – as the form of collective action that serves to construct national identities and both defines and legitimizes national inclusions and exclusions. Since ultimately there is no fundamental difference between ethnic and national movements any more the two concepts are increasingly folded into one (for ethnicity *and* nationalism see Hobsbawm, 1992; Eriksen, 1993; Calhoun, 1993; Smith, 1994; Benda-Beckman and Verkuyten, 1995), or even explicitly merged in the unifying notion of ethno-nationalism (Connor, 1994). This near-congruence relies on the insight that it is impossible to imagine nationalisms devoid of effects on ethnicity.

Identity, to no one's surprise, has also been sent down the road of deconstruction. Like the other categories, identity has been reclaimed from the realm of the static. Identities are no longer interpreted as the outcome of singular socialization efforts leading to fixed and bounded selves but as the provisional result of social interaction. As Martin writes:

> concretely it means that identities are constructed and that the process of construction which makes possible the utterance of an identity narrative implies borrowing from the Other as well as 'correcting the past'. In brief, the production and utterance of an identity narrative transforms the very group it means to preserve and defend . . . Identity means change. (1995: 9)

Once freed from its static elements, identity is conceptualized in such a way that its process-related aspects are emphasized and a link is established automatically between identity construction on the one hand, and *métissage* (Gallissot, 1992), hybridization (Friedman, 1994: 75) and creolization (Hannerz, 1992: 261–267) on the other.

The deconstruction of fundamental categories of the classical social sciences signifies the transition from inertia to process. The new terminology acquired through the critique of the classical concepts is dedicated to movement and change; it also expresses scepticism with respect to what is unmoving and unchanging. Social and cultural worlds are no longer perceived as 'being' but as 'becoming', because static action is a contradiction in terms, as Victor Turner (1974: 24) pointed out a long time ago.

(3) This transition has been in the making for quite some time (Wicker, 1996a: 13–19); it leads away from a view of the world as systemic to an understanding of it as process, from the idea of the 'social system' to the notion of 'social field', from 'society' to 'social formation' (Vincent, 1986: 100). One aspect of this transition is the generous use of terms ending in '-ization' to emphasize the constructed nature of social reality: temporalization, spatialization, substantialization (Alonso, 1994), (de-) territorialization (Appadurai, 1991), (de-) traditionalization (Heelas, Lash and Morris, 1996), racialization (Anthias and Yuval-Davis, 1992), ethnicization, culturalization, globalization and localization.

However, the new world view of the social sciences contains an inconsistency which in my opinion has not been sufficiently addressed so far. Implied in the first step of deconstruction is a second step which the practitioners of deconstructivism regularly fail to execute. By first step I mean the deconstruction of the classical epistemology of totalities. Deconstructivist analyses demonstrate convincingly and in detail that the essentialist and primordialist conceptions of the classical period need to be understood as expressions of the very spirit which eventually ushered in the age of modernity; they conclude that the ultimate driving force behind the closed, coherent, and homogenous totalities developed and essentialized by the humanities and the social sciences was none other than the interests articulated by nation-states, colonial empires and by capitalism of the Fordist mould.

The revealing of hidden conceptual links and of science's function as a generator of legitimacy is no doubt desirable and therefore requires no justification. However, deconstructivism does invite some degree of suspicion when it is applied only retrospectively, and fails to probe the scientific nature of its own post-essentialism. The new meta-language is comprehensible. It is rapidly spreading throughout the disciplines, as even a cursory reading of any number of recent works will demonstrate. It seems fair to assume that the social sciences are once again busy co-generating a new web of meaning which – like others before it – is based on the spirit of a particular time. If we accept the view that functionalism, structuralism and culturalism – the three currents of thought credited with firmly establishing the epistemology of totalities in the social sciences – emerged out of an intense critique of evolutionism at the turn of the century, we should also consider the possibility that the impassioned critique of modern primordialism and essentialism is less about seeking truth than about developing and practising the postmodern meta-language.

In the following section, I propose to retrace the development of the new scientific meta-language to its roots in the today's *Zeitgeist*. In order to succeed we have to revisit the complex of modern ideas once again. Only by uncovering the grammar of modernity can we begin to recognize the equally ideological nature of the grammar of postmodernity.

The Interplay of Capitalism, State and Nationalism

It is generally accepted today that the strength of the nation-state in the nineteenth and early twentieth centuries rested on three fundamental concepts whose complex interplay formed the very characteristics of bourgeois society. The first one was the republican idea; its implementation depended on the existence of citizens and a public administration and, by extension, on a clearly defined territory within whose boundaries the democratic rights were to have validity. Capitalism was the second pillar; its ability to generate technological progress, develop new industries, and accumulate capital provided the element of economic advances which eventually led to a slow rise in the general standard of living. Nation, the third pillar, resulted from the interplay of state and capitalism. To understanding how the modern era functioned, there is no need to discuss the origins of the three pillars. Kleisthenes already mentions the promise of citizens' participation as the basis of 'demo-cracy'. In their time, the Romans were familiar with the idea of the *natio*, even though they didn't apply the term to themselves but used it to designate the 'foreign born' (Greenfeld, 1992: 3–12). Early forms of capitalism can be found in pre-Christian Greece and China, among other places. The pillars of modernity are evidently much older than the historical period they came to symbolize. What is exceptional about the modern era is how these three expressions of human action slowly merged into one powerful totality as from the second half of the eighteenth century. Capitalism, *res publica*, and nation – in this order – are thus the basis of modernity.

Let us take a quick look at the interdependence of capitalism and state. My contention is that a clear grasp of how these two forces interacted is essential if we are to understand the meaning and the function of the nation in modernity – and postmodernity. In the case of modernity, this interdependence implies that capitalism as a project of progress – or in Marxist terms: the project of the accumulation of capital on a higher level – could never have developed without the help of the state; but it also means that the new state would have found it impossible to implement the *res publica* – which ultimately became the welfare state – without the industrialization and division of labour brought about by capitalism. This significant interdependence of state and capitalism found its historical expression in the liberal bourgeoisie, from which both state and capitalist enterprises recruited their leading members.

The economy required many services that could only be provided by the state, including the standardization and homogenization of money, weights and measures, the elimination of domestic tariffs, and the construction of a transport infrastructure to develop domestic markets; the state was expected to take protectionist measures, implement the codification of commercial law and communications, promote trade and industry, and establish systems for the administration of welfare, education, and justice.

While the state served the needs of capitalism, the economy for its part operated largely in the name of the nation-state. In the nineteenth century, the amalgamation of entrepreneurial and national objectives was expressed in terms like 'national economy' and 'Volkswirtschaft'; they indicate the extent to which the political and economic development of societies depended on the including and excluding construct of the nation to clear the way for the progress of civilization heralded by the philosophies of the Enlightenment and the new technologies. As Friedrich List noted early on (1959 (1841): 174), the nation thus inserted itself between the individual and humanity; and by unifying state and capital, it ushered in the concept of totality. List deserves to be reconsidered today inasmuch as his critical assessment of the theories promoted by Quesnay, Say, and other French scientists, who held that economic development would proceed directly to a world economy and a cosmopolitan trading republic without making allowances for the concept of nation, turns out, in retrospect, to have been quite correct (List, 1959 (1841): 133–143). For his part, List maintained that in the play of forces shaping the future, the national economy would serve to educate the nation in matters of economy and prepare it for its eventual entry into the universal community (1959 (1841): 175). As it turns out, List anticipated the very world society that is being discussed today as having developed via the nation-state.

What remains to be pointed out is that the meshing together of state and capitalism continued to dominate the national scene until after World War II. Fordist industrial production paved the way for the development of the welfare state, but it did not yet seriously challenge the national framework. (Although the assembly-line dramatically reduced manufacturing times, thereby making the mass production of cheap consumer goods possible for the first time.) Fordist industry – in a first phase dedicated to generating domestic market potential – continued to operate in a predominantly national context. Labour forces were national, consumers were national and the new prestigious goods were imbued with national symbolism as well. The Fordist model constitutes a highly developed and intricate mesh of the basic principles of market, state, and nation that came to be termed mixed economy and was based on the theoretical tenets of Keynesianism (Jessop, 1994). In this model, government intervention serves to offset the built-in imbalances of a free market economy. In this sense, the model of the mixed economy is the logical successor of the 'national economy' of the nineteenth century.

Not infrequently, the three pillars that constitute the modern state are treated as autonomous entities. In this perspective, nation, capitalism and the democratic state appear in isolation and are each furnished with a separate history. What is lost in the process is the insight that the three pillars depend on each other for their development and proper functioning. Nationalisms are unfinished, self-renewing narratives about topics like: how do capitalism and state interact, what contradictions are generated by the ongoing struggle between these spheres, and how can the resulting paradoxes be dealt with? Modern nationalism draws its strength from two sources. Firstly, from the fact that the mighty web of state and capitalist interests produced by bourgeois society found its adequate expression in the equally powerful concept of the nation-state. Secondly, from the extraordinary social discrepancies generated by the transformation of a predominantly agrarian society into an industrial one. According to Marshall (1950) a strong feeling of national coherence was absolutely indispensable for the preservation of fragmented modern societies torn by deep class antagonisms.

The binding force of the national idea at the time, and its wide-ranging influence on policies, state institutions and everyday living, has by now been extensively documented. The national idea contains the seed of totality, the unifying element in the conceptual complex of modernity; and with its ascribed characteristics – that nations are God-given, homogenous, coherent, and occupy a defined territory – it lends itself easily to essentialization. In the modern age, narratives about the nation contained three major strands of discussion: one describing the nation as totality, another commenting on the necessary inner adjustments to this totality, and a third one discussing the margin of tolerance for deviations from this totality. To illustrate this argument I shall make a brief digression into the history of science. The following example shows the subtle ways in which the social sciences of the classical period contributed to the generation of such narratives. It will help us later to decode the web of meaning that underlies the postmodernist discourse.

Our example begins with two political discourses, separate yet connected, on the issues of immigration and emigration in the second half of the nineteenth century. On the one hand, in immigration countries like the USA, Canada, and Australia immigrants were urged to assimilate very early on because non-assimilation was considered a potential danger to the young nations (Gleason, 1982). European emigration countries, on the other hand – who generally viewed emigration as something beneficial, even inviting it to reduce potential social tension, found it difficult to release their departing citizens from the national fold. Emigrants were often encouraged to com-memorate the home country, to keep their language, to educate their children in the spirit of their home culture – in short, to resist assimilation to their new surroundings. Max Weber's concept of 'belief in ethnic communitarianism' (1956: 306–307) was at least partly based on the author's assumption – Weber was himself a scientist from a country of emigration – that colonists never lose a certain emotional affinity with their native country, fuelled by memories of their youth.

The demands on the individual are reversed as we switch from the immigrant-related discourse of assimilation, which demands flexible individuals, to the discourse about emigrants which assumes that individuals are caught up in feelings of nostalgia and cultural/national loss from which they cannot and should not free themselves. The obvious contradiction between the two discourses is only resolved if we trace it back to the interest-charged totality from which it springs – the nation. The nation-state demands assimilation to create homogeneity inside the national borders, and tries to maintain already essentialized national thinking outside of these borders to extend the national sphere. It would be wrong to reduce these two discourses to regional characteristics – European vs. American – as the example of Switzerland demonstrates. From 1870 to World War I, Switzerland was a country both of immigration and of emigration. By the time the war started, roughly a quarter million Swiss had emigrated, while during the same period half a million foreign immigrants arrived in Switzerland, increasing the foreign population by 15 per cent (Wicker, 1996b: 19–24). As a result, both migration discourses achieved equal prominence during the pre-war period. Immigrant foreigners were exhorted to assimilate (Addor, 1911; 1913; Raymond-Duchosal, 1929), while Swiss colonists who resisted assimilation in their new countries met with great understanding back home (Schuster, 1913; 1929). In other words, the powerful national narrative was applied selectively – to foreign immigrants the second strand and the first to the emigrating Swiss. Though these built-in contradictions of the political discourse are amazing from the epistemological perspective, what is even more astonishing is the fact that these opposing positions both eventually each found their own scientific discipline with scientists ready to work out their respective theoretical foundations.

As is well known, the concept of assimilation was taken up by the school of sociology at the University of Chicago, where it was expanded into a coherent and powerful theory of assimilation. Let us just mention Robert E. Park (Park, 1928; 1950; Park and Burgess, 1921) who developed the sequential assimilation theory, and Milton M. Gordon (1964), who dedicated his energies to the study of the many-layered processes of assimilation that would, in theory, lead to the immigrants' eventual *Americanization*. Ultimately, it was argued, such assimilation processes always led to a complex whole called the nation. The Chicago school evidently contributed substantially to what we earlier called the second strand of the narrative of the nation without, however, acknowledging its nationalist character.

The second discourse on emigrants, which holds that individuals are formed by their national culture and that formations of this kind are not easily discarded, is at the heart of early cultural anthropology (Benedict, 1966 (1935)). Although projected onto foreign peoples or ethnic minorities, the culture concept designed by Benedict, Mead, Whorf, and other ethnologists during the classical period includes most of the meanings and traits which, in a different context, are attributed to the nation: cultures, it was argued, are homogenous, coherent, territorial, suprasubjective entities, and they form the character of individuals subjected to them. Even without explicit references to the concept of the nation, cultural anthropology was instrumental in weaving the first strand of the narrative dedicated to totalities.

Regardless of whether or not it is possible to establish a direct link between social discourses and their scientific transformation – it is easier, presumably, to do so for assimilation than in the case of emigrant longing for their native culture – the fact remains that in the United States, in the first half of this century, two coexisting theoretical directions were crediting human individuals with fundamentally contradictory abilities: one stressing the point that people are extremely flexible and adaptable, the other insisting on the lasting influence of totalities in the life of human beings. The emerging parallels between the discourses of sociology and ethnology on the one hand, and the political discourses that developed the national perspective with their demands on (foreign) immigrants and (native) emigrants, on the other, are striking indeed. This suggests that the concepts proposed by the 'Chicago sociology' and by cultural anthropology can only be fully appreciated if one takes into account the underlying influence of nation-state thinking. Sociology co-developed the process-oriented 'inside view', while anthropology assisted in generating the 'outside view' of nation-state constructions, each inscribing their contribution in a separate theory. Both views are complementary parts of one and the same narrative. An in-depth discussion of classical approaches in the social sciences would probably reveal all three strands of the narrative of the nation. At this point I merely recommend the brilliant essay by Randolph S. Bourne (1996 (1916)), which deals with all three paradigms of totality, of assimilation and of difference in a single coherent argument. From this essay, let us just quote the following, very postmodern-sounding passage: 'Assimilation, in other words, instead of washing out the memories of Europe, made them more and more intensely real' (Bourne, 1996 (1916): 93).

In the modern age, as our example has shown, political discourses and influential social science theories both served the larger requirements of the nation-state in many different ways. Science and the nation-state both essentialized and processualized the very same values and norms. In much of their theorizing, the social sciences were guided by what turns out to have been the prevailing spirit of the age. While this insight may not be particularly astonishing, it does raise some questions that will concern us when we return to the currently fashionable 'flexibilization' of concepts.

After this short digression into the field of the social sciences, I would like to come back to the interplay between the forces of capitalism and the state that characterizes modernity. The element of co-operation between state and economy would deserve less of our attention if it weren't for the fact that it is increasingly called into question in post-industrial and postmodern society, respectively. In order to understand this transition we need to bring in Max Weber's concept of ideal types.

One should not consider the provisional alignment of state and capitalist interests as anything more than a transitory phenomenon, as spheres of society, economy and state are based on entirely different principles. Capitalism stands for competition, for technological progress and rationalization, for the maximization of profits and the accumulation of capital, and consequently, for the uneven distribution of wealth. Its underlying principle is the social inequality of individuals achieved by way of selection. In opposition to this, the constitutional state embodies the principle of equality, where all citizens have the same political rights. The democratic state provides a set of conditions that is necessary to bring about social equality, whether by casting one's ballot in support of parties who work to overcome social inequality, or through union activity. Even though for obvious reasons full equality is never achieved, the constitutional principle which proclaims that all citizens are equal fulfils an important function because it serves to limit the social inequality generated by capitalism. Only a balanced interplay between these maxims prevents excesses on either side. Too much state-decreed 'equality', or too much market-generated 'inequality' that would ultimately undermine the coherence of society, are equally avoided.

In practice the balance between the principles of 'equality' and 'inequality' can only be maintained as long as capitalism works within the complex of the nation-state and does not grow significantly beyond it. This is the state of affairs that was more or less achieved during the modern age. The complementary functioning of capitalism and state in the domestic sphere manifested itself in the balanced progress of technological development, economic growth, a rising standard of living and the expansion of social rights; it was a model development which ultimately brought about the welfare state that relied on a mixed economy. In the non-state sector and in the relations between states, however, the mutual dependency of state and capital brought about increased competition. Strong nationalisms and the Cold War, dominating the world until long after World War II, served as domestic tranquillizers to gloss over the deep social rifts and regional differences that still existed and at the same time regulated the rivalry between states. These two mutually reinforcing functional principles of the nation-state are the reason why modern-age nationalisms mostly developed along national borders.

The one process capable of bringing the project of modernity to fall is known by the magical term of globalization. Ideally, globalization means the shift of economic competition from a national and inter-national level to a global scale. Although this shift has long been in the making, it only developed its full potential with the arrival of the new telecommunication and data processing technologies. Neo-Schumpeterians would say that the information sciences laid the groundwork for all those key industries, that are not only capable of penetrating all other industries but also lead to the 'fifth Kondratiev' (Amin, 1994). The great advances in technology and industrialization in the late nineteenth and early twentieth centuries – along with new possibilities of capitalization – called for the creation, structuring and economization of the national space. In a similar development on a larger scale, the recent leaps in technology and capitalization are announcing the creation, restructuring and economization of the global space. Globalization is tantamount to the ultimate internationalization of the marketplace for goods, finances, symbols, and labour.

Of all the social, political, and economic processes affected by the globalization of markets (see, among others, Robertson, 1992; 1995; Giddens, 1990; Waters, 1995; Mittelman, 1996) we will single out the only one that has any immediate bearing on the subject discussed in this book – the intersection of the national and the global.

It is easy to see how globalization has all the potential to upset the delicate balance, brought to near perfection in the advanced democratic nation-state, between the opposing principles of 'equality' and 'inequality' promoted, as it were, by constitutional and capitalist thinking, respectively. Those productive and speculative capital hold-ings that are powerful enough to transcend the nation-state – and are capable, in other words, of downgrading nation-states to the status of supplicants competing for investments by simply insisting on factors such as 'free choice of location' and 'low labour costs' – are economizing the global space according to marketplace principles. Globalization holds out the promise of fulfilling the old liberal dream of a world in which economic decisions are based purely on consider-ations of supply and demand. Just as early capitalism needed the bourgeois state to liberate itself from the shackles of feudalism, mature capitalism is about to break free from the limitations of the nation or the welfare state in its ascent to the next higher stage of capital concentration.

The ramifications of a neo-liberalism implemented on a global scale are considerable: nation-states are forced to liberalize, competition is increasing, labour markets are becoming more flexible, state intervention is curbed and welfare programs are cut, structures are adjusted and procedures deregulated. *Lean* and *just-in-time production* is bringing in the *lean* and *just-in-time state*.

Since the inequality principle of capitalism is only kept in check by the equality principle of the democratic state, it comes as no surprise that globalization, by boosting the power of capitalism, also leads to a further increase in social stratification. This shift is a result of the creative destruction inherent in the logic of capitalism which, among other things, causes share values – and thus private profits – to increase whenever corporations decide to rationalize away part of their labour force. This kind of downsizing leads to a negative redistribution of wealth, that means an increase of social inequality within individual countries and on a global scale (Gill, 1996: 205). Whereas in the model based on the democratic nation-state the capitalist forces that produced inequality were eventually slowed down because the interests of state and capitalism complemented and controlled each other in important areas, it is obvious that this co-dependence all but vanishes in the global space. Since the voting power of citizens usually extends no further than the nearest national border, capitalist enterprises that manage to escape to the global space are no longer subject to democratic control. The power shift from nation-states to global capitalist enterprises is the main reason behind the overwhelming success of world-wide economic liberalism. Panitch (1996) is deceiving himself when he notes that the large transnational organizations (World Bank, WTO, UN, EC, NAFTA, ASEAN, MERCOSUR) are, after all, the result of agreements between national governments. The fact is that these institutions are not subject to any democratic control whatsoever and, furthermore, that they are quite unapologetic in their dedication to liberal-economic interests. Given that in the modern age it was the growth of democratic structures that reined in capitalism on the level of the nation-state, it is logical to conclude that economic liberalism resulting from globalization can only be controlled by the democratic state writ large, that means by the transnationalization of democratic rights (Held, 1992: 32–34; Kleger, 1995). Only democracy on a global scale – so the argument goes – will restore the balance between state and economy necessary to control, once again, the capitalist principle which generates inequality. Reasonable though they may sound, such proposals are obviously utopian, and they evidently hardly need to be discussed.

Before concluding our analysis, let us take a brief look at another epistemological problem which, as globalization progresses, is becoming more and more evident. It may be remembered that two developments in particular contributed to the demise of Marxist thinking: first, the perversion of Marxism in the communist countries, and second, the enormous economic upswing that was brought about in the west under the aegis of democratic liberalism. The success of the western model seemed to vindicate the theory developed by Keynes, who maintained that the state could soften the negative effects of the market economy's inherent cycles by means of anticyclical interventions. However, as globalization and neo-liberalism progress the Keynesian model is put under increasing stress. The ability of national reserve banks to direct the economic process by monetary intervention is decreasing. This is the result of an enormous dispro-portion between the rapidly growing amount of transnational capital and the relatively stable reserves of the national banks. The accumulation of private assets has reached a level that allows capital to free itself from nation-state dependencies and to impose its own logic – that of pure capitalism – on the global economy. In terms of theory, this shift signifies a victory of Marx over Keynes. This statement obviously begs an explanation since it seems paradoxical to attribute such significance to Marxist theory in a period characterized by the global triumph of market economy and the disappearance of communist systems.

In the era of the Cold War it was easy to disprove Marx. Such statements as (1) the superstructure-substructure-model is too simple, (2) the proletariat – designated principal actor of the world revolution – is about to disappear, (3) large scale impoverishment has failed to materialize, were often enough to dismiss Marxism for good. Guided by the desire to disprove Marx on all counts, discussions of Marxist theory often exhausted themselves in a criticism of his political and philosophical asides while generously overlooking the fact that the main body of his work (Marx, 1969; 1973; 1974) consisted in analysing the functioning of capitalist political economy. What is interesting about Marx in the context of trying to understand globalization, is the fact that he worked from the assumption that capitalism was subject to a logic of its own, which needed to be uncovered and understood. Furthermore, he based his investigation on the existence of a liberal capitalist system – on a form of capitalism, in other words, in which the interests of the owners of capital dominated over all other interests, and in which the free market could function unencumbered by state interventions and other impurities. In other words, Marx analysed a capitalist system which is rapidly gaining in importance again, although on a far vaster scale.

At the centre of the logic perceived to be capitalism's own, Marx made out the 'falling tendency of the rate of profit' (Marx, 1973: 221–227; Luxemburg, 1913; Mattick, 1969; 1970). This is a rule that to the overall reproduction of capital: the continuous development of technological innovation – a necessary prerequisite because it shortens production time, lowers prices and thus affords competitive advantages – leads to a shift in the nature of the capital needed for production. This shift ultimately favours the proportion of 'fixed capital' which is invested in technology and infrastructure, over the proportion of 'variable capital' invested in labour. In other words, labour costs constitute a progressively smaller share of the total capital invested. Since in terms of system theory, the surplus value which eventually results in a profit is exclusively generated by the variable capital – whose proportion of the total is diminishing, as we have seen – the rate of profit tends to sink in the long run. The only effective means to stop this negative development of profits are expansion, rationalization and market restructuring – that means interventions which require an absolute increase in variable capital in order to restart the cycle of capital accumulation on the next higher level. According to Marx, then, accelerating capitalist growth and accelerated capital concentration are the only forces capable of slowing down the fall in the rate of profit. The recurrent crises which appear as periodical business slumps serve primarily to improve profit development by means of market corrections and a phase of intense rationalization and accumulation. Any actual reversal of the downward trend of profits requires new technological input and further increases the proportion of constant capital over variable capital in the overall composition. The fall in the rate of profits is thus merely postponed and the next crisis is in the making (Rolshausen, 1970).

Such a sketch of the systemic aspects of capitalist developments would be pointless if it had no bearing on the topics under discussion in this book. For one thing, it becomes clear – this merely as a remark in passing – that the often repeated postmodernist thesis about the passing out of fashion, if not the outright death of the *grandes theories* (Lyotard, 1984) may well be correct inasmuch as it refers to utopias of redemption or to the universalist and holistic theories of the classical social sciences. With regard to theories, however, that place capitalism at the centre of analysis, this assumption is most certainly false. Lyotard's argument should therefore be modified in the following way: all great narratives today have lost their claim to universal validity except for the meta-narrative which centres on the functioning and the effects of capitalism. This one narrative is so powerful – neo-liberalism and globalization testify to that – that no other narrative can compete with it unless it is a minor variation of the same overriding theme.

The inherent logic of the capitalist system also explains that globalization is far from being an historical accident. From a Marxist point of view one would say that capitalism first developed in a pre-nation-state environment; that it passed through a stage where it depended on the nation-state to unfold its powers; and that it has finally begun to transcend the nation-state in order to rid itself of the social question through a neo-liberalism implemented on a global scale; in this way, it mobilizes yet another, higher stage in the unfolding of market forces. The maximization of profits and the accumulation of capital constitute the driving force at every stage of its development.

We shall now attempt to weave the different threads picked up along the way into a coherent synthesis. In a nutshell, this is what they say:

1. The fact that state and capitalism were linked in the modern era supported the view that nations were totalities, at the same time as it encouraged those forces which attempted to balance the opposing principles of 'equality' and 'inequality'.
2. The classical social sciences were based on the model of totality. Through recent scientific treatment, the narratives about the nation have been 'entextualized' in Ricœur's (1981: 197–221) sense of the word. They are told and retold, made available to multiple 'readers'. Their effects and interpretations are unpredictable; they cannot be controlled by the author, or by the teller of the tale.
3. Due to the possibility and the necessity of the capitalist system to transcend the nation-state and implement the free market through global space, the symbiosis of state and capitalism is progressively coming undone in the postmodern age. As a result, state-generated 'equality' and capitalist-generated 'inequality' are no longer balanced, and social inequality is constantly increasing.

Equipped with this framework of interpretation, we can now return to the problem sketched in the first paragraph. There, we evoked the fact that contemporary social sciences are articulating themselves in an anti-essentialist manner, that they are deconstructing the totality-based thinking of the classical period, and that they have developed, through their critique of the classical ideas of the social sciences, a set of concepts predicated on process and flexibility. We are now confronted with the third of my initial three questions: what is the nature of the *Zeitgeist* that the contemporary social sciences are indebted to, and where are the blind spots in their new world view? The answer can be summarized in three points.

(1) The strength of the deconstructivist approach to the classical theories in the social sciences is that it succeeds in underlining how the concepts of that period relating to culture, ethnic group, society, and identity are based on totalities and essentializations. Its weakness, however, is that its hermeneutic analysis frequently stops at the deconstruction of the individual concepts, and so cuts itself off from the possibility of tracing the totality-based thinking that prevails in the individual disciplines, to that complex whole to which it ultimately owes its existence, and with which – explicitly or not – it shares its ideological roots. Meaning and content of this powerful super-narrative cannot be revealed until the driving force behind totality-based thinking is fully understood as the complex interplay between capitalism, state and nation. It will then become clear that the 'grand' narrators of state and economy have been using the 'small' scientific disciplines to discursively elaborate and enact untold variations of this one great story.

(2) A review of the terminology drawn from the critique of the holistic concepts and used throughout the new social science makes it clear that the former reflects the spirit of the times no less than classical terminology did in its day. The transition recorded in the sciences from structure-based (static) to process-oriented (dynamic) thinking, which is expressed in terms such as flexibility, reflexivity, transitionality, hybridity, creolization, ethnicization, culturalization, racialization, and negotiability cannot be viewed in isolation from the capitalist quantum leap which – aided by the new data processing technologies – has triggered a new phase of intense rationalization and accumulation. In the organization of production processes as well as in the handling of the markets for goods, services, finances, and labour, flexibilization and process-orientation are on the agenda (Hall, 1988). In the context of economy, the transition from static to flexible models indicates that production cycles of goods and reproduction cycles of capital have been shortened to such an extent that they can no longer be perceived as durable (static) but only as being in constant flux (dynamic). The compression of time and space that has so often been described of late, and the concurrent shrinking of the world, are thus most often encountered in the production and reproduction cycles of the capitalist economy. It comes as no surprise, then, that even the post-Fordist accumulation of capital has taken on reflexive aspects (Lash and Urry, 1994: 60–110).

Are we looking at a new reality in the descriptions based on the increasingly flexible categories promoted through the social sciences, or are we seeing a reality that is co-generated by the social sciences? It seems that the answer is yes in both cases. In the same way that the classical sciences were guided by totality-based thinking when they generated those same totalities, so the new social sciences, by trying to get a grip on reality, are helping to construe the new reality and to fill it with meaning. The social sciences, no more than anyone else, are unable to escape the double hermeneutics sketched by Giddens (1984). Since this dual process – interpretation and construction as elements of the same action – does not take place in a ideology-free zone, it is legitimate to ask what kind of ideological current is a science that is implicitly or explicitly committed to reflexivity, flexibility, negotiability and the concept of the decentred subject.

The easiest way to answer this question is again to activate the two ideal types we used earlier: capitalism stands for inequality, the state stands for equality. In the modern era these two principles controlled each other because capitalism was bound up in the nation-state; in the postmodern era the principle of inequality dominates because capitalism transcends the nation-state. The pressure towards flexibility originates in that part of society that is intent on competition and selection and, therefore, on the principle of inequality; it cannot be located in the societal sector represented by the democratic state, whose role is to offer the means of bringing about social equality. The conclusion is simple: whereas the sciences of the modern era focused on totality, systems, structures, function, and the culture-bound subject, and while it gave legitimacy to the integration of state and capitalism, postmodern science, with its emphasis on reflexivity, flexibility, and negotiability, gives legitimacy to the ideology of the free market. Postmodern discourse implicitly naturalizes such principles as 'competition', 'selection', and 'social inequality', and disqualifies the principle of the 'social equality' of people that can be brought about by the state if it works according to democratic principles. The new thinking of the social sciences, steeped as it is in the categories of the flexible, follows – and, I would say, follows quite blindly – in the footsteps of the one remaining universal narrative: that of the free market, of the maximization of profits and unlimited possibilities. At the same time, it dismisses all those discourses that demand social equality through a bounded self, to the dustheap of outmoded conservative ideologies.

(3) The anti-essentialist and anti-primordialist attitude which – as we pointed out in the beginning – has become increasingly prominent in academic circles, is now easier to understand. This attitude communicates two messages, one expressed in words, the other not. Words

are used to criticize the totality-based thinking of classical science and to work out the flexibilization of categories. No words are used as the attitude yields to the *Zeitgeist* and chooses its position in the camp of (neo-) liberal ideology. The epistemology of totalities is succeeded by the epistemology of process.

A process-based world view highlights fundamentally different parameters than a totality-based or structural world view. Unlike 'structural' approaches, which are based on definable ties derived from grammars – on rules through which all concepts that are required for the system to work, are developed out of a predetermined methodology (Lévi-Strauss, 1980 (1964): 41–42) – process-based thinking is committed to an ever expanding universe. Structural thinking points to the existence of strong inner organizations, to universals and constants. Process-based thinking, on the other hand, negates the existence of strong inner organizations, is averse to universalism, and favours particularism (Eco, 1991(1972): 378–392).

Since deconstructivist efforts always involve an ideological positioning from which the interpretation of texts is offered, those who attempt to deconstruct postmodern terminology run the risk of being accused of romanticizing totality-based thinking; in other words, they risk manoeuvring themselves into a conservative corner which postmodernism has set aside for those attempting to resist competition, flexibilization and globalization. But I have no such romanticizing in mind. The only purpose behind my attempt to reveal the underlying pattern of postmodern terminology is to put a finger on the black box that such positioning involves.

Indeed, when we analyse where process-based thinking comes from, we notice that it has a tendency to deny the existence of strong inner organizations that convey stability and durability. When we open this black box, we discover that in the modern era, scientific approaches which defied totality-based thinking caused irritation; today, the irritation is caused by any scientific effort that refuses to make flexibility its fundamental principle. On the level of world events the most visible expression of this paradox are those social movements or social bodies with a stable inner organization whose actors propagate ideologies based on the model of closed, complex totalities, in other words, ideologies that oppose rapid change and advocate durability and continuity instead. To be sure, such ideologies have always existed and it is unlikely that they will disappear. The sole difference between modernity and postmodernity lies in the fact that under the reign of totality-based thinking, such ideologies operated, so to speak, in friendly territory, whereas they now stand in ideological opposition to the dominant postmodern positions. Among these anti-postmodernist forms of articulation we find neo-nationalisms, as well as ethnic and religious movements.

Inclusion, Exclusion and the Problem of Essentialism

The interplay between the production of science and social develop-ment discussed in chapters one and two is significant to the extent that the social sciences of today, much like the scientists of the classical era, are facing a dilemma in trying to understand primordialisms and essentialisms. This dilemma appears as a deep-seated ambivalence towards collective action and its results. On the one hand, no social scientist would deny that collective action – in whatever form, on whatever level, and regardless of how intense and contradictory its manifestations in the life of a society may be – generates the kind of communality which is essential to all forms of what we call human society. On the other hand, there is no denying that collective action also produces 'we'-formations. Some of these formations are weak and some are strong, some are confused, some durable and others short-lived. Without these we-formations, internalized in cognitive and affective patterns and externalized in social institutions, collective action would lack continuity. However – and this is where the problem begins – since every 'we' generates a 'they', since communality encour-ages participation on the inside and erects barriers against participation from outside, there is no collective action without some kind of inclusion and exclusion, and without a dividing line between 'them' and 'us'. Borders of this kind may be visible, as in the case of territorially organized political communities. Many borders exist only in people's minds and remain invisible, as is often the case with markings of social differences. While some of these dividing lines are easily redrawn or stepped across, others are not. Some we-groups are hermetically sealed, others again are transparent and open. In everyday life, most people operate in several interlocking we-groups – and thus in multiple identities – without encountering any difficulties as a result of this.

We can now narrow down the definition of the above dilemma. Social scientists, while taking a benevolent view of collective action as such, tend to be wary of we-constructions generated by collective action. Collective action is usually equated with organization, efficient use of resources, and rationality; but we-groups stand for exclusion, affective ties, intolerance, and, ultimately, irrationality. Since the 'we' evidently has an emotional dimension, it is suspected of lending itself to operations that have no rational underpinning.

The positive rating of collective action and the negative assessment of we-constructions – an exemplary instance of Cartesian dualism – takes on many forms in scientific practice as, for instance, when the idea of the (modern) state is discussed without reference to the idea of the nation; state action is thus equated with reason, national action with unreason. Another case is when religious fundamentalisms are seen as anomalies of the modern age despite the fact that the collective strategies underlying such fundamentalization are quite congruent with modernist strategies. A further form of such dualistic thinking is when ethnic movements are perceived as an expression of reasonable strategic action according to the rational choice theory on the one hand, and as generated by collective identities on the other (Cohen, 1985; Marx Ferree, 1992; Fox Piven and Cloward, 1995; Foweraker, 1995: 9–24); whereby, how could it be otherwise, collective identities of this kind are described as 'blind and even irrational' (Bonacich, 1980: 10), or else as 'purely emotional' (Patterson, 1983: 26), in any case, however, as a form of 'uncontrollable irrationalism' (Dittrich and Radtke, 1990: 24).

The artificial division of human action into 'rational' and 'irrational' parts should at long last be left behind. There are no rational actions without irrational elements and vice versa. Consequently, there is no such thing as a rational strategic action that does not also generate identity, and no collective generation of identity unsupported by rational strategies. Collective identities and collective strategies cannot take shape one without the other, that means collective action requires both strategies and identities. For this reason alone, it is misleading to attempt to analyse identity, strategy, and the construction of meaning separately.

If we accept this premise, primordialism and essentialism lose much of their volatile nature. It is a mistake to assume that we-groups can achieve stability without naturalizing their norms and values. Essentializations stake out the collective action frame by referring to the objectives of we-actions in the future. At the same time, we-action derives legitimacy and strength from narratives about the origin of the we-group. Ethnology teaches us that the ritualizing of we-contents is a uniquely suitable means of lending durability to we-groups. The questioning of essentializations from the inside usually indicates that the we-group is losing its cohesion.

Ethnic, religious, and nationalist movements, contrary to the impression given by scientific literature, are not the only collectivities to provide examples that illustrate the interplay of collective action, of imagined we-identities, and of essentialization. Such examples can be found in the leftist movements of the 1960s (Boggs, 1995) as well as in the feminist discourses of the 1970s and 1980s (Taylor and Whittier, 1995). In fact, I would even say that as an article of faith in the context of neo-liberal thinking the market is as unquestioned and unassailable a principle as the Ten Commandments in biblical thinking.

In the context of the work done by Shils (1957) and Geertz, essentializations were mostly seen till now as relating to those 'assumed givens' which classical thinking attributed to culture – and nation – and which have 'come to be more and more deplored as pathological' (Geertz, 1963: 110) in modern civil society. They include the ties of religion, language, kinship and neighbourhood. In my view this definition of essentialization is too restrictive, and Geertz himself seems to have had his doubts when he says (Ibid.): 'But for virtually every person, in every society, at almost all times, some attachments seem to flow more from a sense of natural – some would say spiritual – affinity than from social interaction'. Ethnicity, religion, language and customs are not the only categories that lend themselves to naturalization; on the contrary, naturalization occurs with virtually every category that can be imagined as independent from social interaction. Nature and gender belong to this group, no less than the belief in freedom, the belief in self-realization, in the laws of the free market, and of equal opportunity.

Once the concept of essentialization is no longer restricted to categories such as ethnic or religious ties – which were left behind yet were far from resolved by modernity – but is broadened instead to include modern and postmodern forms, the question whether essentializations are constructed or not, becomes obsolete. Because we are dealing with 'assumed givens', that means with culture, this question cannot be answered unless it is raised to the level of ontology. Far more pressing than any discussion about the existences or non-existence of essence, it seems to me, is the problem of the degree of essentialization, since the function of essentialization changes with the degree of its intensity. 'Soft' naturalizations as in advertising, Sunday sermons, or marital disputes have little in common with those 'hard' essentializations developed to legitimate civil wars, even though the origins and the mechanisms at work are the same in both cases (on the difference between hard and soft essentializations see Allahar, 1996). Soft essentializations are part of our everyday reality and thus considered normal. They inform everyday living without making our thinking go rigid, and they help us structure, understand, and if necessary endure our lives and render them meaningful. They are part of that common sense which is absolutely vital for social life to develop. Not so the 'hard' essentializations. Their purpose is to generate closed thinking; without them a holocaust, ethnic cleansing, religious or political fundamentalism, or apartheid policies are impossible. Hard essential-izations are at work in all ideologies that replace a 'more-or-less' with an 'either-or' (Imhof, this volume), or substitute 'thin' identity for 'thick' identity (D'Amato and Schieder, this volume).

The stairway leading from soft to hard has many steps. The shifting essentializations that are available between the two extremes are actually more interesting because it is there – depending on context and actual situation – that mobilizations for tangible political objectives occur. With regard to the groups in this middle range the crucial questions are: what kind of social-political conditions, discourses, or interested social actors are conducive to, or capable of weakening and strength-ening essentializations, or shifting them from one object to another? Also: what, if any, connection is there between *actio* and *reactio*; that means between essentialization and counter-essentialization. Inter-mediary forms of essentialization can be analysed on three levels – ideological, social and political.

For the ideological level Pierre Bourdieu offers some elements of a theoretical approach. In his chapter on doxa in *Théorie de la Pratique* (1972) he stresses that every powerful organized whole tends to naturalize its specific forms of arbitrariness by elevating them to the level of orthodoxy; furthermore, that subjected classes – in and through political struggle – attempt to roll back the border of the dominant doxa by challenging the orthodoxy with a heterodoxy of their own. For the social level of analysis, a useful approach is provided by Martiniello (1995: 21–27). By treating the dynamics of inclusion and exclusion based on ethnicity separately for the micro-, meso-, and macrosocial levels respectively, he arrives at a description of how each of these levels has its own forms of inclusion and exclusion, and therefore its own essentializations. The connections between the three levels are particularly interesting since they determine the prevailing manner of ethnicization and essentialization on each level. The model of analysis for the political level is based on Charles Taylor's *The Politics of Recognition* (1992). According to Taylor, a liberal-democratic political order that respects the human dignity of the individual by way of guaranteeing basic civil rights does not preclude the possibility of reflection about 'the good life'. Built into the liberal-democratic model is, by definition, the possibility for any group perceiving itself as a minority, to eschew the majority's demand for homogeneity by developing its own notions of 'the good life' and standing up for its own collective goals in the public arena.

These brief remarks may suffice to show that on the different levels of social action – ideological, social, political – the Hegelian 'I the We and We the I' is broken up by a 'We and You'. Processes based on we-groups cannot be banished from a democratic community because it is in the nature of democratic rights to pave the way for a politics of recognition. Once we-group processes are admitted in a community – in other words, if the community lacks the power to shape a single truth and impose its homogenizing implement-ation, considerable essentializations and counter-essentializations will inevitably occur in such a community.

Nationalism, Ethnicity and Multiculturalism: About the Articles in this Volume

This examination of epistemological problems should deliver the necessary instruments to place the articles collected in this volume in their proper context, without actually reviewing them. Grouped by content, most of them deal with one of four major topics that merit further discussion. For our present purposes these four blocks appear under the following headings: 'Theory', 'Ethnonationalism and Multi-culturalism', and 'Europe'.

Theory

It has frequently been noted that the 'renaissance of nationalism', the 'ethnic revival', and the 'multiculturalization' of modern societies came pretty much as a shock to most social scientists. This seems to suggest that we should go back and carefully review the works of those 'classical' authors who have been considered to be the founding fathers of the modern social sciences and who are said to have predicted the gradual disappearance of ethnic, national and religious bonds in the process of society's modernization. Some articles in this volume are devoted to such historical inquiry. Guibernau probes the writings of Durkheim and Marx with regard to their assessment of nationalism, Imhof takes on Max Weber, and Ålund returns to Simmel and Schutz to re-examine the notions of 'foreignness' and 'identity'. Gutiérrez, on her part, discusses how the more recent theories of Ernest Gellner and Anthony D. Smith relate to the significance of *ethnic revival* within nation-states.

Guibernau and Imhof demonstrate that Marx, Durkheim, and Weber, although they left no coherent theory of nationalism, certainly did consider the issue of the nation-state: Marx saw nationalism as a repressive tool in the hands of the very bourgeoisie that the workers were destined to fight. But, as Guibernau points out, both Marx and Engels brushed aside the principle of internationalism whenever they addressed the practical aspects of the organization of class struggle, and emphasized instead the importance of fighting the domestic bourgeoisie before carrying the banner of the revolution out into the world. Thus, it was through the back door of political practice that the national question eventually found its way into Marxist theory. With his comments about 'state' and 'nation', 'patriotism' and 'collective representations', Durkheim, who focused mainly on questions of societal integration, came very close to understanding the interplay between civil society and the collective ideas about it as expressed in the dualism of state thinking and national thinking. And so it appears that both Marx and Durkheim were not, after all, oblivious to the question of national inclusion and exclusion. Since they held such imagined borders to be merely transitory they never gave nationalism the kind of weight that history has attached to it since.

In academic circles it is now 'de rigueur' to emphasize the universalist character of classical sociology in order to highlight one's own anti-essentialist attitude. I might add, then, that the question of universalism is more complex than is commonly assumed. None of the authors mentioned above were nationalists by any stretch of the imagination, yet, like many other scientists in their day they were unable to transcend the evolutionist mode of thinking. Evolutionism also operated with inclusions and exclusions, but it used civilizational categories instead of national ones to divide humanity into primitive and civilized societies. As we know, these categories provided colonialism with an excellent theoretical structure for its own justification, because in the light of evolutionism it became 'natural' and 'right' for more 'highly' developed societies to colonize their 'primitive' counterparts in order to bring them the boom of civilization. Marx saw the colonialization of India as fully justified because – so he argued – India's ailing oriental despotism had to be destroyed if civilization and progress were eventually to prevail. Or take Durkheim, who found the 'simplest' of all religions among the 'primitive' aborigines of Australia, a discovery that eventually led him to the concept of collective representations. As we can see – and we will take a closer look at this aspect later on – every kind of universalism eventually produces its own particularisms.

Of the three great classical figures of sociology, Weber is clearly the one whose approach is most useful in trying to understand modern nationalisms. His view of human activity as guided by material and immaterial interests that depend on the support and the legitimacy provided by 'ideas' – his discovery, in other words, of a stabilizing dialectic between 'interests' and 'ideas' – answers the question of society's integration. As the organization of interests materializes in the 'idea of the state', so the 'idea of the nation', closely related to the state, symbolizes the belief in some form of community. By linking the two concepts of 'human activity guided by interest' and of the 'belief in national and ethnic communitarianism', Weber overcomes the dichotomy between materialism and idealism. In fact, he could be said to have anticipated the resolution of the contradiction between essentialism and constructivism on the one hand, and identity and strategy on the other.

By extending the Weberian approach and borrowing from Durkheim the concept of anomie, Imhof, in his article, posits a connection between the parallel growth of anomie – an element that encourages communitarianism in society – and the rise of ethnonationalist movements, a thesis that puts him in the vicinity of T. H. Marshall. Given a causality between anomie and the growing ethnicization of politics, the logical question arises: who or what generates anomies? Any attempt to answer this question inevitably takes us back to the uneven distribution of power in society, and to the forces of capitalism that generate inequality. It appears that we will have to turn to Marx once more if we wish to discuss the question of anomie.

If one is not deceived by the rash assertions of those who would claim that ethnic, religious and national bonds are manifestations of a life before modernity, then the theories of Marx, Durkheim, and Weber actually continue to be quite useful in the analysis of nationalisms and ethnicizations. Considering that (1) inclusions and exclusions of this kind appear on different levels of society – indeed, the borders defining 'we' and 'you' often intersect more than once – and that (2) all politics articulating material and immaterial interests will be accompanied by a politics of identity, the persistence of ethnic, religious and national bonds despite the progress of modernity is actually less astonishing than the surprise of those who expected such bonds to simply disappear. Ethnicity never left the political arena and it cannot therefore be brought back on stage as some people seem to believe (Rothschild, 1981: 1). The only thing that has changed are the terms used to describe the processes of inclusion and exclusion.

Ethnonationalism and Multiculturalism

If nationalism is defined as an identity-forming politics generated by the modern territorial state in order to defuse social and regional tensions caused by the new anomies, then every kind of nationalism inevitably has ethnic overtones, and the term ethnonationalism is a pleonastic construction. Whether built around the 'national state' and 'citoyenneté' as in France or around 'Volk', 'Abstammung', and 'Herkunft' as in the German model (Giordano, this volume); or whether used to achieve a domestic unity that is aspired to but remains forever incomplete, as echoed in the 'Americanization' of the USA all nationalisms favour homogeneity and abhor domestic particularisms. Furthermore, nationalisms are contrived and filled with essentialisms, and they are all used to bestow legitimacy on inclusions as well as exclusions. Whereas in pre-nation-state systems of ruling 'divine will' was essentialized to promote identity construction and invoke a spirit of community, the gradual secularization brought about by the modern nation-state has shifted the focus of essentialization to the people, to cultural achievements, to history, and to the institutions of the state. The ideas that feed into nationalism may change in the course of time, and the same is true for nationalism's meanings and functions.

To demand that nationalisms be eliminated or at the very least 'de-ethnicized' (Eriksen, 1993: 116–118) is like asking that all forms of identity politics be abolished. Politicians are no more capable of appealing to voters without recourse to formations of identity than advertisers are of seducing consumers without the promise of identity. What matters is not to find an answer in principle – for or against nationalism – but to reveal the different purposes served by nationalism, and to determine the social circumstances that either strengthen or weaken politics of identity within territorial states at any given moment in history. A weakening of national thinking brings about discourses that promote openness towards the outside, and renounce the ideal of domestic homogenization, that means discourses willing to allow some degree of regionalism and social/cultural pluralism. The reverse is equally true: strong national thinking favours discourses that plead for isolationism, that seek to shut out the world, insist on domestic homogenization, and are openly suspicious of regionalisms and particularisms. This being said, it becomes clear what kind of nationality discourse allows for a discourse of multiculturalism of any significance. Since first and foremost, multiculturalism opposes homogenization, it can only become socially relevant if the demand for assimilation inherent in nationalist thinking is weakened. Multiculturalism confronts the politics of national identity construction with a politics of pluralist identity construction independent of the nation-state. Strong nationalisms and strong multiculturalisms are mutually exclusive. Wherever they do coexist, secessionist desires on the part of those opposing homogenization, are never far below the surface. In such situations, movements originally committed to an ideology of pluralism easily turn into sub-nationalist movements.

In a global context, today, we can make out three major types of nationalism. The first type appears in the context of decolonialization, which promoted the spread of nationalist thinking by creating a large number of new territorial states. In many of these states a weak constitutionality typically coexists with a strong and uncontrolled capitalism. Since such constellations tend to promote social inequality and social unrest, state institutions serve mostly to protect the existing power structures. The groups that control these institutions find that their prestigious position within the state power structure also gives them easy access to lucrative material resources. The struggle for positions of state power becomes a matter of prime political concern among the members of rivalling elites. It is on this level that nationalism is formed and ethnicity activated. Often waged with little regard for democracy, the struggle for state power requires a strong, class-inclusive system of favouritism whose strength depends to no small extent on the power, expressivity, and unifying potential of the symbols used to bind one's clients. Such symbolism tends to be ethnic, since no other set of symbols covers up differences of social standing quite as effectively. The resulting ethnicization of politics (Helbling, this volume) involves sharpening the contours of diffuse ethnic feelings without precluding the possibility of identity switching (Elwert, this volume), inter-ethnic marriages, or the hybridization of social worlds. In situations of extreme ethnic overload, channels of violence are moved from the intra-ethnic to the inter-ethnic level, identity switching and inter-ethnic marriage suddenly count as treason and hybrid social worlds have to be re-segregated along ethnic lines.

Strong nationalisms and strong ethnic currents are not mutually exclusive. On the one hand, an ethnic elite that controls the most important government institutions will continue to apply ethnic strategies domestically, but in its dealings with the outside world it will attempt to turn the ethnic discourse into a national one in order to strengthen its own position of power. Rivalling elites excluded from power, on the other hand, will continue to fly the ethnic flag in the hope of being swept to power by the broad popular constituency thus generated. Elites, whether in positions of power or as brokers between popular constituency and rulers undoubtedly play a central role in forming the principles of ethnic action that accompany the traditionalization and essentialization of culture. In their respective articles, Gutiérrez, Helbling and Elwert refer to this complex of relationships.

The second type of nationalism is typical of formerly centralized, communist-led states with a planned economy that are in the midst of a phase of transition towards a parliamentary democracy and market economy. Here too, the relationship between state power and capitalism determines the actual nature of nationalism, only now we are dealing with what was originally a strong state bureaucracy facing a still fledgling market economy. Under communist regimes 'interests' and 'collective representations' were monopolized by the only actor there was – the state. Questions of nationalities and minorities were thus centrally defined and determined by state sponsored social engineering – Lenin's writings offer ample instruction on how this was done. Today, the decline of the central power and the liberalization of the economy generate a whole new set of actors each tinkering with their own politics of identity in the process of redistributing the country's resources. It would be difficult to overlook the fact that the predatory capitalism exploding in these countries – unchecked by social rights or effective state power – is accompanied by a virulent nationalism of much the same kind that reigned in nineteenth- and early twentieth-century Europe. The revival of old models in situations like this is hardly surprising. The 'Slavic question', for instance, has once again become a burning issue in present-day Russia (Shnirelman and Komarova, this volume) and Herder's notion of a people ('Volk') with its implication of a monoethnic state is currently going through a full-blown revival in Eastern Europe (Giordano, this volume). The resurgence of anti-Semitic currents, of course, is also part of this development (Goldstein, this volume). The revival of national identities and the ethnicization of various social sectors are side-effects of a transformation that inevitably promotes the decline of the state, the elimination of social rights, and the liberalization of the economy. The combined impact of these developments is rapidly sweeping away the last remnants of social solidarity. Although it is striking to see the new nationalisms reaching back to pre-Communist times for meaningful concepts, one should not overlook the fact that the structure of this nationalization is ultimately conditioned by their communist heritage. For example, the old communist elites who once occupied all the important positions within the bureaucracies of party and state and who, in the post-communist era, may suddenly turn into important proponents of nationalist ideas. Indeed, the decline of power at the centre has contributed to the rise of regional elites. Many nationalizations and ethnicizations at the regional level, initially intended to clear the way for independent statehood, are being used by regional elites to secure their share of the bankrupted communist estate. Such processes of regionalization and ethnic valorization have unleashed ethnic wars in former Yugoslavia and in the Caucasus region and have precipitated outright de-Russification movements in the Baltic states.

The third type of nationalism is at home in the highly industrialized countries of Europe and North America. Unlike the first two types, which result from domestic capitalizations of social and economic fields capable of generating massive social tensions and strong nationalisms to match, the nationalisms of highly industrialized countries – paradoxical as it may sound – are actually an expression of transnationalization. The transnational interdependence of institutions, the globalization of economy and media, and an increasing transnational mobility are ushered in the age of the 'nation unbound' (Bash, Glick Schiller and Szanton Blanc, 1994). Although national borders retain their power to admit and exclude, nationality itself is no longer a convincing instrument for the maintenance of the idea of a national community. In retrospect it is safe to say that the nation-state owed its former prominence to the fact that state and economic interests were united in the idea of the nation. The epitome of this union was the bourgeoisie, a class that often closed ranks in support of national politics which it perceived as promoting its own best interests. Today these interests are fragmented. The opinion leaders from the world of business are usually the first to demand an international political perspective at the expense of a national one. This may be the reason why the deconstruction of national myths today has lost much of its power to scandalize.

Increasing transnationalization does not, however, render national thinking obsolete, as one might think; it merely changes the function of such thinking. In the modern era, national thinking primarily served the interests of the nation-state; as transnationalization progresses it is pulled back from the borders of the nation-state and deployed in the heart of society. Nationalism is being deterritorialized: instead of shaping foreign policy, that means regulating inter-state competition, it assumes an ever greater role in domestic matters where, under the guise of right-wing conservative ideologies, it participates in setting up inclusion and exclusion processes. Neo-national thinking, as we can see, is one of those particularisms generated in reaction to transnationalization. In much the same way that the universalism of the eighteenth and nineteenth centuries produced, in an apparently paradoxical effect, strong nation-states, transnationalization is now producing strong intra-societal nationalisms that have great potential precisely because they are operating from a defensive position. This line of thinking can be taken further: just as globalization encourages localization and regionalization, so the emergence of a global culture with unified values, signs, and symbols leads to the development of particularist cultural currents and ultimately to multiculturalism. All these dialectical processes have one thing in common – and here lies the real challenge for the future of all nation-states: they do not reinforce the ideological constructions called nation and state, but actually undermine them by pulling ahead of them on a trajectory of their own.

The concept and phenomenon of globalization itself is not addressed in this collection, but the form of particularization known as multi-culturalism is an important part of our discussion here. Multiculturalism as currently debated in European and North American countries reflects a complex and many-faceted social reality and has provoked an equally bewildering variety of statements from politicians and academics. This might explain why there is still no actual theory to account for the phenomenon, although there clearly is no shortage of analyses and insights that might serve as building blocks for such a theory. Four of the articles in this volume address these issues and are a fair reflection of the breadth of the current discussion. One is by Alexandra Ålund, who, based on the more phenomenological approach of Simmel and Schutz, addresses the situation of foreignness that may result from one's entering a new social environment. Taking the example of immigrant youths in Stockholm, she convincingly demon-strates how being foreign does not necessarily produce multiculture, and that the return to presumably cultural patterns is a reactive process. Phenomena of hybridization and essentialization may interact to constitute each other, as is the case with these youths whose very confrontation with the pressing social issues of the day results in a revival of 'old ghosts'.

Carl-Ulrik Schierup (this volume) chooses an altogether different approach to situate the phenomenon of cultural pluralism. He discusses the type of multiculturalism that has emerged as a master-narrative in postmodern western modernity, and that has come to influence, as a sort of standardized model, the actions of governments and other institutions in some states of Europe and North America. Schierup maintains that this type of multiculturalism is in a state of crisis today because the 'right to be different' has increasingly become a simple 'being different', and that even former advocates are now seeing the pitfalls of their approach. Today, he concludes, there is a greater demand for a more inclusive universalism than for an ever more differentiated multiculturalist approach.

Wicker's conclusions are similar to those of Schierup although he follows a different line of inquiry. Comparing the concepts of multi-culturalism offered by Hannah Arendt and John Rex, he demonstrates that of the three social spheres described in Arendt's model the middle one, marked by competition and discrimination, has encroached on the other two – the 'private' and the 'common' sphere – to such an extent that they are becoming meaningless. Present-day multi-culturalism and ethnicity do not originate in the private sphere – as some maintain despite evidence to the contrary – but in the expanding middle sphere. The battle for identities, therefore, is bound to become more significant. Only by strengthening the sphere of commonality dedicated to the principle of equality can the uncontrolled growth of ethnic and cultural particularisms be reversed.

Matteo Gianni's contribution argues for a more comprehensive politics of difference. He discusses the status of the liberal principles of the constitutional state in a time of growing multiculturalism, and wonders whether these principles may not be in need of reform. In this context he gives extensive consideration to Taylor's politics of recognition, which – brought to its logical conclusion – leads to the concept of dual citizenship. In addition to a general system that defines basic rights applicable to everybody, special rights should exist that articulate the interests of cultural and ethnic groups.

Multiculturalism and ethnicization are expressions of progressive differentiations within society; they each lead to specific politics of identity and, inevitably, to equally specific ethnopolitical conflicts. Ethnopolitical conflicts call for solutions based on identity politics: the circle is completed and the same process starts over again. There is no question in my mind that processes of transnationalization, in other words the de-nationalization of the state, are prerequisites to multiculturalism and ethnicization, for without the gradual disappearance of national assimilation pressures there would be no vacant territories for the various politics of identity to take root. In the following sub-chapter this realignment of the forces of identity politics is illustrated once again.

Europe

Several important and overlapping developments are currently unfolding in Europe. In their unique interactions they are creating a context for a specifically European politics of identity. One current is economic and involves the internationalization of competition. Its side-effects include liberalization and deregulation on a national level, wage cuts and growing unemployment, mounting public debts and the gradual dismantling of the welfare state. Globalization is generating the pressures that are forcing European societies to undergo radical changes *and* it has caused the continent's worst economic recession since World War II.

Social environments torn by crises and depression are sensitive to ideological constructions linking cultural, ethnic, and religious affiliation to visibly deteriorating social conditions. The public articulation of such ideas leads to the type of multiculturalism that Schierup criticizes in this volume. The 'right to be different' becomes a simple 'being different' and this in turn lends credibility to models of sudden insight that seem to explain why immigrants are more often unemployed than natives, why children of immigrants fail more often at school than local children, and why immigrant populations tend to concentrate in certain neighbourhoods. This type of culturalizing and ethnicizing of social problem fields is in evidence throughout Europe and the waves of xenophobia it produces are hardly surprising. Once created, the terms that enable processes of culturalization and ethnicization are readily available to anyone intent on (ab-) using them, whether from the top down or from the bottom up. In the top-down variety governmental and non-governmental institutions typically start operating with cultural and ethnic criteria; they usually justify such procedures by pointing out that it is more efficient to dispense services to ethnically grouped clients. Culturalization and ethnicization from the bottom up is based on a conviction held by many immigrant groups that they will have better access to scarce resources if they articulate their needs in ethnic terms and reactivate ethnic networks. In this volume, only Cristina Allemann-Ghionda discusses issues of culturalization and ethnicization in the social realm. After examining certain aspects of organization and curricula in national educational systems, she concludes that ethnicity plays a major role in practically all of the European countries under scrutiny.

The development of the European Union constitutes the second current that is causing fundamental changes in the social and political landscape of the old continent. Although primarily concerned with economic objectives, the EU is nevertheless causing significant changes in fields unrelated to the economy. It is becoming apparent that the political and economic integration of Europe will be accompanied by a process of identity-building that, no matter how fragile and convoluted at the present time, will ultimately weaken national identities (Shore and Black, 1994; Zetterholm, 1994). The very determination of various groups fighting to maintain a national identity – as evident in certain Euro-sceptical party platforms – or the conflicts building up around the issue of yet-to-be negotiated Euro-meanings indicates that the new Euro-identity construction is already more deeply rooted than is commonly assumed. It takes a major conflict between the EU and other economic powers to reveal just how far the EU has come in building new identities; indeed, nothing moves people to embrace a collective identity, even on a temporary basis, more than an attack from without.

Josep R. Llobera, in his chapter, inquires into the future of European ethnonations in a United Europe. This approach is not nearly as far-fetched as it may appear at first since even for radical ethnonationalist groups the independist option is becoming unimaginable and unappealing. Regardless of the outcome of Project EU the days of national independence are over for Europe because international commitments and global interdependence alone are sufficient to rule out such autonomy nowadays. Yet the weakening of nation-state sovereignty does not mean that nationalism will disappear altogether – in Europe no more than elsewhere. As Llobera points out, the truth is that nationalism can be put to very different uses and that the label nationalism often conceals other realities.

Llobera's argument brings us back full circle to a point I made earlier: that national thinking is retreating from the borders of the nation-state into the heart of society. Nationalism is now free to merge seamlessly with any number of sub-national ethnopolitical movements or, more likely, to be instrumentalized by such movements for their own purposes. On the European level political and economic inte-gration is echoed by the weakening of nation-state sovereignty *and* by the growth of regional ethnopolitical movements. Two such conflicts are investigated in this book. Gianni D'Amato and Siegfried Schieder analyse the genesis, structure, and dynamics of Italy's Northern League, while Marco Martiniello devotes his chapter to the Flemish-Walloon conflict in Belgium. There are other similar movements in Europe: the Scottish and Welsh autonomy movements in Great Britain, the Corse movement in France, the Basque movement in Spain, or the now settled Jura conflict in Switzerland are all of the same basic type. Common to them all are their claims of autonomy from a weakened central government, their way of linking territoriality with sub-nationalism, and their practice of reconstructing ethnic identity. As Llobera correctly points out, the demonization of nationalism pure and simple brings us no closer to any real solution. We need to reveal the root conflicts that generate national movements, to recognize the historical junctions at which they appear, and to understand the specific structural and political constellations that are conducive to their political actualization. There is no longer any doubt that globalization and the political integration of Europe provide a fertile soil for regionalist movements of this type. By the same token, it is quite evident that political systems based on a federalist model offer a far more suitable context for the prevention and handling of ethnopolitical movements than strongly centralized political entities.

Bibliography

Addor, G. (1911), 'De la naturalisation et de l'assimilation des étrangers en Suisse', Offprint *Schweizerisches Zentralblatt für Staats- und Gemeindeverwaltung,* XI, Zurich: Orell Füssli.

——, (1913), 'De l'assimilation des étrangers en Suisse', Offprint *Schweizerisches Zentralblatt für Staats- und Gemeindeverwaltung,* XIV, Zurich: Orell Füssli.

Allahar, A. L. (1996), 'Primordialism and Ethnic Political Mobilization in Modern Society', *New Community,* 22(1), pp. 5–21.

Alonso, A. M. (1994), 'The Politics of Space, Time, and Substance: State Formation, Nationalism, and Ethnicity', *Annual Review of Anthropology,* 23, pp. 379–405.

Amin, A. (1994), 'Post-Fordism: Models, Fantasies and Phantoms of Transition', in A. Amin (ed.), *Post-Fordism: A Reader,* Oxford: Blackwell, pp. 1–39.

Anderson, B. (1991 (1983)), *Imagined Communities,* London: Verso, Revised Edition.

Anthias, F. and Yuval-Davis N. (1992), *Racialized Boundaries,* London: Routledge.

Appadurai, A. (1991), 'Global Ethnoscapes: Notes and Queries for a Transnational Anthropology', in R. Fox (ed.), *Recapturing Anthropology,* Santa Fé: School of American Research Press, pp. 191–210.

Barth, F. (1989), 'The Analysis of Culture in Complex Societies', *Ethnos,* 54, pp. 120–142.

Bash, L., Glick Schiller, N. and Szanton Blanc, C. (1994), *Nations Unbound: Transnational Projects, Postcolonial Predicaments, and Deterritorialized Nation-States,* Langhorne: Gordon and Breach Science Publishers.

Bauman, Z. (1992), 'Soil, Blood and Identity', *Sociological Review,* 40(4), pp. 657–701.

Benda-Beckman, K. and Verkuyten, M. (eds), (1995), *Nationalism, Ethnicity and Cultural Identity in Europe,* Utrecht: ERCOMER.

Benedict, R. (1966 (1935)), *Patterns of Culture,* London: Routledge.

Boggs, C. (1995), 'Rethinking the Sixties Legacy: From New Left to New Social Movements', in S. M. Lyman (ed.), *Social Movements: Critiques, Concepts, Case-Studies,* Houndsmills and London: MacMillan Press, pp. 331–355.

Bonacich, E. (1980), 'Class Approaches to Ethnicity and Race', *The Insurgent Sociologist,* 10(2), pp. 9–23.

Borofsky, R. (1994), 'On the Knowledge and Knowing of Cultural Activities', in R. Borofsky (ed.), *Assessing Cultural Anthropology,* New York: McGraw-Hill, pp. 331–346.

Bourdieu, P. (1972), *Esquisse d'une Théorie de la Pratique,* Geneva: Droz.

Bourne, R. S. (1996 (1916)), 'Trans-National America', in W. Sollors (ed.), *Theories of Ethnicity: A Classical Reader,* Ipswich: The Ipswich Book Company, pp. 93–108.

Calhoun, C. (1993), 'Nationalism and Ethnicity', *Annual Review of Sociology*, 19, pp. 211–239.

Clifford, J. and Marcus, G. E. (eds), (1986), *Writing Culture: The Poetics and Politics of Ethnography*, Berkeley: University of California Press.

Cohen, J. L. (1985), 'Strategy or Identity: New Theoretical Paradigms and Contemporary Social Movements', *Social Research*, 52, pp. 663–716.

Connor, W. (1973), 'The Politics of Ethnonationalism', *Journal of International Affairs*, 27(1), pp. 1–21.

——, (1994), *Ethnonationalism: The Quest for Understanding*, Princeton: Princeton University Press.

Denzin, N. K. (1994), 'Postmodernism and Deconstructionism', in D. R. Dickens and A. Fontana (eds), *Postmodernism and Social Inquiry*, London: The Guilford Press, pp. 182–202.

Dittrich, E. J. and Radtke, F.-O. (1990), 'Der Beitrag der Wissenschaften zur Konstruktion ethnischer Minderheiten', in E. J. Dittrich and F.-O. Radtke (eds), *Ethnizität: Wissenschaft und Minderheiten*, Opladen: Westdeutscher Verlag, pp. 11–40.

Eco, U. (1991 (1972)), *Einführung in die Semiotik*, Munich: W. Fink.

Eller, J. D. and Coughlan, R. M. (1993), 'The Poverty of Primordialism: The Demystification of Ethnic Attachments', *Ethnic and Racial Studies*, 16(2), pp. 183–201.

Eriksen, T. H. (1993), *Ethnicity and Nationalism: Anthropological Perspectives*, London: Pluto.

Foweraker, J. (1995), *Theorizing Social Movements*, London and Boulder: Pluto.

Fox Piven, F. and Cloward, R. A. (1995), 'Collective Protest: A Critique of Resource-Mobilization Theory', in S. M. Lyman (ed.), *Social Movements: Critiques, Concepts, Case-Studies*, Houndsmills and London: MacMillan Press, pp. 137–167.

Friedman, J. (1994), *Cultural Identity and Global Process*, London: Sage.

Gallissot, R. (1992), 'Pluralisme culturel en Europe: identitées nationales et identité européenne. De l'intellectuel métis au métissage culturel de masses', *Informations sur les Sciences Sociales*, 31(1), pp. 117–127.

Geertz, C. (1963), 'The Integrative Revolution: Primordial Sentiments and Civil Politics in the New States', in C. Geertz (ed.), *Old Societies and New States: The Quest for Modernity in Asia and Africa*, New York: The Free Press, pp. 105–157.

Giddens, A. (1984), *The Constitution of Society*, Cambridge: Polity.

——, (1990), *The Consequences of Modernity*, Cambridge: Polity.

Gill, S. (1996), 'Globalization, Democratization, and the Politics of Indifference', in J. H. Mittelman (ed.), *Globalization: Critical Reflections*, Boulder: Lynne Rienner, pp. 205–228.

Glazer, N. and Moynihan, D. P. (eds), (1975), *Ethnicity: Theory and Experience*, Cambridge: Harvard University Press.

Gleason, P. (1982), 'American Identity and Americanization', in W. Peterson,

M. Novak and P. Gleason (eds), *Concepts of Ethnicity*, Cambridge: Harvard University Press, pp. 57–143.

Good, B. (1994), *Medicine, Rationality, and Experience*, Cambridge: Cambridge University Press.

Gordon, M. M. (1964), *Assimilation in American Life: The Role of Race, Religion, and National Origins*, Oxford: Oxford University Press.

Greenfeld, L. (1992), *Nationalism: Five Roads to Modernity*, Cambridge: Harvard University Press.

Hall, S. (1988), 'Brave New World', *Marxism Today*, October Issue, pp. 24–29.

Hannerz, U. (1992), *Cultural Complexity: Studies in the Social Organization of Meaning*, New York: Columbia University Press.

Heelas, P., Lash, S. and Morris, P. (eds), (1996), *Detraditionalization: Critical Reflections on Authority and Identity*, Cambridge: Blackwell.

Held, D. (1992), 'Democracy: From City-States to a Cosmopolitan Order?', *Political Studies*, 40 (Special Issue), pp. 10–39.

Hobsbawm, E. (1990), *Nations and Nationalism since 1780: Programme, Myth, Reality*, New York: Cambridge University Press.

——, (1992), 'Ethnicity and Nationalism in Europe', *Anthropology Today*, 8(1), pp. 3–8.

——, and Ranger, T. (eds), (1983), *The Invention of Tradition*, Cambridge: Cambridge University Press.

Huntington, S. P. (1993), 'The Clash of Civilizations', *Foreign Affairs*, 72, pp. 22–49.

Jessop, B. (1994), 'Post-Fordism and the State', in A. Amin (ed.), *Post-Fordism: A Reader*, Oxford: Blackwell, pp. 251–279.

Keesing, R. M. (1974), 'Theories of Culture', *Annual Review of Anthropology*, 3, pp. 73–97.

——, (1987), 'Anthropology as Interpretative Quest', *Current Anthropology*, 28, pp. 161–176.

——, (1994), 'Theories of Culture Revisited', in R. Borofsky (ed.), *Assessing Cultural Anthropology*, New York: McGraw-Hill, pp. 301–310.

Kleger, H. (1995), 'Transnationale Staatsbürgerschaft: Zur Arbeit an einem europäischen Bürgerstatus', in R. Erne, A. Gross, B. Kaufmann and H. Kleger (eds), *Transnationale Demokratie. Impulse für ein demokratisch verfasstes Europa*, Zurich: Realutopia, pp. 34–59.

Kuper, A. (1988), *The Invention of Primitive Society: Transformations of an Illusion*, London: Routledge.

Lash, S. and Urry, J. (1994), *Economies of Signs and Space*, London: Sage.

Lenoir, R. (1995), 'L'invention de la démographie et la formation de l'état', *Actes de la recherche en sciences sociales*, 108, pp. 36–61.

Lévi-Strauss, C. (1980 (1964)), *Mythologica I*, Frankfurt am Main: Suhrkamp.

List, F. (1959 (1841)), *Das nationale System der politischen Ökonomie*, Basle: Kyklos.

Lury, C. (1992), 'Popular Culture and the Mass Media', in R. Bocock and K. Thompson (eds), *Social and Cultural Forms of Modernity*, Cambridge: Polity, pp. 367–416.

Luxemburg, R. (1913), *Die Akkumulation des Kapitals*, Berlin: Paul Singer.

Lyotard, J.-F. (1984), *The Postmodern Condition*, Manchester: Manchester University Press.

Marshall, T. H. (1950), *Citizenship and the State*, Cambridge: Cambridge University Press.

Martin, D. (1995), 'Choices of Identity', *Social Identities*, 1(1), pp. 5–20.

Martiniello, M. (1995), *L'ethnicité dans les sciences sociales contemporaines*, Paris: Presses Universitaires de France.

Marx Ferree, M. (1992), 'The Political Context of Rationality: Rational Choice Theory and Resource Mobilization', in A. D. Morris and C. McClurg Mueller (eds), *Frontiers in Social Movement Theory*, New Haven and London: Yale University Press, pp. 29–52.

Marx, K. (1969), *Das Kapital*, vols. 1 and 2, Berlin: Dietz.

——, (1973), *Das Kapital*, vol. 3, Berlin: Dietz.

——, (1974), *Grundrisse der Kritik der politischen Ökonomie*, Berlin: Dietz.

Mattick, P. (1969), *Marx and Keynes: The Limits of the Mixed Economy*, Boston: Porter Sargent.

——, (1970), 'Werttheorie und Kapitalakkumulation', in C. Rolshausen (ed.), *Kapitalismus und Krise. Eine Kontroverse um das Gesetz des tendenziellen Falls der Profitrate*, Frankfurt am Main: Europäische Verlagsanstalt.

Mittelman, J. H. (ed.), (1996), *Globalization: Critical Reflections*, Boulder: Lynne Rienner.

Murray, S. O. (1995), 'The Invention of Heterosexuality', *Journal of Sex Research* 32(3), pp. 263–265.

Neckel, S. (1994), 'Die Erfindung des Politischen', *Kölner Zeitschrift für Soziologie und Sozialpsychologie*, 46(4), pp. 738–740.

Noiriel, G. (1991), *La Tyrannie du National: Le droit d'asile en Europe*, Paris: Calmann-Lévy.

Panitch, L. (1996), 'Rethinking the Role of the State', in J. H. Mittelman (ed.), *Globalization: Critical Reflections*, Boulder: Lynne Rienner, pp. 83–113.

Park, R. E. (1928), 'Human Migration and the Marginal Man', *The American Journal of Sociology*, 33(6), pp. 881–893.

——, (1950), *Race and Culture*, Glencoe: Free Press.

——, and Burgess, E. W. (1921), *Introduction to the Science of Sociology*, Chicago: The University of Chicago Press.

Patterson, H. O. (1983), 'The Nature, Causes, and Implications of Ethnic Identification', in C. Fried (ed.), *Minorities: Community and Identity*, Berlin: Dahlem Konferenzen, pp. 25–50.

Popper, K. R. (1945), *The Open Society and its Enemies*, London: Routledge.

Raymond-Duchosal, C. (1929), *Les Etrangers en Suisse*, Paris: Félix Alcan.

Ricœur, P. (1981), *Hermeneutics and the Human Sciences*, Cambridge: Cambridge University Press.

Robertson, R. (1992), *Globalization*, London: Sage.

——, (1995), 'Glocalization: Time-Space and Homogeneity-Heterogeneity', in M. Featherstone, S. Lash and R. Robertson (eds), *Global Modernities*, London: Sage, pp. 24–44.

Rolshausen, C. (ed.), (1970), *Kapitalismus und Krise: Eine Kontroverse um das Gesetz des tendenziellen Falls der Profitrate*, Frankfurt am Main: Europäische Verlagsanstalt.

Roosens, E. (1989), *Creating Ethnicity: The Process of Ethnogenesis*, Newbury Park: Sage.

Rothschild, J. (1981), *Ethnopolitics: A Conceptual Framework*, New York: Columbia University Press.

Said, E. (1978), *Orientalism*, New York: Pantheon.

Sanjek, R. (1991), 'The Ethnographic Present', *Man*, 26(4), pp. 607–628.

Schuster, A. N. (1913), *Argentinien: Land, Volk, Wirtschaftsleben und Kolonisation*, Munich: Huber.

——, (1929), *Paraguay: Land, Volk, Geschichte, Wirtschaftsleben und Kolonisation*, Stuttgart: Strecker und Schröder.

Shils, E. (1957), 'Primordial, Personal, Sacred and Civil Ties', *British Journal of Sociology*, 8(2), pp. 130–145.

Shore, C. and Black, A. (1994), 'Citizen's Europe and the Construction of European Identity', in V. A. Goddard, J. R. Llobera and C. Shore (eds), *The Anthropology of Europe: Identity and Boundaries in Conflict*, Oxford: Berg, pp. 275–298.

Smith, A. D. (1981), *The Ethnic Revival in the Modern World*, Cambridge: Cambridge University Press.

——, (1994), 'The Politics of Culture: Ethnicity and Nationalism', in T. Ingold (ed.), *Companion Encyclopedia of Anthropology: Humanity, Culture and Social Life*, London: Routledge, pp. 706–733.

Staiano, K. V. (1980), 'Ethnicity as Process: The Creation of an Afro-American Identity', *Ethnicity*, 7(1), pp. 27–33.

Swidler, A. (1986), 'Culture in Action: Symbols and Strategies', *American Sociological Review*, 51(2), pp. 273–286.

Taylor, C. (1992), 'The Politics of Recognition', in A. Gutmann (ed.), *Multiculturalism and 'The Politics of Recognition': An Essay by Charles Taylor*, Princeton: Princeton University Press, pp. 25–73.

Taylor, V. and Whittier, N. E. (1995), 'Collective Identity in Social Movement Communities: Lesbian Feminist Mobilization', in A. D. Morris and C. McClurg Mueller (eds), *Frontiers in Social Movement Theory*, New Haven and London: Yale University Press, pp. 104–129.

Tylor, E. B. (1958 (1871)), *Primitive Culture*, New York: Harper Torchbooks.

Touraine, A. (1988), *The Return of the Actor: Social Theory in Post-Industrial Society*, Minneapolis: University of Minnesota Press.

Trautmann, T. R. (1987), *Lewis Henry Morgan and the Invention of Kinship*, Berkeley: University of California Press.

Turner, V. (1974), *Drama, Fields, and Metaphors*, Ithaca: Cornell University Press.

Vayda, A. P. (1994), 'Actions, Variations, and Change: The Emerging Anti-Essentialist View in Anthropology', in R. Borofsky (ed.), *Assessing Cultural Anthropology*, New York: McGraw-Hill, pp. 320–329.

Vervaeck, B. (1984), 'Towards a Semantic-Praxiological Approach to Culture Creation', in R. Pinxten (ed.), *New Perspectives in Belgian Anthropology*, Göttingen: Herodot, pp. 37–62.

Vincent, J. (1986), 'System and Process, 1974–1985', *Annual Review of Anthropology*, 15, pp. 99–119.

Wagner, R. (1981 (1975)), *The Invention of Culture*, Chicago: The University of Chicago Press.

Waters, M. (1995), *Globalization*, London: Routledge.

Weber, M. (1956), *Wirtschaft und Gesellschaft*, Tübingen: Mohr.

Wallman, S. (ed.), (1979), *Ethnicity at Work*, London: The MacMillan Press.

Wicker, H.-R. (1996a), 'Flexible Cultures, Hybrid Identities, and Reflexive Capital', *Anthropological Journal on European Cultures*, 5(1), pp. 7–29.

——, (1996b), 'Einleitung', in H.-R. Wicker, C. Bolzmann, R. Fibbi, K. Imhof and A. Wimmer (eds), *Das Fremde in der Gesellschaft: Migration, Ethnizität und Staat*, Zurich: Seismo Verlag, pp. 11–38.

Wieviorka, M. (1994), 'Ethnicity as Action', in J. Rex (ed.), *Ethnic Mobilization in a Multi-Cultural Europe*, Aldershot: Avebury, pp. 23–29.

Zetterholm, S. (ed.), (1994), *National Cultures and European Integration*, Oxford: Berg.

–1–

The Future of Ethnonations in a United Europe[1]

Josep R. Llobera

As the European Union inexorably moves towards higher levels of economic, political and cultural integration, states, ethnonations, transnational ethnic communities and regions ponder the advantages of such developments. The attitudes that each of these types of units display are obviously diverse and reflect their own different interests and agendas. In the overarching institutions of the European Union, ethnonations tend to see a potentially more sympathetic and flexible framework in which to realize their objective of shared sovereignty than they do in the traditional state in which they find themselves at present. A 'Europe of the regions' – the ambiguity of the word 'region' notwithstanding – is one of the possible outcomes of the current process of unification, though the likelihood of such a development will depend upon the strength that ethnonations and regions can muster in their confrontation with the state and with the emerging European bureaucracy.

Social scientists have recently observed, although not really explained, the apparent paradox that at present, while there is an impetus towards the building of large economic and political units, there is, at the same time, a strong assertion of small-scale regional, ethnic and national identities. This has been taken to signify the death-knell of the nation-state and the coming of a future configuration of Europe in which ethnonational and regional identities dominate the scene in the context of large scale, European-based institutions. Is this wishful thinking on

1. A Catalan version of this paper was published in the collective book *El nacionalisme català a la fi del segle XX*. Barcelona: Edicions de la Revista de Catalunya, 1993, pp. 17–30; the paper has been updated and revised, but not extensively rewritten. For a more detailed treatment of some of the topics dealt with in this paper see Llobera (1993) and (1994) and Goddard, Llobera and Shore (1994).

the part of those who espouse such a thesis, or are there real trends in this direction?

Much has been made of the hegemony of the nation-state in modernity. There appears to be a consensus that the dominant, if not the sole form of political organization in the post 1789 era, and even before that, has been the nation-state. This thesis contains two very different assumptions. Firstly, it conveys the idea that, while in the medieval period a variety of state forms flourished (empires, city-states, theocracies, federations, etc.), modern times see the emergence, consolidation and final domination of a medium-sized, territorial, centralized, sovereign type of polity. Secondly, this new political unit is also characterized by national homogeneity – hence the expression 'nation-state', which means one state, one nation. Both assumptions are problematic, particularly the second one. While there is little doubt that there has been a tendency towards the consolidation of medium-sized, 'modern' types of states in Western Europe, the presence of the Austro-Hungarian and Ottoman empires until World War I, of the German Reich from 1933 to 1945, and of the Russian empire until recently, qualify the idea of the dominance of the nation-state in the modern period when referring to Europe as a whole. In addition, the persistence of small states in Western Europe challenges the assumption of the medium-sized, nation-state as the vessel of modernity.

A much more important critique of the concept of nation-state is that it is regularly used to describe states which are meant to be nationally, that is ethnically homogeneous, when in reality they are not. The idea of a world consisting of states, the boundaries of which coincide with the homelands of cultural groups, is a myth. In a well-known article, W. Connor (1972) remarked that only 9.1 per cent of the world's existing states were ethnically homogeneous, and hence deserved the label 'nation-states'. It would appear, then, that the uninational state is not a common occurrence, but rather a rarity. There are, of course, different degrees of heterogeneity: from the existence of a small national minority within a state to truly multinational states. The point to be emphasized here is the misnomer of the expression nation-state when we are referring to the realities, as opposed to the ideals, of modernity.

To return now to Western Europe, none of the medium-sized classical examples of nation-states (France, Great Britain, Spain) fit the bill; and the newcomers (Italy and Germany) hardly qualify because either the nation is wider than the state (Germany) or because the nation itself is an invention without roots and what has salience are the local identities (Italy). Of course, the word 'nation' is often used in a political sense as equivalent to citizenship in order to signify the democratic incorporation of the population of a country to the political tasks. But the word 'state' should suffice to indicate this reality, particularly in the twentieth century. It is true that there is some ambiguity in the word 'state', which can also mean, as is the case in the USA, a federal union; in this eventuality, the constituent units are referred to as 'states', and hence the use of the expression nation-state is used to refer to the whole. Nevertheless, these so-called states lack one essential characteristic – total sovereignty. It is inescapable that the term 'nation' should have a political and cultural dimension. Only ideally do countries converge towards the perfect congruence between the political (state) and the cultural (nation). As K. Aun has remarked, 'the paradox is that both nation-building by the states and state-building by the nations have the same root – nationalism; and they have the same goal – the nation-state; but as processes they collide with each other' (1980: 72). In fact, the objective of achieving true nation-statehood has proven a slippery, if not unattainable aspiration.

The process of clarification of the concept of nation-state has indicated an unavoidable ambiguity in the use of the term. It is naive to expect that the expression 'nation-state' will ever be used to reflect a univocal reality. The reluctance of social scientists to coin, and to agree to the use of new technical terms, with precise definitions, is notorious; they prefer to stick to everyday language, to redefine old terms and hence to contribute to the ceremony of confusion. But in addition to this, multiple meanings also result through the possibility that a term may be used by different groups to defend political models in the cultural area. In other words, terminological ambiguity may mask attempts to monopolize the symbolic capital of certain ideas which are considered extremely valuable in modernity. This is the case concerning the concept of nation. Many social scientists, particularly in the French tradition, are reluctant to label as 'nations' entities which are not politically independent; Durkheim, Mauss, Dumont, and more recently Schnapper (1994) all appear to agree on this point.

The insistence of multinational states such as the UK and Spain in calling themselves 'nations' should alert us to the appeal of the idea of nation. From the perspective of the submerged ethnonations, there is also an insistence upon asserting their nationhood by using the term 'nation' to refer to themselves. Furthermore, the process of cultural struggle is completed by each group labelling its opponent with a term considered unacceptable by the other – ethnonations do not like being called 'regions' and self-styled nation-states object to being referred to as states.

Certain rigid commentators believe that wherever state and nation do not coincide, there is bound to be a clash of loyalties; it is argued that one cannot serve two masters. Raymond Aron put it the following way: 'Chacun de nous a une patrie et une religion, mais nul ne saurait avoir deux Patries' (1969: 41). This is true in so far as both states and nations try to become nation-states, which is precisely what happens in the era of nationalism. As expressed above, it is fair to say that, on the whole, the idea of a world in which nation-states would be the predominant political type is a mirage. The practice of nationalism in the past two centuries (both state nationalism and nationalism against the state) has shown how illusory the dream is, and how often it can turn into a nightmare. The first fact to be faced is that the reality of any unit, no matter how many subdivisions a state might be subjected to, is likely to still be multinational and multiethnic. This is, of course, a generalization and, as such, it should be qualified. Even if we can agree that, at least in Europe, the nationality principle has radically changed the political map of the continent in the past two centuries, the end is never a set of homogeneous states. A number of reasons account for this.

1. The nationality principle is eminently ambiguous and open to instrumentalization by any group which has an axe to grind. All the key elements involved in the definition of a nation (language, culture, history) can easily be manipulated. Insofar as a national project can gather a degree of popular support, it has a de facto reality. In other words, there is no end to potential fissiparity, though in practice it may be restricted.
2. Once the notion of homogeneous states has been dispelled, the next myth to be challenged is the idea that there exist homogeneous territorial ethnonations. The uneven development of capitalism in the different European states has produced population movements which have undermined the traditional homogeneity of these areas.
3. Some parts of Europe, particularly the East, are traditionally areas of great national and ethnic complexity.
4. Recent migratory processes have brought into Europe, particularly Western Europe, transnational ethnic communities from different parts of the world.

It is interesting to note that the expression 'nation of nations' has made its recent appearance in the literature in order to account for such realities as Spain and the UK. This brings the issue of multiple identity and multiple loyalty into the fore. If it were possible to separate loyalty to the state (a political matter) from emotive attachment to the nation (a psycho-cultural phenomenon), the problem of congruence between state and nation would not be of much consequence.

The problem arises because the state tries to become a nation, and thus has to elicit sentiments of belonging, that is love from its subjects; this is the modern precondition for loyalty. In order to succeed in this, it must attempt to homogenize a multiethnic reality. This is achieved by erasing, with a mixture of coercion and inducement, all cultures other than the dominant one. On the other hand, the nation, in an attempt to preserve its identity, has no other option but to try to become a sovereign, self-governing entity, that is an independent state. This is a rather ideal typical presentation of a much more complex historical reality. In fact, states and nations have to often compromise and accept solutions which are far from their intended objectives. Furthermore, it should already be understood that deviations from the ideal norm are overdetermined by a structural variable hitherto unmentioned – the regional or global interstate system.

It is precisely as a result of this fuzziness between state and nation that a concept such as that of 'nation of nations' could be coined. This expression seems to indicate a supernational reality, usually formed over a long period of time around a cluster of nations which share a state. The new entity would emerge in the context of a sort of pooling of cultures, each essentially preserving its identity, but giving rise to a higher level, national reality. Now, this model can only work if the state is the result of a pact of equals, and it is organized on a federal basis, respecting the national characteristics of the constituent parts. Historically, this is an extreme rarity, with only Switzerland perhaps approximating the model. In the historical context of Europe, even if some states were initially the result of a union of crowns (usually engineered by monarchs in league with sections of the aristocracy), what happens in the long run is that they become centralized, unitarian type of states, with a dominant nationality which tries to impose, to various degrees, its own language, culture, sense of history, religion, etc. on the others. In as far as this process is successful, the expression 'nation of nations' may be appropriate but it implies that the second part of the equation refers mostly to the past. France, originally an 'ethnic mosaic', would perhaps best conform to this model, although one should not forget that the end-product is recent and it contains imperfections.

So what can be said about realities such as Spain and the UK? Can they be envisaged as nations? The two cases are not necessarily the same, although they offer interesting possibilities of comparison. The problem with the UK is that there is no single word to designate the members of the supposed nation – although Tom Narin (1988) has suggested, somewhat jokingly, the term Ukanian. British is, of course, the usual word, but it excludes the peoples of Northern Ireland.

Leaving aside terminological problems, can we say that English, Northern Irish, Scots and Welsh feel the same towards the UK? It is obvious that for the English the UK is England writ large or a Greater England. British culture is essentially English culture, with some minor colourful concessions to the cultural peripheries. The English refer shamelessly to the UK as 'England' (a practice which is even more widespread among foreigners). This should come as no surprise, even if the Scots tried, after the Union of Parliaments, to popularize the expression 'Britain' (and even 'North Britain' to refer to themselves). Scots, Welsh and Irish have lived under the spell of English culture, and have to a certain extent been 'anglicized'. Pressures for the creation of a strong nation-state were stronger in Ireland (a kind of colonial outpost) and led to the creation of the incomplete Republic of Ireland in 1922. The Scots, who had essentially joined the Union of their own will, preserved an array of separate institutions (legal and educational systems, Church, etc.); the Welsh were incorporated into the English crown much earlier and by force, but were not 'anglicized' until well-entered modernity. There have been movements of national self-assertion in both Scotland and Wales since the late nineteenth century. While in the former, this self-assertion is based on a strong sense of history, in the latter, the linguistic and cultural elements predominate.

I tend to agree with B. Crick (1991) when he says that 'British' is a political term and a legal concept best applied to the institutions of the UK state, to common citizenship and common political arrangements. It is not a cultural term, nor does it correspond to any real sense of a nation. And nor should it: '. . . to be British demands a kind of loyalty, but a pragmatic loyalty limited to those civil institutions we have in common' (1991: 97). For the peripheral nations of the UK, there was a sense at the height of the British Empire that being 'British' had 'national' overtones. However, this is hardly the case today, although there is still perhaps a mystical sense of British identity via the Royal Family. Furthermore, at present, the UK consists not only of a disproportionately large dominant nation (England, with 46 million people) and three subordinated nations (Scotland, with 5 million people; Wales, 2.7 million; and Northern Ireland, 1.5 million), but contains a number of transnational ethnic communities making for a polity which is culturally pluralistic in the extreme. A sense of British identity in such a plural society can only be understood in the sense expressed above by Crick. The nationalist demands of the Scottish, Welsh and North Irish peoples are of a different quality and intensity, and may require differing specific solutions. In any case, whatever these solutions may be, they are more likely than not to further erode the idea of a British cultural nation. These developments, and the fear of being swallowed by Europe, are awakening the sleeping beast of English nationalism – a creature which at its worst exhibits xenophobic, chauvinistic and anti-European sentiments.

England is to the UK what Castile is to Spain. However, there is an initial terminological difference that should be noted. While in the British case there is only a cumbersome word to designate the supposed nation-state (United Kingdom of Great Britain and Northern Ireland) and no word at all to refer to their 'nationals', the very opposite occurs in the case of Spain. Although the Spanish state is very much a Castilian invention and creation, the ruling elites and their ideological spokesmen have always insisted on using the term 'Spain' to refer to an indivisible, national reality. In Spanish nationalist discourses, from the post French Revolutionary period to today, if there is one constant it is that Spain is always described as a single and indivisible nation. None of the constituent parts of Spain are recognized with national status (although the 1978 Constitution accepts the existence of 'nationalities') in the sense of entities endowed with contractual powers, among which figures the right to self-determination.

For thirty-five years, the Francoist dictatorship engaged in the most active and aggressive policies of nation-building ever seen within the Spanish state. Its objective was to create a homogeneous national space of Spanishness; to that end, it was essential to erase the national identities of Catalonia and the Basque Country. If Franco failed to achieve his stated goal, it was not for lack of trying; he used all the means that a quasi-totalitarian dictatorship had at its reach – the educational system at all levels, military conscription, the media, political institutions, the fascist syndicates, the Catholic hierarchy, etc. – to project the idea of Spain as a chosen community, with a common past and a common destiny. He only underestimated one thing: the will of the people of Catalonia and the Basque Country to resist the policies of cultural extermination.

In the aftermath of Franco's death, the demands for autonomy in Catalonia and the Basque Country could only go unheeded at the cost of alienating the two most dynamic areas of the Spanish state. A democratization of the country required as a sine qua non the devolution of power. The Constitution of 1978 was a compromise in that it created a moderately decentralized 'state of the autonomies', in which not only Catalonia and the Basque Country, but also all of the constituent parts of the state, were given autonomic powers (although the actual configuration and boundaries of the different autonomous communities were not without problems). This process of decentralization has generated strong regionalist sentiments in most of the autonomous communities and even incipient nationalist feelings in some of them. For the majority of the population, Spain is still a 'state' and a 'nation', although this is not the case in the Basque Country and Catalonia. While it is still too early to foresee the likely developments of nationalist sentiments in Spain, it is unlikely that ethnonationalisms will subside in the near future, given the pending nationalist agenda.

Had I taken Belgium as an example of a 'nation of nations', it would haven been much easier to show the clay feet of such a construct. As a recent state with eight score years of existence, it could only appear as an ideal nation-state in the musings of narrow-minded ideologists. In recent surveys, 'Belgian' identity only comes in third place of choice, after ethnonational identity and European identity.

In any event, I think that the cases of the UK and Spain show how two old European states, with similar processes of state formation, and which are often presented in the literature as successful nation-states (although in the case of the UK, the reference in the literature is often only to 'England'), are in fact multinational realities, even if they exist as 'nations' for a large percentage of the population of both countries; nevertheless, even for those who define themselves in ethnonational terms, the fact of the antiquity of both states and of the concomitant processes of nation-building in which both have engaged, have created an additional layer of national characteristics which live side by side with the ethnonational ones. Whether this entitles us to speak of multiple national identity is problematic, though not totally outlandish. There is, however, a slippery slope which leads us from such an idea to the postmodernist scenario, with a conception of culture as a global supermarket in which individuals choose from a range of cultural artefacts, a combination of the identity flavours of the day according to their conditioning and preferences. Whether the world in general, and Europe in particular, is heading towards such a reality is difficult to foresee, though what is worth exploring is the apparently contradictory double motion towards globalization and fragmentation.

If prior to the collapse of the Soviet order, the trends towards the internationalization of the world economy, the progressive domination on a world level of a transnational 'culture' (initially American in origin) and the impact of the technological revolution (particularly the processing and communication of information) were already obvious, the collapse of the communist world has dispelled the few illusory hopes that existed of a possible alternative to capitalist hegemony on a world scale. Whether we believe in Fukuyama's 'End of History' ideology or not, the reality of the global village seems to be inevitable now, at least in a certain sense. We are told that, in some ways, we are all becoming more the same – or at least we tend to consume the same cultural and material products. Does this mean that we think, feel and behave in the same way? The answer is, of course, a resounding no, because the way in which different nations, ethnic groups and classes react to the global culture are mediated by their very different identities. But even here a certain amount of uniformization must be taking place. After all, we also have very similar educational curricula.

It is in this context of general globalization that the phenomenon of ethnic identity has not disappeared, as modernization theorists had predicted, but rather has become ever more salient. Around the world, people may watch American soap operas, have English as a lingua franca, wear jeans, drink coke, listen to Madonna and read international potboilers, and yet only be 'Americanized' superficially. If they live in a multinational and multiethnic state, as is likely to be the case, they may have a pragmatic allegiance to the governing institutions of the country, but they are also likely to have a strong sense of ethnic or ethnonational identity (in addition to other possible overlapping identities such as gender and class).

For better or for worse, this is a world trend that shows no signs of abating, and which, of course, undermines the stability of unitary and centralized multinational states. I would strongly disagree with Hobsbawm's contention (1990) that these signs should be read as the swan song of nationalism. There is, of course, no way of predicting the future, but we can certainly learn from the past. The foretold death of ethnonationalism has been asserted at least since Marx and Mill in the 1840s. All those 'peoples without history' that Engels had ridiculed – the Basques, the Bretons, the Slovenians, the Welsh, etc. – have come back to haunt him; they are all still here today, with ever growing and stronger identities. I think that, at the very least, this should generate a cautionary attitude towards the vitality of ethnonationalism even in those who are sceptical about the long-term viability of the small, ethnonational identities in a world characterized by uniformity. I think that we must still listen to Mazzini's idea that nationhood is the necessary intermediate identity between individ-ualism and cosmopolitanism. Perhaps in a future 'brave new world', national identities will be totally obsolete; however, this is not the case for the foreseeable future.

It may be worth exploring in some detail the recent reoccurrence of ethnonationalism. First of all, I would like to insist upon the obvious: that in Europe, like elsewhere, there are a good number of unsatisfied ethnonationalist demands which have manifested themselves for quite a long period of time. No doubt, the intensity has varied from period to period according to the structural conditions of the states and the international conjuncture. However, the bottom line is that unless the demands are fulfilled (either through autonomy or secession) the conflict is likely to continue. I should immediately add that in a number of cases the ethnic and national mix in a given territory is such that no easy solutions present themselves. The collapse of rigid and authoritarian political structures has been the immediate detonator of ethnonationalism in the East and West; however, only where there was a previous situation of suppressed ethnonationalities have movements of national emancipation re-emerged (as occurred in Spain, but not in Portugal).

It is difficult to characterize the events that have transformed the Soviet block beyond recognition. Should we talk about revolution, upheaval or simply chaos? More than five years after the beginning of the major visible changes, things are still in a state of flux, although some points can be made with some certainty. There is, first of all, the collapse of the USSR-dominated politico-military block. Second, the idea of a command economy has been abandoned to the gnawing rats, and substituted by more or less rapid moves towards a market economy. Third, there has been a strong assertion of ethnic and national identities and a move towards the (re)creation of nation-states.

It would theoretically be very satisfactory if we could suggest that the revival of nationalism in the West and in the East is the result of a general movement. But this does not seem to be the case. Western ethnonationalism (and regionalism) is taking place in the context of waning nation-states (for the reasons mentioned above) and the appearance of the European Union as a condominium of power. The future shape of the European Union is far from decided and it matters to ethnonations and regions whether it is a centralized federalism (all powers exerted by the centre), confederalism (general government subordinated to constituent states) or federalism (general and regional governments to be each within a clearly defined sphere; co-ordinated but equal; independent; principle of subsidiarity). It is obviously the federalist option, the so called Europe of the regions, that is favoured by ethnonations and regions. Not only does it respond to sound economic arguments, but it is also the adequate framework in which to preserve and develop cultural authenticity and in which to exert a proper, more direct democratic control of political institutions.

As I have repeatedly indicated, in Western Europe the independentist option, pure and simple, is becoming unimaginable and unappealing, even for radical ethnonationalist groups. For example, the slogan coined by the Scottish National Party in 1988 – 'Independence in Europe' – expresses the essence of the compromise forced upon originally secessionist groups which have been induced to rethink their strategy in the light of the momentum towards an even closer European union. The unlikelihood of obtaining enough popular backing for a 'pure' separatist option that is outside the European Union, or the reluctance of the state apparatus to concede it if this were the case, make such a programme unrealistic. In addition, the assumption that the newly independent country would be taken aboard the European Union is not something that can be taken for granted. However, in the eventuality of a major state crisis, the independist option might prove both appealing and feasible.

The federalist perspective, by emphasizing the principles of auto-nomy (that is respecting the right of all the collectivities), co-operation (a union to solve common problems) and subsidiarity (the federation is organized from bottom to top; that is the centre only takes the tasks that have been delegated to it and that it is more efficient at) offers a much better chance of achieving the major objectives of the ethno-nations. However, it should be noted that at present, and particularly after Mastricht, the European Union is far from being or becoming a federal union. Notwithstanding the reluctance of many states to move beyond a confederalist structure (this attitude being particularly strong in the UK), and the dangers of a centralized federalism, the game is open to shape the European Union in different possible ways. A growing pressure from ethnonations and regions to have a more direct say in the decision making of the European Union is the precondition for achieving a federal Europe with a strong democratic Parliament, as well as an ever growing role for the Committee of Regions, which in due course could constitute, along with the Council of Ministers, a 'genuine upper chamber consisting of representatives of the regions and of the existing member states' (McReady, 1991: 18).

It is important to emphasize that, at least in the context of the European Union, the progressive withering away of the nation-state will not mean that ethnonations will succeed in establishing themselves as nation-states. There will certainly be a new nationalism which 'will seek to mobilize new sentiments of resistance and cultural development based on the challenges of the twenty first century' (McCrone, 1991: 8); nevertheless, the old doctrine of sovereignty is in its death-throes, and boundaries of all sorts are likely to become more fluid.

In the aftermath of the collapse of the Soviet Union and Yugoslavia into internecine ethnic/national struggles, it has become *de rigueur* among 'progressive' intellectuals to revamp an old-fashioned distinction between 'good' and 'bad' nationalism under the labels 'civic' and 'ethnic' nationalism respectively (Ignatieff, 1993). While the former is presented as essentially democratic in character, emphasizing loyalty to institutions and to an egalitarian political creed, the latter is depicted as denying individual freedoms and as sacrificing everything to a community often understood in terms of common descent or based on blood ties. Only a small step from such a definition of ethnic nationalism is required in order to conceptualize it as the cause of all ethnic violence and war. This seems to me a rather simplistic conception, if only because it ignores an array of other causes, among which I would point out the lack of liberal and democratic traditions in many of the countries which suffer the so-called ravages of 'ethnic nationalism'. It also glosses over the important role of oppressive states in generating reactive nationalisms. Furthermore, the distinction between civic and ethnic nationalism seems to ignore the peaceful struggle for cultural and linguistic autonomy of stateless nations in the Western world. Last but not least, the term ethnic nationalism introduces an element of confusion in the social scientific literature, because it can be mistaken with the established term 'ethnonationalism', which I have used freely in this chapter to refer to substate nationalisms or nationalisms against the state (Connor, 1972).

To return to the nature of nationalism, it does not help, neither cognitively nor practically, to demonize it; the truth is that nationalism can be put to very different uses and that the label nationalism often conceals other realities. In an article published originally in 1971, Clifford Geertz captured the ambiguous character of nationalism as a begetter of both havoc and creativity, and he added:

> It would seem, then, well to spend less time decrying it – which is a little like cursing the winds – and more in trying to figure out why it takes the forms it does and how it might be prevented from tearing apart even as it creates the societies in which it arises, and beyond that the whole fabric of modern civilization. (Geertz, 1973: 254)

To conclude on a note about the future. There is little doubt that an ethnonationalism which is too obsessed with defining itself in primordialist terms is likely to clash with other potential identities and that ethnic conflict will probably follow; nevertheless, there are democratic mechanisms which can help to regulate this (McGarry and O'Leary, 1993). The notion of territoriality is likely to become more central than are the purely cultural or linguistic features – ethnonational identity will emphasize living and working in a given territory, though, no doubt, there will still be a more or less important ethnic element present.

Bibliography

Aron, R. (1969), *Les désillusions du progrés*, Paris: Calmann-Lévy.

Aun, K. (1980), 'A Critique of the Nation-State', in N. A. Nyiri, and T. Miljan (eds), *Unity and Diversity*, Waterloo, Ontario: W. Laurier University Press.

Connor, W. (1972), 'Nation-Building or Nation-Destroying', *World Politics*, 24, pp. 319–355.

——, (1994), *Ethnonationalism: The Quest for Understanding*. Princeton: Princeton University Press.

Crick, B. (1991), 'The English and the British', in B. Crick (ed.), *National Identities*, Oxford: Blackwell, pp. 90–104.

Geertz, C. (1973), *The Interpretation of Cultures: Selected Essays*, New York: Basic Books.

Goddard, V. A., Llobera, J. R. and Shore, C. (1994), 'Introduction: The Anthropology of Europe', in V. A. Goddard, J. R. Llobera and C. Shore (eds), *The Anthropology of Europe: Identity and Boundaries in Conflict*, Oxford: Berg, pp. 1–40.

Hobsbawm, E. J. (1990), *Nations and Nationalism since 1870*, Cambridge: Cambridge University Press.

Ignatieff, M. (1993), *Blood and Belonging: Journeys into the New Nationalism*, London: Vintage.

Llobera, J. R. (1993), 'The Role of the State and the Nation in Europe', in M. Garcia (ed.), *European Identity and the Search for Legitimacy*, London: Pinter, pp. 64–80.

——, (1994), *The God of Modernity: The Development of Nationalism in Western Europe*, Oxford: Berg.

McCrone, D. (1991), 'Post-Nationalism and the Nation-State', *Radical Scotland*, 49, pp. 6–8.

McGarry, J. and O'Leary, B. (eds), (1993), *The Politics of Ethnic Conflict*, London: Routledge.

McReady, B. (1991), 'Scotland's Ace', *Radical Scotland*, 50, pp. 17–18.

Narin, T. (1988), *The Enchanted Glass: Britain and its Monarchy*, London: Radius.

Schnapper, D. (1994), *La communauté des citoyens*, Paris: Gallimard.

-2-

Nationalism and the Theory of Society

Kurt Imhof

The renaissance of nationalism in both Eastern and Western Europe and the consequences of ethnically-based semantics of difference in South-East Europe have caught sociology off-guard. Western sociology did not consider itself directly responsible for the missing prognosis of the surprising collapse of socialism. Yet the profession has been shaken by the unexpected importance of ethnonationalistic processes of inclusion and exclusion, which appear in the form of separatism and secessionism, virulent racism in the West, war, ethnic cleansing and even genocide in the East. There is talk of 'failure' (Nielsen, 1985: 135; Hondrich, 1992) and a 'deficit of basic theory' in sociology, which for a long time 'hardly concerned itself with subjects like the nation, the nation-state, nationalism or national identity' (Ettrich, 1994: 4; Sterbling, 1994). In a multitude of publications, a debate has begun which concerns the social sciences in general and which could be of paradigmatic importance for the conceptualization of society in the social sciences. If there are deficits in basic theory, then grievances cannot be limited to sociology, because sociology is not the sole administrator of theoretical tradition and development. As far as I can see, this debate is also developing in ethnology, the political sciences, philosophy and history.

In brief, there are two main themes in the sociological debate. Firstly, there is self-criticism, which concerns the most important hypotheses of evolutionary macrotheory, such as functional differentiation, rationalization and individualization. Secondly, there are arguments which refer to the way functionalistic macrotheory in Western sociology developed during the 1950s. This point of view is a repetition of the criticism of modernization theories in the 1970s.

Critics of the evolutionary elements in macrotheory point out that the expectations of increasing modernization have led to the belief that ethnonationalistic movements and social exclusions are premodern phenomena (e.g. Geser, 1981: 165 ff.; Esser, 1988: 235 ff.; Kreckel,

1989: 162 ff.; Nassehi, 1990: 261 ff.; Heckmann, 1991: 51 ff.; Smith, 1991; Imhof, 1993: 32 ff.; Bommes and Halfmann, 1994: 406 ff.; Bommes, 1994: 364 ff.; Richter, 1994: 304 ff.). This refers to the old sociological question about the *social integration* of modern societies (Giddens, 1985; Touraine, 1986; Joas, 1992a; Imhof, 1993; Ettrich, 1994). This question is surfacing again today above all in communitarian circles (Walzer, 1992; Honneth, 1993).

The second type of critics argue that the systematic neglect of ethnonationalistic semantics of inclusion and exclusion and the treatment of the 'Western-society' as the equivalent to the 'sociological ideal type of the modern age' have led to a conceptualization of modern societies as universalistic 'civic nations' whose social integration solely – if at all – rests on 'constitutional patriotism' (i.e. 'Verfassungspatriotismus'; see Sternberger, 1990; Habermas, 1992: 632 ff.; Kreckel, 1994). This means that during the cold war the theory of society analysed the development of Western societies on the basis of this 'universalistic' concept, without reflecting upon the specific historical context (Richter, 1994; Ettrich, 1994). Therefore, it is believed to be impossible to analyse adequately the socio-historical context of the processes of ethnicization (Imhof, 1993; Bommes, 1994).

Bearing in mind the obvious importance of nationalism, i.e. Max Weber's 'idea of the nation-state' (Gellner, 1964; 1991; Francis, 1965; Alter, 1985; Winkler, 1985; Lepsius, 1990; 1994; Elias, 1989; Hobsbawm, 1991), self-criticism with regard to the deficit in fundamental theory is essential for three reasons.

1. Because such declarations of deficit regarding the way the nation-state has structured the modern age contradict sociology's view of itself as *the science of the constitution of this modern age*.
2. Because with ethnonationalistic codes of inclusion and exclusion, sociology is concerned with values which relate directly to the basic sociological question of the 'social integration' of modern societies, and this constituted the central consideration of traditional scholars – especially Durkheim and Tönnies.
3. Due to the fact that the increasing volume of research concerning nationalism and ethnicity is implicitly or explicitly related to Max Weber's point of view. Nevertheless the self-criticism we are seeing also concentrates on a deficit of fundamental theory in the works of the classics (that is the area of social integration of modern societies).

I shall first show why renewing Weber's perspective is worthwhile. With this in mind, it will be necessary to describe the way in which

Weber dealt with 'nationalism' and 'ethnicity' at a time when these beliefs were very important. Secondly, I shall refer to the discourse on fundamental deficits in the theory of society and will illustrate how it is justified. In particular, the trend perspective in wide spheres of the sociological theory of society prevents an adequate understanding of the problem of contingency; that is the crises and radical change in the process of development. In such special periods of social change, an ethnicization of politics as well as a trend towards ethnic conflicts can be observed.

The 'Idea of the Nation'

Pre-modern forms of power were legitimized by the legacy of 'godly right' ('göttliches Recht') and the 'right of the conqueror' ('Recht des Eroberers'). As Max Weber pointed out, the pre-modern process of sociation oscillates between 'charismatic' and 'traditional power'. While the 'charismatic power' rests on a 'belief in the holiness of the extraordinary', 'traditional power' is based on a 'belief in the holiness of the ordinary' (Weber, 1973a: 434). The ethnic composition of the subjects did not play a role in the foundation of the early modern states – with the exception of the legitimization of the privileges of the aristocracy (Geiss, 1988; Sundhaussen, 1994). The integration of the subjects was based on the principle of the stratification of society, which allotted each individual his or her own particular place. The strict confessionalization of the early modern states, with the establishment of new *horizontal* inclusion and exclusion codes, encouraged, however, the territorialization of power and has allowed the mobilization of subjects for collective goals in religious wars since the sixteenth century (Schilling, 1991; Van Dülmen, 1982; Imhof, 1993). The transition from a stratified, unequal society to an equal one creates a problem of definition. The definition of those who are equal, simultaneously defines those who are excluded from this equality.

Nationalism in its different variations proved to be an ideology which is extremely capable of integration. Nationalism was able to assimilate and legitimate power in both forms: in the form of a liberal definition and in the ethnonationalistic definition of the nation. Nationalistic inclusion codes determined the modern nation-state, together with the existing or desired borders as collective *telos*, and integrated the subjects as a national community (Imhof, 1993).

In this process of construction, the sovereignty of the people and the national sovereignty merged to become a state-building maxim which justified the *internal and external* legitimization of the nation-

Kurt Imhof

state. The principle of the nation-state reached its peak at the end of the First World War with implementation of the right of self-determination of the people (Imhof, 1994; Sundhaussen, 1994). The principle of the nation-state as the simultaneous expression of state and individual sovereignty reached 'universal validity' in two ways. Firstly it becomes a 'framework of orientation' into which the ethnic, linguistic, nationalistic, religious or culturalistic 'common beliefs' of minorities were required to fit in order to achieve national sovereignty themselves (Lepsius, 1994; 1990: 233–234, 256; Weber, 1985: 235). Secondly, the idea of the nation-state achieved world validity, because anti-colonial movements arose as nationalistic movements and generated new minorities (Anderson, 1988). The principle of the nation-state is still the most successful export product of Western Society. Ethnicity and nationalism in their various forms of development represent inclusion and exclusion codes of epoch-making potential which have even influenced the modern age.

Max Weber, as a contemporary of 'integral nationalism' (Alter, 1985: 43 ff.), recognized its importance. From a historically-informed perspective, he studied 'ethnicity' and 'nationalism' and used both terms in his sociology of culture. His resistance to German idealism on the one hand and historical materialism and naturalistic evolution theories on the other, allowed him to formulate individual as well as collective action in the *dialectic of ideas and interests*. In German idealism, in the organic approach of protosociology and in materialism, the problem of the social integration of society does not arise, because the action of the actors is regarded as transcendent, naturally evolutive or structurally determined (Habermas, 1981: 220 ff.; Alexander, 1983; Joas, 1992a: 19 ff.; 1992b: 223 ff.). For Durkheim, as for Weber, such negations of the problem of the social integration of society were unacceptable. This problem led Durkheim to the sociology of religion and thereby to the question of the constitution of social categories. Max Weber, by contrast, began with the sociology of religion and from the beginning formulated action in the dialectic of action-oriented and action-legitimizing 'ideas' and 'interests' linked to structured positions.

It is in his *Introduction to the Economic Ethics of the World Religions* that Weber's famous statement is to be found (Weber, 1973a: 414): 'Interests (material and non-material) not ideas directly rule the action of people, but the conceptions of the world, which were formed by "ideas" very often determined the way like junction points, in which the dynamic of interests moved the action'. Weber provides people, on the one hand, with material and non-material interests and, on the other, with dependence on the interpretation of meaning. Material and non-material interests are linked with ideas, which define and legitimize those interests. With material 'deprivation' ('Entbehrungen'), problems of external need arise; with non-material deprivation, problems of internal need, i.e. a lack of orientation, arise.

Ideas and interests alternately stabilize one another. Ideas depend upon socially relevant interests if they are to be maintained; in a 'legitimate order', interests must relate to ideas, which define and justify those interests. The reasoning capability of ideas legitimizes interests. In this way 'main ideas' ('Leitideen') become empirically relevant in a social order precisely through this capability of reasoning and conviction, thereby creating 'junction points' ('Weichensteller') in social change. Thus, Weber is equidistant from materialistic and idealistic positions and far away from removed substantialistic perspective relating to ethnicity and nationalism.

For Weber, societal structures, 'life order' ('Lebensordnungen'), or central institutions are realized through 'main ideas' *if* they are linked to socially relevant interests. The product of ideas and interests achieves power in the form of institutions and it *orients* actions. His terms 'nation' and 'ethnicity' are included in the dialectics of ideas and interests. Max Weber concerns himself with these 'value ideas' ('Wertideen') in 'Economy and Society'. He treats the idea of community of the nation ('Vergemeinschaftungsidee der Nation') similarly, for example, to the idea of predestination in the principles of Protestantism, although he moves the analytical balance between ideas and interests clearly in favour of interests, competition, struggle and conflict.

For Weber, the European nation-state means the *linking* of *two ideas*: the 'idea of state' and the 'idea of nation'. The peer groups which support the idea of state 'as the idea of an imperial power which required unconditional loyalty' and the peer groups which support the idea of the nation are differentiated as follows: those 'who have the power to guide the action within a *political* community' and the group of 'intellectuals' who 'take the leadership within a *cultural* community'. According to Weber, this group of intellectuals is predestined to propagate the 'national idea' (Weber, 1985: 528, 530). The nation-state is therefore *not only the linking of two ideas*, but also of *two peer groups*: the political representatives of power and the intellectuals, the self-appointed representatives of a 'culture'.

The link between the idea of community of the nation and the idea of state is the reason for the power of the nation-state. This link is also the reason why the nation-state is a more important order compared to other forms of social organization (Lepsius, 1990: 233). Both ideas complement one another. The 'idea of nation' includes a belief in *origin* or in a *similarity of nature*. Therefore, the idea of the nation adds to the 'older' idea of the state the definition of 'community' ('Solidargemeinschaft') and defines the territory of the state, should that community be united in a kind of national mission (Weber, 1985: 530). The state, on the other hand, provides a national belief in the community institutional stability and also gives it with a structure within which *interests can be oriented and organized.*[1]

In conclusion: Weber's terms, 'nation', 'nationalism' and 'ethnicity', are rooted in the dialectics of ideas and interests. This is indeed what makes them attractive:

1. They are strictly a part of the 'sphere of values' ('Wertsphäre') and have no presocial or substantialistic character which, in Weber's historical context, is not always evident.
2. They are 'value ideas' which orient the action of the actors in a normative and integrative way towards the common goal, which is the 'imagined order' of the nation-state.
3. They address social positions and their corresponding *interests* as well as the *legitimization and orientation-giving function of ideas.* These terms are therefore useful in any theory of anomie.
4. They are 'open' in space and time; that is they are analytical terms which can be used for different historical situations, and they are sensitive to the problem of contingency in times of crises and radical change.

All of these qualities render Weber's perspective attractive in the context of a differentiated analysis in the social sciences, a realm which denies that nationalistic and ethnic constructs have an ontological characteristic.

The Theory of Society and the Problem of Contingency

It is important to understand, however, that in Weber's sociology of culture the conceptualization of the nation-state is linked to the theory of *rationalization* which characterizes his entire work (Habermas, 1981: 201 ff.; Lepsius, 1990: 44 ff.). The connection between the

1. Max Weber does not emphasize, however, that the idea of the order of the state is changed by the idea of the community of the nation in the direction of participation of power for those understood as 'similar of nature'. In fact, the people's sovereignty cannot be separated from the concept of the nation-state: the nineteenth century of European 'nation building' was at the same time the century of voting right reforms.

ethnonationalistic 'belief in mutuality' or 'community' ('Gemeinsam-keitsglaube') and the modern 'state institution' is of central importance. While the modern state institution represents a 'sphere' of rational administrative actions, the idea of the community of the nation relates to *'traditions'* and *'emotions'*. The nation-state thereby combines 'subjectively felt' *community relations* with rational societal relations. In other words, the modern nation-state combines a rational balance of interests and rational administrative action with the emotionally felt 'national community' (Weber, 1985: 237, 21–22). The nation-state, to use Tönnies' words rather than Weber's, creates the cohabitation of 'community and society'. It is here that the crucial point in the interpretation of Weber's approach lies, because in this way the ethnic 'belief in community' becomes *history* through the 'development of culture'. The 'value ideas' ('Wertideen') of ethnic and national community could therefore be interpreted as *irrational remains* – as the past in the present – in the modern age (Weber, 1985: 237). If ethno-nationalistic ideas can be interpreted as something pre-modern – that is in this context, something irrational – then it is possible to understand Weber's approach as a description of a unique period in the process of modernization (Sigmund and Utz, 1994: 34). Macrosociological sociology has tended to adopt precisely this understanding of Weber's approach.

In his most radical statements about modern societies, Max Weber himself eliminates the relationship between ideas and interests (Weber, 1973b: 357 ff.; 1973c: 311 ff.): 'Experts without spirit' and 'hedonists without a heart' ('Fachmenschen ohne Geist', 'Genussmenschen ohne Herz') will be the principle agents in a world which will be *meaningless*. An orientation towards ideologies is simply an *escape* from a world of pure rationality. This apocalypse is still unsurpassed in the theory of society. Weber did not completely adopt this perspective in his analysis of modern societies, but his point of view is nonetheless influenced by it. He interprets the orientation towards 'irrational' values in some parts of his work as a regressive escape from the 'cold skeletal hands of rational order' (Weber, 1973d: 469). Seen from this perspective, emotional values and charismatic leaders are, unlike in traditional societies, no longer innovative. Their effectiveness is, rather, an indi-cation that people are attempting to escape from the dictates of the increasing degree of rationality in all social relations (Tenbruck, 1975: 685–686; Joas, 1992a: 38).

This final characteristic in Max Weber's theory becomes important in two ways for the further development of the theory of society. Firstly, the Frankfurt school took over Weber's hypothesis of disenchant-ment ('Entzauberungsthese') and increasing rationality (Honneth,

1990). Secondly, and this is even more important, after the Second World War, Talcot Parsons radicalizes in his modernization theory Weber's and Durkheim's assumptions. Until the 1950s, Parsons regarded functional differentiation as a factor which could cause the disintegration of modern societies. From this point of view, he interpreted fascism as an irrational regression from the values of the German romantic period. After the World War II, he changed his perspective (Richter, 1994): He now saw increasing functional differentiation, rationalization and individualization as *the central characteristics of the modern age*. Functional differentiation is interpreted as a structural process which increasingly undermines irrational ethnonationalistic exclusion processes. Modernization is characterized by the fact that distribution of power and status should increasingly follow criteria of achievement (Esser, 1988: 237). The increasing functional differentiation, individualization and rationalization are no longer a problem creating anomic tension. Thus, principles of modernity became the solution to the problem. Ascriptive exclusions are now only an indication of *the past in the present*. In this way, the 'large dichotomy' between 'traditionality' and 'modernity' in modernization theories arises (Wehler, 1975: 16). Modernization and democratization have rationalized the Western-state so that ethnonationalistic semantics no longer play a role. The development of the Western society model then enters the era of a social market economy, while for the rest of the world the Western-state also represents *the future in the present*. The *evolutive elements* which Weber and Durkheim discussed now constitute the inner core of the sociological theory of society. In social science it is now possible to analyse history by looking at contemporary Third World countries. Since the 1950s, it has been possible for the social sciences to function without a past.

In the discussion concerning these arguments about modernization, it has been quite rightly stressed that the genesis of these exceptionally effective perspectives is rooted in the East-West dualism of the Cold War. In the 'battle of the systems', this 'mythos of the good nation' marks the universalistic, Western model of society, which in the process of 'nation building' must necessarily be repeated in the Third World (Richter, 1994: 304). The 'world society' was discovered in East-West dualism. In this dualism, the Western-states, which have their roots either in an ethnic- or a republican-oriented nationalism (Winkler, 1985: 7 ff.; Meinecke, 1962; Kohn, 1962: 309 ff.; Francis, 1965; Alter, 1985: 19 ff.; Lepsius, 1986), were seen in a *convergence process*, which makes of them all *universalistic civic nations*. So the metaphor of the *melting pot* came to represent the developmental pattern of Western society. The analysis of a society dominated by the theory of modernization must therefore systematically interpret ethnic and nationalistic movements as an anomaly, deviation, or anachronism.

Modernization theories consequently lack any notion of the original historical context during the Cold War period. The substitution of ethnonationalistic constructs by anti-communistic concepts of the enemy was overlooked. To put it generally, in the age of anti-communism, the mainstream Western theory of society discovered its research objects on the way to universalism.

Although, above all in the 1970s, these linear-evolutive, fundamental assumptions have been subject to far-reaching criticism since the debate on modernization theory, they still, in large part, constitute the ideology characterizing of the theory of society (e.g. Giddens, 1976; Wehler, 1975). The orientation toward development and progress in the historical philosophies since the beginning of the modern age is reflected in the theory of society *of* the modern age. Furthermore, the *de*-differentiation and *de*-individualization phenomena in the 'Ethnic Revival' in the USA in the 1960s (Imhof, 1994) and in the first post-war wave of xenophobia in connection with the migration of workers to Europe in the 1960s and 1970s (Hoffman-Nowotny, 1973; Esser, 1980) did not fundamentally change the perspective of modernization. The same can be said of the wave of regionalism, autonomism and secessionism in the 1970s, the election successes of nationally oriented conservative parties and the new respectability of nationalistic positions in Europe, above all since the end of the Cold War. Of course, sociological theorists reacted to this unexpected phenomenon – particularly in the sociology of minorities. In principle, this reaction concentrates, however, on the implicit or explicit *reversal* of the assumption that functional differentiation eliminates ethnonationalistic orientations. As with Parsons in his early studies on fascism, the *social costs* of functional differentiation, individualization and rationalization are emphasized. Ethnonationalistic exclusion is therefore either a reaction to anomic tension or a strategy of participation conducted by a minority. Since 'Beyond the Melting Pot' (Glazer and Moynihan, 1963) a discussion has developed which reaches the before mentioned opposite conclusion; namely that both positions *coexist side by side*. Modernization is seen as a power against ethnonationalistic exclusions and modernization causes ethnonationalistic exclusions. This contradiction leads to *a critical survey* of the basic theoretical hypotheses in the profession. The recording of the phenomena of ethnonationalistic collective identities in the late modern age becomes an important test for the theory of society.

It is therefore appropriate to question the evolutive-linear assumptions in the theory of society in the context of an intensified renaissance of ethnonationalistic collective identities. For if it is accepted that the laws of functional differentiation, of individualization and of rationalization determine the modern age, then *de-differentiation and de-individualization* phenomena in the form of ethnonationalistic movements, majority/minority conflicts, secessions and xenophobia can only be interpreted as reactions, regressions, anomalies, secondary forms of differentiation, or 'modernization holes' in the 'master trend' (Esser, 1988; Nassehi, 1990: 263; Luhmann, 1980: 27).

Despite the heuristic use which these axioms of the theory of society may offer, it has been established that these trend hypotheses have led to an *under-estimation* of the importance of ethnonationalistic identities. Furthermore, the lack of a specification of time, which is characteristic of these trend hypotheses, immunises them to empirical research. In this lack of a specification of time, the great distance between these transhistorical axioms and day-to-day history becomes obvious (Joas, 1992a: 332).

From a historico-sociological perspective, it appears however that exclusions on an ascriptive basis, or in other words, the ethnicization of politics, represent a discontinuous phenomenon which correlates with the anything but *linear course* of social change of modern societies. Processes of the ethnicization of politics are not evenly spread over time. They offer an indicator, which is able to distinguish phases of social crisis from structural periods of economic growth and which is able to legitimize social development (Imhof, 1990; 1993). Open, ethnonationalistic movements, which operate under ideologies justifying substantial characteristics of self and other, are successful during periods of high anomic and conflictual tension. Anomie is an element which encourages *community* in society. 'Fear of others' becomes a socially acceptable phobia in the light of an uncertain future and a present which requires a reduction of complexity. Semantics of difference, which distinguish the other from the non-other, are always involved in *overcoming* periods of crises, especially because of their socio-constitutive importance; that is their functions of exclusion and identity creation and their ability to orient interests.

The modern age can therefore be characterized by the discontinuous ethnicization of politics, which is linked to the de-differentiation and de-individualization processes within strongly ideologically oriented social movements. These movements define new areas of conflict in society. These conflict constructions break through the stream of usual conflicts, which modern societies must always overcome. Ideological movements of an ethnic, religious, culturalistic or political nature create conflicts of *'either/or'*. These conflicts create clear (that is polar) orientation and clear opponents in times of insecurity. This conflict type distinguishes itself from *conflicts* of 'more-or-less'.. The 'more-or-less' type can, with time, be solved through civil law procedures in normal periods of social change. While conflicts of 'either/or' do not appear to permit compromises and are not regarded as revisable, conflicts of 'more-or-less' are in principle, only capable of compromise and are limited in time (Hirschmann, 1994; Imhof, 1993).

Since the genesis of the modern nation-state occurring during the crisis of the 1880s, during the crisis of class conflict at the end of the First World War, during the world recession of the 1930s, during the 'culture revolution' at the end of the 1960s and the recession of the early 1970s and again since the second half of the 1980s, the phases of crises and radical social change have been accompanied by conflicts of 'either/or'. These periods are regularly accompanied too by processes of exclusion on the basis of ascriptive characteristics. These exclusion processes are still oriented *toward* the nation-state, which forms the *action framework* through the immanent principle of people's sovereignty (Wimmer, 1994), in order to be able to control the unreasonable demands of unintended effects of social change. The form of this discontinuous ethnicization of politics takes its symbols from history. In periods of change, the past is regularly politicized and the present historicized. In these phases, the collective history is rewritten and the national mythology celebrates a renaissance. During these special periods of social change, the ethnicization of politics offers orientation in a present which has become insecure. This connection with history lends ideological resources from the past an importance in the present and favours everything which appears to be near and uncomplicated. In other words: the ethnicization of political communication through social movements and nationalistic parties produces continuity in discontinuity (Siegenthaler, 1993) as well as inclusion and as exclusion.

Such a perspective, which attempts to record the modern age in its discontinuity, in its contingent breaks in structure and in its succession of different society models (Imhof and Romano, 1996), is nearer to Weber's theory of society than is the traditional theory which was radicalized by Parson's structure functionalism, in Luhmann's theory of functional differentiation (Luhmann, 1994), in the various currents of neo-functionalism and even in Habermas' theory of communicative action. In these theories, evolutive laws still determine the modern age. Despite his theory of rationalization, Weber never lost sight of contingencies, breaks and radical change. After decades of overemphasizing Weber's hypothesis of rationalization, it is possible to rediscover the variability and discontinuity of the modern age.

Kurt Imhof

It is possible, particularly in re-reading Weber, to recognize the susceptibility of modern societies to orientation crises. Compared to pre-modern societies, the disenchantment ('Entzauberung') of the Occident made religious beliefs, which could explain almost any social change, worthless. Secular ideologies replaced the belief in fate and godly leadership. Among these ideologies, ethnonationalistic imaginations as collective identities and common telos play an important role in modern societies. They orient action and legitimize interests and leadership positions.

In conclusion, the discontinuous ethnicization of politics is part of the struggle for the 'right' distribution of scarce material and non-material goods and is a powerful factor in providing orientation in times of an insecure future.

Bibliography

Alexander, J. C. (1983), *Theoretical Logic in Sociology, vol. 3: The Classical Attempt at Theoretical Synthesis: Max Weber*, Berkeley: University of California Press.
Alter, P. (1985), *Nationalismus*, Frankfurt am Main: Suhrkamp Verlag.
Anderson, B. (1988), *Die Erfindung der Nation*, Frankfurt am Main: Campus Verlag.
Bommes, M. (1994), 'Migration und Ethnizität im nationalen Sozialstaat', *Zeitschrift für Soziologie*, 5, pp. 364–377.
——, and Halfmann, J. (1994), 'Migration und Inklusion: Spannungen zwischen Nationalstaat und Wohlfahrtstaat', *Kölner Zeitschrift für Soziologie und Sozialpsychologie*, 3, pp. 406–424.
Elias, N. (1989), *Studien über die Deutschen: Machtkämpfe und Habitusentwicklung im 19. und 20. Jahrhundert*, M. Schrötter (ed.), Frankfurt am Main: Suhrkamp Verlag.
Esser, H. (1980), *Aspekte der Wanderungssoziologie: Assimilation und Integration von Wanderern, ethnischen Gruppen und Minderheiten. Eine handlungstheoretische Analyse*, Darmstadt: Luchterhand.
——, (1988), 'Ethnische Differenzierung und moderne Gesellschaft', *Zeitschrift für Soziologie*, 4, pp. 235–248.
Ettrich, F. (1994), 'Nationalstaat – Nationale Identität – Nationalismus, Editorial', *Berliner Journal für Soziologie*, 1, pp. 3–6.
Francis, E. K. (1965), *Ethnos und Demos*, Berlin: Duncker & Humbolt.
Geiss, I. (1988), *Geschichte des Rassismus*, Frankfurt am Main: Suhrkamp Verlag.
Gellner, E. (1964), *Nationalism in Thought and Change*, London: Weidenfeld & Nicolson.

——, (1991), *Nationalismus und Moderne*, Frankfurt am Main and Berlin: Rotbuch Verlag.

Geser, H. (1981), 'Der "ethnische Faktor" im Prozess gesellschaftlicher Modernisierung', *Schweizerische Zeitschrift für Soziologie*, 7, pp. 165–178.

Giddens, A. (1976), 'Functionalism: Après la lutte', *Social Research*, 43, pp. 325–343.

——, (1985), 'The Nation-State and Violence', in W. W. Powell and R. Robbins (eds), *Conflict and Consensus*, New York: The Free Press, pp. 16–64.

Glazer, N. and Moynihan, D. P. (eds), (1963), *Beyond the Melting Pot: The Negroes, Puerto Ricans, Jews, Italians and Irish of New York City*, Cambridge: The M.I.T. Press.

Habermas, J. (1981), *Theorie des kommunikativen Handelns*, 2 vols, Frankfurt am Main: Suhrkamp Verlag.

——, (1992), *Faktizität und Geltung: Beiträge zur Diskurstheorie des Rechts und des demokratischen Rechtsstaats*, Frankfurt am Main: Suhrkamp Verlag.

Heckmann, F. (1991), 'Ethnos, Demos und Nation oder Woher stammt die Intoleranz des Nationalstaats gegenüber ethnischen Minderheiten?', in U. Bielefeld (ed.), *Das Eigene und das Fremde: Neuer Rassismus in der Alten Welt?*, Hamburg: Junius Verlag, pp. 51–78.

Hirschmann, A. O. (1994), 'Wieviel Gemeinsinn braucht die liberale Gesellschaft?', *Leviathan*, 2, pp. 293–304.

Hobsbawm, E. J. (1991), *Nationen und Nationalismus: Mythos und Realität seit 1780*, Frankfurt am Main: Campus Verlag.

Hoffmann-Nowotny, H.-J. (1973), *Soziologie des Fremdarbeiterproblems: Eine theoretische und empirische Analyse am Beispiel der Schweiz*, Stuttgart: Enke Verlag.

Hondrich, K. O. (1992), 'Wovon wir nichts wissen wollten', *Die Zeit*, 40, September 25.

Honneth, A. (1990), 'Die zerrissene Welt des Sozialen', in A. Honneth (ed.), *Kritische Theorie: Vom Zentrum zur Peripherie einer Denktradition*, Frankfurt am Main: Suhrkamp Verlag, pp. 25–67.

——, (ed.), (1993), *Kommunitarismus: Eine Debatte über die moralischen Grundlagen moderner Gesellschaften*, Frankfurt am Main: Campus Verlag.

Imhof, K. (1990), 'Mythos und Moderne: Zur Fragilität der posttraditionalen Gesellschaft', in V. Bornschier, M. Eisner, K. Imhof, G. Romano and Ch. Suter (eds), *Zur Diskontinuität des sozialen Wandels*, Frankfurt am Main: Campus, pp. 55–90.

——, (1993), 'Nationalismus, Nationalstaat und Minderheiten: Zu einer Soziologie der Minoritäten', *Soziale Welt*, 3, pp. 327–357.

——, (1994), 'Stichwort "Minderheitensoziologie"', in H. Kerber and A. Schneider (eds), *Spezielle Soziologien*, Reinbeck bei Hamburg: Rowohlt, pp. 407–423.

——, and Romano, G. (1996), *Theorie des sozialen Wandels: Zur Diskontinuität der Moderne*, Frankfurt am Main: Campus Verlag.

Joas, S. H. (1992a), *Die Kreativität des Handelns*, Frankfurt am Main: Suhrkamp Verlag.

——, (1992b), *Pragmatismus und Gesellschaftstheorie*, Frankfurt am Main: Suhrkamp Verlag.

Kohn, H. (1962), *Die Idee des Nationalismus*, Frankfurt am Main: Suhrkamp Verlag.

Kreckel, R. (1989), 'Ethnische Differenzierung und "moderne" Gesellschaft', *Zeitschrift für Soziologie*, 2, pp. 162–167.

——, (1994), 'Soziale Integration und nationale Identität', *Berliner Journal für Soziologie*, 1, pp. 13–20.

Lepsius, M. R. (1986), '"Ethnos" und "Demos". Zur Anwendung zweier Kategorien von Emerich Francis auf das nationale Selbstverständnis der Bundesrepublik und auf die Europäische Einigung', *Kölner Zeitschrift für Soziologie und Sozialpsychologie*, 38, pp. 751–759.

——, (1990), *Interessen, Ideen und Institutionen*, Opladen: Westdeutscher Verlag.

——, (1994), 'Die Bundesrepublik – ein neuer Nationalstaat?', *Berliner Journal für Soziologie*, 1, pp. 7–12.

Luhmann, N. (1980), *Gesellschaftsstruktur und Semantik. Studien zur Wissenssoziologie der modernen Gesellschaft*, vol. 1, Frankfurt am Main: Suhrkamp Verlag.

——, (1994), 'Inklusion und Exklusion', in H. Berding (ed.), *Nationales Bewusstsein und kollektive Identität. Studien zur Entwicklung des kollektiven Bewusstseins in der Neuzeit*, Frankfurt am Main: Suhrkamp, pp. 15–83.

Meinecke, F. (1962), *Weltbürgertum und Nationalstaat*, Werke vol. 5, München: Oldenbourg Verlag.

Nassehi, A. (1990), 'Zum Funktionswandel der Ethnizität im Prozess gesellschaftlicher Modernisierung: Ein Beitrag zur Theorie der funktionalen Differenzierung', *Soziale Welt*, 3, pp. 261–282.

Nielsen, F. (1985), 'Toward a Theory of Ethnic Solidarity in Modern Societies', *American Sociological Review*, 50, pp. 133–149.

Richter, D. (1994), 'Der Mythos der "guten" Nation: Zum theoriegeschichtlichen Hintergrund eines folgenschweren Missverständnisses', *Soziale Welt*, 3, pp. 304–321.

Schilling, H. (1991), 'Nationale Identität und Konfession in der europäischen Neuzeit', in B. Giesen (ed.), *Nationale und kulturelle Identität: Studien zur Entwicklung des kollektiven Bewusstseins in der Neuzeit*, Frankfurt am Main: Suhrkamp, pp. 192–252.

Siegenthaler, H. (1993), 'Supranationalität, Nationalismus und regionale Autonomie: Erfahrungen des schweizerischen Bundesstaates – Perspektiven der Europäischen Gemeinschaft', in H. A. Winkler and H. Kaelble (eds), *Nationalismus –Nationalitäten – Supranationalität*, Stuttgart: Klett-Cotta Verlag, pp. 309–333.

Sigmund, S. and Utz, R. (1994), 'Religion und Nationalismus in Irland', *Berliner Journal für Soziologie*, 1, pp. 33–53.

Smith, A. D. (1991), *National Identity*, London: Penguin Book Harmondsworth.

Nationalism and the Theory of Society

Sterbling, A. (1994), 'Rezension von Winkler, Heinrich August, Kaelble Hartmut (Hrsg.), Nationalismus – Nationalitäten / Supranationalität', *Kölner Zeitschrift für Soziologie und Sozialpsychologie*, 3, pp. 528–530.

Sternberger, D. (1990), *Verfassungspatriotismus*, Schriften Band X, Frankfurt am Main: Inselverlag.

Sundhaussen, H. (1994), 'Ethnonationalismus in Aktion: Bemerkungen zum Ende Jugoslawiens', *Geschichte und Gesellschaft*, 3, pp. 402–423.

Tenbruck, F.-H. (1975), 'Das Werk Max Webers', *Kölner Zeitschrift für Soziologie und Sozialpsychologie*, 27, pp. 685–702.

Touraine, A. (1986), 'Krise und Wandel des sozialen Denkens', in J. Berger (ed.), *Die Moderne-Kontinuitäten und Zäsuren*, Special issue of *Soziale Welt*, Göttingen: Otto Schwartz & Co, pp. 15–39.

Van Dülmen, R. (1982), *Entstehung des frühneuzeitlichen Europa 1550–1648*, Frankfurt am Main: Fischer Verlag.

Walzer, M. (1992), *Zivile Gesellschaft und amerikanische Demokratie*, Berlin: Rotbuch-Verlag.

Weber, M. (1973a), 'Einleitung in die Wirtschaftsethik der Weltreligionen', in J. Winckelmann (ed.), *Max Weber: Soziologie, Universalgeschichtliche Analysen, Politik*, Stuttgart: Kröner Verlag, pp. 398–440.

——, (1973b), 'Asketischer Protestantismus und kapitalistischer Geist', in J. Winckelmann (ed.), *Max Weber: Soziologie, Universalgeschichtliche Analysen, Politik*, Stuttgart: Kröner Verlag, pp. 357–381.

——, (1973c), 'Vom inneren Beruf zur Wissenschaft', in J. Winckelmann (ed.), *Max Weber: Soziologie, Universalgeschichtliche Analysen, Politik*, Stuttgart: Kröner Verlag, pp. 311–339.

——, (1973d), 'Richtungen und Stufen religiöser Weltablehnungen', in J. Winckelmann (ed.), *Max Weber: Soziologie, Universalgeschichtliche Analysen, Politik*, Stuttgart: Kröner Verlag, pp. 441–483.

——, (1985), *Wirtschaft und Gesellschaft*, Tübingen: Mohr Verlag.

Wehler, H.-U. (1975), *Modernisierungstheorie und Geschichte*, Göttingen: Vandenhoeck & Ruprecht.

Wimmer, A. (1994), 'Der Kampf um den Staat: Thesen zu einer vergleichenden Analyse interethnischer Konflikte', in H. P. Müller (ed.), *Ethnische Dynamik in der aussereuropäischen Welt*, Zürcher Arbeitspapiere zur Ethnologie 4, Zurich: Argonaut Verlag, pp. 22–48.

Winkler, H. (ed.), (1985), *Nationalismus*, Königstein: Athenäum Verlag.

–3–

Marx and Durkheim on Nationalism

Montserrat Guibernau

Marx

Nationalism and the Bourgeoisie

In the *Communist Manifesto*, Marx describes the history of human society in terms of class struggle (Marx and Engels, 1976: 49): 'Freeman and slave, patrician and plebeian, lord and serf, guild master and journey man, in a word, oppressor and oppressed, stood in constant opposition to one another.' The struggle of 'oppressors and oppressed' ends either in a revolutionary reconstitution of society – where, prior to socialism, the 'oppressed' become 'oppressors' – or in the common ruin of the contending classes. Contemporary society is divided into two great classes, which directly face on another: the bourgeoisie and the proletariat. For Marx, social classes are the proper actors in the historical process. Local and national developments form only a part, and an admittedly insignificant one, unless a nation happens to find itself at the head of the progress of all humanity during a certain turning point in world history. This is a crucial issue in understanding why Marx pays so little attention to nationalism. For him, nations, states and cities need to be studied and evaluated within the context and from the perspective of their place in class relations and in the class struggle occurring on a global scale.

In Marx's view, bluntly stated, nationalism is an expression of bourgeois interests. But as Bloom (1941: 76) rightly points out, the bourgeois 'fatherland' did not refer to the country's potentialities for progress or to the nation regarded democratically, but to the 'aggregate of institutions, customs, laws, and ideas which sanctified the right to property on a considerable scale'. Marx writes (quoted from *Das Kapital* in Bloom, 1941: 77): 'The bourgeoisie conveniently assumed that the "nation" consisted only of capitalists. The country was therefore "theirs".' He considers the nationalistic claims aimed at creating a unified Germany out of the existing thirty-eight states as bourgeois. In his *Contribution to the Critique of Hegel's Philosophy of Right*, he denounces the backwardness of Germany as a fundamental fact. For him, such backwardness revealed itself in the poverty of political aspirations and in the intellectual outlook of the German bourgeoisie. He considered France and Great Britain to be in a more advanced stage of development and for that reason, he saw the abolition of the capitalist system in these two countries as something imminent. In contrast, he regarded Germany as a country in which a capitalist system was yet to be fully realized. However, German backwardness was not all pervasive. Rather, Germany had developed the most up-to-date philosophical framework and was working to place its economy and policy on the same level. Marx advocated a revolution in Germany that would aim not only at elevating it to the same stage as the other most advanced Western nations, but also at enabling it to perform a task which even these nations had yet to accomplish: that is the liberation of individuals as human beings, rather than of Germans as Germans. But how could this liberation be possible if Germany did not have a class capable of acting as 'a negative representative of society', as did the bourgeoisie in France? Was there a real possibility for emancipation in Germany? Marx was aware that in Germany the proletariat was only beginning to emerge under the impact of industrial development, and although he was conscious of the relative youth and weakness of the German proletariat, he was optimistic about the role they might play.

Marx did not write in favour of an 'emancipation of Germany' that would achieve German nationalist goals in the form of a single state. Instead, he sought the abolition of the state. Marx's draft of an article on F. List's *Das nationale System der politischen Ökonomie* provides a detailed elaboration of his position on the 'German Question' and complements the ideas expounded in his *Contribution to a Critique of Hegel's 'Philosophy of Right'*. In his *Critique of List*, Marx views nationalism as a bourgeois ideology and List as its representative (for a detailed explanation, see Szporluk, 1988). He rejects List's attempt to find a national road to capitalism and dismisses the possibility of communism in one country. Furthermore, Marx considers that both capitalism and communism are world-wide systems. List, unlike Marx, bases his entire argument on the recognition of nations as the basic units into which the human race is divided, and argues that nations develop by passing through clearly definable stages.

The German bourgeoisie appealed to 'nationality', but to Marx 'nationality' was a fraud. He argues that the bourgeoisie as a class has a common interest, and 'this community of interest, which is directed against the proletariat inside the country, is directed against the bourgeois of other nations outside the country. This the bourgeois calls his nationality' (Szporluk, 1988: 35). However, Marx does not specify how and why it should be possible for some bourgeois to agree on a common interest in opposition to other bourgeois; nor does he consider why the basis for union and separation should be German nationality.

Nationalism and the Proletariat

In the *German Ideology*, Marx (1978: 78) refers to the proletariat as a class completely unlike any other, 'the class which no longer counts as a class in society, is not recognized as a class, and is in itself the expression of the dissolution of all classes, nationalities, etc. within present society'. For Marx, this is the result of modern industrial labour and modern subjection to capital in a world led by the bourgeoisie. In this world the proletariat has no property, becomes alienated and is a mere instrument in the hands of the bourgeois. The proletarian spends his or her life working, producing goods and benefits for the bourgeoisie. The more he or she works, the more impoverished he or she becomes. Marx denounced this situation and thought that the proletariat all over the world would be able to unite and fight. They would be the 'motor of history', and would have nothing to lose in the struggle since they did not posses anything. In the *Communist Manifesto* he writes (Marx and Engels, 1976: 65): 'The working men have no country . . . National differences and antagonisms between peoples are daily more and more vanishing.' The present conditions of labour and subjection to capital which are 'the same in England as in France, in America as in Germany, have stripped the proletariat of every trace of national character' (Ibid., p. 60):

> The nationality of the worker is neither French, nor English, nor German; it is labour, free slavery and self-huckstering. His government is neither French, nor English, nor German; it is capital. His native air is neither French, nor German, nor English; it is factory air. The land belonging to him is neither French, nor English, nor German; it lies a few feet below the ground. (Marx, 1975: 280)

Engels, in a letter to 'the working classes of Great Britain', expresses the same viewpoint. He addresses the working classes as if they were not English. Instead, he emphasizes the common qualities of being members of the great and universal family of Mankind, who know their interest and that of all the human race to be the same: 'And as much, as members of this family of One and Indivisible Mankind, as Human Beings in the most emphatical meaning of the word, as such I, and many others on the Continent, hail your progress in every direction and wish you speedy success' (Marx and Engels, 1975a: 298).

The working class, as subject of history and social actor *par excellence,* should only think in international terms (Marx and Engels, 1976: 53): 'National one-sidedness and narrow-mindedness become more and more impossible.' Following this line of argument, in his *Account of his speech on Mazzini's attitude towards the International* Engels stresses (Marx and Engels, 1975b: 608): 'The International recognizes no country, it desires to unite; not dissolve. It is opposed to the cry for Nationality, because it tends to separate people from people, and is used by tyrants to create prejudices and antagonism.' Marx argues that the distinctive feature of the communists when compared with other working class parties is that, 'in the national struggles of the proletarians of the different countries, the communists point out and bring to the front the common interests of the entire proletariat, independent of all nationality' (Marx and Engels, 1976: 61).

Nationalism and Proletarian Revolution

In contrast, 1848–1849 seems to herald a major modification of Marx and Engels' original stand on nationalism, through supporting the national causes of the 'historic' or 'great' nations such as Hungary, Poland and Germany, all of which sought to establish large, stable national states. In this sense, nationalism appeared to be compatible with a proletarian revolution in so far as large states would make it easier for the proletariat to advance its class goals. Marx and Engels voiced their hostility towards the aspirations of 'non-historic nationalities' such as the smaller Slavic nations, particularly the Czechs. In an article published in 1852 in the *New York Daily Tribune*, Engels, under Marx's name, referred to the high culture, the high development in science and industry of Germany, compared with that of the Slavs. He argued that the Slavs were living in a condition of backwardness and that their way of life was being dissolved 'by contact with a superior German culture'.

In 1872, Engels recognized one nationality in particular: the Irish. When Great Britain tried to bring the Irish sections under the jurisdiction of the British Federal Council, he argued: 'The Irish form, to all intents and purposes, a distinct nationality of their own, and the fact that they use the English language can not deprive them of the right, common to all, to have an independent national organization within the International.'[1] Engels makes it clear that a nation should be free from its conquerors because only then can the workers think in international terms about a universal working-class solidarity. Internationalism must not be used as an excuse to justify and perpetuate the dominion of the conqueror.

If members of a conquering nation called upon the nation they had conquered and continued to hold it down in order that it forget its specific nationality and position, to 'sink national differences' and so forth, this was not Internationalism. It was nothing more than preaching their submission to the yoke and attempting to justify and to perpetuate the dominion of the conqueror under the cloak of Internationalism (Marx and Engels, 1975c: 155). Accordingly, true Internationalism must necessarily be based upon a distinctly national organization.

The Irish, as well as other oppressed nationalities, could enter the Association only as equals with the members of the conquering nation, and under protest against the conquest. The Irish sections, therefore, were not only justified, but were even under the necessity to state in the preamble to their rules that their first and most pressing duty, as Irishmen, was to establish their own national independence (Ibid., p. 156).

In the *Communist Manifesto*, Marx points out that the struggle of the proletariat with the bourgeoisie is 'at first a national struggle', emphasizing that, 'the proletariat of each country must, of course first of all settle matters with its own bourgeoisie' (Marx and Engels, 1976: 60). He also suggests that, 'the proletariat must first of all acquire political supremacy, must rise to be the leading class of the nation, must constitute itself the nation, it is, so far, itself national, though not in the bourgeois sense of the word' (pp. 65–66). Furthermore, in the *Critique of the Gotha Programme*, Marx argues that 'it is altogether self-evident that, to be able to fight at all, the working class must organise itself at home as a class and that its own country is the immediate arena of its struggle'.[2] In saying this, he does not attempt to formulate any kind of nationalist claim. Marx regarded the working class as an international class to be united above national affiliation, and envisaged the abolition of the State. It is precisely this kind of ambiguous formulation which makes it possible to specify compatibilities between Marxism and nationalism. Marx's internationalism was not an attempt to eliminate cultural differences among societies, nor to favour uniformity. Rather, the assumption of large societies seemed

1. 'Engels' record of his report at the General Council Meeting at May 14, 1872' (Marx and Engels, 1975c: 154).
2. Marx and Engels', Critique of the Gotha Programme (Feuer, 1976: 163).

to him a more effective starting point for the establishment of an harmonious world. He was an internationalist, not only in the sense that he was advocating a system of co-operative world relations, but more specifically because he believed that system to be the outcome or function of the friendly interaction of large nations which were organized harmoniously within. In my view, Marx's goal was not the removal of all national distinctions, but was rather the abolition of the pronounced economic and social inequalities caused by capitalism, as well as the establishment of a world in which the emancipation of all individuals as human beings would be possible.

Marx did not present a theory of nationalism for three main reasons. Firstly, according to him, in class societies the prevailing ideas of any epoch are the ideas of the ruling class. It follows from this proposition that the diffusion of ideas is heavily dependent upon the distribution of economic power in society. In this latter sense, ideology constitutes part of the social 'superstructure': the prevalent ethos at any given time is one which provides legitimation of the interests of the dominant class. Thus, the relations of production, via the mediation of the class system, compose the real foundation on which emerges a legal and political superstructure and to which definite forms of social consciousness correspond. However, Marx does not postulate an unvarying connection between these two modes in which consciousness is moulded by social practice. An individual or group may develop ideas which are partially at variance with the prevalent views of his or her age, but these ideas will not come into prominence unless they correspond with interests held by the dominant class, or with those of a class established in a position from which to challenge the existing authority structure. Marx could see nothing but the economic self-interest of the bourgeoisie in German nationalist claims. He was mainly concerned with the study of the economic relations in society because he thought that to be able to introduce changes in the superstructure, one should be able to change the relations of production and the distribution of economic power. This is one of the reasons which explains why Marx did not pay much attention to the study of nationalism: his primary concern was the study of the economy.

Secondly, Marx's understanding of history as the history of class struggle implies that a proletarian revolution should follow a bourgeois one and should impose the dictatorship of the proletariat as a step on the road towards a communist society. Marx envisaged a stateless society free from class struggle as a long-term goal. This process seems to leave no room for nationalism, particularly since nationalism's main goal is the creation of a state, not its abolition. However, if we consider Marx and Engels' position on Irish nationality, it is possible to find a place for nationalism, at least in the sense that a country needs to be free of its conquerors before engaging in a class struggle. Marx also writes that the working class must first settle matters with 'its own bourgeoisie'. Although he never explains this, it would appear that, at least in the provisional but necessary stages before achieving a 'communist society', a certain form of nationalism and Marxism would be able to be united, especially since the end of this provisional period was not fixed.

The third reason for Marx giving scant attention to nationalism lies in his notion that neither capitalist relations of production, nationality, nor religion should obstruct the liberation of people as human beings. The proletariat should transcend national identities and should be able to recognize itself as 'part of the big family of Mankind'.

Nationalism and Marxism: Similarities and Differences

It is possible to find some similarities between nationalism and Marxism, similarities that have contributed to the union of these two forms of ideology in different countries, especially after Marx (Smith, 1979). Nationalism and Marxism are both what Smith calls 'salvation movements'. They describe the present situation as an oppressive one, in which individuals live alienated lives (Marxism) or have lost their identity (nationalism).

Some of the main differences between nationalism and Marxism are: firstly, while nationalism places primary emphasis on culture, Marxism traces back every phenomenon to its economic roots; secondly, Marxists locate their enemy in the capitalist without considering his or her nationality, while for nationalists, the enemy are those who corrupt and oppress the purity of the nation; and finally, the two forms of ideology espouse a different interpretation of the past. As I have mentioned, Marxists accept the past in order to transcend it, while nationalists seek inspiration from the past in order to link it with the present, thus restoring the original features of the national character.

Émile Durkheim

The State

Durkheim distinguishes between what he calls 'political society' and the 'state'. While the latter refers to 'the agents of the sovereign authority', the former refers to 'the complex group of which the State is the highest organ' (1950: 48).[3] He also separates the state itself from secondary organizations, such as the Law, the army and the Church – in cases where a national church exists – in the immediate field of the state's control. According to Durkheim, the state can be defined as a group of officials *sui generis*, within which representations and acts of volition involving the collectivity are worked out, although they are not the product of the collectivity. It is not accurate to say that the state embodies the collective consciousness, for that goes beyond the state at every point. The representations that derive from the state are characterized by their higher degree of consciousness and reflection. The state does not execute anything; rather, it requires action to be taken. Its main function is to think in order to guide collective conduct (Durkheim, 1958: 437): 'The state is above all a means of reflection . . . it is intelligence taking the place of obscure instinct.'[4]

The Relation Between the Individual and the State

The relation between the individual and the state has changed throughout the course of history. In Durkheim's view, in the beginning, the only aim of the state was to become increasingly powerful, while at the same time ignoring the needs and interests of the individual. The only valuable things were 'collective beliefs', 'collective aspirations' and the traditions and symbols which expressed them: the individual was then completely absorbed into society. As we advance in history, the individual becomes an object of moral consideration. Human beings obtain rights and the state recognizes their 'dignity'. Durkheim's argument can lead to what may seem an antinomy; that is on the one hand, the spread and development of the state, and on the other, the development of individual rights. He rejects this possibility and stresses that our moral individuality is not antagonistic to the state. On the contrary it is a product of it (Durkheim, 1958: 437): 'The state becomes stronger and more active as the individual becomes freer. It is the state that frees the individual.'[5] The state has created and organized individual rights (Durkheim, 1974: 55): 'Man is only man to the degree that he is civilised.' In order to accomplish this function, the State must permeate all secondary groups – family, trade, church, professional association and so on – which tend to absorb the personality of their

3. The author has made all translations from French.
4. Original text: 'L'état est donc avant tout un organe de reflexion . . . c'est l'intelligence mise a la place de l'instinct obscur.'
5. Original text: 'L'état devient fort, actif, plus l'individu devient libre. C'est l'état qui le libère.'

members. 'The state', he writes (1950: 65), 'must therefore enter into the lives of the individuals, it must supervise and keep a check on the way they operate and to do this it must spread its roots in all directions.' Durkheim points out that the rights of the individual are in a state of evolution and it is not possible to set any boundaries on their course. However, he also stresses that the state's action can become despotic if there is nothing between the state and the individual. The state's action can be useful only if it is diversified by a whole system of secondary organs (Durkheim, 1987a: 384). He notes (Durkheim, 1950: 437): 'The state . . . too needs to be restrained by the totality of secondary forces that are subordinate to it but without which like any unrestrained organism, it develops excessively and becomes tyrannical and forceful.'[6]

Features of the State

Durkheim makes a distinction between two types of state actions: external and internal. External action was pre-eminent in former times. Its main features were: violent manifestations, aggression and war (Durkheim, 1950: 435).

Internal action is the main task of the state in modern societies. This action is primarily 'pacifique et morale', and should be understood as a result of the development of 'higher' societies. In his view (Durkheim, 1988: 167), 'the state's attributions become ever more numerous and diverse as one approaches the highest types of society'.

The state is not a mere spectator of social life; rather, it organizes and moralizes society (Durkheim, 1958: 435). The state is also the organ of social thought (Ibid.). Durkheim distinguishes two types: the first is derived from the collective mass of society and is diffused throughout that mass; the second is worked out in the state, has a particular structure and is centralized. He insists that the state thinks in order to guide collective conduct and not for the sake of thinking or building up doctrinal systems. In his view, the state has a positive human and non-transcendent role, which is to free individuals.

The state tends to absorb all forms of activity which are social in nature and is henceforth confronted by nothing but an unstable flux of individuals. In describing our moral situation, Durkheim emphasizes that human beings cannot become attached to higher aims and submit to a rule if they see nothing above them with which they can identify. To free individuals from all social pressure is to abandon them

6. Original text: 'L'état . . . lui aussi a besoin d'être contenu par l'ensemble des forces secondaires qui lui sont subordonnées sans quoi, comme tout organe que rien n'arrête, il se développe sans mesure et devient tyrannique et se force.'

to themselves and to demoralize them. Nowadays, the state is com-
pelled to assume functions for which it is ill-suited and which it has
not been able to satisfactorily carry out: 'while the state becomes
inflated and hypertrophied in order to obtain a firm enough grip
upon individuals, but without succeeding, the latter, without mutual
relationships, tumble over one another like so many liquid molecules,
encountering no central energy to retain, fix and organise them'
(Durkheim, 1987a: 389). To remedy this, he suggests the formation
of corporations, as definite institutions, each one becoming a moral
individuality.

Two further aspects should be mentioned. Firstly, he considers war
as largely a feature of the past and as something that is destined to
disappear. In his view, the glory of the state no longer lies in the
conquest of new territories but in a moral end: the expansion of justice
within society (Durkheim, 1958: 437). Secondly, he sees the state as
an agent that exists and develops in a milieu formed by the assembly
of other states. Each state exists in relation to others, as it forms part
of the international community. No state can exist in opposition to
the rest of humanity. Durkheim stresses this point in *L'Allemagne au-
dessus de tout*, describing the German mentality as an example of
'pathologie sociale' (1915a: 46).

State and Democracy

Durkheim rejects the traditional theory of democracy, according to
which the mass of the population 'participates' in the exercise of
government. For him, this is a situation which is only possible in a
society which is not a 'political society'. He points out that the state
comes into existence by a process of concentration which detaches a
certain group of individuals from the collective mass: government must
be exercised by a minority of individuals. Democracy, therefore, must
concern the relationship between the state and society. A democratic
order exists when citizens are regularly informed of the activities of
the state, and the state is aware of the sentiments and wishes of all
sectors of the population (Durkheim, 1950: 80). In a democratic order,
the role of the state does not simply express the sentiments held in a
diffuse fashion among the population, but is often the origin of new
ideas. In this context, the sphere of the state is larger than in other
periods, and society becomes more flexible. Durkheim argues that
secondary groups are essential if the state is not to oppress the individual; they are also necessary if the state is to be sufficiently free of
the individual (Ibid., p. 96). States become tyrannical if corporations
do not exist (Durkheim, 1958: 437).

Drawing an organic analogy, it is possible to argue, as Durkheim frequently did, that the state is the 'brain' – the conscious, directive centre – which operates via the intermediary organs within the complex nervous system of a differentiated society. A democratic order, he notes, enjoys the same relative superiority over other societies as does the self-conscious being over an animal whose behaviour is unreflective or instinctive. He places considerable emphasis upon the 'cognitive' as opposed to the 'active' significance of the state. The specific role of the democratic state is not to subordinate the individual to itself, but rather to provide for the individual's self-actualization. This can only take place through membership of a society in which the state guarantees and advances the rights embodied in moral individualism.[7] Durkheim's main objection to democracy is that it is difficult to worship a legal order that can be easily changed if the majority of people so decide. In his view, the law should make explicit which are the natural relations among things. The law should be respected simply because it is 'good' (Durkheim, 1950: 104).

The State and Religion

Durkheim considers society to be the source of religion. In *The Elementary Forms of the Religious Life*, he writes: 'religious forces are therefore human forces, moral forces' (1982: 419). The principal object of religion is to act upon the moral life. Religion is the image of society; it reflects all of its aspects, even the most vulgar and the most repulsive. The only characteristics shared equally by all religions are that they correspond to a certain number of people living together and usually show great intensity.

Durkheim argues that, contrary to what would seem to be the case even when religion appears to be entirely within the individual conscience, it is still created by society. He understands religion as an element of unity among believers and points out that when individual minds enter into a close relation and act upon each other, a new kind of psychic life arises from their synthesis. He establishes a basic distinction between the sacred and the profane, stressing the role of the cult. Collective ideas and sentiments which make the unity and personality of a society need to be upheld and reaffirmed at regular intervals. Yet, when Durkheim comments that 'there is no essential difference between an assembly of Christians celebrating the principal dates of the life of Christ, or of Jews remembering the exodus from

7. Giddens remarks this particular point in his book *Durkheim on Politics and the State* (1987).

Egypt or the promulgation of the decalogue, and a reunion of citizens commemorating the promulgation of a new moral or legal system or some great event in the national life', he is not only describing a series of similarities between religious and civil ceremonies; he is emphasizing that both types of ceremonies do not differ 'either in their object, the results which they produce, or the processes employed to attain these results' (1982: 427). He writes, referring to both religious and country rituals, that 'it is by uttering the same cry, pronouncing the same word, or performing the same gesture in regard to some object that they [the people] become and feel themselves to be in unison' (1982: 230). The fact that religion shares common ideas, common obligations and common conduct through ritual means that it creates society in a more important sense than it is created by society. Ritual is not identical in all societies but, as Gellner points out, its underlying role remains the same.

In the crazed frenzy of the collective dance around the totem, each individual psyche is reduced to a trembling suggestible jelly; the ritual then imprints the required shared ideas, the collective representations, on this malleable proto-social human matter. It thereby makes it concept-bound, constrained, and socially clubbable (Gellner, 1991: 36).

Durkheim's theory of religion makes a decisive contribution to the understanding of nationalism since, 'religion has given birth to all that is essential in society' (1982: 419). For if in 'religious worship society adores its own camouflaged image. In a nationalist age', as Gellner (1983: 56) notes, 'societies worship themselves brazenly and openly, spurning the camouflage'. If we replace the term religion by nationalism and take into account the fundamental role of rituals and symbols within the nationalist discourse, we can indeed apply to nationalism the capacity to restrain and instil cohesion within any one community as a means to obtain co-operation and communication. Gellner (Ibid.) argues that in Durkheim's view, 'collective rituals inculcate shared compulsions, thereby quite literally humanizing us. We cooperate because we think alike, and we think alike thanks to ritual.'

Durkheim's Theory of 'Patriotism'

Durkheim's work does not contain an explicit theory of nationalism. In fact, he does not use the term 'nationalism', but instead refers to 'patriotism'. He wrote little directly on nationalism, which means that we need to study his work carefully in order to piece together the comments on it which appear in various parts of his writings.

Durkheim distinguishes between 'nationality', 'state' and 'nation'. He defines 'nationality' as: 'human groups that are united by a community of civilization without being united by a political bond' (Durkheim, 1987b: 206). Durkheim uses the word 'nationality' to refer to large groups of individuals who do not constitute political societies, but who possess a unity. He takes Poland and Finland as examples and stresses that they are not yet states but possess an historical reality. Nationalities are either former states that have not given up the idea of reconstituting themselves, or states in the process of becoming. By 'state', he refers to 'the agents of sovereign authority' (1950: 48), thus implying the existence of a central power. By 'nation' he means a 'group that is both "state" and "nationality"' (1987b: 206).

Durkheim defines patriotism as 'a sentiment that joins the individual to the political society in so far as those who get to make it up feel themselves attached to it by a bond of sentiment' (Ibid.). The 'patrie' (fatherland) is the 'normal milieu which is indispensable to human life' (1973: 103). He has a particular understanding of 'patriotism'. On the one hand, he identifies the 'patrie' as the highest organized society that exists and emphasizes that we cannot dispense with a 'patrie' since we cannot live outside of an organized society. On the other hand, he points out that 'national aims do not lie at the summit of the hierarchy'; rather, 'it is human aims that are destined to be supreme' (Giddens, 1987: 202). On this basis, he notes, it has sometimes been suggested that patriotism could be regarded simply as a phenomenon that would soon disappear. Durkheim recognizes that this idea is problematic (Ibid., p. 203): 'man is a moral being only because he lives within established societies . . . now patriotism is precisely the ideas and feelings as a whole which bind the individual to a certain state. If we suppose it to have weakened or to have ceased to exist, where is an individual to find this moral authority, whose curb is to this extent salutary?'

Durkheim does not see 'patriotism' as a sentiment that will endure. In his view (Ibid., p. 201), a conflict has come about between 'equally high-minded kinds of sentiment – those we associate with a national ideal and the state that embodies it, and those we associate with the human ideal and mankind in general – in a word, between patriotism and world patriotism.' He writes: 'Over and above the patrie there is yet another which is in the process of being formed, which envelops our national patrie. This is the European patrie or the human patrie' (Durkheim, 1973: 101). In his view, 'no matter how devoted men may be to their native land, they all today are aware that beyond the forces of national life there are others, in a highest region and not so transitory, for they are unrelated to conditions peculiar to any given political group and are not bound up with its fortunes' (Giddens, 1987: 201).

It is not clear to Durkheim what attitude individuals should adopt in facing patriotism (Durkheim, 1973: 101): 'to what extent should we desire this other kind of society (human patrie)? Should we try to bring it about, to hasten its coming or indeed, should we jealously maintain the independence of the present home-country to which we belong at all costs?' This dichotomy is partially solved by Durkheim's identification of what he calls the 'national ideal' with the 'human ideal'. He argues that each state becomes an organ of the 'human ideal' insofar as it assumes that its main task is not to expand by extending its borders, but to increase the level of its members' morality. Therefore, societies should place their pride in becoming the best organized and in having the best moral constitution, rather than in being the biggest or richest of all societies.

In the pamphlet *Qui a voulu la guerre?*, Durkheim analyses the causes of the First World War and the attitudes of the different European countries involved, and adopts a French nationalist stance. He blames Germany and writes (Durkheim, 1915b: 61): 'There is not a single serious gesture of peace in Germany, there are only vain words.'[8] In Durkheim's view (Ibid., p. 63), Germany's culpability is obvious. Everything confirms it, and nothing can attenuate it. Furthermore, universal opinion is progressively less reluctant to blame the German government and make it responsible for the terrible calamity that our peoples are suffering today. When describing France's attitude he notes (Ibid., p. 54): 'In fact, France has fought to the end with all her energy to achieve peace . . . France's attitude towards the outside has always been irreproachably correct.'[9]

Durkheim failed in his prediction when he considered 'patriotism' to be a transitory phenomenon: 'as we advance in evolution, we see the ideals men pursue breaking free of the local or ethnic conditions obtaining in a certain region of the world or a certain human group, and rising above all that is particular and so approaching the universal' (Giddens, 1987: 202). According to Durkheim (1987a: 390), 'it is impossible to artificially resuscitate a particularist spirit which no longer has any foundation'. Durkheim stresses the same point in *The Division of Labour* (1988: liv), when he writes: 'an organisation based on territorial groupings becomes progressively weaker . . . geographical divisions are in the main artificial, and no longer arouse deep emotions

---

8. Original text: 'il n'existe pas à l'actif de l'Allemagne un seul geste sérieux de paix, mais rien que de vaines paroles'.

9. Original text: 'en fait, elle a, jusqu'au bout et de toutes ses forces, lutté pour la paix . . . l'attitude extérieure de la France fut toujours d'une irréprochable correction'.

within us. The provincial spirit has vanished beyond recall. "Parish pump" patriotism has become an anachronism that cannot be restored at will.' History has proved Durkheim wrong in his prediction about the transitory character of patriotism. But it is obviously true that the global perception of the world we experience today opens the path towards 'human ideals' and radically transforms both the objectives and content of nationalism.

Conclusion

Marx's theory of the state is derived from his understanding of the history of society as the history of class struggle. Within this framework, he refers to the state as the form of organization which the bourgeoisie necessarily adopts both for internal and external purposes, and for the mutual guarantee of their property and interest. Political power is merely the organized power of one class oppressing another. A basic transition from this point is initiated when Marx appeals to the state as independent from and superior to all social classes and as being the dominant force in society rather than the instrument of a dominant class. His idea that proletarians have to conquer the political power of the state should be understood from this perspective.

Durkheim, by contrast, defines the state as the organ of moral discipline, social justice and social thought. The state gives dignity and rights to individuals while at the same time it imposes restrictions and limitations upon them. For him the state has a moral goal: the expansion of justice within society. Both Durkheim and Marx envisage some kind of peaceful future for humanity. Durkheim's idea that each state becomes an organ of the 'human ideal' as far as it assumes that its main task is not to expand by extending its borders, but to increase the level of its members' morality, can be linked with Marx's goal of the abolition of the sharp economic and social inequalities derived from capitalism, thus establishing a world where the emancipation of all individuals as human beings would be possible. However, neither thinker gives any detailed attention to the nation-state as a generic phenomenon and neither, in a systematic way, connects the nature of the modern state with claims on territoriality and the control of the means of violence – features that will become crucial when discussing nationalism.

Marx considered the nationalist objective of creating one Germany as a bourgeois claim. After 1848, however, Marx and Engels supported the national cause of the 'historic' or 'great' nations, for example

Germany, insofar as large states would make it easier for the proletariat to advance its class goals.

Durkheim and Marx understood nationalism as something which needed to be transcended. Durkheim's and Marx's approaches are slightly different. Durkheim's position could be described as 'pan-nationalist'. By this I mean that his stance puts 'human aims' above 'national' ones. According to him, the 'patrie' has a key role in the process of moralization since it is the 'highest organized society that exists'. He refers to 'patriotism' as a sentiment that is about to disappear and will be replaced by what he calls 'world patriotism'. Marx's attitude can be described as 'internationalist'. His main objective was 'universal emancipation' and he envisaged some kind of world solidarity. But he recognized that this could only be possible if nations were free from their conquerors because only then could the workers think in international terms about a working-class solidarity.

Three main reasons may be discerned to account for the absence of a systematic treatment of nationalism in the work of Marx and Durkheim.

1. Sociology appeared to most of the classical thinkers as closely linked to the rise of industrialization and mainly represented an effort to gain an understanding of the new circumstances human beings had to face as a consequence of a change in the conditions and organization of labour. Classical social thinkers tried to grasp the distinctive features of modern societies and focused on social changes which were the fruit of industrialization processes. The innovations taking place in the economic system produced not only a restructuring of the social bonds concerning the relation between individuals in the social arena, but also a new set of ties linking individuals and political institutions, such as the state. However, nationalism was not seen as a phenomenon that could be connected to the rise of modern nation-states, or as a feature linked to the expansion of industrialism.
2. The attempts of Marx and Durkheim to build a 'grand theory' capable of explaining the evolution of society from its genesis to present times. In this context, it becomes crucial to find a core line of argument that allows for the creation of a theory able to decode the different stages of human history.
3. Marx viewed the concept of class struggle as a central attribute of social systems, present from Ancient Greece to modern times. The centrality he conferred upon class struggle allowed him to construct a general theory of history and explain the social, political and ideological aspects of society in reference to the economy. Econ-

omic life determined social relations more generally and shaped the political sphere. Nationalism was nothing other than a marginal phenomenon. Marx's emphasis upon the political sphere as 'superstructure' led him to downplay both the nation-state and nationalism as major influences upon historical change. Durkheim saw the division of labour as a crucial characteristic in defining society. In his view, changes in the division of labour created different kinds of relations among people: organic solidarity, mechanic solidarity. The political sphere was once more left somewhat marginal. Durkheim made important contributions to the theory of the modern state, but he failed to relate the state to concepts of territoriality and violence. In his description of modern societies, he undervalued the importance of nationalism, because for him 'national aims' are secondary as compared to 'human aims'.

Bibliography

Bloom, S. F. (1941), *The World of Nations: A Study of the National Implications in the Work of K. Marx*, New York: Columbia University Press.

Durkheim, E. (1915a), *L'Allemagne au-dessus de tout: La mentalité allemande et la guerre. Etudes et document sur la guerre*, Paris: Librairie Armand Colin.

——, (1915b), *Qui a voulu la guerre?*, Paris: Librairie Armand Colin.

——, (1950), *Leçons de Sociologie: physique des mœurs et du droit*, Paris: Presses Universitaires de France.

——, (1958), 'L'Etat', *Revue Philosophique*, 83ème année, tome CXLVIII.

——, (1973), 'Pacifisme et Patriotisme', translated by N. Layne, *Sociological Inquiry*, 43(2).

——, (1974), *Sociology and Philosophy*, New York: The Free Press.

——, (1982 (1915)), *The Elementary Forms of the Religious Life*, London: George Allen.

——, (1987a), *Suicide*, London: Routledge & Kegan Paul Ltd.

——, (1987b (1978)), 'A Debate on Nationalism and Patriotism', trans. A. Giddens, in A. Giddens (ed.), *Durkheim on Politics and the State*, London: Fontana Paperbacks.

——, (1988 (1984)), *The Division of Labour in Society*, London: Macmillan.

Feuer, L.S., (ed.), (1976 (1959)), *Marx and Engels Basic Writings on Politics and Philosophy*, Glasgow: The Fontana Library.

Gellner, E. (1983), *Nations and Nationalism*, Oxford: Basil Blackwell.

——, (1991), *Reason and Culture*, Oxford: Blackwell.

Giddens, A. (1987 (1978)), *Durkheim on Politics and the State*, London: Fontana Paperbacks.

Marx, K. (1975), 'Das Nationale System der Politischen Oekonomie', [article on F. List's book], in K. Marx and F. Engels, *Collected Works*, vol. 4, London: Lawrence & Wishart.

——, (1978), *The German Ideology*, C. J. Arthur (ed.), New York: New York International Publishers.

——, and Engels, F. (1975a), *Collected Works*, vol. 4, London: Lawrence & Wishart.

——, and Engels, F. (1975b), *Collected Works*, vol. 22, London: Lawrence & Wishart.

——, and Engels, F. (1975c), *Collected Works*, vol. 23, London: Lawrence & Wishart.

——, and Engels, F. (1976 (1959)), 'Manifesto of the Communist Party', in L. S. Feuer (ed.), *Marx and Engels Basic Writings on Politics and Philosophy*, Glasgow: The Fontana Library.

Smith, A. D. (1979), *Nationalism in the Twentieth Century*, Oxford and New York: Martin Robertson & New York University Press.

Szporluk, R. (1988), *Communism and Nationalism*, Oxford: Oxford University Press.

-4-

The Quest for Identity: Modern Strangers and New/Old Ethnicities in Europe

Aleksandra Ålund

We live in an epoch characterized by a parallelism between centrifugal and centripetal forces, where processes of transnational compression are accompanied by processes of fragmentation. The latter are crucial in the construction of new and new-old individual, local, regional and ethnic identities. These often painful processes are increasingly influenced by wars and crises, as well as by public discourses pregnant with intolerance and exclusivism in relation to 'the other'. This is evident in the current conflicts between different ethnic groups in the new Baltic states and in former Yugoslavia. Russians in the Baltic states and various 'minorities' in Serbia, Croatia and Bosnia no longer 'belong'. They are excluded in legal, cultural or religious terms. Irrespective of whether they define themselves as belonging to the 'people' or to the traditions of the country in which they have lived – sometimes for generations – they are excluded from the newly formed communities, which are reserved for those considered to belong to the dominant national group. The fabrication of new national and often exclusivist identities – which are imbued with regressive ideologies based on an appeal to a 'lost grandeur' in terms of sacrifice, *Blut und Boden* – frames a world of absolutism behind a myth of 'imagined community'. The 'invention of tradition' in these constructed ethno-national histories often carries the vestiges of an instrumentality in the service of unscrupulous power struggles. The victims – the excluded, 'the other' – which stand in the way of territorial, political or economic gains are often forced to join the ranks of the new 'helots' in modernity's stream of refugees.

In a world where the search for roots has become widespread – from new social movements to the building of new nation-states, from identity politics to national identities – the multiple expression of exclusion has spread. A new kind of European citizen, a 'stranger', is being constructed, in the context of a fragmented Yugoslavia as well as in today's Europe in general. The dilemmas and ambiguities of modern society appear in the nexus between bridge-building, multi-cultural, transethnic communities and a fortress Europe that builds new walls around and inside its imagined cultural territories.

Some imaginative reflections from Georg Simmel's essay *Bridge and Door*, written at the beginning of the century, may deepen our understanding of modernity's antagonisms expressed through processes of alterity; closed doors and fragile bridges between different 'others'. 'Belonging', through the accentuation of 'home-space', is a funda-mental human social and cultural marker. The symbolic home has symbolic doors and, following Simmel (1994), *door* signifies, in addition to a necessary psychological and cultural demarcation, the possibility of stepping outside its limitation. A door is a metaphor for the connections between social actors, for the public discourse, for the organization of solidarity and resistance. Modern society's limits – its programmed way of separating in order to connect – is expressed symbolically as a bridge. The multicultural society increasingly stands out as a system of bridge-building between separate parts which are regarded discursively as 'finite' cultural products, with culture regarded as unchanging, as essence – as 'roots'. Understood in this way, bridges of multiculturalism are political and theoretical constructions of petrified structures of connection between human populations in terms of simplified and statically defined culture and ethnicity.

This seems to be the common problem uniting Europe. Not least Sweden, famous in Europe for its Multicultural Politics, is fenced in according to ethnic 'boundaries', and the transethnic is still in its infancy (Ålund and Schierup, 1991). We can also see similar tendencies in, for example, France. Analysing the French context, Michel Wieviorka (1993: 61) argues that 'tendencies to refer to different kinds of boundary creating roots have been stronger than efforts to participate in the birth of new forms of collective actions'. These tendencies reflect contemporary processes connecting the crisis of the welfare state, fundamental societal transformations and a deterioration of social conditions with anxiety over the future European Union, migration, and the spread of racism and its relationship with contemporary nationalism(s). The situation is a hot-bed for the growth of populist movements, localism and boundary-making, the separation of the connected, the simplistic singling-out of 'parts' from the dynamic of the whole, the division of people into Us and the Others, Europeans and Strangers. I have found the sociological notion of the stranger particularly important in this context.

The Stranger: Two Paradigmatic Approaches

Scientific discourses have helped to create the 'stranger' and the 'non-stranger'. I will now discuss two classical lines of thought which, discursively, have branched off in modernity. The one is Alfred Schutz's conception of 'the stranger', which he formulated in the US during his exile from Nazi Germany and Austria. This 'stranger' appears to be an autobiographical reflection of being forced to seek refuge and to live in another world; a stranger who can 'cease to be' and 'gear into', hiding himself in order to avoid being the undesirable 'other'. Schutz's stranger develops a self-effacement in exercizing the skills of adjustment towards total assimilation as the only possible way of saving himself. But between the stranger and the 'group' he meets, yawns an insurmountable gulf – a naturalized breach of cultural and psychological difference.

An alternative line of thought in the discourse of the 'stranger' can be found in the work of Georg Simmel from the turn of the century. Simmel was also, like Schutz, a sociologist of Jewish background. Simmel, however, lived in a kind of inner refuge specific to the Jewish experience of the time. His analysis was a precursor of today's interest in the 'global city' and globalizing 'cultural flows'. From his contemporary 'Metropolis', Simmel (1950b) reflected upon the linkage between the inner and the outer. Proximity and distance, connection and separation – these are the different dimensions of human inter-action. A stranger, a *potential* wanderer, is an important sociological category for the study of the process of interaction. In contrast to Schutz, however, Simmel does not see the stranger as a person outside the perceived natural continuity of the group. Rather, Simmel's stranger takes part in a dialogue. Being a stranger is 'a very positive relation: it is a specific form of interaction. The inhabitants of Sirius are not really strangers to us, at least not in any sociologically relevant sense: they do not exist for us at all; they are beyond far and near' (Simmel, 1950a: 402). The stranger is the person who comes today and stays tomorrow. His 'position is determined, essentially', according to Simmel, 'by the fact that he has not belonged to it [the group] from the beginning', but 'he imports qualities into it, which do not and cannot stem from the group itself' (Ibid., p. 402).

This specific form of interaction can, however, create special ten-sions. The stranger, Simmel says, is 'fixed within a group whose boundaries are similar to spatial boundaries'. Thus, he calls attention to how the stranger is an element of the group itself – 'like the poor and like sundry "inner enemies". His position as a full-fledged member involves both being outside of and confronting it' (Ibid., pp. 402–403). Addressing the peculiar unity of the stranger's position '. . . composed of certain measures of nearness and distance' (Ibid., p. 408), Simmel focuses on the problematic character of this relational peculiarity; 'a special proportion' of specific conditions behind 'its uniform life', which are then related to 'reciprocal tensions'. Together, these processes produce the particular and formal relation to the 'stranger' which goes beyond general 'human commonness'. The stranger is not really thought of as an individual, but rather becomes 'itself' – a constructed human category, a 'strangeness'. Through the specificity of the relationship between proximity and distance, Simmel attaches a positional category with an identity and a cultural dynamic. 'There arises a specific tension when the consciousness that only the quite general is common, stresses that which is not common.' This '. . . non-common element is once more not individual, but merely the strangeness of origin' which in turn becomes 'common to many strangers' (Ibid., p. 407).

This understanding goes beyond incompatibility between cultures, beyond a perception of cultures as well-defined modules, and even beyond limits in the mainstream discourse of cultural bridging in the real multiculturalism of the present – where, to use Simmel's terms, bridges are seen as connecting 'the finite within the finite' (Simmel, 1994: 8). Hence, instead of perceiving bridging as 'the line stretched between two points' (Ibid., p. 8) which connects isolated entities, interaction and the relationship between the social and the cultural are emphasized. At the turn of the century, accordingly, modern life was perceived as an 'open door' – 'life flows forth out of the door from the limitation of isolated separate existence into the limitlessness of all possible directions' (Ibid., p. 8).

While bridging seems to represent an attempt to connect solid points in a search for 'unconditional security and direction' (Ibid., p. 8), the door displays an agency encompassing both entering and exiting. Closing the door is (culturally) a separation from 'the uniform, continuous unity of natural being' (Ibid., p. 9), which at the same time means that 'a piece of space was thereby brought together and separated from the whole remaining world' (Ibid., p. 7). After that, however, a kind of demarcation takes place, 'its limitedness finds its significance and dignity only in . . . the possibility at any moment of stepping out of this limitation into freedom' (Ibid., p. 10). The door subsequently becomes a central metaphor for agency; it represents a subtle dialectical relationship between humankind's need to demarcate its unique being culturally, and the ability socially to transgress borders between human beings. The human being is 'the bordering creature who has no border' (Ibid., p. 10).

The contemporary search for roots reflects the kind of bordering of which Simmel speaks, and it mirrors our contemporary social crises and cultural delusions as well. The latter seem to have more to do with the difficulties of connecting 'the finite with the finite' culturally, as discursively formulated in the phenomenology of Alfred Schutz in his essay on 'The Stranger'. Cultural essentialism is becoming widespread, and it finds resonance in neo-liberalism's celebration of the private and the particular. The culturalization of modern life that should be 'liberated' – in an academic and political sense – from social relationships of dependence (on the institutions of the welfare state, and on the 'structural' in general) goes hand-in-hand with the spread of market styles and the celebration of the full expression of our natural instincts. The 'natural' and the 'authentic' form the frame of reference for the national, regional and local. Like a contemporary echo of Schutz's words (1976: 95), 'thinking as usual' appears to be based on a 'relatively natural conception of the world'. The naturalization of a cultural 'us' is accompanied by a demarcation of a 'them'; an immigrant's atavistic ethnicity and a discursive banishment to its pre-modern roots. Boundaries are drawn, and the question is *whether* rather than *how* separate cultures can be connected.

'The Stranger', Schutz (1976: 103) writes in his classic essay, 'constructs a social world of pseudo-anonymity, pseudo-intimacy, and pseudo-typicality. He is outplaced from his "home"' and uprooted both geographically and culturally, which renders him invalid in the dialogue on the new social environment. The stranger lives on in an 'unbroken' connection with 'the cultural pattern of his home group' (Ibid.) which becomes an unquestioned, *natural* frame of reference. In his lecture on *The Cultural Construction of the 'Stranger' in Social Scientific Thought*, Jonathan Schwartz (1994: 6) argues: 'This is Scheler's phrase. Scheler spoke of "the opening and closing of the sluice gates of the spirit" to describe the "relatively natural" ideas and cultural styles.' According to Schwartz, the phenomenological core of Schutz's stranger is an abstracted essence – 'Home' or rather *Heimat*; nostalgia for the *Gemeinschaft* of a rural village, *Heimat*. The notion has its roots in Romantic German philosophy and is readily evident in Schutz's essentialistic concept of culture. Paradoxically enough, Schutz – himself an immigrant in the US – creates the 'stranger' for whom it becomes impossible to belong or feel at home, as a consequence of his own and others' *Heimatization*.

While the exiled individual stubbornly preserves an 'ex-world', and thus a (self-inflicted) psychological trauma of pseudo-existence, the *Heimat* he encounters is perceived as embodied in the group that, as a stranger, he is to approach. Here he is stopped by the rules of 'naturalness'. The result of the naturalness of 'thinking as usual' is again the cultural pattern excluding the stranger. He cannot share the 'essence' owned by the group he meets. 'Any member born or reared within the group accepts the ready-made standardised scheme of the cultural pattern handed down to him by ancestors, teachers, and authorities as an unquestioned and unquestionable guide in all the situations which normally occur within the social world' (Schutz, 1976: 95). The group the stranger encounters appears to be monitored by the unwritten rules of culturally inherited recipes – that is 'recipes for interpreting the social world' (Ibid.). Cultural recipes acquire hereby 'the function of the cultural pattern of eliminating troublesome inquiries by offering ready-made directions for use' (Ibid.). While helping group members avoid 'undesirable consequences', recipes serve ultimately as guardians of a social order.

The preservation of the social order can thus be seen as the reason why '. . . only members of the in-group, *having a definite status in its hierarchy* and also being aware of it, can use its cultural pattern as a natural and trustworthy scheme of orientation' (Ibid., p. 99, my emphasis). This also seems to explain why the 'stranger' can only live in a pseudo-world. He can never take part in the mysterious 'belonging' to the deep roots surrounding graves not his own; 'graves and reminiscence can neither be transferred nor conquered' (Ibid., p. 97). This is also why the stranger, 'a border case outside the territory' (Ibid., p. 99), only approaches the group superficially, and in vivid and immediate experience. While he remains excluded from the foundations of the past, he is also excluded from 'home' and from 'belonging'.

Thus, as Schwartz (1994: 8) observes, 'phenomenology, because it claimed to dig deeply into the roots of existence – to care for them, and not to tear them up – had natural affinities for *Gemeinschaft* and *Heimat* as ideals'. Mediated through Schutz, this exposes the irony of the rootlessness of the stranger who is uprooted and who cannot – on account of his cultivation of old roots – be rooted in the new environment. He is, instead, to remain rooted as a stranger in the new plantations of latter so-called urban villages. *Gemeinschaft*, Schwartz argues (Ibid., pp. 8–9), 'survives in Chicago immigrant milieu and the research of the Chicago school'. In Jewish ghettos, Little Sicilies, Little Polands and so on, Schwartz continues, we are confronted with research which – with 'ethnographic detail and its fieldwork quality' (Ibid., p. 9) – represents a paradigm which 'was not the blazing hot melting pot of Henry Ford's Americanization; it seemed more like an amalgam of rural community and emancipated urbanity' (Ibid.).

But rather than an amalgam, maybe, what is at stake here is the immigrants' second exile – to excluded and in turn exclusivist urban ethnic communities. In the face of the devastating effects of urbanization and modernization upon the old worlds, the little worlds of *Heimat* disappear. 'The century of exile', as Schwartz (1993) calls it, then begins. The uncertainties which develop are 'organized' through the intolerance of modernity and the various kinds of rigidity and inequality within the *Heimat* of the future – 'havens in a heartless world'. The social psychology of cultural encounters has been reduced to a psychology of the culturally absolute and impregnable. Schutz's phenomenology lays the ground for a type of psychologized and naturalized cultural fundamentalism, which in many ways traverses contemporary academic and popular discourses dealing with the stranger and with cultural 'collisions'.

In a world where the search for roots has become widespread – from new social movements to the building of new nation-states, from identity politics to national cultural identities – Alfred Schutz's phenomenology can provide food for thought. A cultural panic has spread in the wake of a globalization of uncertainties. This essentially social crisis has become a worship of the cultural as it fosters a quest for pluralization and ethnicization in an implosive 'roots' radicalism. 'The explosion of invented communities and "reactive" identities is taking place in a situation of hegemonic cultural homogenisation and scattered revolt' (Karlsson, 1994). The doors are closing, while possible bridges seek to connect points of scattered ethnic separateness – along the route of prescribed multicultural security and direction (Ålund and Schierup, 1991).

New Ethnicities

New boundaries and barriers to the transgression of boundaries illustrate the inner tensions of contemporary multicultural society. We are faced with the choice between an open and a closed society. No modern open society can exist as ethnically pure. Modern identities are formed in a dynamic interplay of different cultural elements from the composite living world which stresses the meaning of the transethnic in the construction of modern identities and the process of belonging.

Still, more often than not, cultures are classified and ordered in line with prevailing ethnocentric norms. This results, at our northern latitudes, in a Eurocentric system of hierarchical classification, in which the perceived cultural distance of the 'others' from the (Swedish) centre is decisive. (One example of this classification in Sweden may be found in Charles Westin's *Den toleranta opinionen* (1987) [The Tolerant Public Opinion].) How far apart *we* and *they* are is expressed in terms of cultural distance and collision. The periphery seems to be associated with the traditional, moreover, and the centre with modernity.

The culturally classified and ethnocentrically ordered functions as a discriminatory standard – as when, for example, determining suitability within a labour market divided increasingly along lines of ethnic origin. Despite the egalitarian discourse of Swedish cultural pluralism, cultural segregation is constructed on a status-oriented basis, and in accordance with stereotypical and deterministic notions. It leaves the field open for social inequalities and intense tensions between population groups.

I believe that representing ethnic relations exclusively in terms of culture or attitudes does not lead to a proper understanding of integration and disintegration in modern multicultural societies. In this multifarious, sometimes mixed and often divided world of ours, the notion of ethnicity is a central one. What do we mean? How do we use it? Ethnicity has become a key question in the discussion of multicultural and immigrant policy in Sweden and all over Europe. What we have learned thus far is that ethnicity is an obscure concept – it is used, for example, in contexts relating not only to culture but also to structure, and it addresses both purity and mixture, both imagined closed communities and the imaginative processes through which culture is created and boundaries are transgressed.

Immigrant ethnicity is not now – if indeed it ever was – solely the expression of pluralism in the cultural sense. Whatever we mean by 'the cultural' associated with ethnicity, the structural constraints of the societal majority are rapidly infecting it. Ethnicity is becoming an expression of specific reactions to the growing experiences of multiple exile among a majority of Scandinavian immigrants. The social petrification of a hierarchical ethnic division of labour and the social/ political marginalization of immigrant populations are cardinal factors in the development of ethnicity.

The widespread static view of ethnicity, with its emphasis upon cultural difference, has come under increasing criticism as a deterministic view that portrays cultural preservation as a goal in itself, while presenting social inequality as cultural deviance. Ethnicity, and indeed race as well, have come to be understood as social constructions (Gorelick, 1989; Ålund and Schierup, 1991). Different types of ethnicity always historically appear – to use the expression of Stuart Hall (commenting on race in *New Ethnicities*) – in articulation, in a formation, with other categories and divisions in society. Being closely related to socio-cultural tensions, ethnicity is 'constantly crossed and recrossed' (Hall, 1992: 255) by the categories of race, gender and class. The primordialist concept (and practice) of ethnicity seems to me to be related, both historically and at present (as in the new states of ex-Yugoslavia, for example) to the same type of theoretical and 'empirical' problems of exclusion. Indeed, as Stuart Hall warns us, there can be no simple 'return' or 'recovery' of the ancestral past which is not re-experienced through the categories of the present. Modern history also teaches us that clean cultures are too often cleansed according to 'blood', and sometimes also with blood. Distant or not, these 'issues' are related to the problem of cultural analysis (i.e. the cultivation of differences), the present (harmonized) politics of immigration, (culturally exclusive) Eurocentrism, and the obscure multiculturalisms of Western Europe. Culture is obviously a battlefield, embodying contradictions in political and mainstream intellectual discourse, in which the rhetoric of the liberal democratic politics of recognition tends to neglect the hierarchical dissonance of social inequality, and explains structurally conditioned pluralism (Gordon, 1970) in terms of culturally derived ethnic stereotypes.

The problems with a culturally reductionist understanding of ethnic processes were brought to attention as early as 1974 in Abner Cohen's introduction to *Urban Ethnicity*. He argued that, even if the concept of ethnicity is usually associated with minority status, lower-class position or 'migrancy', the complex socio-cultural dynamics of ethnicity are seldom the focus of analysis. Instead, the social and the cultural are cast in terms of static and discriminating stereotypes. In this way, the social-structural and class aspects of ethnicity are rendered invisible in favour of the perspective of 'cultural conflict' predominating among both researchers and the general public. The social construction of ethnicity remains concealed, and many of its important aspects escape observation: e.g. the complex processes of group formation, inversion, boundary-drawing, myth activation, fusion and the symbolic representation of cultural markers. However, this neglect of the socio-cultural complexity of ethnic processes has increasingly attracted attention, particularly in contemporary migration research in Western Europe and North America.

Ethnicity is a concept derived from the construction of ethnic groups and their dynamic relations with each other and their societal environment. Ethnicity has two fundamental determining criteria. Cultural solidarity, to begin with, is required, i.e. members of the group must feel a subjective sense of belonging and of shared values, norms and patterns of behaviour. In addition, certain structural preconditions must be fulfilled, i.e. objective material conditions must obtain which generate common interests, group organization and sometimes political action. In this interplay between the 'structural' and the 'cultural', one can in varying degrees find ethnicity expressed with political, religious or cultural overtones (depending on the platform of interests of the ethnic group in question). Ethnicity is often regarded as situationally and contextually determined, and as symbolically charged. If, for example, the platform for solidarity is defined and understood in structural terms – as in the case of 'political Blacks' – the result may be transethnic identities and mobilization on the basis of politically articulated solidarities. Similar experiences related to oppression, discrimination and racism can, independently of conspicuous cultural differences, form the basis for solidarity and a broad social mobilization and construction of collective identity.

Ethnicity and class are not related to each other in any immediate or automatic way. We find many examples of how the invocation of cultural similarity can become an integrative factor for a range of social groups which are far from one another as regards class position. The 'cultural' can function as symbolically integrative (through myths, signs, etc.) and as a basis for solidaristic mobilization, or against a collectively perceived threat or commonly experienced degradation. A culturally defined religious sense of belonging – e.g. Muslim, Jewish, Christian – are clear examples of the integrative force of the 'cultural'. At the same time, many contemporary forms of ethnic mobilization and conflict point towards a complex interplay between structural tensions (local, regional, national and global) and culturally expressed forms of mobilization (e.g. reactive strategies in connection with inclusion/ exclusion). A complex and dynamic perspective of ethnicity is therefore necessary and relevant if one is to analyse the fundamental social conflicts associated with ethnicity and culture. The social dimension has too often been overshadowed by cultural stereotypes in both scientific and popular discourse.

Culturalism, culturalization and ethnicization are notions that have been used to criticize a type of disguised hierarchizing ideology which is premised on a simplified antinomy between civilized/modern and primitive/traditional. Cultural differences are cultivated and polarized. Fuel is furnished for the increasingly common political and popular argumentation focusing on whether various groups among refugees and immigrants are suitable or unsuitable, or adaptable in higher or lower degrees, or 'foreign' to a greater or lesser extent. Here is the basis for a differentiation and selection among people in cultural terms; its extension supplies the basis of legitimacy for what has been termed 'Fortress Europe' and the 'Mediterranean wall'.

The structural processes must be explained if the underlying tensions in the social construction of ethnicity are not to be masked. Thus, we see an interconnection between reinforced external barriers (Fortress Europe) and internal constraints like the discrimination on the job market, segregation in housing areas, political marginalization and growing racism in everyday life. Behind the labels of refugee, immigrant ('invandrare') and the New Underclass, a new kind of second-class citizen is appearing in Europe.

The risk that the culturalization of social disparities will become a type of 'new racism' has been pointed out. While differing from a compromised racial-biological discourse, the 'new racism' focuses on cultural differences, in a simplified and naturalized form. Culture is made to function as nature. 'New Racism' appeals to notions of cultural apartheid and repatriation.

In the mid-September 1993 issue of the Swedish newspaper *Expressen*, a new lift-the-lid politics finds clear expression − 'Kör ut dom' − drive them out. This seems rather symptomatic of the present ideological climate − in the whole of Scandinavia, I believe − where, in a rough interplay, the extreme right, new populist movements and the mass media join in announcing the character and type of exclusion. The process of constituting ethnicity behind the popular rhetoric about the refugee (and purportedly Muslim) 'invasion' is − to use the expression of Stuart Hall − dividing the West from the Rest.

In this historical setting, the making of 'home from home' (Phil Cohen, 1991) has to be done under the besieged conditions of multiple exile. I would now like to connect the question of exile with that of the integration of society, and to relate this to the processes of identity-formation in modern, polyethnic society.

Quest for Identity

The question of social integration appears to be as loaded today as at the beginning of the century. Academic representations of this issue seem today to be polarized between, on the one hand, the theoretical heritage of the 'lonely crowd' − the massification of publics, the undermining of collective morality, growing anonymity, modern individualism, etc., and on the other, the recognition of new forms of cohesion, social bonds, and identity-building. These latter aspects have usually been associated with the meaning of cohesion on the micro-social level.

The notion of community has been fundamental in this context, if not unproblematic. It frames the wide area of the potential of civil society, another notion with multiple resonance. The position of civil society has usually been placed in the conflicting perspective of centre-periphery tensions, and explained in the context of power relations, autonomy and identity-forming processes. Emerging associations, networks and new social movements have been discussed as a zone of mediation and a buffer between the family and the state. This has, by no means seldom, led to overestimating the potential of institutions and movements on the level of civil society (in contrast to the alleged suppressiveness and hegemony of the state). In the discussion of new social movements in particular, the meaning of coherence becomes problematic. It relates increasingly to the particularism of identity or place, and celebrates differences and uniqueness in a world of migration, globalization, cultural amalgamation and merging.

During the 1980s and 1990s, the quest for identity – as well as its complex relationship to modernity – has become one of the most central characteristics of our civilization's transformation. Crisis, the 'end of history', the demise of the grand narratives of modernity, and the social and cultural meaning of life have come to dominate the academic debate. Transnational amalgamations in the shadow of a new international order, together with Eastern Europe's ideological and territorial transformation, have created the background for identity crises in both an individual and collective sense.

The quest for identity thus seems increasingly to be mediated through the fragmenting symbols and rhetoric of ethnicity, regionalism and localism, while the national shows tendencies of leaving the universal behind. Civic policies excluding 'the other' are promulgated. The present also includes, however, the relaxation of social and cultural boundaries, the expansion of a 'world culture', the fusion of cultures, and meetings across boundaries. New boundary-transcending cultures and lifestyles are emerging in the inner cities of Britain, in the Kreuzberg neighbourhood of Berlin, in Sweden's multicultural suburbs, in Paris, etc. Parallel to the forces of exclusion and ethnic absolutism, the processes of merging present us with a multiplicity of answers to the crises of modernity, identity and integration.

It has often been pointed out that insecurities and crises in the West generally are created by the fragmentation of close social ties, the erosion of meta-social guarantees (Touraine), and the dissolution of the more or less homogeneous identities and ideologies of classes and nations. In addition to marginalization, discrimination, and the racism of structure and of everyday life, a more profound feeling of social and cultural erosion is most likely relevant, especially in diasporic immigrant settings.

Given the context of this crisis of modern consciousness in the course of the erosion of systems of integration, a turning towards history is appearing, which has shown itself to be both reflexive and reactive. On the one hand, we see the emergence of increasing societal reflexivity in the identity-forming processes on both individual and collective levels. On the other, we see new enclosures following ethnic lines. Processes of identity-formation around exclusion resemble what is going on in the so-called new-born democracies rising from the ashes of the Soviet Union, ex-Yugoslavia and eastern Europe.

While the nationalists of new-born states appeal to the glory of a purified ethnic past of old victories, heroes and other ghosts, thus demonstrating a sclerotic symbolism of old imperial dreams, the umbilical cord (or bondage rather) to the hinterland helps reflect these tendencies among immigrants in Europe. Thus, in the processes of identity- and community-building among immigrants in European polyethnic settings, we meet an echo that in a way mirrors the hinterland type of ethic revival, but which also – and this needs to be stressed – frequently calls it into question.

Thus, Janus-faced dynamics in the development of ethnic consciousness among immigrants include – besides the processes of purification – ethnic amalgamation and merging. This very often takes on, especially among youth, the character of wrestling with the ghosts of the past – in the present (Schierup and Ålund, 1987).

The metaphorical expression of these processes, deeply embedded in the autobiographical stories that I have collected during my current fieldwork in Rinkeby, a suburb of Stockholm, demonstrates the delicate character of modern ethnic consciousness. Present dilemmas and struggles are often expressed through the mediation of old ghosts. In the specific intersection between the old and new antagonisms faced by immigrants, novel insights are released and 'amalgamated' into new forms of collective identity and social community – in which the symbols of tradition attain their place, not seldom in the service of modern solidarities. Emerging mixtures of cultures and cultural innovations, as well as a variety of identities (in an individual and a collective sense) illustrate the diversity of contemporary multicultural society and its potential for change. In Rinkeby, however, we do not find a 'multiculture', i.e. a kind of 'pluralist order of discrete patches of culture, all somehow, equally valid within the polity', as Roger Hewitt (1992: 29) has observed about Britain. Rather, we find here a variety of cultures which are 'active together and hence bound up with change' (p. 30). Rinkeby became famous for, among other things, its new language – Rinkebyska (or Rinkeby Swedish). This dialect consolidates a composite local identity and sense of belonging to a community which, ethnically speaking, also includes Swedishness. A widely announced Rinkeby 'spirit' — a sort of transethnic collective identity expressed through the locally produced label 'Rinkeby: a village in the world' — alludes to the manifold relationships between the local and the global, and to the inventiveness of the ways in which the people there make a home from home — their local sense of their place in the world. I also became aware of how centripetal forces of togetherness act beyond fragmentation, and of the political importance — beyond the social and psychological — of popular culture like rap music, hip-hop and samba-group, all of which have to do with the formation of new urban social movements and processes of identity.

Individual interviews repeatedly expose a destabilization of fixed ethnicities in the process. In contrast to the dominant Swedish stereo-types of rootlessness and ethnic conflicts in the 'concrete ghettos' of the suburbs, young men and women there seem to share a tendency towards an extensive transcultural identity. Young people mediate experiences anchored in several social and cultural worlds. In their reflexive relation to the 'self' and the 'other', they expose a type of ethnic consciousness that relates in complex ways to present tensions in the countries of emigration, to major structural tensions in the society of immigration, to shared inequality, and to a common outsider identity among modern youths. Thus, to paraphrase Anthony Giddens (1991), social events and social relations 'at a distance' are interlacing with local contextualities.

Referring to the society in which they are growing up, and which they want to consider their own, young people expose the traumas of modern diaspora — not by expressing feelings of displacement, but rather by referring to obstacles in such a way that their wish becomes to make a home of their actual homes. They do not belong to one single world, nor are they telling one particular history, or developing straight-line cultural identities. Their stories are traversed by a multi-plicity of histories, connecting their own memories and those of others with dreams of overcoming the experienced boundaries of the 'multicultural' society.

The complex interplay between ethnicity, class, gender and gener-ation forms the implosive force for a reflexive rejection of both old and new forms of oppression, and for the creation of new forms of solidarity and collective identity. Here we find a social force which has until recently been neglected. The reflexive relation to tradition to which Marshall Berman (1983) calls our attention, and the 'recog-nition' binding time and space to which Paul Gilroy (1987) refers, places modern ethnic consciousness, syncretic culture and transethnic social movements at the front-line of research. New hybrid cultures are building upon history as the carrier of meaning in the diaspora present. Contemporary experiences are welded to life-forms in and through transcultural movements that transpose the historical symbols of tradition on to the symbolic decor of the contemporary inner city's public space.

The psychological, cultural and political importance of a world of mixture and boundary transgression is often overlooked in favour of an overwhelming scientific interest in differences and boundaries. By crossing boundaries, in both a social and cultural sense, young people are throwing light on the complexity of lived realities. There are experiences of hybridity between social worlds and identities that must be heard – beyond the ongoing polarization between 'us' and 'them'; beyond the disparity between, on the one hand, the official rhetoric of tolerance and, on the other, the lack of recognition and the brutal reality of growing intolerance, marginalization, discrimination and racism; beyond the more or less clearly announced purification of the mainstream, of the majority and nowadays also of the minority. Otherwise, we run the risk not only of veiling the emergence of new ethnicities arising from interaction and merging, or of camouflaging 'the inventive act itself', to use the expression of Werner Sollors (1989). We also run the risk of finding ourselves behind the wall(s).

Mediation and Struggle

I will attempt to summarize the diasporic experiences of trying to belong in not belonging. Processes of belonging are filled with tensions between dreams and realities – realities of merging, exclusion and exile. Identity is not fixed or unchanging, of course, but given the character of the social experience of the majority of the migrant population in Scandinavia and elsewhere in Europe, there is a danger of the petrification of stigmatizing images of the stereotypical 'other' based on the existing social order. This can contribute – further down the line – to releasing reactive or defensive feelings in the service of new forms of ethnic purification and absolutism. It can also effectualize a partition of the public space into separate ethnic territories. In that case, the broken bridges of Mostar and Sarajevo will not just be metaphors for distant barbarism.

During the summer of 1993, a mosque and a Greek Orthodox church were set on fire in Sweden. Countless attacks on refugee centres, fires, and plundered ethnic businesses are seen on our TV screens. Politicians march in torchlight demonstrations against racist terror and the desecration of Jewish graves. The police mobilize massive force to meet the confrontations between racists and antiracists occurring in connection with the celebration of the great Swedish cosmopolitian and conqueror, King Charles XII. The racists celebrate, rather paradoxically, the memory of an adventurer who internationalized Swedish culture and political praxis. The racists, by contrast, want to rid Sweden of all 'foreign races'. The police meet them with the same irritation they show towards 'unruly' antiracists (Löwander, 1993). The most important goal on the part of the police seems to be keeping the streets of Stockholm clean, quiet and free of people (Ålund, 1992). Stockholm's streets and squares are no longer safe. The memory of the 'Laser man' who killed and wounded a number of men of foreign appearance has spread terror throughout that part of the Swedish population with a 'foreign' and 'non-Swedish' appearance. Isolated 'nutcases' are running amok at a time when organized racism is on the rise and cultural racism is spreading in insidious forms throughout society – from the street to parliament.

At the same time, new voices are spreading like rings on the water. The local rap artist, Lucco, sings: 'Because they have the name of the country . . . no somos criminales no nos traten como animales . . . fuck the gringo con el sabor de latino, Huh . . .'

Gringos and Latinos meet in Sweden, and the history of colonial oppression relates to closed doors, disco security guards, and patronizing glances here and now. 'Flows in space' of rhythm and resistance are televised to private rooms, redrafted in texts about the local and particular, and mediated through meeting places to embrace the unifying and common, as a collective insight of outsider status and as a challenge to resistance. Young racists in the hardrock group, *Ultima Thule*, sing 'out with the riffraff' on a TV program about racism, while the TV camera zooms in on a Nazi flag. While Jan, a young member of this group, says that 'we need very high walls around Sweden', the young immigrant rap artist Dogge, from the group *Latin Kings*, answers: 'Brown Latino with black hair, ten fingers and ten toes, just like you, here and now . . .' In an interview on another occasion, Dogge explains, 'skinheads and "blackheads", they are really the same', and adds, 'we are all idiots who go against each other . . . instead we should, skinheads and "blackheads", come together against politicians and all those damn big dudes that have money and power. First when we come together and do something together are we a threat' (Moe, 1994; Ålund, 1995).

Like the racist skinheads, Jan and Roger in *Ultima Thule*, the antiracist rap artists Lucco and Dogge are children of their time, children of the same struggle. The former want to build walls, the latter want to build bridges. The former lock themselves in. The latter leave the door ajar and are on their way out. Both groups mirror the same world in the texts of their songs – where are we going?

The sociology of complex societies allows for no automatic answers. Amongst all of us who are more or less exposed to the expansion of 'alterity', alienation and the search for identity, the different effects of the uncertainty caused by the demise of the welfare state, weakened collective identities, economic crises and the broken promises of universalism are ramified. In the face of transnational capital accumulation and hypernational political processes, anonymous forms of control, and legitimacy crises for the nation-state and its system of political representation, the conditions are created for uncertain identities and new ethnicizations. We are all ethnicized, at a rapid pace and in different ways – exclusively or inclusively. An increasingly common result of these processes is reactive flight into regional and local imagined communities.

'Culture' has become a universal ideological category in the political struggle, an indispensable tool for the techno-scientific administration and organization of differences, a general common-sense popular cliché celebrating the separateness of 'cultural belonging' as a 'natural' right. The cultural has acquired an independent role. Cultural explanations in a bare and distorted form have colonized the social by means of culturization. The social space has been reduced to a site for the production of identities or merely differentiated entities.

The conditions are developing for the emergence of collective identities which are ethnicized in a flora of variations (from exclusive ethnic absolutism to inclusive transethnic syncretism). This ethnicization is 'new' in that it assumes its form in relation to the social and cultural boundary-making of modern societies. That is through inventive processes rather than repetitive practices governed by ritual or tradition – even if the latter can appear as old symbols (actual or invented) injected with new meanings for purposes other than traditional ones, albeit in the name of 'tradition'. The symbols of tradition often assume their place in the service of modern solidarities. Emerging mixtures of cultures and of cultural innovations, new boundaries and transgressions of boundaries, and a variety of new identities (in an individual and collective sense) illustrate the diversity of contemporary multiethnic society, its potential for change, and its inner tensions.

Among immigrant ethnic minorities, the ambivalence is strengthened by a cross-breeding between the general cultural crisis and the specific discriminatory and stigmatizing practices of an increasingly racialized society. 'Immigration' is developing into a dilemma joining far-flung times and places, Europe and America. It is a European dilemma resembling what Myrdal (1962 (1944)) terms the 'Negro problem', but without an automatic connection to skin colour. It is a matter, in Balibar's terms, of 'racism without race' (1992).

It should be stressed, finally, that new transethnic identities are developing, not least among youth in the multiethnic environments of the cities. These new European identities are besieged, however. The social contexts and immediate life-worlds, with their inequalities and tensions, carry fundamental conflictual forces, which are particularly important for young people who still are called 'immigrants' and strangers. The young contest their 'not belonging' status more sharply than do their first-generation immigrant parents. Like Simmel's 'stranger', they are near yet far away (1950a). They are, to paraphrase Simmel again, an element of the group itself, constructed not to be part of it fully. They are equipped to mediate but forced to struggle.

Bibliography

Ålund, A. (1992), 'Immigrantenkultur als Barriere der Kooperation', in A. Kalpaka and N. Räthzel (eds), *Rassismus und Migration in Europa*, Hamburg: Argument, pp. 174–189.

——, (1995), 'Alterity in Modernity', *Acta Sociologica*, 38, pp. 311–322.

——, and Schierup, C.-U. (1991), *Paradoxes of Multiculturalism: Essays on Swedish Society*, Aldershot: Gower.

Balibar, E. (1992), *Les frontiers de la democratie*, Paris: La Decouverte.

Berman, M. (1983), *All That is Solid Melts into Air: The Experience of Modernity*, London: Verso.

Cohen, A. (ed.), (1974), *Urban Ethnicity*, London: Tavistock.

Cohen, P. (1991), 'The Migration of Identity', revised paper for the Conference on 'Rassismus und Migration in Europa', Hamburg 1991.

Giddens, A. (1991), *Modernity and Self-Identity*, Oxford: Polity.

Gilroy, P. (1987), *There Ain't No Black in the Union Jack*, London: Hutchinson.

——, (1993), *The Black Atlantic: Modernity and Double Consciousness*, London: Verso.

Gordon, M. (1970), 'Assimilation in America: Theory and Reality', in B. W. Hawkins and R. A. Lorinskas (eds), *The Ethnic Factor in American Politics*, Columbus, Ohio: Merrill Publishing Co, pp. 24–45.

Gorelick, S. (1989), 'Ethnic Feminism: Beyond the Pseudo-Pluralists', *Feminist Review*, 32, pp. 111–118.

Hall, S. (1992), 'Introduction', in S. Hall and B. Gieben (eds), *Formations of Modernity*, Cambridge: The Open University Press.

Hewitt, R. (1992), 'Language, Youth and the Destabilisation of Ethnicity', in Palmgren et al. (eds), *Ethnicity in Youth Culture*, Stockholm: Stockholm University, pp. 27–43.

Karlsson, L.-G. (1994), 'Hegemonic Cultural Homogenisation', unpublished manuscript, Department of Sociology, University of Umeå.

Löwander, B. (1993), 'Massmedierapportering om etniska relationer', *Invandrare & Minoriteter*, 1/93, pp. 7–11.

Moe, A. M. (1994), 'Intervju med Dogge', unpublished manuscript, Department of Sociology, University of Umeå.

Myrdal, G. (1962 (1944)), *An American Dilemma: The Negro Problem and Modern Democracy*, New York: Harper & Row.

Schierup, C.-U. and Ålund, A. (1987), *Will They Still be Dancing? Integration and Ethnic Transformation Among Yugoslav Immigrants in Scandinavia*, Stockholm: Almqvist & Wiksell International.

Schutz, A. (1976 (1944)), 'The Stranger: An Essay in Social Psychology', in A. Brodersen (ed.), *Collected Papers II*, The Hague: Martinus Nijhoff, pp. 91–106.

Schwartz, J. (1993), 'A Century in Exile: Social Science as Witness', *Rescue-43: Xenophobia and Exile*, Copenhagen: Munksgaard, pp. 125–137.

——, (1994), 'The Cultural Construction of "the Stranger" in Social Scientific Thought', lecture at University of Umeå, February.

Simmel, G. (1950a), 'The Stranger', in H. K. Wolff (ed.), *The Sociology of Georg Simmel*, New York: The Free Press, pp. 402–409.

——, (1950b), 'The Metropolis and Mental Life', in H. K. Wolff (ed.), *The Sociology of Georg Simmel*, New York: The Free Press, pp. 409–427.

——, (1994), 'Bridge and Door', *Theory, Culture & Society*, 11, pp. 5–11.

Sollors, W. (ed.), (1989), *The Invention of Ethnicity*, Oxford: Oxford University Press.

Westin, C. (1987), *Den toleranta opinionen. Rapport No. 8. CEIFO*, Stockholm: Stockholms Universitet.

Wieviorka, M. (1993), 'Tendencies to Racism in Europe', in J. Wrench and J. Solomos (eds), *Racism and Migration in Western Europe*, Oxford: Berg Publishers, pp. 55–67.

Multiculturalism and Universalism in the United States and EU-Europe

Carl-Ulrik Schierup

'Multiculturalism' has become an increasingly influential framework for the conceptualization of the contingencies of global migration and ethnic relations. It is a notion buttressed by a moral ideal of the good society. Having developed into an increasingly influential political-ideological doctrine, this moral ideal appears to aspire to the position of the hegemonic *credo* of our times. As represented in numerous practices within education, science, politics and administration, a real institutionalized multiculturalism, to an increasing extent, creates and reproduces society. This is at least so at our own pole of the contemporary world system; a setting where the culturalist relativism of postmodernity has emerged as a paramount hallmark of modern times (Friedman, 1988).

Although the notion of multiculturalism appears to be influential in thought and institutional practice, its meaning remains vague.

Multiculturalism is one of those 'plastic words', fit for the casting of new models, writes Hans-Rudolf Wicker (1993). After having been processed by science, it has traversed a range of social sectors, where it becomes implemented in the creation of a new reality. It represents one of those new world-wide floating concepts, which, travelling from continent to continent, are 'communicated easily and quickly to sometimes unexpected recipients and with sometimes surprising results' (Radtke, 1992: 1).

After having in the beginning of the 1970s developed into an explicit political strategy in Canada, the idea of multiculturalism spread to the US, Australia and to Western Europe. It became instrumental as a notion helping to formulate politics and policies of and for the so-called 'new immigration'. Centring on what has become known as 'identity politics', a new radical multiculturalism in the US of the 1970s and 1980s broke with the affiliation to the American universalism which had informed the integrationist civil rights movement in the 1960s. Allegations about the existence of an American creed based on *The Declaration of Independence* and *The Constitution* began to generally be perceived as a cloak for the white power-block and institutions; those Eurocentrically focused institutions – in culture, education and politics – that had always served to silence the genuine voices of the subaltern. Radical US 'multiculturalists' equally distanced themselves from what, following in the footsteps of Horace Kallen (1915), represented a liberal, cultural pluralism's implicit, minimal, universalist assumption concerning the reality of certain shared American public values.

In Europe we have, since the 1970s, seen the birth of a whole variety of conceptions of multiculturalism. In some places, we find multiculturalism to mean a legitimate political ideology, officially acknowledging the cultural heritage and permanence of ethnic minority groups. In others, the doctrine still represents more of a heretical and oppositional position in politics, or an avantguardist strategy in local administration. At a higher super-national level, we find multiculturalism being purported as a morally and politically superior doctrine for an integrated Europe; a framework of positive humanistic values and democratic political governance (Keane, 1992; Crowley, 1992; Council of Europe, 1991). The more multiculturalism seems to aspire to the position of a master narrative for a postmodern western modernity, however, the more the gap between creed and reality appears to widen. This seems to hold true whether the creed is disseminated from the political centre as in, for example, Canada and Sweden, or from oppositional movements and the strongholds of local councils such as in the case, for example, in the US, Germany and France.

The Crisis of Multiculturalism

After a spectacular upsurge of multiculturalism in the 1980s, the 1990s give witness to an evident crisis of multiculturalist models. We are confronted by increasing doubt in their adequacy as frameworks for a liberal democracy.[1] Rather than an overall harmonious orchestration of mankind, as suggested by Horace Kallen, the culture of multiculturalism has (paraphrasing Wallerstein, 1991) become an important 'ideological battleground' of the modern world system. This is a condition reflected by a number of contemporary critical discussions concerning the relationship between multicultural theory and prac-

1. For a discussion of problems of multiculturalism and democracy see, for example, Crowley (1992).

tice (e.g. Castles, Kalantzis, Cope and Morrissey, 1988; Rath, 1990; Escoffier, 1991; Ålund and Schierup, 1991; Higham, 1993; Marable, 1993). Under a culturalist and relativist veneer, this battleground articulates the deep and increasingly complex structurally grounded disjunctions and conflicts characteristic of modern capitalist society. Seen from this perspective, 'multiculturalism' signifies a social condition where, together with a politization of the 'cultural', a general 'culturalization' of the political language has taken place. Here, strategies of dominance as well as those of rebellion become increasingly phrased in the culturalized terms of ethnic particularity. This takes place in manners that often act to displace the articulation of more general cleavages contained in the constitution of modern society. A truly existing multiculturalism often appears to function as an institutional practice for the structuration of enforced cultural enclavization and a culturally justified and ethnically stratified social inequality (Schierup, 1991). The conspicuous upsurge of an identitarian discourse on 'ethnicity' and culture has come to be marked by profound ambiguity. This ambiguity is articulated in different ways in every country, depending upon the overall societal conditions and the particular role of multicultural discourse and politics.

A Cacophony of the Subaltern

In the US, multiculturalism became a powerful policy issue during the 1980s. The movement mostly distanced itself from what Horace Kallen (1915), founder of an established US tradition of 'cultural pluralism', had named 'the symphony of civilization': a claim implicitly assuming a consensus around certain common values belonging to an American national public culture. A plethora of 'liberation movements', professing a radical and divisive 'cultural nationalism' (such as, for example, Louis Farrakhan's 'Nation of Islam') did away with any affiliation to a shared American creed, which came to be understood as representative of those Eurocentric institutions in the realms of culture, education and the polity, that had always served to silence the voices of the 'subaltern'. The mythology of the American nation and of all of its established public rituals came to be seen as so many instruments designed to beat racial, ethnic, cultural and sexual minorities into a submerged and subservient position in an inherently racist and discriminatory society. The purpose of identity politics became to reconstruct 'authentic narratives' which would restore the dignity, self-confidence and trajectory lost with bereft, submerged or appropriated identities. This retelling of American and world history needed, in turn, appropriate institutional set-ups: racial and ethnic awareness training institutions, multilingual teaching, Afrocentric and Hispanic curricula, schools fostering ethnic self-confidence and self-reliance, and culturally sensitive social work.

The product of radical multiculturalism must definitely did not become an 'orchestration of mankind', another of Kallen's (1915) celebrated expressions; nor even a polyphony of the subaltern. What resulted was more of a cacophony, while the trajectories of individual ethnically or racially defined collectivities tended to become as sealed off from one another as from the white hegemony. Lack of solidarity and political fragmentation was followed by a general marginalization in national politics.[2]

The social mobility, the empowerment associated with restored or constructed ethnic identities, the cultural awareness and human dignity which the actually existing multiculturalism, indeed, helped to bring forth, came to stand out in contrast to extended political marginality and urban violence. The co-optation and institutionalization of various of the new identitarian movement's claims certainly helped the ascent to local, and occasionally also national, positions of influence of black and ethnic minority elites. But, notwithstanding the repeated efforts to form composite 'rainbow coalitions', this did not materialize in the stabilization of a broad and aggregate political movement; an indispensable position from where a new battle against poverty and a struggle or extended social rights could be waged. This became particularly problematic as – against a background of economic restructuring and unemployment, and following the Reagan and Bush administrations' onslaught against federal social policy programmes – a deepening poverty hit broad sections of the ethnically and racially defined minorities.

'Les Trentes Glorieuses Adieu'

This dismantlement of existing welfare compacts is gaining an acute actuality, not only in America, but also in Europe. Together

2. This conception of the predicaments of multiculturalism in the United States is particularly influenced by the comprehensive analysis done by John Higham (1993), but also by other critical and self-critical receptions like those of Giroux (1993a; 1993b), Davis (1993a; 1993b), Escoffier (1991), Gooding-Williams (1993), Mclaren (1993), and Marable (1993). Together with Aleksandra Ålund, I developed a similar analysis concerning *Paradoxes of Multiculturalism* (Ålund and Schierup, 1991) in the European context. Our discussion centred particularly on the Swedish case with Britain as the main comparative point of reference.

with Canada and Australia, Sweden represents one of the those three advanced liberal democracies that have, in their official self understanding and major policy documents, declared themselves 'multicultural societies'. Sweden's state sponsored multiculturalism is, in this sense, unique in Europe. By the mid-1970s, it was spelled out in the primary long-term perspectives of 'Equality, partnership and freedom of choice'. This powerful slogan, boldly paraphrasing the French revolution's 'Liberté, Egalité, Fraternité', came to mean a multiculturalism as a hegemonic condition. A general moral and political consensus was inaugurated. It embraced government and state institutions and political parties across the traditional left-right spectrum. It incorporated powerful socio-political organizations and movements like the Swedish federation of trade unions (LO) and the national association of local municipal administrations ('Kommunförbundet').

This policy's basic commitments corresponded rather well with the axioms of that programmatic leftist 'Concept of a Multicultural Society' which has been spelled out in sociological terms by John Rex (1985). The preconditions for the working of this model are those of an already existing welfare state compact. It is, using Rex's words, a society which in its 'main structures' is already firmly committed to 'equality of opportunity'. A multicultural society, being in this sense already a welfare society, represents a formation which in its main structures finds 'a place for both diversity and equality of opportunity'. It is a liberal democratic society where historical compromises have already produced powerful institutions designed to deal with the class-based injustices of capitalism. New consensual solutions now lead to the cumulative development of institutions that are capable of dealing with the injustices produced by racism.

This vision of modern polyethnic democracy was not only at the base of Swedish multicultural politics and policies during the 1970s. It was also the type of vision that informed policy making in Canada and particularly in Australia (Castles et al., 1988; Vasta, 1993). In Sweden during the 1980s, it became increasingly clear, however, that it was a reductionist discourse centred around 'freedom of choice' – the last axiom of the Swedish multicultural slogan – that should come to dominate public discourse and actual political and institutional practice. 'Freedom of Choice' has, in turn, been equalled to a formalized 'right to be different', culturally speaking; the right to be different tends to be equalled with actually 'being different' (Ålund and Schierup, 1991). A paradigmatic shift in public discourse articulates with general forms of socio-economic restructuration, cultural change and the establishment of new, more sophisticated forms of public agency under postmodern conditions (Schierup, 1991). An ethnicization of the public discourse creates and reproduces, through the faculty of ramifying multicultural institutional practices, an increasingly differentiated and stratified cultural division of labour coupled with an ethnically enclavized society. Paramount for an adequate institutional performance is the inert competence to structure a complex production and distribution process that effectuates, just in time, the assignment of human articles with different skin-colours and the relevant 'culture'.

We are confronted here with discourses and institutional apparatuses of multiculturalism becoming media for the marketing of commodified ethnic lifestyles, for managing an ethnically stratified labour market and, concerning certain minority elites, a political-ideological vehicle for the successful advancement of powerful diasporic business networks. These are the general trends in the modern postmodern West which have (with particular reference to Canada) given rise to the striking aphorism: 'Multiculturalism: the united colours of capitalism' (Mitchell, 1993). Even in a number of countries where a real multiculturalism, so far, signifies localized institutional strategies rather than canonized national policies, a culturalist discourse and institutional practice has taken over a central role in the structuring of society. The upsurge of identity politics in Europe, observes Michel Wieviorka (1992) when discussing the case of France, is matched by the demise of the particular type of universalism characterizing the welfare state, for which the labour movement used to be the chief ideological and political anchoring point.

This signifies more than the crisis of a movement and a political ideology. We experience the transgression of a social order. We are confronted with a great transformation; a transformation circumscribed by the transnationalization of capitalism; a transformation implicating the collapse of the political compacts that were at the basis of the relative economic and social stability in north-western Europe from 1945 to 1975. We are witnessing the collapse of a pattern of political integration that, on the verge of its deroute, had still embodied the strength to bring the southern European periphery beyond dictatorship (Poulantzas, 1975). What the French call *les trentes glorieuses* are now, more or less, history. We do not live in a post-industrial era. But, seen from a Eurocentric perspective, the transnational restructuration of the global division of labour makes it look as if we did. The dominant identitarian space of EU-Europe is becoming occupied by the postmodern pole of a transformed, transnational system of modernity. In the same instance, the central role – politically, ideologically and culturally – of the old working class has been taken over by new middle professional strata (Naïr, 1992; Hjarnø, 1993). In addition, certain elites among ethnically and racially defined communities may enter this postmodern identitarian space and take advantage of institutional restructuration. But any universalist horizon and the integrative power belonging to the kind of welfare state compact of which John Rex speaks, is being replaced by a fragmented occupation with particular cultural identities. Confronted with social deroute, urban decay and deteriorating living conditions, a politically fragmented underclass has become preoccupied with constructing a compensatory national identity. This takes place at the expense of the equally marginalized immigrant other.

An enclavization of society is taking place.[3] We live in a time of political-economic *deshérence* (Naïr, 1992). The programme is, through policies of blaming the victim, to reverse any strategy purporting broad social solidarities. It is this postmodern ethos that supports up the predominant culturalist conception of 'multiculturalism', according to which existing social inequalities and social conflicts between ethnic groups are invariably interpreted, in essentialist and fragmentary terms, as 'cultural difference'. In this perspective, the dominant ideological construction of 'multiculturalism' becomes itself part of the problem of constituting a democratic multiethnic society.

A More Inclusive Universalism

The paradoxes and dilemmas implicated by the crisis of a truly existing multiculturalism present a problem much akin to the difficulty posed to the left by a defamed 'real socialism'. Intellectuals, having been absorbed by the breeding of theories and politics of identity,[4] become increasingly aware of the pitfalls of real multiculturalism. This has set the scene for protracted discussions of 'particularism versus universalism' (e.g. Taguieff, 1987; 1991). The problem of the moral and legal recognition of a set of universal human rights and the imperative of recognizing 'difference' within that frame of reference have moved to the centre of current debates within the social sciences (e.g. Taylor, 1992; Taguieff, 1991; Crowley, 1992; Bauman, 1989; Silverman, 1992). The discussion tends, in line with liberal contract theory, to see this question as a matter of *choice between* identitarian particularism and enlightenment universalism; or it is seen as a matter of *choosing* adequate ways for merging them. The focus is on the *will* to form a certain social compact, a hegemonic moral consensus, in the abstract.

---

3. One aspect of this is a growing dualization of the social insurance systems. See for example Hjarnø (1993) who discusses the case of Denmark.
4. See the critical intervention of Sivanandan (1990).

Carl-Ulrik Schierup

But an analysis of the limitations and opportunities presented by changing national and global social structures and relationships of power remains bracketed.

It would now appear urgent to proceed beyond the blind alleys of an abstract, postmodernist identitarianism and an equally abstract universalism, into which so much of the contemporary debate has become stuck. The focus could be less one-sidedly oriented toward 'culture'. More attention could be devoted towards structural dimensions of social cohesion and conflict. A scrutiny of the societal contingencies of the political and the social dimensions of citizenship, according to Marshall's (1973) tripartite division, could be central. This will demand the erection of a critical perspective on '[t]he cultural and by implication intellectual fragmentation of the world which has undermined any attempt at a single interpretation of the current situation' (Friedman, 1992: 311). 'Ethnic and cultural fragmentation and modernist homogenisation are', quoting Jonathan Friedman, 'not two arguments, two opposing views of what is happening in the world today, but two constitutive trends of global reality . . .' (1992: 311). Modernity is a convoluted condition and world systems theory should, if anything, have taught us that, in a global perspective, the same grand diachronic movement – the accumulation of capital – may help to produce apparently opposite contingencies.

The Memento of LA

The inter-ethnic urban feuding in Los Angeles in 1992 demonstrated the urgency of an already ongoing rethinking of multiculturalist positions within a wider framework of changing national and global power relationships (Giroux, 1993a; Davis, 1993a; 1993b; Escoffier, 1991). 'Reading the urban uprising' (Gooding-Williams, 1993) from this perspective came to represent a memo for reconnecting the intellectually and politically refractured contingencies of capital, race, culture and ethnicity (Giroux, 1993b). It made clear the imperative of reconciling the micropolitics of 'difference' with the macropolitics of structural organization (Mclaren, 1993), deconstructivism with Marx (e.g. Derrida, 1994); the necessity of retrieving trails towards broadening forms of transethnic agency.

Manning Marable (1993: 127) concludes his plea for a 'liberation theory for multicultural democracy beyond racial identity politics', as follows:

Our ability to transcend racial chauvinism, inter-ethnic hatred and the old definitions of 'race', to recognize the class commonalties and joint social justice interests of all groups in the restructuring of this nation's economy and social order, will be key in constructing a nonracist democracy, which will break down the ancient walls of white violence, corporate power and class privilege. By dismantling the narrow politics of racial identity and selective self-interest, by going beyond 'black' and 'white', we may construct new values, new institutions and new visions.

It would seem, indeed, to be a restatement of *An American Creed* for new times; a plea for a new, more inclusive universalism.

Another American social scientist, John Higham (1993), argues in an illuminating manner for the historical realism of this sort of project. Its realism is, he asserts, planted in what he calls the 'invigorating paradox' of the American universalist tradition. 'What was theoretically and potentially universal' in the declaration of independence and the constitution, indeed soon came to be understood as 'the very lynchpin of identity . . . of a peculiar people' (Higham, 1993: 198). However, the coupling, in national icons, of a 'distinctively American bird of prey with a transnational symbol of freedom cannot be fully understood as a smokescreen or a delusion' (Ibid.). It reflects 'the inescapable locatedness of any universalistic perspective' (Ibid.). This displays, more specifically, an enduring tension in American universalism 'between closure and openness, between separateness and inclusion' (Ibid.). From the time of the American Revolution onward, concludes Higham, 'a principle way of managing this tension has been to extend the circle of those who are acknowledged as makers of an American nationality and to project each incremental addition as a promise of still wider inclusiveness' (Ibid.). In this sense, American universalism has passed through several phases of crisis and remoulding. The upsurge of radical multiculturalism may be seen as an indicator of and as one possible reaction to a deep crisis for this incremental inclusivism.

The crisis has its roots in the restructuration of capitalism, globally and nationally. It reflects, as well, the dismantlement of the grand coalition of liberal democratic forces which held a hegemonic position in American politics during the 1940s and 1950s. It speaks of the continued refusal of a white power-block to accord civil and political rights of citizenship to all of its subaltern minorities. It recounts the demise of Afro American integrationism during the 1960s, culminating in King's failure in 1966 and 1967 to 'turn his civil rights crusade into a broader class coalition', and consummated by his murder in Memphis in 1968 (Higham, 1993: 200).

American multiculturalism could, however, according to its leftist critics, recognize its own universalist roots and build a more inclusive universalism. A new social compact for full rights of citizenship built on a syncretic and transethnic universalism and aligned across racially and culturally defined divides, could offer a verified and transethnic movement a common purpose and horizon. With this in mind, we may turn our attention towards a concluding discussion of the current dilemmas of the United States of America and of the United States of Europe *in spe*.

New Dilemmas

American universalism is threatened, first and foremost, by multi-culturalism, alleges Arthur M. Schlesinger (1992) in one of the most quoted books in the US of recent years. The claims of radical multiculturalists are *Disuniting America*. By disavowing the universalism of the American Creed, multicultural policies are exposing Afro-Americans and ethnic minorities of Third World origin to identitarian pathology, to under-education, to professional failure, to social and cultural marginalization, to segregation, to racist stigma. The culture of the subaltern Other is, thus – in the spirit of a conventional 'blame the victim' discourse – spotted as the basic cause of this Other's social misery.

But the 'disuniting of America' cannot be stated, simply, in terms of a problem to be accounted for by the politics of multiculturalism. We may understand multiculturalist fragmentation as a token rather than as a cause. We may, alternatively, see the *disuniting of America* as the symptom of a series of paradoxical disjunctions, of discourse and structure, traversing American civilization and a new world disorder in general.

There is the continuing need for the import of cheap and docile third and second world labour, paradoxically coupled in symbiotic disjuncture with the populist cry for immigration control and the official oratory constructing the new immigration as a problem of integration (Brochman, 1994; Collinson, 1993). There are the sweat-shops and an extended service sector exposed to third world exploitation levels and, door by door in the 'global city', the hyper-concentrated power-nuclei of transnational financial networks (Sassen, 1994a; 1994b; Cross, 1992); that is the multifaceted appearance of a new type of polarized, segmented and sealed off 'division of labour', dividing the polity and making any official appeal to social cohesion sound increasingly hollow. There are, contingent upon this, extended sectors of society being turned into permanently marginalized and enclavized ethnically and racially defined segments and the incremental formation of multiethnic agglomerates suing for welfare provisions, while at the same time any mentioning of a social dimension for all is being obstructed by a conservative power block in conjunction with new nationalist-racist coalitions on the right. There is the growing sector of the subaltern new immigration, bereft of any rights of citizenship whatsoever, rendering traditional mechanisms and strategies for societal integration impotent. There are the emphatic appeals to universalist allegiance and national or hyper-national integration, while, at the same time, the agony and anger produced by poverty, disenfranchisement and social marginality is systematically being channelled into a plethora of microscopic urban wars (Enzensberger, 1993) or the segmenting claims of radical multiculturalism. There is the rhetoric of a new world order and human rights and economic reforms as remedies for stemming immigration pressure. We are confronted with the contradiction seen in the perspective of transnational restructuration, market theological super-austerity measures, and neo-imperialist interventionism, which every second day raises another local internal war in the third world and in a disintegrating second world (Schierup, 1994; Duffield, 1994); all which spawns new global legions of uprooted helots.

We may – alluding to Gunnar Myrdal's (1962 (1944)) famous book, published now fifty years ago – sum up all of these paradoxes and disjunctures in the sense of a contemporary *American Dilemma*. The essence of this *American Dilemma* of new times is the incompatibility of elitist appeals for social cohesion and universalist allegiances with all of the powerful political and economic interests that both require and create growing segments of the population as ethnicized, enclavized and bereft of rights of citizenship. Unwilling or unable to face this dilemma, hegemonic coalitions are themselves forced to keep straddling between declaratory appeals to an abstract universalism and a realpolitik of manipulative particularism; that is politics and policies occupied with the management of a disintegrating nation, which are cast in culturalizing and ethnicizing categories (compare Ålund and Schierup, 1991). As structurally embedded disjunctures become increasingly critical, such a balance becomes increasingly untenable.

In addition, subaltern America is confronted with a political crux of universalism versus particularism. The dilemma centres around the urgency of reconciling the myriad of particular interests and strategies embodied in real multiculturalism's 'fixity on diversity, autonomy, and otherness' (Higham, 1993: 214) with the arduous task of reconstructing a universalist tradition. This American dilemma of the subaltern appears to call for the compliance of a multitude of localist movements and their particular strategies for identity appropriation and for survival or mobility with the establishment of an embracing political compact; an inclusive compact to enforce the constitutional commitment and necessary institutions for a promotion of extended civil, political and social rights of citizenship.

These are still most characteristically American dilemmas. This is so, from whatever side of the a changing class and ethnic spectrum of postmodern modernity they may be seen. But they are becoming the increasingly shared dilemmas of western Eurocentric civilization, on both sides of the Atlantic; of Europe as well as of North America.

They are questions with an increasingly common relevance for the 'new' and for the 'old world'. These questions need to be restated, reformulated and elucidated in the global context of a new 'great transformation'. 'The old world is turning new' (Therborn, 1987). All the shared problems and paradoxes of the transnational restructuration of capitalism in the silicon age (Sivanandan, 1979) have made the new worlds of Europe and America increasingly similar. We are living in a 'world of new worlds' as expressed by Edward Tiryakian (1994). This demands that we, in Europe as well as in America, clarify and restate the values upon which our paradigms of theory and research rest. Nevertheless, we must also scrutinize their societal contingencies.

However, there are important differences. The confluence of racial and social inequality is still most typical for the US. However, the enigmatic problem of the nation conceivably poses particularly obstinate complications for utopian visions of a so-called 'integrated Europe' as a harmonious poly-national, poly-ethnic concert – *le nouveau concert Européen* – and these obstacles lie at the heart of a truly paradoxical and precarious constitution of EU-Europe itself. While 'turning new', the Old World may get the worst of both worlds (Therborn, 1987: 1187). Institutionalized social and cultural exclusivism is currently creating underclass ghettos reminiscent of the New World. Parallel to this, the traditional cultural closure of the Old World is expressed in new forms of racism. These racisms are legitimized by ethnic-nationalist ideologies with conceivably more powerful sources of legitimacy than their North American counterparts in the 1980s and 1990s.

Ambiguous Integration

An ambiguous super-national condition of EU-Europe penetrates all of our lives. Meanwhile, the political processes associated with the gains of liberal democracy continue to be centred on the struggles surrounding the definition of hegemonic compromises within every single national state. This paradox is historically and structurally grounded. But its reverberations increasingly jeopardize the political scene of each single country and of the Union as a whole. Attempts at social and political reform, nationally as well as on a Community level, are easily blocked (Hjarnø, 1993). The image is that of a zero-sum game staggering between national impotence and community paralysis. This amplifies an always present Eurocentric public stigmatization of the Third and Second World Other, addressed alternately in terms of the 'aliens', the 'Muslim peril' or the 'immigrant problem' (Schierup, 1993). But the immigrant problem is not its own cause. The immigrant problem is a problem of the constitution of EU-Europe. The immigrant problem is the symptom of a situation where cultural and social creativity is being blocked by the unhappy articulation of continued inter-state rivalry with mounting structural disjunctures, with social disintegration, with a nostalgic and reactive ethnic-nationalist narcissism of difference. This culturally argued racism is, within each single national state, tacitly instrumentalized or actively encouraged by official pragmatism. An ideological hegemony of a diffuse, but politically potent merger of universalism and particularism ensues (Balibar, 1993; Silverman, 1992). Evoking, alternatively, an imagined community of ethnic-nationalist peculiarities and enlightened universalism, the focus is on the cultural clash between a 'traditional' other and European modernity.

A contemporary European universalism must, however, by virtue and by necessity, be more inclusive than the idea of Europe shared by most of today's Europeanists following in the footsteps of Saint Simon or Ralph Dahrendorf. It is not enough to plea for a transplantation of the essentials defining a national bureaucratic welfare compact to the setting of a growing 'Commonwealth of Ethnocentrism' (Schmid, 1992) uncoupling itself from the distressing purview of deteriorating north-south relationships; a Fortress Europe, divided by inner trenches; an EU-Europe excluding the internal third world Other from essential dimensions of citizenship. Contemporary questions of race, ethnicity, class and culture are circumscribed by an increasing pluralization of society. They are contingent on growing polarizations of our current condition of globalization.

The setting up of a Europe distinguished by reconstructed social solidarities needs to go beyond a EU-centric perspective. The problems and dilemmas circumscribing social injustice and inequality are increasingly contingent on structural and institutional racism, and the clue to structural racism is more than ever the polarization of a generalized North and a generalized South. Most of the Other, of Post-Communist

Europe, has become enrolled in the eschelons of the new helots of this new generalized South. Seen in this inclusive perspective, the multi-cultural cliché, 'Europe begins in Sarajevo!', harbours a convoluted ambiguity. It camouflages the multiple dimensions of an internally divided Europe.

Bibliography

Ålund, A. and Schierup, C.-U. (1991), *Paradoxes of Multiculturalism: Essays on Swedish Society*, Aldershot: Gower.

Balibar, E. (1993), 'Racism and Nationalism', in E. Balibar and I. Wallerstein (eds), *Race, Nation, Class: Ambiguous Identities*, London: Verso, pp. 37–68.

Bauman, Z. (1989), *Modernity and the Holocaust*, Cambridge: Polity Press.

Brochman, G. (1994), 'Immigration Policies in Europe: Control of Democracy or Democracy out of Control', Paper presented at the XIII World Congress of Sociology, Bielefeld, July 18–23.

Castles, S., Kalantzis, M., Cope, B. and Morrissey, M. (1988), *Mistaken Identity: Multiculturalism and the Demise of Nationalism in Australia*, Sidney: Pluto Press.

Collinson, S. (1993), *Beyond Borders: West European Migration Policy Towards the 21st Century*, London: Royal Institute of International Affairs.

Council of Europe (1991), *Community and Ethnic Relations in Europe*, Final report of the Community relations Project of the Council of Europe, Strasbourg: The Council of Europe.

Cross, M. (1992), *Racism, the City and the State*, London: Routledge.

Crowley, J. (1992), 'Ethnicity, Democratic Theory and the Nation State', Paper for the conference, Mass Migration in Europe. Implications in East and West, Vienna, March 5–7.

Davis, Mike (1993a), 'Who Killed LA? A Political Autopsy', *New Left Review*, 197, pp. 3–28.

———, (1993b), 'Who Killed LA? Part Two: The Verdict is Given', *New Left Review*, 199, pp. 29–54.

Derrida, J. (1994), 'Spectres of Marx', *New Left Review*, 205, pp. 31–58.

Duffield, M. (1994), 'The Political Economy of Internal War: Asset Transfer, Complex Emergencies and International Aid', in J. Macrae and A. Zwi (eds), *War and Hunger: Rethinking International Responses to Complex Emergencies*, London: Zed Books, pp. 50–59.

Enzensberger, H. M. (1993), *Aussichten auf den Bürgerkrieg*, Frankfurt am Main: Suhrkamp.

Escoffier, J. (1991), 'The Limits of Multiculturalism', *Socialist Review*, 21 (3–4), pp. 61–73.

Friedman, J. (1988), 'Cultural Logics of the Global System: A Sketch', *Theory, Culture & Society*, 5, pp. 447–460.

——, (1992), 'Being in the World: Globalization and Localization', *Theory, Culture & Society*, 7, pp. 311–328.

Giroux, H. A. (1993a), 'The Politics of Insurgent Multiculturalism in the Era of the Los Angeles Uprising', *Bulletin of the Midwest Modern Language Association*, 26 (1), pp. 12–30.

——, (1993b), 'Living dangerously: Identity politics and the new cultural racism: towards a critical pedagogy of representation', *Cultural Studies*, 7(1), pp. 1–27.

Gooding-Williams, R. (1993), *Reading Rodney King. Reading Urban Uprising*, New York and London: Routledge.

Higham, J. (1993), 'Multiculturalism and Universalism: A History and Critique', *American Quarterly*, 45(2), pp. 195–219.

Hjarnø, J. (1993), 'Causes of the Increase in Xenophobia in Denmark', *Migration*, 2, pp. 41–62.

Kallen, H. (1915), 'Democracy Versus the Melting Pot', *The Nation*, 100, pp. 190–194, 217–220.

Keane, J. (1992), 'Questions for Europe', in B. Nelson, D. Roberts and W. Veit (eds), *The Idea of Europe*, New York and Oxford: Berg Publishers, pp. 55–60.

Kofman, E. and Sales, R. (1992), 'Towards Fortress Europe?', *Women's Studies International Forum*, 15(1), pp. 29–39.

Marable, M. (1993), 'Beyond Racial Identity Politics: Towards a Liberation Theory for Multicultural Democracy', *Race and Class*, 35(1), pp. 115–130.

Marshall, T. H. (1973), *Class, Citizenship and Social Development*, Westport: Greenwood Press.

Mclaren, P. (1993), 'Multiculturalism and the Postmodern Critique: Towards a Pedagogy of Resistance and Transformation', *Cultural Studies*, 7, pp. 118–146.

Mitchell, K. (1993), 'Multiculturalism, or the United Colors of Capitalism?', *Antipode*, 25(4), pp. 263–294.

Myrdal, G. (1962 (1944)), *An American Dilemma: The Negro Problem and Modern Democracy*, New York: Harper & Row.

Naïr, S. (1992), *Le regard des vainqueurs: les enjeux francais de l'immigration*, Paris: Grasset.

Poulantzas, N. (1975), *La crise des dictatures*, Paris: Seuil.

Radtke, F.-O. (1992), Unpublished Notes on Multiculturalism, Bielefeld (Without title, quoted with permission from the author).

Rath, W. (1990), 'Minorization: The Political and Ideological Construction of "Ethnic Minorities" in the Netherlands', Paper for the Conference on Migration and Racism in Europe, Hamburg, September.

Rex, J. (1985), *The Concept of a Multi-Cultural Society*, Occasional Papers in Ethnic Relations no. 3, Warwick: Centre for Research in Ethnic Relations.

Sassen, S. (1994a), 'Urban Marginality in Transnational Perspective: Comparing

New York and Tokyo', Paper for the international conference, Migration, Social Exclusion and the European city, Utrecht: ERCOMER.

———, (1994b), 'The Urban Complex in a World Economy', *International Social Science Journal*, 139, pp. 43–94.

Schierup, C.-U. (1991), 'The Puzzle of Transethnic Society', in A. Ålund and C.-U. Schierup (eds), *Paradoxes of Multiculturalism: Essays of Swedish Society*, Aldershot: Avenbury, pp. 137–167.

———, (1993), *På kulturens slagmark – mindretal og størretal taler om Danmark*, Esbjerg: Sydjysk Universitetsforlag.

———, (1994), 'Eurobalkanism: Ethnic Cleansing and the Post Cold War Order', in S. Bianchini (ed.), *The Yugoslav War, Europe and the Balkans: How to Achieve Security*, Ravenna: Longo Editore, pp. 31–44.

Schlesinger, A. M. Jr. (1992), *The Disuniting of America*, New York: W. W. Norton & Company.

Schmid, G. (1992), 'The Development of Migration Policies and Their Contradictions', *Innovation in Social Sciences Research*, 5 (2), pp. 41–50.

Silverman, M. (1992), *Deconstructing the Nation: Immigration, Racism and Citizenship in Modern France*, London: Routledge.

Sivanandan, A. (1979), 'Imperialism and Disorganic Development in the Silicon Age', *Race and Class*, 21(2), pp. 111–126.

———, (1990), 'All That Melts into Air is Solid: The Hokum of New Times', *Race and Class*, 31(3), pp. 2–29.

Taguieff, P.-A. (1987), *La force du préjugé: essai sur le racisme et ses doubles*, Paris: Editions la Découverte.

———, (1991), *Face au racisme 1–2*, Paris: Editions la Découverte.

Taylor, C. (1992), 'The Politics of Recognition', in A. Gutmann (ed.), *Multiculturalism and 'The Politics of Recognition': An Essay by Charles Taylor*, Princeton: Princeton University Press, pp. 25–73.

Therborn, G. (1987), 'Migration and Western Europe: The Old World Turning New', *Science*, 237(4), pp. 1183–1188.

Tiryakian, E. A. (1994), 'The New Worlds and Sociology: An Overview', *International Sociology*, 9(2), pp. 131–148.

Vasta, E. (1993), 'Multiculturalism and Ethnic Identity: The Relationship Between Racism and Resistance', *The Australian and New Zealand Journal of Sociology*, 29(2), pp. 209–225

Wallerstein, I. (1991), *Geopolitics and Geoculture: Essays on the Changing World-System*, Cambridge: Cambridge University Press.

Wicker, H.-R. (1993), 'Migration, Ethnizität und Paradoxien des Multikulturalismus in industrialisierten Gesellschaften', in W. Kälin and R. Moser (eds), *Migration aus der Dritten Welt*, Berne: Haupt, pp. 205–220.

Wieviorka, M. (1992), 'Tendencies to Racism in Europe: Is the French Experience Unique or Exemplary?', Paper for the conference Racism and Migration in Europe in the 1990s, Warwick: University of Warwick, September 20–22.

– 6 –

Multiculturalism and Political Integration: The Need for a Differentiated Citizenship?

Matteo Gianni

Although multiculturalism cannot be considered a new phenomenon, its political relevance in the western democracies seems to be increasing. The problems posed by immigration, the resurgence of nationalist movements and the claims of disadvantaged sociocultural groups most likely represent, 'the greatest challenge facing democracies today' (Kymlicka, 1995b: 1). Multiculturalism poses a very large range of political, economic, social and anthropological questions. In this paper, I will primarily focus my attention upon those questions which are political in nature. More precisely, I will examine the theoretical relationship between multiculturalism and citizenship. After having established the descriptive characteristics of the phenomenon, I intend to discuss the relevance of certain procedural and substantial principles which could (or should) govern liberal and democratic multicultural societies. My analysis aims to propose answers to two basic questions: does multiculturalism implicate theoretical changes in the normative construction of citizenship? How can a political community preserve its integration and social unity while acknowledging the claims of the ethnic, national, religious and other cultural groups which are a part of it?

According to Taylor, one important way to take the claims of cultural minorities seriously is to offer political recognition to these minorities. For him, multicultural societies 'can break up, in large part because of a lack of (perceived) recognition of the equal worth of one group by another' (1994: 64). The politics of difference represent a new way of understanding citizenship. The claim for recognition by the liberal state of the groups' cultural specificity involves a reappraisal of the universalistic categories underlying the liberal conception of

Matteo Gianni

citizenship. As Taylor puts it, the politics of difference 'asks that we give acknowledgement and status to something that is not universally shared' (1994: 39). Therefore, the politics of difference propose an alternative conception of political integration. This form of integration is not based upon a model of citizenship and equality blind to the cultural attributes of individuals, but rather takes these differences into account. Such is the notion of 'differentiated citizenship'. It expresses the idea that persons have to be integrated into the political community not only as individuals, but also as members of a cultural group. In such a case, citizenship would depend, in part, upon cultural identity. According to Young (1990: 174), 'a culturally pluralist democratic ideal supports group-conscious policies not only as means to the end of equality, but also as intrinsic to the ideal of social equality itself. Groups cannot be socially equal unless their specific experience, culture and social contributions are publicly affirmed and recognized'. According to this perspective, it is possible to define a complex model of citizenship based upon a dual system of rights, namely 'a general system of rights which are the same for all, and a more specific system of group-conscious policies and rights'.

Many criticisms have been formulated concerning this idea of differentiated citizenship.[1] The most recurrent of these criticisms is the idea that differentiated citizenship is based upon a paradox. According to the traditional liberal paradigm, political integration requires equality and universal rights in order to be effective. For liberals, political integration is realized by citizenship, which creates 'a community under law; it makes those who belong a part of the system of rules which protects them from each other, by creating a sort of club from outsiders' (Dahrendorf, 1974: 672). In other words, citizenship is a form of identity, whose purpose is to unify (by a minimal common denominator) the heterogeneity of society. It is the treatment of people as individuals with equal rights under the law that distinguishes democratic citizenship from views that determine 'people's political status by their religious, ethnic or class membership' (Kymlicka and Norman, 1994: 370). Therefore, differentiating citizenship would lead to the destruction of the only common status in an already deeply divided society. However, is this situation necessarily dangerous for the stability of the liberal democratic political system or is it possible to achieve a fair, differentiated citizenship without engendering even more divisions, conflicts and social disintegration? Is it possible to create unity (namely political integration) on the basis of recognized difference?

1. For a presentation of these criticisms, see Kymlicka and Norman (1995: 370 ff.) and Kymlicka (1995a).

I agree with Kymlicka and Norman (1994) that the idea of differentiated citizenship constitutes a radical development in the theory of citizenship. In my opinion, the project of a differentiated citizenship (and its political translations) is useful in trying to conceive a model of 'democracy through difference . . . [which] neither denies nor capitulates to the particularity of the group identities' (Philipps, 1993: 5). More precisely, the concept of differentiated citizenship may help provide ways of limiting the gap between the abstract universality of liberal principles and the very concrete conflicts of democratic civil societies. In fact, according to several scholars, instead of being an area where integration is constructed, liberal citizenship thus becomes more and more a space of fear and exclusion. This creates conditions for the rejection (or the non integration) of the 'other', for the production of prejudice and for the destruction of social solidarity. In such a context, differentiated citizenship would permit theorists and politicians to explore new ways of revitalizing the bonds of citizenship.

Kymlicka (1995b) has recently written a very interesting book explaining the compatibility between cultural rights and liberal values.[2] Even if the premises are very different, the same conclusions may be reached by following a communitarian (Taylor, 1994) or postmodern approach (Young, 1990; Mouffe, 1994). It would seem that in theory the politics of recognition – if well understood – may be an important way to regulate the social and political dynamic of multiculturalism. I believe that the theory of citizenship offers some interesting insights into improving our understanding of this type of social and political regulation, namely a space within which there is room for diverse and even conflicting understandings of individuality, community and public identity.

The Specificity of Multiculturalism as a Social Fact

In social science literature, many concepts are used to express various sorts of cultural difference: multiculturalism, cultural pluralism, radical pluralism, pluralism, multinational, multiethnic, multiracial, multireligious, multilinguistic, etc. Much confusion results from the fact that these notions are often used as synonyms. There are two basic concepts which are important to distinguish, namely plural society and multicultural society. Both express the idea that there is an under-

2. 'Liberals should accept a wide range of group-differentiated rights for national minorities and ethnic groups, without sacrificing their core commitment to individual freedom and social equality' (Kymlicka, 1995a: 126).

lying conflict in society; however, they differ as to what this conflict is. For pluralist theorists, 'as a consequence of diversity, . . . conflict is an inevitable aspect of political life, and political thought and practices tend to accept conflict as a normal and not aberrant feature of politics' (Dahl, 1989: 218). Multicultural conflicts, on the contrary, are seen as potentially destructive (Taylor, 1994). They entail a social dynamic which is important in defusing and regulating. Thus, in multicultural societies, the conflicts are often harsher than in societies marked by the 'fact of pluralism' (Rawls, 1993).

An implicit assumption underlying the pluralist conception of society is that conflicts basically concern individual or collective interests. As Connolly writes, from this perspective, 'all major groups share a broad system of beliefs and values which encourages conflict to proceed within established channels and allows initial disagreements to dissolve into compromise solutions' (1971: 3). Therefore, in a plural society, conflicts arise within a given structure of political identities. Individuals and groups struggle among themselves in order to satisfy their respective interests. Nevertheless, they are presumed to accept the rules and the symbolic 'intuitive ideas' everybody agrees upon (Rawls, 1993) and which govern the democratic system.

I assert that multicultural societies are based on a different kind of conflict, which is not related to interests, but rather to cultural identities. According to Pizzorno's conceptualization (1993: 195–200), I believe that multicultural societies are primarily marked by conflicts of recognition, by which some cultural minorities (nationalist movements, ethnic groups, sociocultural groups) come into conflict with others in order to be recognized. In liberal democratic systems, this struggle is mainly oriented against the state, while in other contexts it involves different groups that fight against one another. Generally speaking the goal consists in both cases of imposing or obtaining recognition concerning the value of the cultural specificity of the group. The kind of identities at stake here are identities considered symbolically and anthropologically very rich, 'thick'; they are perceived by the members of the group as virtually non-negotiable. These identities are the product of what Kymlicka (1995a) calls 'societal culture', which provides its members with meaningful ways of life across the range of human activities. However, why are the conflicts between social actors advocating strong particularistic cultural loyalties (based on religion, nationalism or ethnicity) seen as dangerous and virtually destructive for the democratic order (Elshtain, 1994; Rawls, 1993)? What is the main difference between these two perceptions of the social conflict?

In order to elaborate upon this opposition, I will base my reasoning on the (ideal-typical) dichotomy between negotiable and non-negotiable identities (Pizzorno, 1993). According to social science literature, the forms of individual and collective identification may differ in intensity, depth or flexibility. Some identities are considered stronger than others. For example, ascriptive identities (like ethnic, gender or sexual) are stronger than pragmatic identities based on individual choice. The negotiable identities are built on the promotion of particular, chosen, thus virtually changeable, interests, while the non-negotiable identities are based on belonging to a cultural (mostly ascriptive) community. Concerning this last type of identity, the possibilities of individual choices are reduced. Following this assumption, I argue that in multicultural societies the main conflict centres around identities which are considered to be 'non-negotiable', while in plural society the social conflict lies in interests which are, by definition, 'negotiable'. In others words, if in plural societies there exists a relative homogeneity of collective identities (primarily founded upon the fiction of the nation-state in the European context or upon civil religion in the United States), multicultural societies are characterized by a very differentiated network of collective identities. According to these differences, the way the political institutions regulate a political dynamic based on conflicts of interest is not suited to a situation within which the conflicts concern non-negotiable cultural identities and values.

Therefore, taking cultural differences seriously is a necessary condition when rethinking a conception of citizenship which works in a multicultural society. This means adopting a less optimistic conception concerning the regulation of society than the pluralist one. Moreover, as far as a pluralistic conception of society is concerned, the problems arising from social differences (including the ethnic, linguistic and sexual) are ignored, because relevant differences are basically treated as if they were matters of choice, which implies that ascriptive differences as such are not recognized (Galeotti, 1993: 590).[3] Put in a different way, following the pluralist perspective, every component of cultural identity is considered virtually negotiable. This postulate is based upon a liberal anthropology which considers the self autonomous, rational and critical with regard to collective identities, social boundaries

3. For Horton (1993: 2 ff.) 'pluralism is misleading precisely because it fails to distinguish the kind of differences implied by multiculturalism from the much more restricted and ethically often less problematic differences of tastes and pursuits which the term "pluralism" also encompasses . . . Multiculturalism becomes a problem when conflicts between groups about values or their interpretation cannot be comfortably accommodated within a particular social structure'.

and cultural values.[4] Communitarian anthropology, conversely, assumes that the members of a given society conceive of their identity as, to a certain extent, defined by the community to which they belong. Therefore, it is very difficult for individuals to negotiate the value and the narratives that 'constitute' their identity.[5]

To say that some identities are perceived as non-negotiable does not mean that they are essential or perpetual nor that the individual is defined exclusively in terms of belonging and not in terms of being and acting. As the result of an interactive process of social construction, each identity, from an anthropological point of view, is virtually open to change and re-examination and thus to negotiation. The relation between negotiable and non-negotiable identities is best expressed by the idea of a continuum rather than a dichotomy. Some empirical research has shown that, for different reasons and in different contexts, certain identities are perceived as non-negotiable. From a political perspective, the main problem is to know how to deal with groups which express and demand recognition for a supposed non-negotiable identity. Is it legitimate and open-minded for the liberal state to consider that each identity (each cultural value) is virtually negotiable and thus open to political compromise? Is it possible for all of the actors to negotiate cultural values into the political sphere? Does a liberal multicultural society offer all of the conditions (equality of political and social resources) for fair negotiation between different cultural groups? Is there a political (and democratic) way to defuse the production of radical identity claims?

I believe that the liberal approach is wrong about the unlimited extent of the negotiability of the components of cultural identity in culturally fragmented societies. As Bohman (1995: 268) correctly writes,

> bargaining is an inappropriate model for such conflicts, since it asks what cannot be done: if members of a culture could treat their deep commitments like negotiable interests or shifting preferences, there would be no deep conflict. Removing the contentious issues from the public agenda is also possible, but parties have to agree to do so. This solution already requires a compromise.

In his latest book on political liberalism, Rawls (1993) argues that only 'reasonable' conceptions of good can reach an 'overlapping

---

4. For a remarkable discussion of the liberal conception, see Kymlicka (1995a).

5. I have discussed the liberal and communitarian conceptions of citizenship in Gianni (1994) more thoroughly.

consensus' in a liberal society. In others words, for Rawls, a 'reasonable' comprehensive conception must be *sufficiently* negotiable in order to reach the minimum moral consensus on which a just and democratic society can be built. The problem is that in social reality some groups do not agree with this assumption of 'reasonableness'; rather, they perceive this political condition to be an imposition from a state which denies their specificity as a cultural group or to be a form of domination from the cultural majority.

Identity Politics as a Criticism of Liberal Citizenship

Confrontation in the public sphere of groups claiming non-negotiable identities undermines the possibility of citizenship as the medium for political integration. Elshtain (1994: 9–10) argues that even if 'the recognition of difference represents a legitimate, modern concern, and some form of equal recognition must form the very lifeblood of a democracy', the democratic system is threatened by a 'politics of displacement' which 'disdains all distinctions between citizenship and any other identity and seeks full public recognition, not as citizen but as a person with a handicap, as [person] having a particular sexual orientation, as a member of ethnic or racial groups, or as a man or a woman'. It is correct to believe that citizenship – considered to be the principle of common membership – is denied when there is no room for negotiation and agreement between cultural groups. As Barber (1995: 3) says, 'seeking a repository for identity, everyone belongs to one tribe. But no one is a citizen. Without citizens, how can there be democracy?'

In Western democracies, the possibilities of negotiation among the different cultural tribes seems to be limited by what we call the ethos of identity, which arose in the sixties (especially in the United States). The advent of forms of existential politics expressed by the New social movements and the rhetoric of authenticity have created a basis for the politics of recognition: 'it is the identity obsessions, all of them, each fuelling the others, that give the question of multiculturalism its charge and its venom' (Gitlin, 1995: 227). According to Taylor (1994), recognition of the personal authenticity constitutes a major feature of the liberal democratic project.[6] For him,

---

6. 'Being true to myself means being true to my own originality, which is something only I can articulate and discover. In articulating it, I am also defining myself' (Taylor, 1994: 31).

with the politics of difference, what we are asked to recognize is the unique identity of this individual or group, their distinctness from everyone else. The idea is that it is precisely this distinctness that has been ignored, glossed over, assimilated to a dominant or majority identity. And this assimilation is the cardinal sin against the ideal of authenticity. (Taylor 1994: 38)

But, as Appiah rightly responds, 'the rhetoric of authenticity proposes not only that I have a way of being that is all my own, but that in developing it I must fight against the family, organized religions, society, the school, the state – all the forces of convention' (1994: 154). Following this perspective, the authentic community is not what is constructed artificially (as is, for example, the nation of citizens) or what is supposed to be morally right. The real community is what *I* feel, the subjective experience. From a political viewpoint, problems arise when the constitution of the authentic community and the expression of the authentic self require violence against the 'others', against the entity which is supposed to threaten or to make impossible authentic self-realization.[7] However, even a non-confrontational exit from citizenship represents an important challenge to the democratic order.[8]

Generally speaking, the search for authenticity leads to a situation in which the idea of common citizenship as an existential experience dissolves (Beiner, 1995; Miller, 1995). This tendency virtually brings us to the well-known slogan: the personal is political. In order to preserve democracy, there must be some limits to the claims based on cultural identities. The crucial political question is how to establish these limits while still respecting the liberal principles of liberty and equality. In fact, the liberal state, through the meta-rule of freedom of expression, promotes and protects the creation of cultural identities. The neutrality of the liberal state is supposed to promote and defend the expression of difference in the private sphere through the attribution of civil, political and social individual rights. Gutmann (1994: 4) summarizes this idea clearly: for the classical conception of liberalism, 'our lack of identification with institutions that serve public purposes, the impersonality of public institutions, is the price that citizens should be willing to pay for living in a society that treat us all as equals, regardless of our particular ethnic, religious, racial or sexual identities'. This means that cultural differences can flourish in the private realm, but have nothing to do with being a citizen (Walzer, 1992).

7. For a book concerning the notions of identity and difference and their theoretical relationships, see Connolly (1991).

8. 'For identity-based movements, the margins is the place to be. Within each margin, there are always margins to carve out' (Gitlin, 1995: 150).

Nevertheless, the practical neutrality of the liberal institutions has been harshly criticized by several scholars. Postmodernists voice the strongest objections against the neutrality of the liberal state. Put succinctly, liberalism demands citizens and individuals to be neutral toward structures of power which are not in and of themselves neutral. Liberal citizenship is a form of identity which pretends to be the centre of political integration. But, as Gitlin (1995: 150) summarizes, 'the centre, if there is one, is the malevolent Other'. Liberal institutions, far from being neutral, express a universal mask carried by very particular individuals; they create strangers and enemies of those who do not fit into their categories. These 'others' are marginalized; they do not possess the same social and political resources as do the members of the dominant cultural group(s). Thus, liberal universalism is nothing other than a form of exclusive particularism and a form of alienation, considering that each universal category is in fact an attempt to homogenize the subjectivity of the social actors. According to this perspective, however, 'if democracy is a medium through which difference can establish space for itself as alter-identity, it is also a means by which the dogmatization of identity can be politically legitimized' (Connolly, 1991: x).

In my opinion, the strength of the postmodern criticism of liberalism depends more on its empirical analysis than on its normative conclusions, which sometimes seem contradictory to me.[9] Postmodernists are right when they affirm that, on the one hand, there are cultures which confer social power(s) and, on the other, there are cultures which confine people to social inferiority.[10] That there are different degrees of citizenship in a given political system has been demonstrated by political scientists (Zincone, 1992). What is important to underline here is that cultural membership often has an influence on this process.

9. For example, according to Mouffe (1994) 'our belonging to the political association cannot be conceived as one more identity at the same level as the others' and 'modern democracy [has to be] understood as a specific regime whose political principles are the assertion of liberty and equality'. Why? Why should the political identity be more important than other kinds of identity, if these are perceived by the subjects as more authentic? Why should we accept the values of liberty and equality if we have to deconstruct all the universal categories?

10. For example, analysing the racial problem in the United States, Steele (1990: 43) – who is not a postmodernist – argues that 'the condition of being black in America means that one will likely endure more wounds to one's self-esteem than others and that the capacity for self-doubt born of these wounds will be compounded and expanded by the black race's reputation of inferiority.'

To put it crudely, being culturally different implies political weakness, i.e. fewer resources to influence the political will to change the causes of his or her own marginalization. This trend seriously affects the intrinsic quality of the liberal democratic system: it under-mines the equality of citizenship and the legitimacy of representative democracy.

It is, therefore, a radical criticism of the conception of liberal citizenship which underlies the politics of identity. As we have seen before from a liberal perspective, citizenship represents the foundation of the public identity. Citizenship is the area where unity is created in a society marked by cultural differences. This kind of unity is never-theless 'thin'. It is based on the anthropological assumption that citizens are able to adopt a public and neutral standpoint which allows them to make common decisions concerning individuals who do not share the same conceptions of good (Rawls, 1993). Moreover, this assumption implies a sharp distinction between the private and the public sphere. Individuals are considered able to distinguish properly between their private interests and identities and their public status as citizens. In this conception of citizenship, it is difficult to conceive of any community other than a functional one based on weak collective commitments. As Miller (1995: 437) asserts, 'so long as one can adopt the citizens perspective in thought, one may live an entirely private existence'. Put differently, the liberal conception implicitly admits the negotiation of citizenship as a form of collective identity.[11] In fact, liberals unsatisfactorily explain why people with strong, 'thick' and non-negotiable private identities should give priority to an unencum-bered, 'thin' public identity which could conflict with their deep private commitments.

More generally, it seems to me that, blind to the political implications of identity claims, the liberal paradigm is not able to propose a model of citizenship which coincides with the notion of multiculturalism. According to Kymlicka and Norman (1994: 372), there are three types of social and cultural actors which demand recognition of their differences: (1) national minorities; (2) immigrant and religious groups; (3) disadvantaged groups. The normative recognition of these groups should lead to the attribution of three kinds of rights: (1) self-government rights for national minorities; (2) multicultural rights for ethnic and religious communities; (3) special representation rights for disadvantaged and marginalized groups. It seems to me possible to distinguish four political attitudes toward citizenship:

---

11. This point has been further developed in Gianni (1995).

1. The 'good' citizens, who are loyal toward the values expressed by citizenship and respect the separation between private and public spheres.
2. The 'different' citizens, who do not recognize the values and the symbolic meanings expressed by citizenship. These citizens, on one hand, may feel excluded from the membership represented by citizenship and, on the other, may not fit into this form of identity and may try – by political action – to abjure from its implications (Alejandro, 1993). For example, groups such as national minorities (Kurds or former Palestinians) and ethnic groups (for example, the Harkis in France or certain groups of gypsies) are, despite their formal status, culturally and socially marginalized. Further examples are those who desire independence (Amish and Orthodox Jews in the United States), or cultural groups composed of individuals who struggle against a model of citizenship perceived as alienating or dominating (women, sexual minorities, and the disabled). As suggested by Hirschman, these groups are characterized by an attitude of 'exit' or 'voice'.
3. The 'good aliens', who aspire to be culturally and socially integrated into the host community. Even if they are not part of the political community, these actors display loyalty concerning the cultural values expressed by citizenship. Much empirical research has shown that this is the dominant trend in western democracies.
4. The 'different aliens', who intend to preserve their cultural identity and do not want to be integrated more than functionally into the host community. For some ethnic minorities, this means obtaining access to the welfare of the host community; for national communities, this means, for example, entering into a multinational structure while retaining their own forms of citizenship.

In proposing these four types of possible political integration, I do not presume to have had exhausted all of the possible empirical situations which exist. Nevertheless, this classification seems to me interesting because it shows the contradictory tension between integration and disintegration which underlies the struggle for citizenship in multicultural societies. It is important for liberals to recognize that the problem of citizenship in western democracies goes beyond the question of control by the state concerning the size of the political community (i.e. the problem of politics of immigration and naturalization). They must also address the danger of destroying citizenship as a form of membership and as a space of mediation for conflicting identities, loyalties and conceptions of the good. Between the myth of community as a civic nation of equal citizens (Schnapper,

1994) or the ideal of a community without unity (Corlett, 1989), there is room to reflect upon concrete strategies for democratic political integration. The revitalization of citizenship and the possibilities of mediation it involves may contribute to a definition of a complex unity built out of different and potentially conflicting loyalties. As Habermas (1994: 137) maintains, 'a nation of citizens can sustain the institutions of freedom only by developing a certain measure of loyalty to their own state, a loyalty that cannot be legally enforced'. Nevertheless, the state must also deserve the loyalty of its subjects. Instead of being a sphere of exclusion, citizenship must take on the function of integration. I believe that the differentiated citizenship constitutes an important theoretical and political step in this direction.

Differentiated Citizenship as a Form of Integration

It is not my intention here to establish a model of multicultural citizenship, nor do I wish to establish a typology of multicultural rights to be incorporated into a model of differentiated citizenship. Concerning this point, I agree with Kymlicka (1995a: 130) that there is no simple formula for deciding exactly which rights should be accorded to which groups. What I wish to suggest are certain elements for reflection concerning the ways differentiated citizenship can lead to a better political integration of citizens. How can the liberal ideal of the maximum negotiability of identities be politically promoted without destroying the notion of citizen-identity on which political community and modern democracy are constructed?

I believe that to answer this question, it is conceptually interesting to distinguish two general notions of citizenship. The first considers citizenship an organizational 'rule', while the second sees it as a 'content', namely a substantial value which individuals must promote by their behaviour. As a 'rule', citizenship is the place within which deliberation and political will can be constructed. The public sphere, juridically protected by rights and rules, allows for a mediation between the different interests and identities expressed by social actors. Conversely, citizenship as a 'content' provides a teleological meaning to citizenship. Thus, citizenship is not only a kind of organizational procedure, but also a way of morally participating in community life for the preservation of its memory and well-being. These two types of citizenship involve different conceptions of political and cultural identity. The first one is based on a 'thin' identity, which aims at obtaining an extensive membership, while the second one aims at creating an intensive membership, thus embodying a 'thick' identity.

The first one is based on rights; the second one on duties. Intensive citizenship requires a certain proximity between social actors. In other words, in order to preserve this proximity, the state must limit the extent of citizenship. Thus, intensive citizenship is exclusive. On the contrary, extensive citizenship is inclusive, but requires certain forms of commonality in order to preserve social and political bonds. If it is necessary to rethink forms of democracy which coincide with multi-cultural societies, conceiving 'rules' without 'contents' and 'contents' without 'rules' is not a viable solution from a sociological and political point of view. As I have shown, in multicultural societies, social actors consider *both* conceptions of citizenship as negotiable. I believe that if it is normal (and correct from a normative point of view) that the 'content' of citizenship is viewed as negotiable, political problems arise when citizenship as a 'rule' is perceived as negotiable. Put another way, if in modern societies the 'content' of citizenship is in an endless process of definition, the question of negotiability of citizenship as the 'rule' of the creation of integration and representation could weaken the foundations of the democratic system. As Habermas (1994: 135) rightly maintains, 'citizenry as a whole can no longer be held together by a substantive consensus on values but only by a consensus on the procedures for the legitimate enactment of laws and the legitimate exercise of power'.

I conceive differentiated citizenship primarily as a way of promoting greater inclusion in the sphere of citizenship, and not as a way of imposing a fixed content of membership. It is sensible to believe that an attribution of rights in the context of differentiated citizenship would reduce the negotiability of the liberal rules of citizenship due to the fact the recognition of some cultural specificities would remove important factors of struggle between cultural groups and the state. Moreover, the conditions for the negotiation of 'contents' of citizenship are made easier when rights have been granted. There are two types of cultural rights which seem to me necessary in order to improve political and social integration. The first one consists in granting particular rights to some groups, thus allowing them to realize their conception of the good. The purpose of these groups should be integrated despite their cultural difference, in the name of liberal tolerance. There are many examples of this kind of recognition, namely the exemptions from mandatory schooling laws for the Amish in the United States or motorcycle helmet laws for Sikhs in England. Levy (1995: 11) speaks about 'exemption' rights, which allow minorities to engage in practices different from those of the majority culture. The second situation concerns groups which are marginalized or, according to Young, oppressed by the dominant cultural majority. In this case, the main goal is not to obtain 'external protections' (ways of limiting the vulnerability of the groups from decisions of the larger society) but to achieve true integration into the community (Kymlicka, 1995a). Levy (1995) calls these practices 'assistance rights', whose purpose is to overcome obstacles in engaging in common practices. This would mean giving these groups certain representational rights in order to maximize their political participation (Bohman, 1995) attributing language rights, or introducing specific rights in an attempt to reduce the effects of the persistent structural discriminations, for example quotas for women or affirmative action and reverse discrimination for Afro-Americans in the United-States.[12]

The goal of these types of rights is to integrate people despite their cultural difference, without renouncing the liberal commitments of individual liberty and equality. Nevertheless, in order to be consistent with these liberal assumptions, rights must respect one condition: the forms of recognition should not call into question the basic individual rights of citizenship. In my opinion, the main purpose of differentiated citizenship is not to protect cultures,[13] as some argue (Taylor, 1994) but rather to protect individuals as members of a cultural group. Put in another way, I believe that a differentiated citizenship should entail an enrichment of rights for the individual, but never a diminution of those rights due to membership in a cultural group. A classical situation in which individual rights could be weakened by the political recognition of difference would be the case in which the community is allowed to exercise certain 'internal restrictions' (Kymlicka, 1995a) on individuals, namely ways of limiting the freedom of members to promote collective goals of the community. It is important to be very careful in attributing these kinds of rights: the possibilities which members have to exit from the community have not only to be formal, but real. Differentiated citizenship should to lead national minorities, ethnic groups and other cultural groups toward a better integration

12. As Galeotti (1993: 597) rightly asserts, in this case 'the quest for public recognition of collective identities, asserting social differences, in fact, underlies a fundamental demand for equality. The kind of equality at stake here is equality of respect. If a social difference is denied public visibility and legitimacy in the polity, the group associated with it inevitably bears social stigmata.'

13. I completely agree with Habermas (1994: 130): 'The protection of forms of life and traditions in which identities are formed is supposed to serve the recognition of their members; it does not represent a kind of preservation of species by administrative means . . ..The constitutional state can make this hermeneutic achievement of the cultural reproduction of life-worlds possible, but it cannot guarantee it.'

into the political community, but should not do so at the expense of the rights and integration of the individuals.

Bibliography

Alejandro, R. (1993), *Hermeneutics, Citizenship, and the Public Sphere*, Albany: State University of New York Press.

Appiah, K. A. (1994), 'Identity, Authenticity, Survival: Multicultural Societies and Social Reproduction', in A. Gutmann (ed.), *Multiculturalism: Examining the Politics of Recognition, Charles Taylor et al.*, Princeton: Princeton University Press, pp. 149–163.

Barber, B. (1995), *Jihad vs. McWorld*, New York: Times Books.

Beiner, R. (ed.), (1995), *Theorizing Citizenship*, Albany: State University New York Press.

Bohman, J. (1995), 'Public Reason and Cultural Pluralism', *Political Theory*, 23(2), pp. 253–279.

Connolly, W. (ed.), (1971), *The Bias of Pluralism*, New York: Atherton Press.

——, (1991), *Identity / Difference: Democratic Negotiations of Political Paradox*, Ithaca: Cornell University Press.

Corlett, W. (1989), *Community Without Unity*, Durham: Duke University Press.

Dahl, R. (1989), *Democracy and its Critics*, New Haven and London: Yale University Press.

Dahrendorf, R. (1974), 'Citizenship and Beyond: The Social Dynamics of an Idea', *Social Research*, 41(4), pp. 673–701.

Elshtain, J. B. (1994), 'Democracy and the Politics of Difference', *The Responsive Community*, 4(2), pp. 9–20.

Galeotti, A-E. (1993), 'Citizenship and Equality: The Place for Toleration', *Political Theory*, 21(4), pp. 585–605.

Gianni, M. (1994), *Les liens entre citoyenneté et démocratie sur la base du débat 'Libéraux-Communautariens'*, Genève: Département de Science politique, Etudes et Recherches, No. 24.

——, (1995), 'Multiculturalisme et Démocratie: quelques implications pour la théorie de la citoyenneté', *Revue Suisse de Science Politique*, 1(4), pp. 3–40.

Gitlin, T. (1995), *The Twilight of Common Dreams*, New York: Metropolitan Books.

Gutmann, A. (1994), 'Introduction', in A. Gutmann (ed.), *Multiculturalism: Examining the Politics of Recognition, Charles Taylor et al.*, Princeton: Princeton University Press, pp. 3–24.

Habermas, J. (1994), 'Struggles for Recognition in The Democratic Constitutional State', in A. Gutmann (ed.), *Multiculturalism: Examining the Politics of Recognition*, Charles Taylor et al., Princeton: Princeton University Press, pp. 107–148.

Horton, J. (ed.), (1993), *Liberalism, Multiculturalism and Toleration*, New York: St. Martin's Press.

Kymlicka, W. (1995a), *Multicultural Citizenship*, Oxford: Oxford University Press.

——, (ed.), (1995b), *The Rights of Minority Cultures*, Oxford: Oxford University Press.

——, and Norman, W. (1994), 'Return of the Citizen: A Survey of Recent Work on Citizenship Theory', *Ethics*, 104(2), pp. 352–381.

Levy, J. (1995), *Classifying Cultural Rights*, Paper Presented at the APSA Meeting, Chicago.

Miller, D. (1995), 'Citizenship and Pluralism', *Political Studies*, 43, pp. 432–450.

Mouffe, C. (1994), *Citizenship, democratic politics and the question of identity*, New Brunswick: Working paper of the Walt Whitman Centre, Rutgers University.

Phillips, A. (1993), *Democracy and Difference*, Cambridge: Polity Press.

Pizzorno, A. (1993), *Le radici della politica assoluta*, Milano: Feltrinelli.

Rawls, J. (1993), *Political Liberalism*, New York: Columbia University Press.

Schnapper, D. (1994), *La communauté des citoyens*, Paris: Gallimard.

Steele, S. (1990), *The Content of Our Character*, New York: St. Martin's Press.

Taylor, C. (1994), 'Politics of Recognition', in A. Gutmann (ed.), *Multiculturalism. Examining the Politics of Recognition*, Charles Taylor et al., Princeton: Princeton University Press, pp. 25–73.

Walzer, M. (1992), *Cosa significa essere americani*, Venezia: Marsilio.

Zincone, G. (1992), *Da sudditi a cittadini*, Bologna: Il Mulino.

Young, I. (1990), *Justice and the Politics of Difference*, Princeton: Princeton University Press.

–7–

Multiculturalism and the Sphere Theories of Hannah Arendt and John Rex

Hans-Rudolf Wicker

Introduction

They're crawling out of the woodwork again, those elusive spirits whom most people – blinded by the post-war economic boom – believed had been safely consigned to history and who express themselves through nationalist ideologies, cultural fundamentalism, and even occasionally through racist attacks. Convictions and ideologies based on strong group feelings are thought to be legitimated by invoking the existence of the 'other', the 'foreign', the 'culturally alien' and the 'ethnically different'. Such subtle categories of incompatibility would – if they didn't already exist – have to be invented by their adherents, for without them the closure of thinking is not possible. Because we-groups of this kind depend on labelling, stigmatizing, marginalizing and segregating a discernible 'other' to confirm their own ideologies – and thus their identities – processes of fundamentalization inevitably promote the ethnic and cultural differentiation of societies. Advocates of nationalisms cannot accomplish their self-prescribed task of strengthening the domestic integration of the nation-state unless they can invoke the existence of enemies of the nation at home and abroad. Ethnic integration and ethnic marginalization are two sides of a coin, and forms of racism that are not based on the construed notion of an inferior people do not exist.

Social and political movements whose immediate purpose is to generate a sense of belonging are once again on the rise as our century draws to a close. The upsurge of integrisms is usually perceived as the result of manifest disturbances in the social and political fabric that are beyond the reach of conventional crisis management and encroach on society's consciousness to the point of causing irrational reactions. In this perspective, integrative currents reflect the destruction of obsolete political structures, the disintegration of the social realm, as well as the loss of spiritual orientation. As such, they are classified among those transitory phenomena which bind the anxieties resulting from the collapse of traditional structures, and impose a search for new rules of social coexistence. The collapse of the Soviet empire, the reunification of Germany, the emergence of the European Union and the rapid development towards a world society by way of the globalization of the economy and the media are some of the anomie-generating revolutions that contribute to the disruption of formerly valid identities. By extension, the fundamentalization of we-processes thus constitutes another expression of the crisis management of identity vacua.

Blinded by the assumption that rapid economic development, rationalization, and a widespread increase in individualism, consciousness and reflexivity would eventually wipe out all forms of 'irrational' communitarization, the social sciences were very late in recognizing what was, in fact, becoming evident already in the latter half of the nineteenth century, namely that the enlightened modern age, far from eliminating such 'irrational' communitarizations, was actively evoking and modifying them according to the exigencies of the moment. The most striking evidence for the complementarity of societal development and community beliefs is provided by the fact that the genesis of the modern age itself is unthinkable without the synchronous genesis of national thinking. Today it is evident that the 'project of modernity' – epitomized by technological progress, accelerated industrialization and the emergence of democratic structures – could not have come about without the nation-state. In other words: the birth of civil society and the birth of the nation are two aspects of one and the same development. From the age of Enlightenment, the processes leading to the formation of civil society thus find themselves trapped in the paradox of having to rely on 'irrational' mechanisms of communitarization in order to promote a development guided by reason. Expansive modernist development and the generation of communal and national limitations are by no means mutually exclusive or conflicting currents. On the contrary, they actually constitute each other. Depending on the historical constellation – a society's domestic social tensions and dislocations being the main determining factors – the pendulum sways from civil to the national aspects and vice versa. When the structures of the welfare state cease to ensure the integration of civil society, nationalism rises to counteract the fragmentation of society.

Seen from this perspective, some of the hypotheses that currently enjoy considerable popularity both in the media and in the social sciences seem highly questionable. Take for instance the assumption that ethnic conflicts such as the wars in ex-Yugoslavia or in Rwanda and Burundi can be explained by pointing to the existence of 'pre-modern' ethnic ties that were temporarily suppressed and are now reasserting themselves in a cataclysm of extreme violence; or that fundamentalist Islamic dignitaries attempting to subject their countries to the rule of God are succeeding in their efforts because the Islamic world has never known an age of Enlightenment. Such interpretations are reductionist because they fail to take into account that 'irrational' communitarizations are an integral part of the development of modernity, and that the struggle for national, ethnic and cultural integration is always intimately connected with the struggle for access to general goods such as housing and living space, education, jobs, etc. The scarcer these goods are and the stronger the competition is for access to them, the greater the odds are that ethnic, cultural, and national categories are seized as resources in staging such conflicts and fights. Far from being causes of conflict these categories merely provide the forms under which such struggles are enacted. The search for the 'origin of ethnic conflicts' always yields the wrong answers because it mistakenly conceives ethnicity as some sort of primordial category. One does wonder, obviously, why so many social, political, and economic conflicts in the modern age – examples abound in eastern Europe, Russia, the Caucasian republics, Afghanistan, Sri Lanka and other parts of the world – parade in the robes of ethnicity, culture and nationality. Evidently the articulation of social tensions and conflicts in terms of ethnicity generates social and political movements which are not only often notable advantages in comparison to earlier models of conflict – socialist class struggle, for instance – but are also much more in tune with the social conditions that prevail at the end of this century. In my subsequent analysis of the interdependence of modernization and ethnicization, I have applied two models that offer distinctly different approaches to an interpretation of this phenomenon. The first – known to social scientists as the model of the three spheres (Radtke, 1990; Steiner-Khamsi, 1996) – was developed by Hannah Arendt (1959). The second – repeatedly taken up and discussed by John Rex (1986; 1993) whose interpretation I will be following for the most part – is known as the theory of the two domains.

I begin by examining the possibility of applying the sphere and domain theories proposed by Hannah Arendt and John Rex respectively to interpret present-day ethnic and multicultural phenomena. I then enquire what the nature is of the societal changes that increasingly cause contemporary social movements to appear in the guise of ethnic and cultural patterns of signification.

Multiculture and Sphere Theories

In her book *The Human Condition* the social philosopher Arendt (1959: 23–69) develops a model which subdivides social entities into a 'public', a 'social' and a 'private' sphere. The model assumes that the democratic state has a different set of controlling functions in each of the three spheres, whose contours – translated into contemporary scientific terminology – are as follows. In the 'public' sphere – where political cohesion is produced – equality among individuals is the defining principle. Equality under the law and equal opportunity for all individuals belonging to the community are maintained on this level. In the modern constitutional state this is achieved by way of the political rights to which all citizens are entitled. In the 'social' sphere – a space no longer private but not yet political where most of society's activity takes place, where goods are produced and traded, and where capital is being transformed – the free market is the defining mechanism. Since competition is permitted, a certain amount of discrimination is inevitable while the state, at best, undertakes to contain some of its more detrimental effects; or, in terms of the welfare state, equal opportunity in the social sphere will, in the best of cases, be achieved through the elimination of starting level inequalities for the benefit of underprivileged individuals. The private sphere is characterized by the protection it extends to human qualities that could not survive in public, such as intimacy, trust, goodness – qualities, in other words, which are indispensable to the mutually supportive creation of meaning and communitarization. In this social space individual actors must be at liberty to engage in relationships, to cultivate friendships and to start neighbourly relations. Translated into modern terminology it means that the state has no right to intervene in the private sphere of its citizens, unless constitutional laws are being violated. However, this implies that one accepts the fact that communitarizations occurring in this space may be determined by class, religious or ethnic criteria and may lead to the exclusion of third parties. The private sphere thus stands for both the principle of integration as well as the principle of exclusion.

The full significance of this liberal–democratic model can only be appreciated if one understands the implications of its cardinal rule: none of the specific characteristics of each sphere – equality, competition and discrimination, inclusion and exclusion – may be carried over into another sphere because this may lead to a loss of meaning and a perversion of the different levels. Moving the principle of equality from the public-political sphere to the social sphere would restrict competition and ultimately lead to social paralysis. If the same principle were to be expanded further to the private level, the state would assume totalitarian traits. Conversely, if the exclusion of certain groups is tolerated on the social level, competition and social progress are in jeopardy. Allowing the principle of exclusion to function in the public-political sphere would constitute a serious breach of the principle of equality; to tolerate a politics based on ethnic prejudice – as we might say today – would ultimately undermine the constitutional state. The value of Hannah Arendt's sphere theory, worded carefully and using generalizations sparingly, lies mainly in its function as an analytical tool. While the author convincingly illustrates to what extent the meaning of human activity depends on the place in which it occurs, she also points out that a strict separation of the spheres and their respective principles is impossible because the activity of doing good works apparently 'is not even at home in the realm of privacy . . .' (Arendt, 1959: 69).

Despite the fact that it does not lend itself to generalizations, Arendt's model is helpful in attempting to identify the field of tension which is currently causing much controversy between universalists and particularists in the social sciences and humanities. What is striking about this debate in the present context, is the incompatibility of the respective positions of those who promote a wide-ranging relativism and multiculturalism (Rex, 1986; Taylor, 1992) and those who perceive multiculturalism as an unpardonable betrayal of the principles and values of the enlightenment – all men are equal – (Finkielkraut, 1987; Radtke, 1990), and who therefore insist on a strictly universalist politics. Arguing from Arendt's perspective one is inclined to point out that it depends on where a particular human activity takes place if one is to assess whether universalist or particularist action makes sense and thus deserves to be tolerated or even protected. Advocates of an unrestricted multiculturalist politics, by introducing particularisms where they do not belong, violate the principle of universalism. Theoreticians of modernization who essentialize the equality-principle by attempting to introduce it into spheres where equality is restrictive and limiting, violate the principle of particularism. According to Hannah Arendt universalism and particularism are complementary and mutually supportive principles that each require their proper, separate spaces if they are to be of any use as controlling and, at the same time, liberating social maxims.

While Arendt arrived at her sphere theory by way of social-philosophical and historical reflexions, John Rex (1986) treats multiculturalism in a comparative and topical manner. Where Arendt anchors the antagonism between universalism and particularism in a three-sphere theory, Rex, focusing on the same dualism, activates a concept known in the social sciences as the theory of two domains. Rex divides society into two domains – the 'public-political' and the 'private'. By a combination of different possibilities he tries to arrive at four basic types of society (1986: 120): Type A guarantees equal opportunity (universalism) in the public-political domain and allows for multiculturalism (particularism) in the private domain; Type B imposes the equality principle in both the public-political and the private domain and leads to monoculture; Type C allows for ethnic differences and ethnic lobbying in the public-political domain and combines these with multiculturalism in the private domain; Type D, finally, imposes a monoculture in the private but not in the public-political. In the following pages I will analyse the models offered by Arendt and Rex – possibly even over-interpreting them – in order to arrive at certain insights which might lead us to a better understanding of the meaning and function of ethnicity and multiculture.

Switzerland from the Perspective of John Rex's Theory of Two Domains

When we apply Rex's typological matrix to Switzerland we can see that the country has gone through a transition from Type B to Types C and A. Until the 1950s, Type B was the dominant mode. A very distinct federalism guaranteed that cantons and language regions have an even and balanced access to political power. Segmented 'language culture' was transformed, on a political level, into a dictate of regional equal opportunity that prevented a demographically dominant region from imposing itself by simple popular majority on another region either immediately or in the long run. The potential for fragmentation implicit in language-regional disparities – translated into functional-sociological terms: excessive integration pressure triggers centrifugal movement – was partially neutralized by a high degree of autonomy granted to the federal states and by federalist principles. Yet, without an additional, overarching national culture the danger of disintegration could not have been fully contained; or conversely: It was precisely by becoming a 'nation' that the Swiss Confederation could afford a high degree of regional and local autonomy (Siegenthaler, 1994: 118).

For the federalist principle and the concordance of political parties to actually work on a power-sharing level, a strong uniting principle was required to keep social, regional, and linguistic contrasts as well as diverging interests at bay. The nation-state – manifested in the individual's civil rights – provided such a principle. Constructs of inclusion lacking such primordial justifications as a common language, a common religion, or common descent required a national ideology to underline the shared attributes and mutual obligations that did exist. Whatever adjustments and communicating this monocultural national image – which reached far into the private lives of citizens – did require was performed by what were then the major national institutions – the federal administration and the army militia – both of which rested firmly in the hands of the bourgeoisie.

Totalities that use integrative pressure to produce inner harmony and homogeneity tend to overemphasize the process of assimilation and often develop a vivid imagery of domestic and foreign enemies. Assimilation aspires to 'making things similar' to an imagined (national) whole. Even before World War I, foreigners living on Swiss territory were frequently exhorted to assimilate because their presence was seen as endangering the unity of the Swiss nation. In fact, the influence of the assimilation paradigm was so pervasive in those days that its integration into the country's liberal naturalization policy is hardly surprising. Since the obligations imposed by the nation-state on its citizens were seen as outweighing the rights it granted to them, naturalization appeared as an effective instrument to make foreigners assimilate Swiss norms and values. In 1912, in an inquiry into the naturalization of foreigners, all cantons without exception – some almost enthusiastically, others hesitantly at best – opted in favour of facilitating the naturalization of foreigners. Humanitarian concerns were not what prompted such liberal thinking which, incidentally, was to be replaced by a restrictive immigration policy during World War One. Instead, it was the desire to force foreigners to internalize 'Swissness' to the point where they would develop that inner loyalty towards the Swiss state which was seen as crucial for its preservation (Raymond-Duchosal, 1929). The cup of citizenship was filled, as was customary at the time, with national essences. The democratic rights to which every citizen was entitled – symbol of the equality principle – were thus subordinated to a thoroughly monocultural and morally binding idea of the nation. The search for a Swiss national character – an imaginary construction in which the individual characteristics of each Swiss citizen are seen as immediately relating to a higher national essence of being – was a telling expression of the times. These, then, are the major elements which allow us to classify Switzerland as it presented itself in the first half of the century as a society of the B-Type. Starting from here we can now attempt to show how the country then developed in the direction of Types C and A.

The emergence of multicultural demands – at least in Europe – is usually placed in the context of a growing presence of new immigrants from 'foreign cultures'. In Switzerland, this hypothesis receives further affirmation by the shift in the regional origins of migrants which did indeed occur during the seventies and which led to an increase in – as it was unfortunately and absurdly termed (Hoffmann-Nowotny, 1992: 84) – 'cultural distance' between the new immigrants and Switzerland. Unlike the 'guest workers' of the post-war period who were mainly recruited in southern Europe, the migrants and asylum seekers whose presence the migration discourse of the eighties and nineties chiefly addresses – even though they constitute but a fraction of the foreign population in Switzerland – arrived overwhelmingly from regions in south-eastern Europe, Asia and Africa. It is true that the presence of these groups of people has contributed to the process of hetero-geneization in Switzerland. It cannot be denied that most advocates of a multicultural Switzerland demand that these new immigrants, respectively their religions, languages and customs, be given more credit and more recognition. The old obligation to assimilate has been replaced in recent years by a new idea of integration: insofar as the migrant is still expected to assimilate, the scope of this obligation is now limited to a recognition of the country's laws and social structure (labour market, social insurance, etc.) and it no longer automatically applies to cultural matters as well. In this way, the right to be different that is implied in multiculturalism is immediately linked to the presence of the new migrant groups, and is interpreted as an expression of the legitimate needs that foreign people bring with them from their respective cultures. Such a perspective suggests an intimate connection between multiculturalism and xenophobia since both ideologies – one in the guise of tolerance, the other in the guise of aversion – are focused on the same object, 'the foreigners in one's own country'. But the attempt to understand multiculturalism merely as a result of the presence of foreign and, specifically, 'culturally foreign' people yields a partial truth at best, a truth whose other half is to be found on an altogether different level.

At this second level are developments which – regardless of the presence of migrants – lead to the fragmentation of social and political fields in industrial societies. These developments include a continuing functional differentiation, the increasing flexibility of production and markets, the transition from national to transnational forms of organization, the emerging shift from vertical to horizontal segmentation and identity building, the development of different lifestyles and the rise of new social movements (gender, environment, religious fundamentalism, radicalism of the right, etc.); processes which, more than anything, help to expose supra-subjective entities as imagined communities (Anderson, 1983). The particularization of social reality ultimately results in the deconstruction of national imagery which until after World War II was the guiding principle for Switzerland and other countries and which – as we have demonstrated above – generated the idea of a national monoculture and gave rise to the demand for assimilation. Switzerland could only be conceived as a fragmented society once the idea that defined our country as a coherent entity, i.e. as a closed nation, was dismantled. The old image – national identity fills the foreground and is linked to the requirement of assimilation – and the new image – focused on the existence of a fragmented social reality held together by the fabric of the welfare state that no longer insists on cultural assimilation but is satisfied with mere structural integration – are both inscribed in the current contradictory political discourses. In recent statements regarding naturalization, Switzerland's New Right still insists on a principle which derives from the model of *jus sanguinis*: naturalization is seen as a reward for cultural assimilation achieved and demonstrated. The left, on the other hand, favours the model of *jus soli*, which releases citizenship from all cultural content and emphasizes instead the motto of 'integration through participation' (Ossipow, 1996). In both discourses the beginnings of a transition from type B to type C is clearly discernible.

By attaching the term multiculture to a progressive fragmentation of modern civil-social processes – a localization that has long been a common feature of the social sciences in traditional countries of immigration such as the USA, Canada, and Australia – we can now apply the domain-model to Switzerland at a further level of discussion. The following conclusions can now be drawn:

According to the theory of two domains, multiculturalism in the private domain is tolerable and may even be encouraged without endangering the principle of universal equality in the public-political domain. In applying these standards to Switzerland one obvious inconsistency immediately comes to mind: multiculture refers primarily to the populations of foreign origin who have no political rights in the public domain. According to John Rex's classification Switzerland is a Type C society with regard to this aspect: a more or less tolerated multiculturalism in the private lives of migrants clashes with a politics of ethnicity – predicated on marginalization and ultimately justified by the argument of 'cultural distance' – on the public-legal level. This combination, as John Rex points out, is typically found only in apartheid states. In the contemporary case of Switzerland's resident foreigners, naturalization would be the only means of favouring a transformation from the discriminatory Type B to an acceptable multiculturalism of the Type A.

If, however, we disregard the multicultural scene of migrants and consider multiculturalism only as embodied by its citizens, then Switzerland is clearly a Type-A society. The political rights are fully guaranteed, fragmentation is permitted in the private domain – not least in the realm of cultural expression, as the language article in the constitution, recently approved by popular vote, clearly demonstrates. With the exception of the right wing the political classes are no longer attempting to communicate to the citizenry the image of a homogenous national monoculture. The principle of the universal equality of all humans on the one hand, and the idea of particularization and differentiation on the other exist in their proper, respective domains and complement each other.

By the standards of the two-domains-theory, Switzerland thus contains two distinct types of multiculturalism that obviously operate along separate lines, each with a different significance. The divide between them is expressed in terms of belonging to the nation-state and being excluded from it, respectively. In the first case, multiculture is fully integrated in the ideal of a multicultural society as sketched by John Rex (1986). The second form, linking multiculturalism in the private domain with marginalization in the public domain, is highly dubious, if only because in this configuration the combined effects of multiculturalism are played out on highly sensitive territory. Located outside the public-legal domain and thus under pressure to demonstrate its legitimacy, multiculturalism easily assumes provocative traits which, under certain conditions, are sufficient to activate the spectre of national unity as a form of defence mechanism. In this way, the expression of cultural difference assumes an importance which in substance it does not deserve. It is obvious that multicultural desires in societies of the B-type make excellent *Ersatz*-surfaces for projections of a political nature.

As the above analysis shows, the two-domains theory has its limits. On the one hand it serves well enough to illuminate the positioning of the multicultural in the context of a more politically oriented sociology. But Rex's structural model also reveals the weak point of the multiculturalism debate. Depending on one's point of view – multiculturalism within a community versus multiculturalism as the characterization of the excluded other – particularism takes on significantly different shades of meaning. One of the disadvantages of the Rex approach turns out to be that its typology remains inconclusive with respect to the question why multicultural and ethnic aspects have assumed such importance in present-day society. The need for multicultural expression remains confined to the private domain by definition and in no way relates to changes in the society at large. Without the insertion of Hannah Arendt's sphere of the 'social' the two poles of the 'public' and the 'private' lack the element that produces contradictions, tension and change in the first place.

Ethnic Movements and the Theory of the Three Spheres

Hannah Arendt indicates in her analysis of the *vita activa* that the three spheres are by no means immutable but change in the course of time. In fact, the expansion of the middle sphere at the expense of the two adjoining spheres is one of the defining traits of the modern age. The middle space – a field distinguished by division of labour, wage labour, market, capital and profit where every form of social interaction is tinged by competition, and individual, short-term advantages can only be gained at the expense of others – is growing to such an extent that the spheres of the 'private' and 'common', progressively drained of their substance, may disappear altogether. Our perception of the world has narrowed to where market and competition are all we can see – even in those spaces which should be off-limits to the principle of competition.

It is not difficult to see that Hannah Arendt is proposing a different kind of approach to multiculturalism, one which is fundamentally at odds with the direction taken by John Rex. If multiculturalism, in all its manifestations and values, were primarily a fact of the private sphere as the two-domains theory suggests, one would expect the significance of modern-age multicultural concerns to dwindle at the same rate as privateness itself. Obviously, this is not the case. On the contrary: multiculturalism becomes relevant at the very moment in history when the last residues of the private sphere are about to be completely 'socialized' – and thus cancelled – by new technologies of consumption and organized leisure activities. In the logic of Arendt, then, multi-culturalism is undoubtedly an element of the middle and not of the private sphere: The inflation of the 'social' sphere at the expense of the 'private' and 'common' spheres is paralleled by the growth of multiculturality in modern times. This insight reveals another paradox which is rooted in Arendt's sphere model and requires an explanation: apparently, multiculture is not directly related to the 'principle of exclusion' which Arendt observed in the private sphere and which can (but need not) lead to ethnic neighbourhoods within complex societies. In this model, 'ethnic exclusion' in the private sphere and 'multiculturalism' in the social sphere are not congruent, each refers to its own origin and function.[1] How is this discrepancy to be understood and what conclusions does it lead to?

As we have seen, the social sphere in these times of liberal-democratic societies is the locus of the *vita activa* which includes, on the one hand, the production and distribution of goods according to the principles of a market economy including the attendant material-technological development, and, on the other, the production of wealth and poverty. In this sphere the equality principle cannot be enforced without running the risk of limiting competition and strangling the liberal market economy. The social sphere favours people with competitive advantages – in the words of Bourdieu (1972): people equipped with social (connections), cultural (education), and economic capital. By way of the 'public-communitarian' sphere which is committed to the principle of equality, attempts can be made to eliminate the initial handicaps of disadvantaged people and to prevent excessive discrimination.

In this middle sphere, which is organized by way of market laws and where social behaviour must be interpreted primarily in terms of profitable strategies, social actors can secure additional competitive advantages by forming alliances and discrediting their opponents. In this way, competition provides an opportunity to transfer the practices of integration and exclusion – originally intended for the private sphere – to the social level and of using them there to one's best advantage. Included in the catalogue of extraneous options which can be applied in the social sphere are all the forms of communitarization commonly subsumed under the term multiculturalism. As a result of their transfer to the competitive social field they are now capable of appearing

---

1. Incidentally, in my view the mostly pointless debate surrounding the question whether multiculturalism should be considered a blessing because it guarantees diversity and demands tolerance, or a danger because – depending on one's reading – it jeopardizes the unity of the nation-state (Hoffmann-Nowotny, 1992), mocks human rights and the principles of enlightenment (Finkielkraut, 1987), or constitutes a modern form of racism (Radtke, 1990), is bound to remain unresolved because the opponents start from different assumptions. The advocates of multiculturalism usually have in mind the private sphere where cultural expression is to be considered as part of the democratically guaranteed liberties. Critics of multiculturalism, on the other hand, bemoan its occurrence in the social sphere where it is indeed closely linked to competition and discrimination. As we have seen above, according to Arendt both sides are right and wrong at the same time.

under the sign of exclusion, i.e. they can readily assume ethnicizing, xenophobic and racist forms. The linking of these different expressions of symbolic and habitual difference is legitimate inasmuch as they, by virtue of the attribution of identity by oneself or others, mark actual cultural, ethnic and/or racial borders, both on a symbolic and on a practical level. Ultimately, multiculturalism in the social sphere is merely one instrument among many used by individuals and groups to form and reinforce alliances in order to hold one's own in the fight for social, cultural and economic capital.

As mentioned above, in the private sphere integration and exclusion have a different meaning. In the realm of the private, multiculture is part of the naturalized everyday and requires no ideological justification. This may be the reason why cultural difference in the private sphere is readily crossed. Border zones of culture, religion, language and values generally tend towards hybridization because, as Serres (1977) states, learning and interaction invariably generate *métissage* and because, in the words of Friedman (1994: 75), culture has a hybrid nature. As a result, definite borders that permit a definition and separation of cultural and ethnic totalities are hard to find in the private sphere.

In the social sphere this same phenomenon takes on a different aspect. Since, by definition, competition includes the struggle for resources and positions, ethnic and cultural traits appear no longer as part of an unreflected everyday but as an element of the strategies and ideologies used to contrive and resolve competition. This opens the possibility for discourses to emerge that provide cultures and ethnic groups with coherent histories and definite borders, and that relate ethnic and cultural affiliation to innate mentalities and immutable identities. As such ideologies encroach on the private sphere privateness as defined by Arendt is dissolved. Examples that follow this pattern abound. In former Yugoslavia, for instance, bi-ethnic marriages were common and hybridity thus part of everyday life. With the decline of the centralized state and the ensuing political fight for positions and resources the ethnic element in the social sphere was fundamentalized. With loyalty and treason being defined along ethnic lines it became necessary for the hybrid forms of the private sphere to be 'un-mixed'. Bi-ethnic marriages were divorced, hybrid neighbourhoods were broken up and reorganized along ethnic lines. In the process of this conflictive development 'culture' and ethnicity assumed new meanings and new political weight.

In the private sphere a grammar of multiculturalism can give actions shape without ever having been explicitly stated. This 'household'-multiculturalism, which is not the same as an 'official' multiculturalism, leaves plenty of room for practices of negotiation and hybridization.

Only after it has been inscribed in people's collective consciousness does a multicultural grammar acquire the ability to guide people's actions; cultural borders and identities are now being created and the ability to hybridize is reduced. The formation of such a grammar requires a process of political negotiation that can only take place in an ideologically charged debate – in other words: a multicultural grammar is not generated in the private but in the social-political sphere. One example may serve to illuminate this point. In 'multicultural' diction deceased Muslims may not be buried in Swiss cemeteries because the graves there rarely face east. In such 'official' diction the demand for Muslim cemeteries is the logical consequence. Experience shows, however, that 'privately negotiated' compromises between Muslim mourners and Christian ministers or priests are not uncommon. Such agreements may provide for burial in a Christian cemetery but with special permission to have the grave face east or at least to lay the deceased to rest in such a way that his/her face looks east. The demand for Muslim cemeteries originates in the social sphere. It derives its legitimacy from the right to be different and the uncon-ciliatory nature of Christian and Muslim tradition. The 'compromises', on the other hand, originate in the private sphere. If such negotiated agreements were to become more commonplace they would sooner or later lead to a hybrid Christian-Muslim tradition. Only the multicultural discourse of the middle sphere, charged with ethical convictions and insisting on separate developments, can prevent this from happening. These insights allow us to draw certain conclusions regarding the origin and significance given to ethnic movements in the model of the three spheres.

First of all, the model sketched by Hannah Arendt and expanded by me allows us to clear up a misunderstanding which in recent years has repeatedly generated misguided solutions. The fallacy lies in the assumption that because multiculture belongs to the private sphere, intercultural frictions have to be resolved in the private sphere as well. If, however, multiculture originates in the social sphere, the problems it generates cannot be resolved in the private sphere. The demand put forth by the conservative right, that individual assimilation of the values, norms and cultures of the host-society is needed as a means of defusing multicultural conflicts, is as fallacious as the left-liberal claim that racism and ethnic ghettoization could be resisted by increasing private tolerance towards the culturally other.

Because the social sphere in modern times is expanding at the expense of the 'private' and the 'common', and because the struggle for resources and positions takes place in it, social movements are increasingly caused by the anomies that have come to dominate this middle ground. Most important in shaping the contours of this new type of social movement are the contradictions and injustices caused by the liberal market economy and the inequitable distribution of economic, social and cultural starting capital, the possession of which alone enables groups and individuals to compete successfully. In this context the following point requires clarification: the fault lines that determine the formation of social movements have shifted. In earlier periods these faults were mostly horizontal and generated social movements which were typically dominated by contrasts such as poor-rich, unpropertied-propertied, lower-higher, worker-bourgeois. Although the movements expressing a class–dichotomy have by no means disappeared they are being superseded by forms of protest that form along vertical faults. The women's movement is an example of this type, as are the various gay and ecological movements.

With class affiliation no longer the dominant generator of solidarity, attributes that rely solely – in Weber's terms (1956: 307) on 'believed community' are given more space. This type includes all movements that use religious, ethnic, cultural, and national categories to integrate people. Both protest discourses formulated along vertical incisions and mobilizations based on 'irrational' attributes are characteristic of the more recent social movements. With the help of Hannah Arendt's model we can at least offer a partial answer as to why this change has occurred.

While the spheres of the 'private' and the 'common' naturally favour continuity and durability as their underlying principle, the middle sphere, by contrast, functions increasingly better as binding structures are dismantled to make room for process, since after all – as Arendt (1959: 60) put it very succinctly and to the point – the very purpose of structure is to resist process. The reason for the priority of process in the social sphere is easily found: the principle of capitalism, as Marx and others have repeatedly pointed out, is to draw profit from the 'work' of the capital that its owners have injected into the cycle of the production and circulation of goods. Investments lose both value and meaning if the flow from work to merchandise, from merchandise to profit, and from profit to capital is paralysed, i.e. if structure dominates process, as is the case in socialism. While socialist and state-capitalist societies are at pains to reduce unyielding structures to the point of allowing at least a minimum of productive flow in the social sphere, market-oriented societies face the problem of how to contain the processual mushrooming of productive capital in order to preserve at least some parts of the 'common'. Based on the production of goods, signs and meaning, the processualizing of the social sphere ultimately implies the dismantling of rigid and determinant structures. On the social level the consequences of such changes appear as a tendency to transcend all types of (structural) constraints, to de-traditionalize all formerly valid metaphors, theories and blueprints for living, to hybridize social fields, and liquefy and to relativize and fragment identities.

A social field thus processualized and governed by competition favours ideological conceptions capable of occupying the spaces cleared by the retreat of the 'common' with new and authenticated identities. Open spaces invite constructions of identity which are almost completely divorced from the structural givens of the 'common' and, therefore, all the more suited to what Taylor (1992) aptly terms the *politics of recognition*. Asserting oneself in the competitive field of the social sphere in order to gain access to positions, resources and competitive advantages becomes a fundamental feature of the modern age. On such terrain the social movement becomes an important social-technical instrument in the fight for recognition. In their quest for legitimacy, such movements no longer have recourse to symbols from the fund of the 'common' whose ultimate dogma is 'universal justice', they are forced to create new allegories of communality which tend to emphasize the particular. It is at this point that the door opens onto categories sufficiently charged with emotion to overcome the fragmentation of the social landscape in their striving for identity, and to be transformed into purposeful homogenous movements; once the lines of integration and exclusion are drawn, such categories will also appear sufficiently authentic to resist critical reasoning and deconstruction. The ethnic, the cultural, the religious, the national and the sexual are such categories, or in the words of Zygmunt Bauman (1996: 57): 'Ethnic herding and confessional flocking together take over when collective responsibility of the *polis* fizzles out. The dissipation of the social rebounds in the consolidation of the tribal. As identities go, privatization means tribalization.'

Conclusions

Some conclusions may be drawn from the arguments above that will be helpful in understanding and localizing the revival of the ethnic and the cultural in the modern age. The Arendt model demonstrates the intimate correlation that exists between the expansion of the 'social' and the way ethnic and cultural categories reclaim the social fields. Such categories offer themselves as new ways of shaping the increasingly harsh struggle for scarce goods – a struggle which can be waged from the bottom up as well as from the top down. On the one hand the American civil rights movement *(black, red power)*, the women's movement and minority movements in general are 'ethnic' movements striving for social advancement, and are therefore based on a bottom-to-top ideology. The ethnicization of former Yugoslavia, on the other hand, originates in regional political castes fighting for supremacy after the decline of the central state; to promote their own private interests, they mobilize the masses with a top-down ethnic ideology. Much the same could be said of ethnic conflicts in some African states and of the construction of nationalist ideologies in states of the former USSR. The swell of xenophobic and racist currents in many European countries in recent years also constitutes a top-down ethnic strategy aimed at stigmatizing and, ultimately, keeping out marginal groups who are also competing for their share of benefit from the welfare state. Arendt's model performs exceedingly well in bringing out the process- and interest-related aspects of the new social movements.

John Rex, on the other hand, in explaining multiculturalism with his two-domains theory tends to emphasize the agencies that mediate between the 'private' and the 'public' domain. Included among these agencies are legislative, political, and administrative controls which regulate membership as well as civil and political rights and obligations in and towards the welfare state but also state institutions responsible for the safeguarding and/or advancement of equal opportunities. Notably included in the latter group are agencies and institutions active in the fields of education, welfare and public health as well as institutions which, by their interventions, regulate the economy and the labour market. In Rex's approach – unlike in Arendt's model – multiculturalism appears less as an effect of the development of market forces than as a consequence of political and institutional regulations. Rex's perspective thus includes the option that cultural expression, although rooted in the private domain, is subject to modification through political and institutional channels. Any discussion of multi-culturalism should therefore include a discussion of the political ethics which ultimately help to generate it: a politics of multiculturalism is legitimate only while it serves to advance equal opportunity (Castles, 1993; Rex, 1993). A form of multiculturalism that does not manifest itself politically is questionable for the simple reason that it can easily be manipulated to justify existing inequalities (of opportunity).

The two models discussed in this chapter address different but complementary fields in which multiculturalism becomes significant. While Arendt's model is superior in explaining the general causes of multiculturalism and ethnicity, Rex's approach addresses the fact that phenomena of culture and ethnicity are to be viewed in the context of real politics and may not be discussed without considering the actual social-political mechanisms of inclusion and exclusion. In summarizing our findings we get the following picture:

1. If multiculturalism and ethnic conflicts are perceived as a result of a toughening competition for scarce resources, it seems logical to assume that future developments resting on market-oriented liberal ethics will promote multiculturalization and the enacting of social and regional conflicts in ethnic terms. Politicians clamouring for less state intervention and more competition would be well advised to consider the available options for the prevention and resolution of the ethnic conflicts that are the inevitable consequence of their politics.

2. Only a politics aimed at reinforcing the 'common' sphere, and unwavering in its insistence on the promotion of equal opportunity will be capable of keeping in check the excessive growth of process spilling over from the social sphere; indeed, this form of process is causing a critical loss of social competency and undermining society's capacity for integration. Paradoxically enough, it is precisely the strengthening of the 'common' sphere which most effectively prevents the particularization, ethnicization and nationalization of social fields. Such a politics requires the mediating agencies of the state that are emphasized by Rex, and whose pre-eminent objective must be equal opportunity.

Bibliography

Anderson, B. (1983), *Imagined Communities*, London: Verso.

Arendt, H. (1959 (1958)), *The Human Condition*, New York: A Doubleday Anchor Book.

Bauman, Z. (1996), 'Morality in the Age of Contingency', in P. Heelas, S. Lash and P. Morris (eds), *Detraditionalization*, Cambridge: Blackwell, pp. 49–58.

Bourdieu, P. (1972), *Esquisse d'une Théorie de la Pratique*, Geneva: Droz.

Castles, S. (1993), 'Migrations and Minorities in Europe: Perspectives for the 1990s: Eleven Hypotheses', in J. Wrench and J. Solomos (eds), *Racism and Migration in Western Europe*, Oxford: Berg, pp. 17–34.

Finkielkraut, A. (1987), *La défaite de la pensée*, Paris: Editions Gallimard.

Friedman, J. (1994), *Cultural Identity and Global Process*, London: Sage.

Hoffmann-Nowotny, H.-J. (1992), *Chancen und Risiken multikultureller Einwanderungsgesellschaften*, Berne: Schweizerischer Wissenschaftsrat.

Ossipow, L. (1996), 'Citoyenneté et nationalité: pratiques et représentations de l'intégration en Suisse chez les candidats à la naturalisation et des responsables de la procédure', in H.-R. Wicker, J.-L. Alber, C. Bolzman, R. Fibbi, K. Imhof and A. Wimmer (eds), *Das Fremde in der Gesellschaft: Migration, Ethnizität und Staat*, Zurich: Seismo, pp. 229–242.

Radtke, F.-O. (1990), 'Multikulturell – Das Gesellschaftsdesign der 90er Jahre?', *Informationsdienst zur Ausländerarbeit*, 4, pp. 27–34.

Raymond-Duchosal, C. (1929), *Les Etrangers en Suisse*, Paris: Felix Alcan.

Rex, J. (1986), *Race and Ethnicity*, Milton Keynes: Open University Press.

——, (1993), 'The Political Sociology of a Multi-Cultural Society', in D. Kós-Dienes and A. Sander (eds), *Multiculturality – Warfare or Welfare*, Göteborg: Papers in Anthropological Linguistics 26, pp. 1–26.

Serres, M. (1977), 'Discours et parcours', in *L'identité, Séminaire interdisciplinaire dirigé par Claude Lévi-Strauss*, Paris: Grasset, pp. 25–29.

Siegenthaler, H. (1994), 'Supranationalität, Nationalismus und regionale Autonomie. Erfahrungen des schweizerischen Bundesstaates – Perspektiven der Europäischen Gemeinschaft', *Traverse – Zeitschrift für Geschichte*, 3, pp. 117–142.

Steiner-Khamsi, G. (1996), 'Universalismus vor Partikularismus? Gleichheit vor Differenz?', in H.-R. Wicker, J.-L. Alber, C. Bolzman, R. Fibbi, K. Imhof and A. Wimmer (eds), *Das Fremde in der Gesellschaft: Migration, Ethnizität und Staat*, Zurich: Seismo, pp. 353–372.

Taylor, C. (1992), 'The Politics of Recognition', in A. Gutmann (ed.), *Multiculturalism and 'The Politics of Recognition'. An Essay by Charles Taylor*, Princeton: Princeton University Press, pp. 25–73.

Weber, M. (1956), *Wirtschaft und Gesellschaft*, Tübingen: Mohr.

8

Ethnic Revivals Within Nation-States?
The Theories of E. Gellner
and A. D. Smith Revisited

Natividad Gutiérrez

To the memory of Professor E. Gellner

Culture and ethnicity are rapidly overlapping, to the extent that the fragile (or imaginary) line that used to separate these two key concepts of the social sciences is now becoming redundant. The interpretation of ethnicity as a host of representations of the subjectivity and social practices of minority peoples (stateless peoples) is beginning to lose its conventional attributes of cultural inferiority and social marginality, attributes attached to the ways of life of rural or non-industrialized sectors, and reproduced in the ambience of domestic life by national or international immigrants, either in host or national states. During the age of nation-building, despite systematic assimilation or extermination, unwanted ethnicity managed to survive, and gradually, it is becoming visible, organized and militant. Culture, on the other hand, as the medium of communication and cohesion of peoples of industrial nations, also claims ethnicity. A nation's display of a prestigious ethnic past which recollects solid experience and tradition, not artifice, invention or fabrication, is the source that provides authenticity and a collective desire for renovation and posterity.

How can we explain today's renewed interest in the ethnic element and its corollary, ethnicity, when it was dumped onto the fringe of modernism and when it became the antithesis of progress and a symbol of backwardness? A number of factors taking place towards the beginning of the 1990s may help provide an answer: namely, the emergence of new ethnic states after the conditions propitiated by the end of the Cold War; scholarly re-consideration of relentless local expressions of pride in language, tradition, or nostalgia, largely discredited by the positivistic schools of scientificism and international socialism; the emergence of transnational markets and the demise of commercial frontiers; as well as the debate concerning free identity expression advanced by globalization and postmodernist thesis.

In this chapter, I argue that the renewal of ethnicity is less a result of external forces, than a process of self-discovery and assertiveness of ethnic ties due to the gradual access of minorities to the culture of nationalism fostered by the modern state. It is essential for this discussion, however, to clarify a contrasting theoretical trait common to studies of nationalism, this being the establishment of a dividing line between ethno-nationalism and ethnic revivalism. Ethno-nationalism is understood here to mean politicized demands of stateless ethnic groups via negotiation or coercion (e.g. political parties or armed movements) seeking to achieve sovereignty and self-rule. Ethnic revivalisms, on the other hand, are organized demands of ethnic peoples pressing for cultural and linguistic recognition within the administrative and territorial boundaries of a nation-state.

Leaders or intellectuals of ethnic revivalisms, through organized campaigns, cultural groups, public meetings and publications, seek to obtain adequate official treatment concerning the special needs of complex ethnic ways of life, by demanding the implementation of effective bureaucratic action (e.g. multiculturalist policies and tolerance to ethnic diversity). While ethno-nationalisms theoretically represent a threat to the national state, ethnic revivalisms do not pose an end to the nation-state. Rather, they exhaust the nation-building project based on the assimilation or exclusion of ethnicity.

The access of marginal ethnic peoples to the modernity of the nation-state will be explored through a comparison of two leading methodologies of nationalism which emerged in the 1980s: the 'modernist' school, particularly the model delineated by Ernest Gellner (1926-1995) and a second school, which I call the 'historical-culturalist' approach associated with the work of Anthony D. Smith (born 1933).[1] I propose that it is possible to use these models in a complementary fashion, despite their antagonistic conceptualizations. The reason for this is that both exponents concentrate on two vital factors essential to perceiving the problematic nature of nations and nationalism: namely, how is the transmission of a modern culture possible and necessary, and why does ethnicity prevail? In constructing a complementary theoretical approach, it is also important to underline the

---

1. Professor Gellner's sad death occurred only days later, after his last public debate with A. D. Smith in a series of meetings entitled 'The Warwick Debates' (University of Warwick, 24 October, 1995).

fact that the authors in question have systematically divulged their arguments in an abundant and specialized bibliography which has emerged since the late 1970s (Gutiérrez, 1995a).

Nationalism in Gellner's view epitomizes the culture of modernity. A society permeated by modern nationalism is characterized by high levels of communication, a common language, anonymity, and an increasingly complex division of labour to meet the changing demands of the industrial era. This type of advanced socialization is not the result of spontaneous or natural evolutions. Thus, Gellner has firmly argued that nationalism is a process of 'social engineering' which requires the eager intervention of the welfare state playing one of its most unmistakable roles: the monopolization of standardized education in order to create upward social mobility and to inculcate citizens with common loyalties and goals (Gellner, 1981; 1983).

The argument underlying this perspective is that nationalism's main social function is the gradual creation of a compact correspondence between politics, culture and territory in one single entity, i.e. the archetype of the nation-state. Basically, the backbone of Gellner's theory is constituted by the argument that the existence of a uniform educational system exists which is the primary state agent employed as a progenitor of nationalism and cultural homogeneity. Therefore, Gellner, like other 'modernists', implicitly denies the relevance of primordial explanations explaining the formation of nations and nationalism. In order to exemplify such an argument, Gellner uses a dichotomy, that is the recurrent sociological polarization between agrarian and rural versus industrial and urban. In his opinion, the agrarian-rural realm cannot generate nationalism, nor is this necessary for rural life because agrarian societies lack the means of enhancing social cohesion, and cohesion explains the emergence of nationalism which comes into existence through state education in order to facilitate communication beyond local boundaries (1983: 35).

A conceptualization of this type remains antithetical to other characterizations of nationalism, such as political movements for self-determination as a result of shared ethnic awareness. Truly, in Gellner's interpretation of nationalism, the discussion on ethnic assertiveness for independent self-rule occupies a role of secondary importance since ethnic 'sub-units' of society lack capacity for exercizing cohesion and thus for helping to shape the borders of a given ethnic group. The possession of a state as a promoter in the instigation of cohesion (a key indicator of the culture of modernity or 'high culture'), does not appear to be possible for all ethnic 'sub-units' (Gellner, 1979; 1983). Internally fragmented and stateless ethnic groups have little control over their future and face inevitable assimilation. This interpretation poses two possibilities: firstly, Gellner underestimates ethnicity because it does not constitute the primary social mechanism by which a nation-state is formed. However, and as a second case in point, despite generalized predictions towards the effective policies of assimilation of the nation-state, this form of modern polity has not obliterated ethnicity.

What make the persistence and reproduction of ethnicity possible, despite the compelling force of modernity, is, in my view, one of the most fascinating riddles in the field of sociological studies of nations and nationalism. A more reliable ground on which to begin to build part of the answer is provided by Gellner's theory delineated above. The role of the state is to bring about modernity which becomes materialized through a long-term planned strategy of providing the masses with social mobility and a medium of communication. Policies which exclude ethnicity may contradict the complex task of all embracing integration; thus, ethnic groups are driven to form part of the national core. Members of some ethnic groups assimilate, but some others make use of this modernity (access to school, labour employment, mass media) in order to reconstruct a discourse of ethnicity which enables them to maintain a separate cultural identity in the light of political negotiation. Indeed, objective conditions of modernity in the Gellnerian tradition have fostered the resurgence of ethnicity expressed in a specialized type of project put forward by educated and socially mobile members of ethnic groups (i.e. the ethnic intelligentsia). What remains to be explained is, interestingly enough, the aspect that Gellner left out of his analysis: the components of ethnicity and their capacity for survival and reproduction. In order to underpin arguments for this complementary discussion we shall now turn to Anthony D. Smith's theory of nationalism.

The theoretical relevance of Smith is the polemical importance which, in the view of modernists and instrumentalists, he ascribes to subjective factors which determine the power of the symbolic past that preceded the modern nation. This concern for demonstrating the impact produced by ethnic genealogies and origins of present nations is clearly opposed to Gellner's view that nationalism is a purely modern phenomenon detached from 'folk' or the past (1964: 151; 1983: 5).

It is the importance attributed to the ethnic historicity of nations that opens a theoretical rift between Gellner and Smith. A simple way to fully understand the nature of this controversy, which will continue to inspire further debates, is to take a look at these author's different interpretations of nationalism. Nationalism, for Gellner, is the vehicle for forging efficient and cohesive societies. Therefore, reality implies a break with the past. For Smith, nationalism is the ideological formulation which gets in motion the setting for a modern collectivity; nationalism is, then, expressed, in the fervent desire for independence, possession of territory, and self-rule, stimulated by emotional and powerful memories of the past (Smith, 1984; 1993).

Having clarified key areas of these important discrepancies, we can now continue with our argument. Since our discussion centres around the reconstruction of ethnicity by ethnic groups within nation-states, it is of decisive interest to investigate which elements conform to such ethnicity. A useful starting point is provided by the method implicit in Smith's approach. This methodology basically refers to the study of the constitution and influence of the ethnic past on modern nations through an understanding of the ideological impact of ancient history and mythologies (Smith, 1985; 1986; 1989). In his numerous writings aimed at demonstrating the scholarly impossibility of ignoring both history and ethnic memory, Smith has vehemently argued in favour of cultural or 'subjective' factors, relegating to secondary importance purely 'objective' or economic explanations. Unlike Gellner's dichotomous approach, Smith proposes a *continuum*, expressed in the so-called power of the collective memory which allows for the reproduction over centuries or generations of a sense of 'self' in the form of ethnocentrism. From this formulation, Smith (1984; 1986; 1991a) argues that nationalism is the politicization and territorialization of an earlier sense of ethnocentrism expressed in the '*myth-symbol* complex' and '*mythomoteur*' (i.e. myths of descent and origin).

If, in Gellner's interpretation, the state is the progenitor of nationalism, myths in Smith's conceptualization serve a similar purpose: they have the power to inspire amongst the population a variety of messages of continuity and solidarity in times of mobilization or crisis, such as common goals, desire for survival and cultural uniqueness. Although we learn from Gellner that a monopolized force is necessary to shape the efficiency and loyalty of the masses, it follows that such a shape is not produced from thin air: traditions, language, history, mythical stories and heroic events are adapted to modern curriculas of standard systems of education. We may briefly anticipate one aspect of our conclusion by pointing out that both Gellner and Smith's approaches complement on another: a comprehensive explanation of nation formation involves the forceful interplay of modernity and ethnicity as expressed by the dissemination of historical and cultural information via national educational systems.

If attention is drawn to myths as the basis of ethnicity, a fascinating paradox emerges. Moreover, such a paradox will also be helpful in delimiting the alleged ethnicity of ethnic groups. In doing so, it is useful to briefly list the components of Smith's definition of nation: 'a population sharing common myths and historical memories, mass public culture, historic homeland, common economy and citizenship' (1991a: 14; 1995: 56–57). To find out what could be the shared 'common myth' of a modern nation is the beginning of the paradox. Although Smith has placed conceptual weight on the 'myth of origin and descent'[2] manifested both in history and the arts, the paradox is that it is indeed difficult to locate which industrial European nation is openly pursuing a cult of common ancestry. Memories of origin may exist in the form of records or oral traditions, but this information (presumably shared by the peoples of the nation) is largely lost, interrupted or eroded by the long-lasting effects of a myriad of invasions, migrations, conquests, wars, religions and ideologies, to mention only a few. Smith has also supplied some historical examples (Jews, Greeks, Armenians) which seem to confirm the nature of his reflections and enquiries, although these cases are the exception rather than the norm (1984; 1991b; 1992; 1993).

The rest of the paradox is that Smith's approach would better suit cases stemming from cases originating outside the scope of his theoretical analysis. For example, the nation of Mexico would be inconceivable if consideration were not granted to the fabrication of a myth of common ethnic origin, initiated after the Spanish conquest of 1521 (i.e. the *mestizo* people – a mixed race people resulting from European, African and Amerindian interbreeding), and legitimized as an official ideology of ethno-racial unification throughout the twentieth century (i.e. the 'cosmic race') (Gutiérrez, 1995b). To discern whether this myth propagated by the state is putative and fictitious is, within the terms of the present discussion, of minor importance. What matters is that such a mythologized story of conquest and renewal contains an enormous inspirational power which helps to organize the ethnic cleavages (native and immigrant) of modern Mexico. Furthermore, and in connection with the above mentioned paradox, the discretionary possession of a wealth of mythological information eulogizing origin and descent is to be found, not necessarily among certain nation-states, but rather in the system of ideas of certain indigenous peoples (e.g. Amerindian and/or Aboriginal peoples) inhabiting various parts of today's world. Therefore, we are now able to lay the foundations of the constituents of ethnicity of the ethnic groups: a thread of continuity

2. On the discussion of myths which evoke collective transcendence, Stasiulius and Yuval-Davis (1995) have recently drawn new interest to the 'myth of destiny' popularized by the Austro Marxist, Otto Bauer (see 'Introduction').

starts with a myth of origin. These stories do not derive from Judeo–Christian traditions – e.g. descent of woman-goddess-trees, caves and so on, as the purveyor of the groups' existential explanations concerning, for example, why they wear a traditional dress and speak a non-national language, or why they live in such a particular territory and follow ancestral traditions. Thus, the identification of a story represents the nucleus from which visible markers of identity emerge (e.g. dress, language). The type of ethnicity that ethnic groups nurture is based on mythological material, as suggested by Smith's scheme; to this we may add the experience of conflict and socialization under unprivileged conditions during the nation-building process. We must also include other components of ethnicity which have been widely argued and commented upon in Smith's extensive bibliography, and which also adequately reflect the state of identity of contemporary ethnic groups; for example values and memories expressed in symbols and memories and legends. Ethnic groups seem to possess abundant mythological information in support of Smith's formulations but, returning to Gellner's key argument, their prospects as potential modern nations are extremely poor because they lack their own educational and communication systems necessary to engender cohesion. No disagreement seems to exist concerning the view that villages or 'tribal segments' manage to retain their own patterns of reproduction and perpetuation, despite the fact that Gellner has insisted that this cannot be considered as nationalism ('A Nuer village produces a Nuer, but it does not produce a Sudanese citizen'). It follows that for Gellner (1964: 158) nationalism emerges only to meet the demands of modern circumstances, and does not arise where there is an absence of the state, but rather appears only for *some* states (1983: 5).

At this point, a clarification would seem to be in order: nationalism is an affair of the state. Consequently, it is not a pragmatic device easily found among stateless ethnic groups. However, the view regarding the nationalistic integration of ethnic sub-units may be treated as polemical, as full assimilation and cultural homogeneity are extremely difficult to measure, given that such features are, certainly, not typical of most nations. This is the reason for my proposal to reconsider the emergence of revivalisms as channels of expression of modern ethnicity. My argument is that the nationalist project has not been completed with the ongoing expansion of industrialization. Conversely, technology and mass communication, standard education and the division of labour introduced at an exponential rate to meet the demands of industrialization are generating new waves of potential and as yet unknown expressions of ethnic revivals. Such a process takes place because the existence of modern nations is due to the quantitative expansion of educational services; a uniformity of training not only expands literacy rates, but also the 'educational pyramid' (e.g. teachers and bureaucratic staff) is turned into a vehicle for upward social mobility for people of working class (and peasant) origins (Gellner, 1983: 34).

The emergence of an ethnic intelligentsia formed by trained professionals who are members of ethnic groups may be seen as the result of the benefits brought about by modernization and uniformity. However, I am also suggesting that the appearance of the ethnic intelligentsia is motivated by the awareness of ethnic identity which seeks to find adequate channels of expression, continuity and renovation. What makes the transmission of ethnic information over generations possible? How does the 'myth-symbol complex' manage to survive the modern phase of nation-building? For Smith, part of the answer is to be found in the role of intellectuals and the intelligentsia who act as spokespeople for the group, and who play a vital role in collecting, reshaping, recombining, idealizing and organizing the content of ancestral memories. Modern disciplines also play a part in helping to recreate and amplify the historicity of the nation or ethnic group (Smith, 1986). Ethnic intellectuals (i.e. members of non-dominant cultures who retain some of their cultural attributes but who have received modern education and have proposed solutions in modern contexts) are the progenitors of a new type of revival within nation-states (Shils, 1976; Feierman, 1990). I list three *ad hoc* cases of such revivalism: firstly, campaigns seeking the implementation of bureaucratic policies allowing the inclusion of either language, culture or religion in the educational curriculas; secondly, formation of a printing press for ethnic editors, journalists and writers, who target specific ethnic audiences; thirdly, creation of associations of writers and ideologues in ethnic languages.

My own studies on the revivalism of indigenous ethnic groups in Mexico is the initial empirical basis of my argument. However, it can also be used to understand the nature of other revivalisms in other parts of the world. A salient case in point is the current Islamic revival that is apparent in many parts of the globe – for the Islamic ideologues this spread is messianic, world-wide. The means by which this revival is making itself evident, in some regions and cities of the industrial world (e.g. Chicago, California and London), is through the organization of rallies and massive concentrations of Islamic followers, as well as the 'global' edition of a collection of pamphlets, cassettes and video cassettes which aim at disseminating the spread of a religious dogma: 'Islam once again will flourish and blossom to provide the leadership for humankind in all areas of man's life' (e.g. Al-Khilafah

Publications). By no means is it possible to argue that these examples have similar ideological goals: the campaigns of the indigenous groups of Mexico basically demand political recognition, while the Islamic revival has a pungent fundamentalist appeal of indoctrination. However, what they have in common is that both cases utilise similar techniques of dissemination, and these mobilizations have emerged (and seek accommodation) within the boundaries of nation-states.

It is through the intellectual endeavours of an ethnic intelligentsia that organized ethnicity acquires political or cultural visibility. Nevertheless, I would like to suggest that the sole identification of intellectuals as progenitors of ethnicist appeals seem to be an insufficient explanation. Here again, there is room for exploring another complex aspect derived from Smith's scheme. Since 'ethnic memories' by no means remain unaltered, the implication is that they have to be somehow located either in records of some sort, or oral traditions. Specifically, I refer to the methods by which the transmission of ethnic information is successfully carried out, and how a rediscovery of 'ethnocentrism' (or the process on unravelling 'ancestral memories') takes place.

Reference to my empirical research will once again prove useful. The tiny intellectual elite of Amerindian peoples of Mexico, formed by teachers, journalists or writers have claimed, not without romantic and apologetic overtones, to have in their families, communities and villages, the source of their 'autonomous' knowledge, where the ethnocentrism suggested by Smith is likely to be found. Present ethnic revivalisms, despite their vigorous creativity and emerging militancy, face the challenge of discovering, systematizing and diffusing ethnic information; a task of monumental proportions. This is basically due to the lack of resources available to ethnic groups which would enable them to facilitate mechanisms of internal cohesion. The search for a kind of indigenous ethnocentrism is hampered by the fact that, even if elites reshape and adapt suitable mythology, ordinary ethnic peoples are very likely to have blurred memories of an uncontaminated past, simply because ethnicity, like culture, depends on efficient forms of transmission. Available anthropological techniques, such as collection of testimonies and oral history, have propagated the belief that a valuable source of information is to be found in the memories of the elderly. However, most of this information refers to memories of a recent past, or adaptations of stories recalling impressionistic interpretations of various events.

Ethnic peoples, immigrant or indigenous, are placing renewed importance on the search for their own roots, either because they have a desire for continuity or, perhaps, more convincingly, because they are becoming aware that the instrumental practice of ethnicity holds a great negotiating value to overcoming two limitations imposed by the nation-state: to achieve cultural recognition (or tolerance), and to improve their marginal livelihoods. Another unprecedented implication for future cultural configurations of nation-states, is that revivalisms are first and foremost encouraged by ethnic peoples' interest in rediscovering and learning about their ethnicity, a multifarious reality largely suppressed, inasmuch as the nation-building project has sought its erection on the imaginary base of homogeneity.

Conclusion

In this chapter, I have argued that the nation-state, instead of hastening the disappearance of so-called obsolete ethnic identities, is gradually facing a phenomenal circumstance posed by the fact that ethnic peoples are forming their own cultural elites and intelligentsia in order to launch and disseminate autonomous and semi-autonomous revivalist movements. The theoretical backdrop to this formulation is supplied by my own methodology aimed at contrasting the merits and short-comings of two leading sociological theories of nationalism. Ethnicity is proving to be a more elusive and ambiguous phenomenon than was initially predicted. Through the construction of a complementary approach which seeks to reunite antagonistic conceptualizations, I have put forward an argument which seeks to restore the balance between the ethnicist and modernist trajectories of nations.

By the time a society achieves a sustainable level of industrialization and homogenization as a nationalist requirement, groups within that society may have already generated other alternative goals and agendas. Contrary to modernist predictions, so called 'low cultures' – instead of assimilating with the 'high culture' – are taking advantage of modern circumstances such as mobility, mass media and standardized education systems. However, ethnic intelligentsias (and peoples) enjoying the unprecedented opportunity of experiencing a certain tolerance, and even encouragement to diversity, are still faced with the task of finding suitable ways of helping themselves to rediscover their largely oppressed ethnocentrism brought about by the spread of modernism.

Bibliography

Feierman, S. (1990), *Peasant Intellectuals: Anthropology and History in Tanzania*, Madison: University of Wisconsin Press.

Gellner, E. (1964), *Thought and Change*, Chicago: University of Chicago Press.

——, (1979), 'Nationalism or the Confessions of a Justified Edinburgh Sinner', in E. Gellner, *Spectacles and Predicaments: Essays in Social Theory*, Cambridge: Cambridge University Press, pp. 265–276.

——, (1981), 'Nationalism', *Theory and Society*, 10, pp. 753–776.

——, (1983), *Nations and Nationalism*, Ithaca: Cornell University Press.

Gutiérrez, N. (1995a), 'The Culture of the Nation: The Ethnic Past and Official Nationalism in 20th Century Mexico', Ph.D. dissertation, London School of Economics, University of London.

——, (1995b), 'Dismantling Cultural Archetypes: A Critical View of Key Terms of Mexican Nationalism', *Bulletin of Latin American Research*, forthcoming.

Shils, E. (1976), 'The Intellectuals in the Political Development of the New States', in J. Kautsky (ed.), *Political Change in Underdeveloped Countries*, New York: Robert Kriedger.

Smith, A. D. (1984), 'Ethnic Myths and Ethnic Revivals', *European Journal of Sociology*, XXV, pp. 283–305.

——, (1985), 'Ethnie and Nation in the Modern World!', *Millenium*, 14, pp. 127–142.

——, (1986), *The Ethnic Origins of Nations*, Oxford: Basil Blackwell.

——, (1989), 'The Origins of Nations', *Ethnic and Racial Studies*, 12(3), pp. 340–367.

——, (1991a), 'Chosen Peoples: Why Ethnic Groups Survive', *Ethnic and Racial Studies*, 15(3), pp. 436–456.

——, (1991b), 'States and Peoples: Ethnic Nationalism in Multicultural Societies', *Soviet and Jewish Affairs*, 21(1), pp. 7–21.

——, (1992), 'The Question of Jewish Identity', in P. Y. Medding (ed.), *A New Jewry? America since the Second World War*, Oxford: The Hebrew University of Jerusalem and Oxford University Press.

——, (1993), 'Ethnic Election and Cultural Identity', *Ethnic Studies*, 10, pp. 9–25.

——, (1995), *Nations and Nationalism in a Global Era*, Cambridge: Polity Press.

Stasiulius, D. and Yuval-Davis, N. (eds), (1995), *Unsettling Settler Societies*, London: Sage.

9

Affiliation, Exclusion and the National State: 'Ethnic Discourses' and Minorities in East Central Europe

Christian Giordano

National State and 'Ethnic Discourse'

The National State has been seen far too often exclusively as a geographical entity. The sociological implications of this type of organization are often forgotten and the fact that the National State is also an association of citizens who belong to it on the strength of well defined characteristics which, according to the case, can be acquired or ascribed, is neglected. Not everyone can indiscriminately belong to a specific National State and, to take a well-known formula of Max Weber, one can say that the National State is an association which is only partially open towards the outside (Weber, 1956: 26). Naturally, this limited opening towards the outside, i.e. towards the 'other' or towards the 'foreigner', entails the creation of institutional mechanisms of social selection which regulate affiliation and exclusion. Citizenship and nationality represent the fundamental tools which define who has the complete right to belong to the National State and who is excluded from it.

However, what interests me is not so much the analysis of these mechanisms which regulate the relations between the National State, on the one hand, and minorities and foreigners on the other, but rather the reconstruction of the 'ethnic philosophy' which is at the base of the aforementioned tools of social selection. We are not so much dealing with examining the judicial content of constitutional acts, laws and decrees which are laid down by the National State in order to recognize, limit or even deny the rights of minorities and foreigners, as we are specifying the characteristics of the 'ethnic discourses', which are in evidence to a greater or lesser degree, and which condition the sense of the judicial purviews sanctioned by the institutions of the National State. If one begins with this premise, one realizes that in Continental Europe a common, unified concept of the National State has not developed. Rather, according to the 'ethnic philosophy', one can deduce that there are, broadly speaking, two principal models of the National State: the French model and the German model (Brubaker, 1994). There are certainly many analogies and overlapping areas between these two models. Nevertheless, they substantially differ from one another as far as the recognition of 'diversity' and, more specifically, the status of minorities and foreigners (immigrants, refugees, etc.) are concerned.

Since we will be concentrating on the 'ethnic philosophy' in the countries of East Central Europe, I shall, however, add some annotations on the 'ethnic discourse' which developed in the Soviet Union, as this had a strong influence on the 'ethnic philosophy' in the Popular Republics at the time of real socialism and is still material for 'hot' discussion in some ex-Eastern Block countries. I would like to say that recourse to the above mentioned models and discourses is to be understood in an ideal-typical way in the Weberian sense of the word.

The French 'Ethnic Discourse': National State and 'Citoyenneté'

The French historian Michel Vovelle has shown that the originality of the French Revolution consists in having known how to unite the formation of the National conscience with the idea of emancipation and liberty. The movement tried to rethink the 'roots' by, above all, placing in doubt their implied 'inevitability' (Vovelle, 1989: 209). In this sense, although it is almost banal to say it, the French Revolution is directly tied to illuministic universalism and is clearly in opposition with the particularism of the 'nationalist' logic. Under the influence of revolutionary cosmopolitism from the first, the concept of the 'nation" assumes a very 'open' character which dates back to the definition of 'nation' proposed by the *Académie française* in 1694. The 'openness' of this term is extremely clear: one belongs to the 'nation' by living inside the confines of a certain State, by being subjected to a common legislative system and by making use of the same language which, at a stretch, can also be a lingua franca. There is no mention of ethnic or religious affiliation, either real or presumed. Robespierre's idea of 'patrie ouverte' pointed in the same direction as does the above-mentioned concept of 'nation'.

At the end of the eighteenth century, during a period of full-blown revolution, the concept of nation was used more and more in a 'closed' manner, thus becoming – as some French authors have noted – a true and proper machine used for the exclusion of the individual (Lochak, 1988: 78). More specifically, one can say that if, in the revolutionary constitutions of 1791 and 1793, a foreigner first entered as a citizen and consequently acquired nationality over the years, the terms were inverted, a situation which is still true today (Weil, 1988: 192). This fact provoked the expansion of an 'ethnic philosophy' in France since defining the affiliation to a social group or to a political community primarily on the basis of the concept of nationality implies the use of 'ethnic criteria' as canons of differentiation between 'native' and 'foreigner'.

However, one must add that although the idea of 'citoyenneté' may have been weakened, it has not been completely abandoned. This has certainly helped in France the persistence of a concept of nationality which is less rigid and more open than in other countries. In principle, the French 'ethnic philosophy' is still 'assimilationist' and not 'differentialist', meaning that it allows a 'foreigner' to become a citizen on the condition that he or she can demonstrate a certain degree of cultural integration in the host country. It thus seems clear to me, in spite of the evident 'exclusivism' inherent in the concept of nationality, that the French 'ethnic philosophy' is universalistic in character and oriented toward the unity of mankind. Ethnic frontiers exist, but they are not impassable: everybody, in as far as he or she belongs to mankind, is able – if he or she so desires – to assimilate or to become a full member of the 'Cité' inside of which all relations between individuals and between individuals and public institutions are regulated by a social contract.

Ethnic and national affiliation in French discourse is thus never inescapably invariable but is, on the contrary, always modifiable by way of acculturation processes which favour social integration and assimilation. Thanks to these changes in affiliation, which also naturally involve certain modifications of the cultural identity of the person, the foreigner can enter into the process of 'naturalization' and can be deemed 'worthy' of being received into the bosom of the community of citizens.

The fact that the ethnic affiliation of an individual is not defined once and for all also gives a specific connotation to the idea of the French term 'peuple' which, as we shall shortly see, is substantially different from the Germanic concept of 'Volk'. The 'peuple' is not an entity defined by pure ethnic commonness, but is rather a community of citizens, all of whom have the equal right to leave ethnic or racial origins outside the realm of consideration.

The French 'ethnic philosophy', in spite of its obvious tendencies towards the exclusion of foreigners, is, nevertheless not as closed as many other philosophies due to the fact that it finds its judicial expression in the 'jus soli'. Recently however, France has further restricted the limits of the 'jus soli' and has automatically reinforced those of the 'jus sanguinis', the latest measures having been taken and put into effect by the Minister of the Interior in 1993, i.e. the controversial and now famous 'Pasqua Law' concerning the acquisition of nationality/citizenship. Sami Naïr is most likely correct when he claims that in France, due to an internal policy of immigration, a strategy is being delineated which aims at suppressing the 'jus soli' and thus of transforming France into a nation based on extraction and blood (Naïr, 1992: 141).

Consequently, French 'assimilationism' ignores a 'geography of ethnicity' inside its own national territory. This has undoubtedly had and still has important consequences, to return to our initial theme, on the policy concerning the statute of ethnic minorities. In fact, in the French 'ethnic discourse', minorities, understood as ethno-cultural entities inside the National State, practically do not exist: they are systematically ignored, concealed, or, at best, represent an uncomfortable reality which is accepted with unease. The logic of this position is very simple: Either one is outside the national community or, if one does belong to it, is French, primarily due to reasons of assimilation.

The German 'Ethnic Discourse': National State and 'Volk'

The 'ethnic discourse' linked to the construction and to the character of the National State in Germany hinges on the concept of 'Volk', understood as an ethnic entity and not as a union of citizens who do not necessarily have a common origin. This primary, brief assertion already makes clear the fundamental difference to the French 'ethnic discourse'. If the latter places the 'inevitability of roots' in doubt, then the German 'ethnic discourse' underlines it and, as National Socialism shows, may obsessively exasperate it.

However, in order to avoid misunderstanding, it is better to be more precise and say that when I speak of the German 'ethnic discourse', I am referring to an ideal-typical construction of a Weberian stamp from which the current trends in the reunited Germany are distancing themselves, although they still retain, even at a judicial level, certain elements which are certainly not marginal.

Nevertheless, let us first proceed with order. It has often been said that the idea of 'Volk', organized politically and territorially on the basis of the National State, spread throughout Germany during the period between Humanism at the end of the eighteenth century and nineteenth century Romanticism (Greverus, 1987: 160 ff.). It is well known that the great divulgers of this concept were Herder and the brothers Grimm.

However, contrary to the suppositions of certain authors, it seems rather rash to me to consider Herder as the one who transformed the universalist concept of culture into the particularist concept of 'my' culture (Benda, 1965: 52; Finkielkraut, 1987: 14). Rather, it was certain successors of Herder, of whom only some were Germans, who transformed the idea of 'Volksgeist' into the ' most dangerous explosive of modern times' (Talmon, 1967: 224; Finkielkraut, 1987: 56 ff.). When I briefly speak of Herderian reminiscence or of 'Herderianism', above all in regard to the present situation in East Central Europe, I will be referring not so much to Herder himself as to all those who, in the wake of Herder, constructed their own 'ethnic discourse' based upon the idea of 'Volk' and 'Volkgeist' in such a way as to perhaps trust his thinking.

Herder certainly never imagined the resonance which his proposals would have not only in the German environment, but also in those East Central European societies still integrated in the Imperial 'Vielvölkerstaaten' (Austria-Hungary, Russia, Turkey) which were involved in the arduous and wearisome undertaking of realizing their respective national unities.

In Germany, Herder, in any case, provoked colourful discussions in which politicians, jurists, philosophers, men of letters and folklorists of an extremely high level participated. Almost all of these intellectuals tried to specify the rather vague and elusive concept of 'Volk', and the overwhelming majority underlined to one extent or another the importance of extraction and common origins (Veiter, 1984: 16). 'Abstammung' and 'Herkunft' thus became the essential physiological attributes necessary to characterise the 'Volk' as an ethnic entity.

There is consequently an almost generalized agreement in Germany according to which extraction and common origins have something to do with the character of the 'Volk'. This supposition, considered by all to be a certainty, has had a definite influence on the German 'ethnic discourse' linked to the project as well as on the realization of the National State in Germany.

In fact, if we look at the development in this country of the judicial doctrines concerning the definition/acquisition of citizenship, which always seem to me emblematic of the 'ethnic philosophy' of a National State, we realize that these are dominated by the formula: 'Das Volk ist der Inbegriff der vollberechtigten Staatsbürger' i.e. 'The people as an ethnic entity are the essence of citizens with full rights' (Grawert, 1973: 166). In this way, extraction and origin become two fundamental criteria in defining who is 'native' and who is 'foreign'.

This biological course, emphasized by the strict application of the 'jus sanguinis', has only been found in Germany in a radical and perverse form in national socialism, which notoriously infused a clear racialist component in the 'ethnic discourse'. If the ethnocratic concept of 'Volk' championed by national socialism evokes, beyond measure, the value of genealogy and blood, the post-war legislation of the Federal Republic has never completely denied the relationship between 'Volk', extraction and 'jus sanguinis'. The most emblematic example which brings to the fore these characteristics of the present German 'ethnic discourse', is without a shadow of doubt, the different treatment reserved for the children of emigrants in Germany or, in other words, for the so-called second and third generations and the 'Aussiedler', i.e. those people of German origin who intend to permanently settle in the Federal Republic. While the former, although having grown up or even having been born in Germany, must take part in a long bureaucratic procedure before obtaining citizenship, the 'Aussiedler', because they are able to show specific and even very distant biological links of extraction and consanguinity, are given nationality almost automatically. The former are therefore considered as outsiders, while the latter are considered as belonging to the 'Volk'.

Exclusion of one and integration of the other come about by virtue of one's origin, which in the case of the 'Aussiedler' must be biologically proven; proof in the case of immigrants is not even required since in fact, it wouldn't be documentable. Consequently, in the given example, no reference whatsoever is made to the possibility of assimilation or integration: everything is inescapably defined by the family tree.

Hence, one can find oneself confronted by paradoxical cases, e.g. fully 'Germanized' children of immigrants who remain foreigners and 'Aussiedler', particularly those originating from the Asian Republics of the ex-Soviet Union who, in spite of rapidly becoming 'natives', are neither able to express themselves in what may be considered their mother-tongue and who are not able to adapt to today's German life-style and culture (Römhild, 1994: 107 ff.; Graudenz and Römhild, 1990: 313 ff.; 1993: 17 ff.).

In the preceding chapter, we underlined how the principle of 'jus soli' in French 'ethnic philosophy' tends to dedramatize the tie between consanguinity or extraction on the one hand and territoriality on the other. In the German 'ethnic discourse', one might maintain just the opposite, i.e. to rigidly conform to the 'jus sanguinis' doctrine emphasizes the relationship between genealogy and territory.

To conclude this chapter, it can be said that all of the elements thus far exposed, from the specific concept of 'Volk' to the principle of 'jus sanguinis' and ultimately to the idea of ethnic, homogenous space, indicate the existence of a pronounced 'geography of ethnicity and mono-ethnic territoriality' in the German 'ethnic discourse'. This makes, for different or even opposing, reasons to that of the French 'ethnic philosophy', the recognition of minorities, particularly immigrants, difficulty achieved in the Federal Republic.

'Ethnic Discourse' in the Soviet Union: Citizenship and Nationality

Certainly the Soviet Union, as the Russian Empire, cannot be classified as one of the National States but should rather be seen as a pluri-ethnic community. The fathers of the October Revolution realized this, and the so-called 'solution to the National question' was one of the first worries of the Bolsheviks after power was seized in 1917. All the most visible leaders of the Communist Party formulated 'ethnic discourses' which were in part expressed through the political strategies designed to solve this same problem.

Both Lenin and Stalin particularly distinguished themselves as theoreticians on the National question, and Stalin, up to his death in 1953, was considered a peerless expert on this subject (Skalnik, 1990: 183; Tishkov, 1989: 10). It was, in fact, these men who, by way of theoretical reflections and corresponding political decisions, 'definitively solved', according to the official version, this thorny problem. Due to the strength of the positions taken by Lenin and then by Stalin, it was recognized that the Soviet Union was a pluri-ethnic entity, a fact which was sanctioned by the founding treaty of the country in 1923. This multi-ethnicity, however, was considered transitory since socialism would set irreversible processes of fusion and assimilation into motion. From these dynamics would come the birth of the 'Soviet people', i.e. an ethnically homogenous social aggregation which would cancel out all national differences. Quite paradoxically, although not entirely, the thoughts of Lenin and Stalin were reminiscent of the nineteenth century liberal theoreticians who saw in the national movements and in the formation of vast National States the characteristics of a transitory epoch on the path toward a planetary society without ethno-cultural differences (Hobsbawm, 1992: 45). The 'ethnic discourse' in the Soviet Union after the death of Stalin was largely dictated by the Communist Party, most particularly by the Institute for Marxism/Leninism at the Central Committee. Even the anthropologists played their part, although to a lesser degree. For years, Soviet 'etnografija' took delight in developing a specific theory of 'etnos' which painted an idyllic picture of inter-ethnic relations within the country, thus implicitly guaranteeing the aforementioned evolutionist arguments (Skalnik, 1990: 184 ff.). In fact, in this way, Soviet 'etnografija' systematically concealed all of the conflicts which had always existed and which exploded at the end of the eighties, thus revealing how the theories of Lenin and Stalin had been incorrect or mystifying.

Nevertheless, admitting the pluri-ethnicity, albeit transitory, of the Soviet Union meant recognizing, if only on paper, the national specificity of the various members of the Federation while at the same time acknowledging the existence of a Soviet identity. Thus, one could be Ukrainian, Armenian or Belorussian and at the same time Soviet.

In this way, a double regime was created which distinguished between citizenship and nationality. One cannot omit the fact that this Soviet 'solution in a nutshell', in reality, had its roots in sociological thinking bearing a bourgeois stamp. The regime of double affiliation implicitly tries to conciliate the famous elaborated dichotomies of Durkheim and Tönnies. In fact, Soviet citizenship is part of the universalist sphere linked to the macrostructure of 'organic solidarity' and 'Gesellschaft', while nationality, in as much as it deals with 'etnos', concerns the particularistic dimension inherent in the microstructure of the 'mechanic solidarity' and 'Gemeinschaft'. It is not by chance that in Soviet 'etnografija' the term 'ethnic community' ('etničeskaja obščnost') is synonymous with 'ethnos' (Bromlej, 1977: 25; Tokarev, 1964; Kozlov, 1967).

Furthermore, it should be remembered that reflections evoking dual affiliation and linked to the democratic movements, although unrelated to socialism, had already, long before the October Revolution been expressed by Russian exiles. Schnapper mentions the names of Dubnov and Dragomanov who, between the end of the nineteenth century and the beginning of the new century, proposed, albeit somewhat embryonically, the separation between citizenship and nationality with the objective of peacefully resolving the tension between Imperial centralism and ethnic particularism existing in the Russia at that time (Schnapper, 1994: 75 ff.). According to Schnapper, this need for cultural autonomy was particularly felt by the Jewish population of Imperial Russia (Schnapper, 1994: 76).

Finally, I would like to stress that the regime of dual affiliation is not uniquely Soviet, but is rather an attempt to combine the German 'ethnic discourse' with that of the French.

Schnapper sees a certain line of continuity between the ideas of Dubnov and Dragomanov and consequently between those of the Soviet 'ethnic discourse', on the one hand, and the 'post-national' projects, such as those of the currently much talked about Jean-Marc Ferry and Jürgen Habermas, on the other (Schnapper, 1994: 77 ff.). This compels one to believe that the Soviet 'ethnic philosophy' was, at least for a certain time, a 'solution in a nutshell', able to make Socialist Universalism compatible with the particularist needs of 'etnos'. Surely, this impression cannot be attributed to this French author who is certainly not suspected of being pro-Soviet, but rather it can be attributed (1) to the fact that the 'ethnic discourse' which revolves around dual affiliation has its own undeniable fascination and (2) to the fact that the model for itself seems, from a purely theoretical point of view, to authentically function.

Setting aside the true intentions of the Soviet political and cultural managers, whose good faith is rightly put in doubt by Schnapper (Schnapper, 1994: 74), the practice of dual affiliation showed itself to be an appalling machine of segregation, discrimination and stigmatization.

The passport in which both Soviet citizenship and national affiliation was registered and in which the Soviet citizen was shown to be 'Latvian', 'Russian', 'Georgian' or 'Jew' was one of the primary instruments used in applying the principle of 'two loads and two measures'. Ideally, dual affiliation should have guaranteed the recognition of rights which were culturally defined and inherent in the minority ethnic communities; in reality, what it did was to reinforce prejudices, rivalry and hatred between the different groups due to the fact that it became a source of clear injustice and favouritism which worked its way into everyday life. Being a Soviet citizen of 'Russian' nationality thus opened the door to many privileges, among which were the rapid acquisition of accommodation, transfer to a more economically developed region such as, for example, the three Baltic countries (Lithuania, Latvia and Estonia) or the rapid accomplishment of certain bureaucratic practice. Being a Soviet citizen of 'Jewish' nationality meant, in a society characterized by chronic shortages, further oppression as well as vexations of every kind, e.g. being refused a telephone line, being assigned an apartment in the extreme periphery of the city, etc.

In fact, the model of dual affiliation contributed to the construction of the Soviet 'ethnocracy' and, by way of selection processes which in principle should never have existed, helped to cement social hierarchies defined by the 'ethnic factor'.

In any case, the Soviet model seems to once again confirm an elementary sociological rule formulated some decades ago by W. E.

Mühlmann, according to which the everyday immediacy of the 'ethnic factor' would seem to possess a greater potential in mobilizing the social actors of abstract concepts such as class consciousness, the state of law or human rights (Mühlmann, 1962: 404; Mühlmann, 1982: 61; Schnapper, 1994: 79). The distinction between citizenship and nationality was even applied, although in different versions, in the satellite countries of East Central Europe. Even in these cases, however, the aforementioned model made itself more noticeable because it was extremely easy to manipulate in accordance with the political opportunities which presented themselves.

It is interesting to take a look at the case of Bulgaria, during which the regime of dual affiliation was maintained up to the eighties when forced Bulgarization and, as an alternative to that, expulsion of Turkish minorities occurred. In fact, as long as the Popular Republic of Bulgaria tolerated the Turkish community, also in an attempt to illustrate to the capitalist West its role as provider of the rights of ethnic minorities in the country, dual appurtenance was maintained, even in identity documents. The distinction between citizenship and nationality was eliminated when it became politically convenient to declare, due to a pretence of spontaneous assimilation into the majority group, that the problem of the minorities had been resolved and that Bulgaria had thus become a mono-ethnic country. It would be well, however, to remember that the Bulgarization of the Turks was a forced process carried out in such a meticulous and capillary way as to touch even personal identity, since these individuals were obliged to change both their first name and surname.

Putting aside this political problem, one could say in conclusion that the Soviet 'ethnic discourse' which materialized as a result of dual affiliation is also characterized by its own intrinsic staticity which, in a certain way, has something in common with the German 'ethnic philosophy', the difference being that the latter generally parts from the presupposition of mono-ethnic territoriality.

The Soviet Union, a pluri-national and multi-ethnic State, recognized even by official ideology as being such, was not subdivided into stagnant compartments which rendered the borders between the different groups of which it was made up ethnically impermeable. Migratory movements, perhaps also partially encouraged and planned with the intention of 'Russianizing' entire regions considered strategic, and mass deportation for political reasons have not been without consequence but rather have led to the formation of nuclei of binational families whose descendents, in their turn, have entered into matrimony with members of other nationalities. On the other hand, migratory processes always carry with them phenomena of acculturation and of variation of identity. How does one then 'cage' someone e.g. in his supposed 'Ukrainity', knowing full well that his mother is 'Russian', that his grandmother came from Central Asia, that he speaks Russian prevalently in his everyday life, that he only has a rudimentary knowledge of what the authorities have saddled him with as his mother-tongue and that he has lived and worked for a quarter of a century in Latvia?

In spite of the declarations made by the Soviet ethnographers, according to whom 'etnos' should be considered a dynamic entity (Eidlitz Kuoljok, 1985: 28 ff.), the above mentioned 'ethnic discourse' is imbued with an 'essentialism' and 'primordialism' which do not take into consideration the 'situational' dimension of identity.

'Ethnic Discourses' in Post-Communist Countries between Historic Reversibility and Mono-Ethnic Territoriality

The collapse of Communist totalitarianism has brought about in practically all of the countries of East Central Europe a radical modification of the 'ethnic discourses' which, during the forty-five years of Socialism, were based upon the model of the Soviet 'ethnic philosophy' I have just mentioned.

The new 'ethnic discourses' in the post-Communist countries, as with many reformatory activities ranging from agrarian reforms to the reprivatization of various political-economic sectors, are part of the general evaluation which has been made, officially or otherwise, during the period between 1945 and 1989.

It is superfluous to recall the mass enthusiasm which followed the fall of the Berlin Wall and the subsequent certainty of a quick and painless transition. Today, five years later, those convictions have given way to perplexity and disappointment, proof of which is the rise to power of governments dominated by ex-communist politicians such as exist in Lithuania, Poland, Hungary, Bulgaria and Latvia.

Nevertheless, the 'ethnic discourses' which have shaped some of the new laws concerning nationality/citizenship remain linked, at least for the moment, to the first phase of transition, i.e. to when, with iconoclastic passion, every last testimony to the past regime was cancelled. From this perspective, the aforementioned 'ethnic discourses' are founded on a concept of 'historic reversibility' which puts forward the idea of a return to a pre-socialist stage in which the social-political order is not contaminated by Communist experience. Socialism is thus interpreted by means of the metaphor of a 'blind alley' from which one can escape only by returning to the starting point; at the same time, the period between 1945 and 1989 is considered a 'black hole', during which history doesn't show evolutionary processes able to produce social-economic progress.

Following the myth of 'historic reversibility', the 'ethnic discourses' in the countries of post-socialist transformation reject the Soviet model of dual affiliation and tend to restore the concepts of nationality/citizenship which were in force in the pre-socialist period and which, to a large extent, referred to the German 'ethnic philosophy' which, as already shown, was based upon the idea of 'Volk'. One must also remember that up to the end of the Second World War, the National States of East Central Europe considered themselves to be the political-territorial expression of an ethnic group defined by a common culture and language, as well as by the same origins and genealogy. One must add, however, that in many cases these States were oriented towards French administrative centralism, as was partly the case in Bulgaria, which was possibly mediated by the Italian experience.

This was so despite the marked linguistic, religious and cultural heterogeneity of almost all of the countries of this region which were and are distinguished by a lack of accord between real political frontiers and imagined ethnic confines. In accordance with the German 'ethnic discourse', the National States of pre-socialist East Central Europe never developed a true sensitivity towards the problem faced by the minorities in their territory, in spite of the fact that each citizen was aware of these minority individuals' existence (Bibó, 1993: 169 ff.).

In fact, in many countries of East Central Europe of that time, the minorities were objects of marginalization, oppression, forced assimilation, expulsion or of conquests on the part of vindictive neighbours who wanted to restore the 'historic borders'. Bibó analysed in particular the situation of three countries, i.e. Poland, Czechoslovakia and Hungary, thereby revealing the various discriminatory strategies, both on an official level and occurring in everyday life.

In Poland, a profound sense of diffidence reigned towards the Catholic Lithuanians and the Orthodox Belorussians resident in the North East of the country; these sentiments were notably accentuated in regard to the six million Ukrainian residents living in the territories conquered during the war against the Soviet Union which began with the 'Miracle on the Vistula' and ended 1920 with peace in Riga (Bibó, 1993: 141 ff.).

Analogous attitudes towards specific minorities could also be seen in Czechoslovakia, to which were added measures aimed at discouraging cultural and linguistic autonomy as well as extremist projects which petitioned for the expulsion of populations which didn't belong to the Slav world, such as the Hungarians of Slovakia (Bibó, 1993: 146 ff.).

However, in Hungary, the great loser of the First World War in East Central Europe, a hatred of those ex-minorities (Croatians, Romanians, Russians, etc.) who repudiated the 'historic borders' of the country to unite with the other States, developed. The official policy, the intellectual 'elites' connected with 'identity management' and vast strata of the Hungarian population consequently cultivated not only irredentist ideas with the aim of annexing the territories inhabited by Magyar populations, but also the dream of forcefully reconquering the 'treacherous', alien populations and of thus re-establishing the 'Great Hungary' in its 'historic borders' (Bibó, 1993: 145).

This catalogue of negative sentiments and discriminatory official measures in regard to minorities or ex-minorities is even more extensive when taking into consideration Romania, Bulgaria, and the Kingdom of Yugoslavia. All three of these countries were characterized by the presence of a majority ethnic group which aspired, without compromise, to a political-cultural hegemony, haughtily ignoring the minority communities on National territory.

The indifference or even outright scorn of the problems of the minorities was not, however, only palpable in everyday ethnic relations and in the question of internal policy, but was also so on a level of international relations. The presupposed National States of pre-socialist East Central Europe, being obliged to draw up international agreements concerning the rights of minorities, which in turn were guaranteed, at least in theory, by the League of Nations, put on a brave face. However, even after having accepted the principles of the various treaties, conventions and declarations, they almost always categorically refused to respect the commitments they had made.

Horak shows us that practically every State of this region, from Estonia to Bulgaria, signed documents of a diverse nature concerning the defence of minority groups ('Minderheitenschutz'), but adds that between 1920 and 1931 the League of Nations had to register a good 525 petitions connected with the violation of the cited agreements. The four countries which were most implicated in these violations were Poland (155 petitions), Romania (63 petitions), Czechoslovakia (60 petitions) and Yugoslavia (53 petitions) (Horak, 1985: 7 ff.). As one can already see from this desultory data, the 'defence' of minorities on the part of the League of Nations was not very effective and in practice was essentially limited to a pathetic 'moral pressure'. The societies of this region thus became, almost without exception, 'ethnocracies' in which the majority community, both on a level of 'ethnic discourse' and on a level of everyday inter-ethnic relations, expressed a clear sentiment of superiority towards the other groups (Veiter, 1984: 24; Bibó, 1993: 172). According to Bibó, this presumed 'right to supremacy' which one finds in the 'ethnic discourses' of East Central Europe before socialism is a slightly modified version of the German concept of 'Herrenvolk', in virtue of which a 'people' or a 'nation' understood as an ethnic entity are called to carry out a 'mission' of dominion over others (Bibó, 1993: 172).

However, insensitivity to the ethno-cultural 'difference' doesn't always automatically carry with it processes of marginalization and discrimination. It has, in fact, been historically demonstrated that, in certain cases such as those of pre-war Estonia and Latvia, where at least six culturally, linguistically and religiously different populations have lived together, everyday life has gone on with a surprising reciprocal respect and mutual understanding between majority and minority groups. There was a common effort to limit clashing interests, although many authors stress the fact that, in spite of these attempts, there continued to be a 'plate glass wall' between the various groups (Pistohlkors, 1994: 452 ff.; Bosse, 1986: 329 ff.). The case of the two Baltic countries is particularly interesting, above all in regard to the Germans who were a minority ethnic group but who, up to the end of the First World War, were economically dominant since they made up the great land-owning class. With the independence of Estonia and Latvia, they were dispossessed of their land through agrarian reforms and thus lost their economic predominance. They easily acquired, however, either Estonian or Latvian citizenship and were able to organize themselves politically. In addition, only a few decided to emigrate (Pistohlkors, 1994: 482 ff.).

Nevertheless, the most recurrent theme in the above-mentioned 'ethnic discourses' is still that of 'mono-ethnic space' inhabited, from a cultural point of view, by a homogenous people. Bibó rightly points out that the history of East Central Europe after the fall of the multi-national empires is characterized by continual territorial vindications of the new States (Bibó, 1993: 171).

The project inherent in these vindications is usually the materialization of imagined ethnic borders, for which reason 'ethnic discourses' take on, in this perspective, a clear 'territoriocentric' character. The territorial argument, which often takes on an extremely obsessive tone, thus becomes fundamental. For this reason, the rebirth, strength, power and prosperity of the nation is exclusively seen in map terms, that is in terms of a definition of borders (Bibó, 1993: 171).

The fact that the components of a similar 'philosophy' hark back, explicitly or implicitly, to Herder or other German authors in his wake appears incontestable. In fact, the ideas of Herder had a remarkable impact, albeit indirectly, in East Central Europe; one could almost say that he was better received in this region than in his own country. In relation to this, it is enough to recall a strong personality such as Vuk S. Karadzic (1787–1864), the most important ideologist of Serb nationalism in the last century, or of brothers Dimiter and Konstantin Miladinov in Bulgaria. However, this shouldn't surprise us since the 'Herderian' authors of East Central Europe spent long periods in Germany and Austria (Grmek, Gjidara and Simac, 1993: 39). Nevertheless, examples of many other 'Herderians' in East Central Europe exist, amongst whom were folklorists, philologists, historians of law as well as other national identity 'builders' or 'managers' such as artists or pedagogues. I would, however, like to point out that, in the countries mentioned, Herder has undergone a substantial reinterpretation, by which the romantic, particularist and differentialist ideas present in Herder's work clearly had the upper hand over the general establishment which had received, as already mentioned, a stamp of illuministic universalism. It is not so much Herderian thought as the 'Herderianism' of many intellectuals which is at the root of the 'ethnic discourses' of pre-socialist East Central Europe.

Let us, however, return to the present situation. The myth of 'historic reversibility' has certainly reactualized the 'ethnic discourses' of the 'status quo ante'. It is for this reason that the types of ethnicism in East Central Europe to which we bear witness today appear 'archaic' or 'romantic'; we tend to assimilate them just because their 'Herderianism' is reminiscent of the nationalism of a nineteenth century matrix.

In East Central Europe today, 'territoriocentrism', which revolves around an ideal of 'mono-ethnic space', has once again become extremely topical. It is enough to think how important territorial controversy has once again become as, for example, the Hungarian covert vindications in regard to Slovakia and Romania, the contention between the Baltic countries and Russia over the possession of microscopic territories attributed to the latter by Stalinist despotism, the unappeased interest of Romania for South Dobrudzha which belongs to Bulgaria, the contention between Greece and Albania, and finally the Macedonian question in which almost all of the Balkan States have become involved. 'Territorial-centralism' and the idea of 'mono-ethnic space' are particularly palpable in ex-Yugoslavia, where territorial vindications and the myth of 'ethnic purity' are the inseparable binomial of the different 'ethnic philosophies' expressed by various 'warlords'.

However, there are substantial differences between the 'ethnic discourses' of the past and those of the present, some of which have been lucidly highlighted by Hobsbawm and which are particularly pertinent to East Central Europe (Hobsbawm, 1992).

The first thing to remember is that the 'ethnic discourses' of the last century concerning the formation of the National States were of an aggregative nature and were projected towards the future. The idea was to create the most extensive, political-territorial entities as possible, while the National State, seen as a necessary institution, would remain transitory, focusing upon a homogenous planetary society (Hobsbawm, 1992: 43 ff.). In the name of a greater 'purity' and 'genuineness', the current 'ethnic discourses' in East Central Europe are of a much more dissociative and differentialist nature, as is exemplified by the divisions in ex-Czechoslovakia, ex-Yugoslavia, ex-Sovietic Moldavia and in the Caucasian Republics (Georgia, Armenia). When it comes right down to it, schismatic tendencies prevail over associative ones.

In respect to the nationalism of the nineteenth century, one notices a substantial radicalization in the 'ethnic discourses' of East Central Europe in that the ideal of 'mono-ethnic territoriality' is accentuated. The result is that one tends to be less disposed to accept foreigners or minorities in what is considered one's 'own' space. The example of the two Baltic countries, Latvia and Estonia, despite being noted for their openness in the pre-war period and currently otherwise known for just the opposite in regard to alien groups, is surely a symbolic and unsettling illustration of this assertion.

Conclusion

Our analysis of the 'ethnic discourses' in Europe which, at least in part, represented and in fact still represents the ideological basis for the legitimacy of the National States, shows us that, at present on our continent, neither a cultural tradition nor institutional tools exist which can adequately address the problem of minorities. Both French 'assimilationism' and German 'differentialism' leave little space for an acceptable solution. In addition, the Soviet model has, for intrinsic reasons and political motives, shown itself to be largely unfeasible. It is therefore necessary to abandon the idea of a National State and of a pluri-national State and to begin to familiarize ourselves in reasoning within the framework of an 'anational' State. This would introduce a new 'discourse' which would take into consideration the 'diversities' beyond the 'contemporary ethnic hysteria', particularly in the countries of East Central Europe.

Bibliography

Benda, J. (1965), *La trahison des clercs*, Paris: Pauvert.

Bibó, I. (1993), *Misère des petits Etats d'Europe de l'Est*, Paris: Albin Michel.

Bosse, H. (1986), 'Die gläserne Wand: Der lettische Mensch in der deutsch-baltischen Literatur', *Journal of Baltic Studies*, 17, pp. 329–349.

Bromlej, J. V. (1977), *Ethos und Ethnographie*, Berlin: Akademie Verlag.

Brubaker, R. (1994), *Staats-Bürger: Deutschland und Frankreich im historischen Vergleich*, Hamburg: Junius.

Eidlitz Kuoljok, K. (1985), *The Revolution in the North: Soviet Ethnography and Nationality Policy*, Uppsala: Acta Universitatis Upsaliensis, Studia Multiethnica Upsaliensia.

Finkielkraut, A. (1987), *La défaite de la pensée*, Paris: Gallimard.

Graudenz, I. and Römhild, R. (1990), 'Kulturkontakt unter Deutschen: Zur interaktiven Identitätsarbeit von Spätaussiedlern', *Bildung und Erziehung*, 3, pp. 313–324.

——, and Römhild, R. (1993), 'Fremde Deutsche: Aussiedler und Fremdenfeinklichkeit – eine Herausforderung an das bundesrepublikanische Selbstverständnis', in P. Döbrich and G. Rutz (eds), *Fremdenhass und politischer Extremismus – was kann die Schule tun?*, Frankfurt am Main: Gesellschaft zur Förderung der pädagogischen Forschung, pp. 17–29.

Grawert, R. (1973), *Staat und Staatsangehörigkeit. Verfassungsgeschichtliche Unter-suchung zur Entstehung der Staatsangehörigkeit*, Berlin: Duncker und Humbolt.

Greverus, I.-M. (1987), *Kultur und Alltagswelt. Einführung in Fragen der Kulturanthropologie*, Frankfurt am Main: Notizen, Institut für Kulturanthropologie und Europäische Ethnologie.

Grmek, M., Gjidara, M. and Simac, N. (ed.), (1993), *Le nettoyage ethnique: Documents historiques sur une idéologie serbe*, Paris: Fayard.

Hobsbawm, E. J. (1992), *Nationen und Nationalismus: Mythos und Realität seit 1780*, Frankfurt am Main: Campus.

Horak, M. (ed.), (1985), *Eastern European National Minorities 1919–1980: A Handbook*, Littleton: Libraries Unlimited.

Kozlov, W. I. (1967), *O poniatii etničeskoi obščnosti*, Moskwa.

Lochak, D. (1988), 'Etrangers et citoyens au regard du droit', in C. Wihtol de Wenden (ed.), *La citoyenneté*, Paris: Edilig–Fondation Diderot, pp. 73–85.

Mühlmann, W.-E. (1962), *Homo Creator: Abhandlungen zur Soziologie, Anthropologie und Ethnologie*, Wiesbaden: Harassowitz.

——, (1982), 'Zur Soziologie komplexer Gesellschaften', *Schweizerische Zeitschrift für Soziologie*, 8(1), pp. 53–62.

Naïr, S. (1992), *Le regard des vainqueurs: Les enjeux français de l'immigration*, Paris: Grasset.

Pistohlkors, G. v. (ed.), (1994), *Deutsche Geschichte im Osten Europas: Baltische Länder*, Berlin: Siedler Verlag.

Christian Giordano

Römhild, R. (1994), 'Staying or Leaving? Experience and Expectations of the German Minority in the Former Soviet Union', *Anthropological Journal on European Cultures*, 3(1), pp. 107–121.

Schnapper, D. (1994), *La communauté des citoyens: Sur l'idée moderne de nation*, Paris: Gallimard.

Skalnik, P. (1990), 'Soviet "etnografiia" and the National(ities) Question', *Cahiers du monde russe et soviétique*, XXXI(2–3), pp. 183–191.

Talmon, J.-L. (1967), *Destin d'Israel*, Paris: Calmann-Lévy.

Tishkov, V. A. (1989), 'O novych podchodach v teorii i pratike mežnacionalnich otnošenii', *Sovetskaia etnografiia*, 5, pp. 10–18.

Tokarev, S. A. (1964), *Problema tipov etničeskich obščnosti (k metodologičeskim problemam etnografii)*, Moskwa.

Veiter, T. (1984), *Nationalitätenkonflikt und Volksgruppenrecht im ausgehenden 20. Jahrhundert*, München: Bayerische Landeszentrale für politische Bildung.

Vovelle, M. (1989), 'Révolution, Liberté, Europe', in Institut de Recherches et d'éducation permanente du Territoire de Belfort (ed.), *L'idée de nation et de citoyenneté en France et dans les pays de langue allemande sous la Révolution*, Belfort, pp. 195–210.

Weber, M. (1956), *Wirtschaft und Gesellschaft*, Tübingen: J.C.B. Mohr.

Weil, P. (1988), 'La Politique française d'immigration (entre 1974 et 1986) et la Citoyenneté', in C. Withol de Wenden (ed.), *La citoyenneté*, Paris: Edilig-Fondation Diderot, pp. 187–200.

–10–

Re-Imagining the Jew in Hungary: The Reconstruction of Ethnicity through Political Affiliation[1]

Donna Meryl Goldstein

Introduction

Why are Hungarians of Jewish background still culturally constructed as foreigners in Hungary despite their attempts, during the last forty years, to assimilate and self-censor any revitalization of Jewish identity either in religious or ethnic terms? Why has contemporary nationalism in Hungary accelerated both the rise of democratic institutions and a publicly legitimized form of anti-Semitism? Also, why are Hungarian-ness and Jewish-ness, in popular definitions of Hungarian citizenship, mutually exclusive? In order to come to a better understanding of these questions, there is the need to come to grips with the Hungarian concept of citizenship, how it has shifted at various historical moments, and, specifically for this case, how it has been used and applied to Hungarians of Jewish background. In the following sections, I explore the changing concepts of cultural citizenship in Hungary in recent manifestations of right-wing and popular discourse, despite the accommodating behaviour of a large proportion of urban assimilated Hungarians of Jewish background. For many Hungarians, Jews are still assumed to be entirely culturally different than the 'real

1. An early version of this chapter was presented at the Annual Meeting of the American Anthropological Association, Washington D.C. 1993, on a panel titled, 'Citizenship Contested: Cultural Difference, Belonging and Not Belonging in Nation-States'. I would like to thank Anna Werner and her family for their insights and support, Eric Hirsch for early conversations on this topic, and Gita Steiner-Khamsi for her comments. I also thank Vera H. and her network in Budapest for research and translation support of all kinds. I take responsibility for all interpretations made here.

Hungarians', and on these grounds are discriminated against.[2]

In 1993, approximately three years after the radical economic changes from a centrally planned economy to a free market economy, and in the midst of a political rhetoric of anti-communism and demo-cracy, Hungary seemed to be experiencing a rebirth of anti-Semitic discourse. The leader of the ruling government's party (Hungarian Democratic Forum), Istvan Csurka, announced that there was an international, Zionist-inspired conspiracy against Hungary that included the International Monetary Fund.[3] During that year, I interviewed twenty middle- and upper-class citizens of ages varying from fourteen to eighty-four, most of whom felt some connection to a Jewish past or a Jewish background. I hoped that an understanding of this particular group's subject position, that is how they viewed themselves and their own identity as Hungarian citizens, would somehow provide a clue to understanding the resurgent nationalism and anti-Semitic discourse which seemed to characterize the changing notions of citizenship accompanying the Hungarian political and economic transitions. It seemed that the image of the Jew as 'foreigner' and 'outsider' in Hungary was historically persistent despite changing circumstances.

The Hungarian construction of alterity, for example, seems to have changed drastically in the post-Communist era. Jewish Hungarians in the post-1989 period, it seems, are seen as the generalized 'Others' on the grounds of their location in metropolitan areas as well as their past political alliances with the Communist Party. These characteristics ought to be examined not simply as chance happenings, but rather as a 'defining' feature for many of those Jews who reconstituted their lives in Budapest at the end of the Second World War and who opted to stay in Hungary after the events of 1956 (where an attempt was made to reform Communist politics by a broad spectrum of alliances from the political left and right). Additionally, their metropolitanism, which connects them to westernization/modernization processes and new joint-venture capitalism projects, characterize them as 'new' enemies within a developing post-communist society which is exper-iencing new levels of unemployment and capitalist forms of insecurity.

2. The rhetoric of exclusion which uses cultural difference rather than racial difference has been noted recently in the literature on European integration and immigration, most recently and cogently in anthropology by Stolcke (1995). This chapter offers a preliminary investigation of one case concerning one particular group which has already passed through various exclusionary moments based on shifting conceptualizations of 'foreignness' and 'otherness'.

3. 'Hungarian Steps Up Attack on Rightist Opponent', *New York Times*, 9 March, 1993, p. A7.

In the Hungarian case, Jews are simultaneously re-imagined as both 'new capitalists' and 'old communists', both potential enemies within the new Hungary.

Cultural Citizenship Along Religious, Linguistic and Political Lines

Rosaldo (1994: 402) has used the notion of 'cultural citizenship' to refer to 'the right to be different and to belong in a participatory democratic sense'. According to Rosaldo, the idea of cultural citizenship assumes that, 'in a democracy, social justice calls for equity among all citizens, even when such differences as race, religion, class, gender, or sexual orientation potentially could be used to make certain people less equal or inferior to others'. Rosaldo uses the term to speak about the North American context and the lines of exclusion that have been historically drawn in cases which excluded women from voting and, more recently, excluded polyglot citizens from standard citizenship by imagining a 'one language–one nation' model as the prototype of the nation-state. I find this construction of cultural citizenship useful in tracking the shifting case of Hungarian notions of belonging with regard to Hungarians of Jewish background. In this case, notions of citizenship have moved from religious to linguistic markers, and in the contemporary case, towards political lines of demarcation, each time reconstructing notions of citizenship in a manner that made dual identity, or in Rosaldo's terms, 'polyglot' citizenship a conceptual and real impossibility.

Jews in the Age of Linguistic Nationalism

In the mid-1800s, Jews that found themselves living within the boundaries of the Austro-Hungarian Empire were able to choose an identity as Hungarian citizens. According to Deák (1983: 1), the Habsburg Monarchy, and its army, although German-speaking, 'showed no preference for any one nationality during the entire period of its existence'. Rather, in the Compromise Agreement of 1867, which divided the territory into the Austrian Empire and the Hungarian Kingdom, what counted was that Magyar became the official language for the Hungarian Kingdom and, hence, linguistic commitment became the sole prerequisite to claim citizenship. In this period, what could be called the 'nationalization' of the Jews of East Central Europe occurred. By 1880, 58.5 per cent of all Jews (within the borders of

Hungary at that time) indicated Magyar as their mother tongue, and by 1910, 77.8 per cent (Deák, 1983: 7). Deák (1983) estimates that between the 1780s and 1914, over 700,000 Jews became Magyars and thus citizens on the basis of language choice. Another important feature of the construction of alterity concerning Jews in Hungarian history is that Jews who came to Budapest in the nineteenth century were not identified as a separate ethnic group, but were usually counted as Germans (Deák, 1983: 11). The situation could be described in the following manner:

> Prior to 1848, Jews were forbidden, at least theoretically, to settle in most Hungarian cities. Then came emancipation, thanks to the efforts of Magyar liberal nationalists, and within a few decades the situation had changed fundamentally. By 1900, one out of every four inhabitants of Budapest, a metropolis of close to one million inhabitants, was Jewish, and so was every other voter. (Deák, 1983: 14)

Historians have noted that many of the Jews in this context willingly gave up religious practice and spoke Magyar as a sign of loyalty to the Hungarian nation-state and as a sign of their willingness to become Hungarian citizens. We don't have a set of documents to tell us exactly what these subjects in this particular position felt in these times. However, part of the standard interpretation by my contemporary elderly informants concerning their own ancestors was that Jews in the Austro-Hungarian Empire were already highly assimilated and never very religious. They were always, to borrow Rosaldo's notion, 'polyglot citizens'. Many of the elderly Jews I interviewed spoke with pride about parents who spoke German and Magyar equally well. According to Deák (1983), because of the numerical decline via assimilation, the representation of both Germans and Jews as separate ethnic groups in Hungary occurred long before the 1940s:

> The Jewish communities in the Habsburg Monarchy flourished as much as the German, thanks to the successful urbanization of the Jewish rural population and the influx of immigrants from Russia. But parallel emigration to the West, a declining birth rate, and the total assimilation of many into the Gentile world caused the Jewish population to diminish in some parts of East Central Europe even before the end of the Habsburg Monarchy. (Deák, 1983: 2–3)

It is important to consider this early assimilation mode of Hungarian Jews via language choice and the promise of Hungarian citizenship. In this first round of becoming Hungarian in the mid-1800s, Jews in urban settings gave up any vestiges of religious identity and made Magyar their language of choice in order to belong. In this particular 'social contract' between the liberal ruling class and assimilating Jews, the categories declared Jews to be Magyars in *nationality* and Israelites in *denomination* (Várdy, 1986: 137). According to Várdy, this construction gave rise to a long-term identity crisis among assimilated Jews in Hungary:

> The distortions of assimilation gave rise to examples of grossly overdoing 'Magyarism', to abject conformity or a feeling of hopeless outsiderhood. The gentrified Jew, the Jewish contractor raised to the peerage, the rancorous internationalist, the bourgeois closet-Bolshevik, the international celebrity writing in several languages at once, the Habsburg partisan, irredentist, Stalinist, and anti-Zionist Jew – not to speak of the secretly observing high Party functionary – have all been conspicuous examples of a crisis of identity of the whole Hungarian society which has especially been dogging assimilating Jews for more than a century. (Várdy, 1986: 137)

Várdy also views 'modern' anti-Semitism as having emerged in Hungary by about 1880 and as having been based on the idea of 'race', which in its particular Hungarian form culminated with the vision of Arrow Cross fascists in 1944.

Jews as Capitalists

As the new Hungary turns toward the capitalist West for economic aid, it is the urban and educated middle class who are in the position to enter into the joint-venture craze. To some Hungarians, this group looks overwhelmingly Jewish. So much of the literature analysing the Holocaust has explored this dimension of anti-Semitism and the accompanying representation of Jews, which promoted the imagery of the 'Jew as capitalist' in pre-war Europe, and how this imagery helped to flame the anti-Semitic programme of the time. In Hungary, the statistics concerning the class position of Jews before the war have been analysed as part of an ethnicity/class model for explaining anti-Semitism. According to Karady (1986), in 1945 only about a third of the Jews of Budapest were working class, and this despite the 1920 *numerus clausus*[4] which forced many Jews to emigrate or to take menial jobs. An institutionalized selection process beginning in 1920 and

4. *Numerus clausus* officially limited the number of Jews permitted to enter the University system.

continuing through to the anti-Jewish Laws of the 1930s, in varying degrees restricted the employment of Jews in certain professions and limited their access to university education.

One of the recurring 'self-descriptors' used by informants of Jewish background to describe their ancestors was that of being 'talented' and 'clever'. Given the many institutionalized barriers to Jewish survivorship and mobility in Budapest since 1920, it makes sense as to why these words so frequently emerge in oral history reports. If there is any common thread of identification among these individuals, it lies in the great deal of pride each of them express about some 'clever and talented' relative that persevered in spite of difficult historical circumstances, including the events of 1944–45, where Hungarians of Jewish origin were forced into ghettos and over 500,000 perished in labour and Nazi concentration camps.

Jews as Communists

It is of interest to note that although the great majority of Hungarian Jews perished in the last months of the Second World War, some did survive and, rather than emigrating, re-established their lives in Hungary and more specifically in Budapest. Várdy (1986) estimates that 60 per cent of Jews within the area of present-day Hungary perished and almost 80 per cent of provincial Jewry was exterminated (Várdy, 1986: 134–135). Since there have been no separate census figures since 1949 indicating religious or racial origin, the numbers suggest that approximately 80,000–100,000 Jews have survived and most are in Budapest. Karady (1986: 87) argues that Jews who survived the Holocaust and returned to Hungary after the war were, in some cases, seeking 'compensatory' education for their situation before the war, and many of the new institutions were Party schools which produced a new power elite.

The children of survivors, who were either very young during the war years or born immediately after the war, generally celebrate Christmas, are atheists, and are thoroughly urban – and most of them claim they did not know they were Jewish or of Jewish origin until they were adolescents. Their parents, many of whom became Communist Party members after the war, hoped that the question of Jewish identity would be erased by complete devotion to the Party, and they shrouded their Jewish origins in self-censorship and vague references to the past, especially with regard to the war years. That second generation of adults, who are today in their forties and fifties, explain almost ritualistically the surprise that they felt as teenagers when they found out that they were 'of Jewish origin'. Many of them replicated this strategy with their own children, delaying the mention of a Jewish past to this next generation. The consistency of these stories of 'closeted identities' is interesting to consider. It highlights the extent to which, in many cases, Jewish identity was and continues to be a label maintained externally rather than by the subjects themselves. Hence, as Magyar was the marker for citizenship within the nation-state, in the Communist era, political allegiance to the Party became the marker and the guarantor of citizenship. For many Jews of this generation, claiming devotion to the Communist Party was not only a form of claiming citizenship as it was constructed at the time, but was also a final assimilatory note into an ideological stance which made Party affiliation and Jewish identity incompatible. From the subject of Jewish background's position, the definition of assimilation shifted in these different contexts, and compliance rather than simple existence meant access to social mobility and the rights of citizenship.

One particularly compelling explanation for why Jews were successful Communists in the aftermath of the war had to do simply with how they collectively experienced the war. One must remember the role of Russian soldiers in liberating Budapest from the Germans and from Hungary's own Arrow Cross fascists. Likewise, in terms of 'political reliability', as far as the Soviets were concerned, 'by virtue of their past harassments and thus, indirectly, of their origins, surviving Jews became the possessors of this new kind of inherited social capital' (Karady, 1986: 79). Since so many of these survivors felt no particular religious feelings, having been assimilated and given up religious identity in an earlier round of citizenship politics, they felt that there was no reason to make any specific claim of a Jewish identity. For my informants it was clear that claiming a Jewish identity necessitates a religious faith, one that these informants did not share. They were more comfortable describing themselves in terms of having 'a Jewish background'. At the same time, however, they had seen labour and concentration camps or been forced into the ghetto during the war years and their lives were forever transformed by these collective experiences. In this context, the collective biography of suffering and the political choice to support Communist Party politics led to a new level of erasure of Jewish identity in any overtly ethnic or religious sense. An important aspect of Communist Party politics, it ought to be remembered, was that they were anti-nationalist and, for the most part, prohibited overt manifestations of anti-Semitism. The formal meritocratic language which sought to abolish class and status privileges as well as anti-Jewish restrictions was an attractive ideology to this surviving cohort (Karady, 1986: 77).

Communist Party doctrine itself strictly forbade anti-Semitism as well as nationalisms of any kind, substituting nationalist discourse with a discourse of 'Communist brotherhood' with neighbouring nations and thereby suppressing particularistic religious sentiments or national identity questions concerning Hungarianness. In practice, religious and ethnic affiliations were supplanted by Communist Party activities. Jews in the Communist Party willingly accepted the unofficial form of anti-Semitism within the Party which they say 'kept anyone with a Jewish face outside of the public view'. They also accepted the Party's attempt to promote members from non-bourgeois roots, and, in this construction, urban bourgeois survivors of Jewish origin were perhaps hindered from mainstream advancement within the Party. Religious and ethnic affiliations were explicitly discouraged and replaced. In this non-religious, non-ethnic world, Jews in the Hungarian Communist Party could feel as Hungarian as anybody else and would swallow what they considered rather muted anti-Semitism in exchange for full citizenship. The elimination of the religious question in the form of 'We are all Communists' for once allowed Jew and non-Jew to claim equal rights of citizenship, although not necessarily to Hungarianness.

The discourse of assimilated Jews in Budapest in 1993 partially reflects this early history: informants mention the participation of their ancestors in the founding of the Hungarian nation, and especially of the glory of ancestors who served in the military as proof of their Hungarianness. This, in turn, is usually cited as proof of their own personal distance from any Jewish cultural or religious identity.

For assimilated Jews in Budapest who became Communists (and Hungarian from their own perspective), the 'Others' were the Ortho-dox Jews who remained isolated from mainstream Hungarian life, spoke Yiddish and not Magyar, and whose religious life, it was believed, made it impossible for them to be 'true' Magyars. From this perspective, one could not be a religious Jew and a secular Hungarian at the same time, and this dichotomy still exists in the minds of most Hungarians today. The ambivalence about the Budapest Jews, however, is likewise expressed not only by contemporary nationalists who construct them as foreign, but also by the few remaining religious Jews in Hungary who question the 'Jewishness' of these survivors in Budapest. One Orthodox Jew who is part of a religious community of 1,000 people in the small city of Debrecen in Northern Hungary said this of the Budapest Jews: 'They don't know anything about the Jewish religion – you cannot separate culture and religion. They celebrate Christmas, intermarry with non-Jews, and they know nothing of the traditions. Most of them are Communists. So, what makes them Jewish anymore?'

The Reinvention of the Past in Times of Political Transition

The 1950s brought an increasingly Stalinist-style Party and group of leaders to power in Hungary, including Rákosi, the Soviet-appointed chief widely known both for his Jewish origins and equally well-known for his own anti-Semitic purges. For most Hungarians, however, he was known ironically as the 'first Jewish king of Hungary' and despised as the pinnacle of *foreign* Soviet domination over sovereign Hungary. (Rákosi had spent many years in exile in the Soviet Union prior to taking power.) For many Hungarians, the continuity and autonomy of the nation was symbolically broken during this particular reign of 'Jewish' terror.

For non-Jewish Hungarians, this confluence of the images, epitomized during the 1950s reign of Rákosi, of the 'Jew as foreigner' and of the 'Jew as Communist', was and remains a very well accepted idea – as accepted as the 'Jew as capitalist' image had been in the years preceding World War II. At the same time, it is, seemingly more in the construction of the folk and 'authentic' folk tradition that Hungarians are searching for a new sense of national identity in the context of a rapidly changing Europe.

Hungarians, at specific moments of re-imagining their past, trace themselves back to ancestry with Mongolian plains tribes and to warriors such as 'Attila the Hun'. Hofer (1991) outlines the way in which rival notions of Hungarianness have been developed by competing groups of elite during the last century and argues that the history of national ethnography in Hungary helped develop different symbolic economies including that of modernist/traditionalist, East/West, and populist/communist. Hofer (1991: 153), for example, discusses the 1909 picture entitled 'Attila's Palace' as 'linking the popular and Far Eastern motifs with ancient Hungarian history and with the Huns suggest[ing] that peasant culture retained ancient Oriental traditions and that the predecessors of Hungarians and the Huns earlier lived like the Hungarian peasants and herdsmen of a more recent past'. Hofer's (1991) description of different symbolic economies are interesting to apply to the construction of Jewish identity within a post-communist and emerging nationalist consciousness.

The historical re-imaginings and constructions of the Jew as 'other' continually challenge the dual possibility of Jew as Hungarian, and over time these constructions have encouraged Hungarians of Jewish background to censor the Jewish question from their lives completely. The possibility of a dual identity as both Jew and Hungarian was non-existent, as was the identity as both Jew and Communist. This is illustrated in various practices by the subjects themselves, including conversion to Christianity, the practice of changing one's name, and hiding the details of 1944 from later generations. In their wish to distance themselves from a Jewish identity, this last generation also avoided talking excessively of the war years to their children and grandchildren. The newest manifestation of 'assimilation' is to avoid mentioning loyalty to Communist Party politics and of one's sentiments concerning the events of 1956.

The Uprising of 1956 and the Struggle for the Interpretation of the Past

Especially potent is the interpretation that is assigned to the uprising of 1956 (which briefly began as a reform movement within the Communist Party and meant to move it away from Soviet domination) and its aftermath: Hungarian nationalists have attempted to co-opt the interpretation of 1956, emphasizing its nationalist and revolutionary nature – as something expressive of the first wave of discontent with the Soviet system. Hungarian Communists, and especially those of Jewish origin, are less eager to celebrate the meaning of 1956. While many recognize some of the reformist potentials expressed in the 1956 movement, they generally tend to emphasize the criminal and fascist elements that participated in the uprising; they also have tended to justify the Soviet domination that followed 1956 because of the participation of fascists in the movement. The attempt to claim 1956 in any specific way is so heatedly debated that recently an institute was set up in Budapest to study day by day, and hour by hour the events that occurred during late October and early November in 1956.

The interpretation of 1956 has also embedded within it a piece of 'the Jewish question'. It is tacitly recognized that the fear of the fascist elements in 1956 is what led to the lessening of support by some in the Communist Party. Communist Party members of Jewish origin are recognized as having been influential in emphasizing the fascist elements that participated in the 1956 uprising. This issue continues to be important in terms of defining political identity in the new Hungary. Where you were and which group you ultimately sided with politically during the events of 1956 are partially indicative of one's present political ideology. For many Hungarians of Jewish background who supported the Soviets, it was also a sign of political reliability influenced by their previous experiences during the reign of the Arrow Cross in the 1940s.

In October of 1993, the '1956 Uprising' (as it is known in the

West) was celebrated in Hungary; it has, since the fall of the Communist Party in 1989, become a symbol of Hungarian nationalism and independence from the Soviet Bloc. During the 1992 celebration, skinheads bearing swastikas appeared at the national celebration and forced the president to leave the podium without speaking. The appearance of these young neo-fascists at the celebration confirmed for many in Hungary that feelings of national independence and autonomy from the former Soviet Union are linked to the rise of nationalism, fascism, and increasing anti-Semitism.

In October 1993, the struggle for ownership of the meaning of 1956 continued when a journalist and his oppositional news-team were dismissed because they had allegedly doctored a tape of the celebration of the year before. This journalist, widely respected and also known to be 'of Jewish origin', was accused of exaggerating the strength of the skinhead participation in the 1992 events, and was thus accused of tainting the government's image at home and abroad by implying that the government tolerated support of fascist skinheads. The coverage of events by this press group was also fuelled by the explicit nationalist and anti-Semitic language used by one of the far-right parties, which until late in 1993 was part of the coalition government. The opposition television news programme, the only alternative to the pro-government programme, was thus closed down, leaving all of Hungary with only one pro-government channel. The dismissed journalist was replaced by a right-wing pro-government director who is quoted as saying that Hungarian television had been (until now) 'ruled by the bleating sing-song of Yiddishism'.[5]

The New Nationalism after 1989

Many factors influence the contemporary position of Jews in Hungary. These include a collective history not necessarily determined by feelings of collective identity by the subjects themselves, as well as the changes in Hungary since 1989. These changes include a peaceful abdication of power by the Soviet-aligned Communist Party and the resurgence of Hungarian nationalism in the aftermath of forty years of Communism. Another important factor is that Hungary lost 67 per cent of its national territory and over 3 million ethnic Hungarians in the border shifts at the end of World War I, thus positioning Hungarians

---

5. Zygotian, Dork, 'Anthro 212: To Know or Not to Know', Editorial, The *Hungarian Times*, Monday November 1, 1993, Issue No. 23, p. 1.

as ethnic minorities within neighbouring Romania and the Slovak Republic. The pain of this loss is periodically rekindled by nationalists. Additionally, the continual re-imagining of Hungarian culture as something purely folk rather than urban ('népy' rather than 'urbános'), and which defines 'authentic' Hungarianness within the mythic peasant rural past, is a set of images which right-wing nationalists have drawn upon in a discourse of exclusion. It seems that one form of developing Hungarian national consciousness, perhaps best illustrated in the configuration of images used by extreme right-wing leaders such as Csurka (quoted above), draws upon a construction of Hungarianness that celebrates the existence of a pure Hungarian peasant, is anti-Communist, and is reactive against the forced 'Communist brotherhood' ideology that marked periods of Hungarian post-war history. In this construction of national identity, the ethnic Hungarians who live within the boundaries of present-day Romania represent an integral part of Hungarian authenticity, including their folk dances and musical traditions, which are imagined as 'untouched' by the Soviet period of influence.

The combination of the particular circumstances of Jewish history in the Hungarian context and the post-Communist search for a new identity not tied to Soviet era iconography, has once more situated the Jew as 'Other'. One interpretation of this coinciding of particular histories and the reactivation of peasant imagery, which necessarily excludes Hungarians of Jewish descent, is that in times of rapid political change (which are also accompanied by economic hardships often downplayed by Western commentators), minority groups are excluded from the image of citizenship so that a coherent (if imagined) image of 'we' can emerge (Dominguez, 1993). The two alterity markers labelling Hungarians of Jewish background as both metropolitans and communists in the post-war period and more recently as metropolitans and capitalists in the post-Communist period, although seemingly mutually exclusive at any one point in time, contrast deeply with the image of the rural Hungarian peasant folk tradition and imagery recently being drawn upon.

Recently, Hungary has been experiencing the arrival of new immigrant groups, especially to Budapest, thus continuing the challenge to narrow notions of belonging. The experience of Hungarian Jews and the construction of Hungarian nationalism is key to understanding the possibility of creating a multicultural state, one that is politically democratic but which also provides full cultural citizenship to all. The experience of Jews in Hungary can thus be compared and contrasted with the experiences of newly arriving immigrants in order to understand the processes of assimilation, ethnic identity formation, and the re-creation of nationalism and anti-foreigner sentiment under contemporary circumstances. Despite the highly assimilated nature of contemporary Hungarian Jewry and their historically accommodating behaviour, rising anti-Semitism has recently been reported there.[6] National diversity, even in an imagined form, is potentially threatening to the identity of the nation.

Erasing the Communist Past and the New Nationalism

Since 1989 and the fall of the original Communist Party from power, Hungarians have achieved a new level of social, economic, and political autonomy, are busy erasing the memory of Soviet occupation, and are recovering an independent political and economic structure. Surrounded by the continual disintegration of former Yugoslavia and the Soviet Union, post-Communist Hungary struggles to achieve economic reforms and democratic institutions which bear a uniquely Hungarian national identity. All over Budapest, street names have changed from Soviet-era names to the names of Hungarian poets and national heroes, red stars are being replaced by the Hungarian coat of arms, and statues of Lenin and Soviet soldiers liberating Hungary from Nazi control now reside in a cemetery for Soviet-era monuments far from the city's centre.

Not only public symbols of the Soviet era are being reconstituted, however. There has been a resurgence of religious feelings, and new churches are vying for members in all corners of Hungary. Hungarian nationalism has also emerged as a strong force, and much of the democratic coalition is simultaneously democratic, nationalist, and explicitly anti-Semitic. The Jews of Budapest provide a good example of how Hungarian citizenship is constructed and re-imagined in the post-Communist world. It illustrates that there can be a 'Jewish question' and anti-Semitism even without the presence of a group that self-identifies strongly as Jews, and that Hungarians have been unable to forge a notion of dual identity, whether under fascist, liberal nationalist, or Communist Party rule. The question remains open as to whether in this democratic environment Hungarians will continue to ascribe onto the Jew the identity of foreigner or re-imagine the possibility of a Hungarian who is somehow Jewish. Even more problematic, however, is the realization by many Hungarians of Jewish

6. 'Hungarian Steps Up Attack on Rightist Opponent', *New York Times*, 19 March, 1993, p. A7.

origin that even without an explicit religious or ethnic identity, their urban roots, anti-nationalist sentiments, and political affiliations label them as Jews and as foreign elements from the perspective of a conservative nationalist discourse.

Hungarian nationalism can be felt and seen in various forms. Besides the change in street names and the covering of red stars, museum exhibits of Hungarian folk culture use maps which proudly display the Hungarian borders pre-Trianon treaty. In the theatre, revivals of the Hungarian nationalist play 'Bank Ban' and a new rock musical 'Attila' celebrate Hungarian autonomy and independence from *foreign* invaders, which include Jews. There is a revival of Hungarian folk songs and dress of a particular style which attempts to distinguish itself from the parallel forms promoted during the Soviet era – these 'true' Hungarian symbols are perceived as having been preserved by the folk in the provinces, and especially in the rural areas of Transylvania, which contain a large population of Hungarian speakers but presently exists within the borders of Romania. Prime Minister Josef Antall had been known to say that he was the guarantor of all Magyars, and not just those living in Hungary itself.[7]

At the same time that urban middle-class Jews are constructed as foreigners, Magyar speaking peasants living in Romania are hailed as the 'authentic Magyars'. Budapest, in the discourse of right-wing nationalist intellectuals, is named a 'foreign' city, one dominated by Jews and other international invaders. At the same time, there is a great hopefulness and optimism concerning the possibility of joint-venture business projects with Western European and American companies. There is, simultaneously, a battle for the return of Hungary to the Hungarians – a desire to return Hungary to some mythic past of pureness which would exclude both Jews and others perceived as foreigners. At the same time, the city looks westward for models of capitalist economic miracles.

The Jew's image since the Second World War is now permanently connected with urban culture, a symbolic economy which celebrates the rural only and excludes anyone with a Jewish history from being 'truly Hungarian'. Thus, coming from Communist Party/survivor Jewish urban background contrasts with rural land-owning non-Communist Party origins. While the Jew can be seen as simultaneously communist and capitalist because of the urban connection, the Jew cannot be seen as also Hungarian and folk.

---

7. 'Meciar conciliatory toward Magyars', *Budapest Week*, 14-20 October, 1993, Volume III, No. 32, p. 9.

In this post-Communist search for identity, the third generation of Hungarian Jews are facing an interesting array of possibilities. Recently, Jewish organizations from abroad have arrived and are attempting to bring the grandchildren of assimilated Communist Jews back into Judaism and Jewish culture. Two schools have opened, one religiously oriented and the other not religious but which teaches Jewish history and which is attempting to re-create the possibility of being both Hungarian and somehow Jewish at the same time. Many of the students at the school speak of the resistance that they encountered from some of their own family members in choosing this school. One young student (age fourteen) told me, 'My grandmother said that I was now willingly entering the ghetto and that her mother told her, 'I am afraid that if you go to this school – if it happens again, they will know who you are'. The girl told me proudly, though, that her mother had in fact named her Miriam and that she was the first person to be named Miriam in Hungary since 1945. She said that for her generation, 'Being Jewish is just a fact, like being born male or female – I am Jewish and there is nothing I can do about that. I am not religious, but I feel that I am different, that I am Jewish as well as Hungarian.'

Ironically, what has preserved whatever remains of Jewish identity in Hungary is the continued construction, whether under Communist Party rule or democratic rule, of the Jew as somehow not belonging. Despite all attempts by the Communist Jewish survivors to end the so-called Jewish question and thus practice a form of self-erasure, it is precisely their grandchildren who are embracing a Jewish identity as something compatible with their identity as Hungarians. They are, perhaps, one group that can forge a dual or polyglot identity that would not threaten their rights to citizenship within contemporary Hungary. It is too soon to know exactly what exactly this cohort will choose.

The 'Closeted Jew'

Historically, Hungarians of Jewish descent have attempted to abide by the strict rules of citizenship governing the ethos of the times: they converted to Christianity or gave up religious practices, adhered to Magyar over German and other minority languages, and became Communists during the era of Soviet influence in Hungary. Such an extreme case of accommodating behaviour can be interpreted as a reflection of the specific demands of assimilation and the requirements of citizenship made on this group during different historical periods, and this can be seen as having flamed the production of what appear to be 'closeted Jews' (Mouffe, 1993). Jews have been literally alternately marked as 'other' by 'yellow stars' during the period of Nazi occupation and then symbolically by 'red stars' in the post-Communist period. Both historical experiences could be said to perpetuate 'the closet' as part of a survival strategy. Because documentation such as diaries, reflections, and memoirs of subjects at these different historical junctures are lacking, we can only imagine from our contemporary positioning at what level and to what extent this mode of assimilation was self-imposed or externally conditioned. There is too much data on the politics of exclusion and anti-Semitism in all of these historical periods to ignore the external conditions. Re-examining the politics of cultural citizenship concerning Jews in Hungarian history, however, can perhaps shed light on the contemporary attempts to understand the structure of ethno-nationalism and ethnic tolerance in Hungary more generally. It also points to new directions, such as political affiliation, in understanding ethnicity, which functions even in the absence of an explicit religious or group feeling, as in the case of Communists of Jewish background.

If we examine the construction of Jewish alterity over time, a paradox exists which fuels an old conspiracy theory concerning anti-Semitism that postulates that the actual presence of Jews is unnecessary for anti-Semitism; it exists *sui generis*. In pre-war Europe, Jews were constructed as capitalists and representative of the corruptions accompanying modernity and industrialization. Today, in post-Soviet Hungary, they are constructed as both 'old communists' and 'new capitalists', two categories which contrast with the rural peasant and which provoke, in the first case, ambivalence about past Soviet domination, and in the second case, ambivalence about the economic reforms and possible hardships brought on within a newly promoted capitalism. Moreover, in the construction of Jewish subjects, there is no longer certainty or agreement about what exactly constitutes this category. At one level of analysis, it seems reasonable to assert that anti-Semitism could exist without a single Jew in the country. But, here, I would like to move away from conspiracy theories and attempt to broaden our understanding of anti-Semitism within the context of the notion of cultural citizenship, since this notion could perhaps encompass the cases of other minority groups who also find themselves in the New Europe struggling for the right to belong. If we understand the Hungarian search for identity as one that has shifted over time, sometimes looking West, other times looking East, sometimes celebrating modernity and other times the traditional, we notice that there is, more often, clarity about who shouldn't belong rather than who should belong. Mouffe (1993: 3–4) argues that in times of political transition, and in the case of the Communist bloc countries, there is a 'resurgence of old antagonisms – ethnic, national, religious and others'. To some extent, it may be a misnomer to call what is emerging presently in Hungary and in other parts of Eastern Europe the 'new' nationalism (Jakubowska, 1993) since so many of these antagonisms have long histories. On the other hand, in the case of Jews in Hungary, we see the emergence of old antagonisms in what appear to be new forms. We also witness that even extreme forms of assimilation do not abolish the construction of Jew as 'Other'.

I have tried to understand the strands of identity linking Hungarians of Jewish background to the climate in which lines of cultural citizenship were drawn. One common strand of these different historical moments is the fact that ambiguity, or even duality, were inconceivable concepts. One had to be Christian and Hungarian rather than Jewish and Hungarian; one had to favour Magyar and not another language in order to be Hungarian; one could not be simultaneously a practising Jew and a Communist; one could not be folk and urban. Today, the same Jews who historically accommodated to these changing pre-requisites for citizenship are now excluded because of their Communist past, or their metropolitan location, or even for their perceived links to the West.

In the North American context, we are witnessing the intensification of social movements and identity politics which are demanding the rights of cultural citizenship for polyglots. I wonder, from this context, who is left in Hungary to re-imagine and to demand, simply, the Hungarian who is also Jewish?

Bibliography

Deák, I. (1983), 'Assimilation and Nationalism in East Central Europe During the Last Century of Habsburg Rule', *The Carl Beck Papers in Russian and East European Studies*. NTIS, Paper No. 202.

Dominguez, V. R. (1993), 'Questioning Jews', *American Ethnologist*, 20(3), pp. 618–624.

Hofer, T. (1991), 'Construction of the "Folk Cultural Heritage" in Hungary', *Ethnologia Europaea*, 21, pp. 145–170.

Jakubowska, L. (1993), 'Writing About Eastern Europe: Perspectives from ethnography and anthropology', *Nijmegen Studies in Development and Cultural*

Change (The Politics of Ethnographic Reading and Writing), Nijmegen, pp. 143–159.

Karady, V. (1986), 'Some Social Aspects of Jewish Assimilation in Socialist Hungary, 1945–1956', in R. L. Braham (ed.), *The Tragedy of Hungarian Jewry*, New York: Columbia University Press, pp. 73–131.

Mouffe, C. (1993), *The Return of the Political*, London, New York: Verso.

Rosaldo, R. (1994), 'Cultural Citizenship and Educational Democracy', *Cultural Anthropology*, 9(3), pp. 402–411.

Stolcke, V. (1995), 'Talking Culture: New Boundaries, New Rhetorics of Exclusion in Europe', *Current Anthropology*, 36(1), pp. 1–24.

Várdy, P. (1986), 'The Unfinished Past-Jewish Realities in Postwar Hungary', in R. L. Braham (ed.), *The Tragedy of Hungarian Jewry*, New York: Columbia University Press, pp. 133–189.

–11–

Majority as a Minority: The Russian Ethno-Nationalism and its Ideology in the 1970–1990s

Victor Shnirelman and Galina Komarova

The Russian issue is unique in the context of minority problems. A complexity inherent in this issue is that, despite their numbers and their political and social dominance in the Russian Federation, Russians are currently experiencing an identity crisis as a result of the disintegration of the USSR and certain attendant circumstances. Thus, in subjective terms many ethnic Russians view themselves as a minority. Why is this so? We will first address a number of crucial objective factors which negatively affected the Russians during the past few decades. Next, an ideological response of the Russian ethno-nationalists to these processes will be analysed. Finally, we will argue that the current growth of Russian ethno-nationalism is not accidental and that it may have serious political consequences in the future. It is well-known that the Russians were a dominant majority in both the Russian Empire and the USSR not only in numbers but in terms of political power, education, and cultural achievements. Until very recently, they primarily associated themselves with the state rather than with any particular culture and did not separate their history from the history of the state.

The ill-born, contradictory demographic trends manifested themselves in the development of the Russian community during approximately the last thirty years (Bernstam, 1986) at which time the Russians began to feel as if they were divorcing themselves from both their culture and their state. On the one hand, the growing dispersion of the Russians due to their engagement in the industrialization and urbanization of the marginal zones of the USSR, as well as forced resettlement to remote areas above all in the 1930s, caused the devastation of Central Russia, the historical core of the Russian community, and consequently a decline of Russian traditional folk culture. For instance, the number of Russians in the Soviet Republics other than the Russian Federation has grown from 5.2 million to 23.9 million between 1926–1979, i.e. from 6.7 per cent to 17.4 per cent of the entire population of the non-Russian Republics. On the other hand, the number of Russians within the Russian Federation decreased 3.2 per cent in 1959–1979 as a result of the low birth-rate among the Russians, their extensive resettlement outside the Russian Federation, and a slight growth of the non-Russian populations within the Russian Federation (Arutiunian, 1992: 18–22, 28–32). The situation in the rural areas of Central Russia is especially unfavourable. The number of the local rural residents has dropped by 60–70 per cent during approximately the last fifty years. Today a ghost-village is by no means a rare phenomenon in Northern Russia. The middle-aged and elderly account for the bulk of the rural population in modern Central Russia (Arutiunian, 1992: 39; Savoskul, 1992: 103).

Simultaneously the opposite trend has occurred during the past decades, namely by retreat of the Russians from former Soviet Central Asia, Caucasus and several other areas. The number of Russians decreased by 66,700 in Georgia between 1959–1989, by 117,800 in Azerbaijan between 1970–1989, by 18,700 in Armenia between 1979–1989, by 15,300 in Turkmenia in between 1979–1989 and by 12,200 in Uzbekistan between 1979–1989. The local Russian populations also shrunk in the 1970s in Northern Caucasus, Mordvinia, Komi-Permian Autonomous Okrug, Ust'-Orda Autonomous Okrug, Mountainous-Altai Autonomous Oblast'. The Russian community in Kalmykia began to decline in the 1980s (Arutiunian, 1992: 19–20, 43; Ostapenko and Subbotina, 1992; Komarova, 1993; Tishkov, 1993).

At the same time, modernized Russian culture and, in particular, the Russian language (Russification) spread among non-Russian populations all over the country. This was encouraged by the state in an attempt to build up a homogeneous Soviet community and caused a trend of 'deculturation' among those Russians who felt a loss of distinction between themselves and the many non-Russians in the country who were attempting to mobilize their own cultural resources in order to withstand Russification. These feelings were above all inspired by the brutal campaign against the Russian Orthodox Church launched in the early 1960s which has since led to closure of many churches and monasteries (Simon, 1974: 73–75). This provided the background for the growth since the 1960s of a Russian ethno-nationalism along two trajectories, namely, the growth of the open activity of the so-called 'ruralists' ('derevenshchiki') and other patriotic-oriented Russian writers (Arutiunian, 1992: 372–377, 385 ff.), as well as the emergence of the Russian underground ethno-nationalist movement (Kheifetz, 1981a; Dunlop, 1983: 35 ff.; Barghoorn, 1986; Yanov, 1987: 91 ff.; Laqueur, 1993).

The perestroika period was a time characterized by the rapid uprise of an anti-Russian mood ('Russophobia') among the many non-Russians in the country who identified the Russians with the Communist Bureaucratic State and charged them with all of the failures of the Communist regime. Finally, after the collapse of the USSR in the fall of 1991, a new Russian diaspora of 25 million people who suffered from implicit prejudices and explicit discrimination in the newly established states suddenly emerged (Elliott, 1994; Savoskul, 1994). This resulted in the early 1990s in a mass exodus of Russians from the non-Russian Republics and regions (Zajonchkovskaja, 1995: 45–47). In January 1994, 1,097,100 ethnic Russian refugees and migrants were officially registered in the Russian Federation, accounting for more than 80 per cent of the total number of migrants. This figure by no means represents the true situation since 298,800 Russian-speakers left Kyrgyzstan only in 1989–1993 (197,000 in 1992–1993!), accounting for one third of all the Russian-speakers in this area in 1989. During the early 1990s, Armenia lost 42 per cent of its Russian population, Azerbaijan 30 per cent , Georgia 27 per cent and Tajikistan 35 per cent.

Simultaneously in 1991, for the first time in modern Russian history, Russians experienced a significant decline in their population, whereby the death rate exceeded the birth rate. A growth in the death rate and a decline of the life-span have been observed in the Russian Federation during the last twenty-five years (Morozova, 1994: 25–26). Among all of the ethnic communities in the Russian Federation, Russians now have the lowest birth rate and one of the highest mortality rates. The situation is especially alarming in Moscow at the present, where the decline of the population increased by more than sixteen fold (from minus 0.6 to minus 9.9 per 1,000 persons) between 1989 and 1994 (Bol'nye . . ., 1995). Some scholars predict a demographic catastrophe provided that the given trend remains constant (Rybakovskij and Zakharova, 1992: 91). On the other hand, in the past few decades, the growth rate of the Muslim populations has remained high (Bernstam, 1986: 324–325), which has frightened those Russian ethnonationalists (Artemov, 1992: 141; Lysenko, 1992: 130) oriented toward resistance to de-ethnicization of the Russians (Mialo, 1992).

All of these negative trends in question are of much concern to nationalist-oriented Russian scholars. One of these scholars goes so far as to argue that 'a spatial shift of the nationalities and a consequent growth of the mixed families in numbers (there were 9.9 millions of

Victor Shnirelman and Galina Komarova

them in 1979, or 15 per cent of all the families in the USSR) contributed . . . to a spread of the Russian-speaking "Soviet" culture, i.e.
to the erosion of the Russian ethnos, and undermined its uniqueness'
(Kozlov, 1992: 106). Since the late 1980s, the Russian patriotic-
oriented writers have been particularly concerned about what they
called 'a depersonalization of the Russian culture' and 'a destruction
of the Russian historical memory', which they linked with the idea
of a conspiracy to destroy the Russian people (Arutiunian, 1992: 382–
383). Paranoia became a permanent feature of the Russian ethno-
nationalist ideology, which was being developed in order to protect
the Russian culture, i.e. the Russian people, from some 'evil forces'
(Kheifetz, 1981b: 159–160).

In order to block centrifugal trends and to stimulate Russian consolidation some Russian ethno-nationalists began to develop in the
late 1960s and early 1970s a new non-sanctioned, non-orthodox
ideology. Already in their first Manifesto, 'A Word to the Nation',
which began to circulate in Samizdat in December 1970, they complained, in contrast to common opinion, that the Russians were
the most non-privileged people in the USSR, that they played a
disproportionally small role in the country, that the Russian lands
were appropriated by other peoples and that the Russians were
under-represented in science and culture. They were already scaring
themselves with 'the threat of biological degeneration of the white
race' and demanded 'to put an end to random hybridization'. They
stressed that by 'Russian people' they meant 'those people who are
true Russians by blood and in spirit' (A word . . ., 1971; Yanov, 1987:
155–165).

Since that time, the Russian ethno-nationalists have tried to develop
and encourage a self-esteem and pride for their glorious Russian
ancestors. Some of them occupied themselves, in particular, with re-
writing early Russian history and with the invention of 'Russian
prehistory' in an attempt to establish a special role for the 'Russian
Slavs' in human evolution. It is curious that this movement was, even
by serious scholars, treated in Russia as an awakening or restoration
of 'a people's historical memory' (see, for instance, Arutiunian, 1992:
386). Actually, what really happened was more an invention of the
past, to paraphrase a famous idea of Eric Hobsbawm (1983). According
to A. D. Smith, the intellectuals helped to 'recreate' a sense of ethnicity
out of the artefacts at their disposal (1984: 119).

In this chapter, we will outline the ways a neo-Pagan faction of the
Russian ethno-nationalists used to build up mythological versions of
the Slavic ethnogenesis. We will demonstrate how these versions
reflected the contemporary ethno-demographic, social and political

– 214 –

processes within the country as well as the ethno-nationalist evaluations of the Russians' role in the world community. We will also demonstrate how these highly primordialist concepts manage to overcome the problems of discontinuities and breaks in order to prove the immortal nature of the Russian cultural community and to encourage Russian identity.

It seems useful to make a distinction between four different approaches to Russian history which have recently been intensively exploited by various factions of the Russian ethno-nationalists. One of these approaches follows an official Soviet historiography and is rooted in pre-Soviet Imperial Russia. It is, at least partly, based on the slogan 'Orthodoxy, Autocracy, Peoplehood', which, since the early 1830s, developed a core theory of 'official peoplehood' (*narodnost'*). A second approach focuses upon the extensive search for Russian prehistoric roots. The modern Russian neo-Pagans adopted this approach primarily from certain emigrant amateur authors in the early 1970s. A third approach emphasizes a historical and cultural unity of all individuals residing in the USSR as if they were naturally fated to live together. This particular approach attempts to re-establish a famous interpretation of Russian history invented in the 1920s by the Eurasianists, a group of Russian emigrants. Finally, a fourth 'metahistorical' approach treats modern Russia as the main stronghold of Eurasianism in its everlasting struggle against Atlanticism.

This chapter focuses upon the second approach which is, firstly, less-known, and which secondly, represents an extreme wing of Russian ethno-nationalism – neo-Paganism. The approach in question clearly demonstrates what may be called 'an invention of the past', an attempt to artificially create a framework of the Russian past, both in time and space, in order to legitimate the everlasting existence of the Soviet/Russian Empire. This greatly contrasts with the common conservative response to modern changes which, until very recently, expressed itself in nostalgic addresses to a local medieval past (Nisbet, 1986: 18–19, 35 ff.).

'Russian prehistory' was initially 'discovered' in the early 1970s by certain Russian writers who made themselves familiar with the so-called, 'Book of Vles', a famous falsification produced by certain Russian emigrants (Kaganskaja, 1987; Tvorogov, 1990). Since that time, this book and its ideas have become the true Scripture of the Russian neo-Pagans. The neo-Pagans treated Christianity as if it was a disruptive ideology, forged by the Jews in order to subjugate the world (Yanov, 1987: 141–144). They therefore linked the most glorious pages of Russian history with the pre-Christian period, praised Russian paganism as its most important human intellectual achievement (see, for instance, Gusev, 1993), and charged Christianity with the most brutal crimes committed against various peoples, in particular, the Russians (see, for instance, Vedomysl, 1993; Barabash, 1993). One of them goes so far as to argue that the destruction of the true Russian culture already began in the Kievan Rus', i.e. in the tenth century. He appeals for a restoration of the Pagan Rus' and its Empire, which, in his view, flourished long before the ninth century (Gusev, 1993: 14). In brief, the approach in question is based on the notion that the most glorious episodes of Russian history were written before the tenth century, i.e. during a period which left almost no written sources concerning Slavic history, let alone Rus'. Thus, there is ample room for speculation, fantasy and invention of the past. In this respect, 'the Book of Vles' is very helpful for the Russian neo-Pagans, who treat it as the earliest and the most reliably written source concerning the early history of the Slavs. It is worth mentioning that, initially, the approach in question was developed in science-fiction literature, which was less controlled by censorship. The main ideas of the newly established 'Russian prehistory' were as follows.

1. The Rus' Slavs should be identified with the proto-Indo-Iranians or even with the proto-Indo-Europeans. They were mighty nomadic pastoralists who roamed all over the Eurasian steppe belt and who, from time to time, invaded adjacent regions. According to some authors, the Slavs (i.e. the Russians, in their view) inhabited Europe up to the British Isles, Northern Africa, Near East, Asia Minor, Caucasus, Arabia, Iran, and the Indus valley during certain prehistoric periods (Skurlatov and Nikolajev, 1976; Skurlatov, 1977a; 1977b; 1987; Shcherbakov, 1987; 1988; 1991; Milov, 1991; 1993). Indeed, it is argued, that 'not the Pripiat' marshes, where some archaeologists attempt to drive us, but the vast space of the Eurasian steppes up to the Amur river is our true homeland. Four hundred years ago the Russians returned to the native Russian grounds which belonged to our ancestors for millennia (Skurlatova, 1979: 57). This approach introduces a new dimension to Russian history and 'prehistory' – an idea of cyclical expansions and shrinkages (Milov, 1991).

2. The Slavs are an everlasting immortal population known from at least Early or Middle Holocene times, i.e. one of the most ancient populations in the world (Milov, 1991; 1993; Grinevich, 1993).

3. They have made a great contribution to the formation of many other peoples of the world. In order to prove this idea, the Russian neo-Pagans identify the proto-Slavs with certain well-known, ancient, extinct peoples. Skurlatov (1987) treats the proto-Slavs as

proto-Indo-Europeans or 'Aryans', whose particular segments provided a starting point for the formation of the peoples of the Caucasus, Great Bulgaria, Asia Minor and even Levant. In Shcherbakov's view, the Slavs, the Etruscans and, above all, 'the Eastern Atlantians' were one and the same population who survived after the destruction of the legendary Atlantis. They made a contribution to the formation of both Ancient Egyptian and Levantine civilizations and even sailed to Mesoamerica where they influenced the Maya and the Aztecs (Shcherbakov, 1987). He believes that they can be identified with the pre-Sumerian inhabitants of Mesopotamia, who spread from Libia up to Northern India, China and Japan (Shcherbakov, 1990: 204; Grinevich, 1993: 243–250). Milov goes so far as to state that the Khmers of Cambodia and the Ainu of Northern Japan are the offspring of these proto-Slavs (Milov, 1991: 6; 1993).

4. While roaming around the world, these 'proto-Slavs' invented crucial cultural elements which represented the foundation of modern civilization. The neo-Pagans search for the deep roots of the Slavic writing system (Skurlatova, 1979: 56; Zhukova, 1989; Beliakova, 1991) and go so far as to state that it was the proto-Slavs who introduced the original proto-writing, which was the foundation of other writing systems of the world (Skurlatov, 1987: 215; Shcherbakov, 1987: 198–200; 1991: 237; Zhuravskij, 1988; Grinevich, 1993). The proto-Slavs are pictured as the bearers of the original Vedic religion (Skurlatov, 1977b; Milov, 1993), as if the latter had been borrowed from them by the Indians and the Tibetans (Iz glubiny . . ., 1993). And finally, it was they who built the first states in many regions of the world (Shcherbakov, 1991: 236, 254; Grinevich, 1993; Milov, 1993).

5. The ideology in question bears clear racist connotations. Skurlatov believes in the supremacy of the Indo-European ('Aryan') 'ethnocultural' chromosomes whose purity was maintained, in particular, by the priests. In his view, the Indo-European warriors have spread these chromosomes all over the world (Skurlatov, 1987: 215). Shcherbakov blames archaeologists, as if they have consciously kept silent about the 'Slavic skulls' discovered in Armenia (1991: 254). He particularly insists upon blood relationships between the Slavs and the Germans, as if it were this fact which encouraged them to live in peace and friendship. Due to this fact, like many other modern Russian ethno-nationalists (Yanov, 1987: 158; Moroz, 1992: 72), he treats German aggression against the USSR as Hitler's fatal error (Shcherbakov, 1991: 135). This line of reasoning leads to the idea of the existence of a fraternal unity among the white

race and of harmful consequences of mixed marriages. Significantly enough, Shcherbakov, on the one hand, praises the Cro-Magnon people as having made the most important achievements in modern civilization (1991: 141), and on the other hand, argues against mixed marriages (1991: 235). All the arguments in question lay the foundation for the open racism which is embedded in the ideology of the extreme wing of modern Russian ethno-nationalism (see, for instance, Otkrytaja doktrina, 1993; Dugin, 1993).

6. The patriotic-oriented Russian authors rely upon concepts in question in order to legitimate the Russian claims to all territories in the former Russian Empire and the USSR. This is, Skurlatov argues, why the proto-Slavs built Tbilisi, the capital of modern Georgia (1977a: 328), and why Shcherbakov (1991: 207–224; 238–254) insists, they established the Urartian state in the Transcaucasia and the Parthian Kingdom in the Transcaspian region. Nevertheless, the main concerns of the Russian ethno-nationalists revolve around the North-Western, in particular, Baltic regions. Shcherbakov (1991: 134) reminds us of the Lithuanian, Estonian and Latvian nationalists who collaborated with the Nazis during the Second World War, considering them to be the worst enemies of the Russians. Other authors treat the Baltic and Northern lands as indisputably Slavic and as being where the Finnish groups, let alone the Balts, came at a much later period (Kuz'min, 1993; Milov, 1991: 6). This argument was made by the Chair of the Russian communities in the Baltics, D. A. Ragozin, who used it in his interview for the Moscow broadcast program 'Majak' on July 9, 1993. At that time, his statement manifested a response by the new Russian diaspora concerning the discriminating anti-Russian legislation adopted in Estonia and Latvia in the early 1990s.

7. Finally, regardless of slight internal differences, almost all Russian ethno-nationalists are advocates of anti-Semitism (Yanov, 1987; Moroz, 1992; Pribylovskij, 1992: 168–169; Laqueur, 1993: 106–111). This should not be surprising since, in their view, the Jewish people naturally compete with Russians for the truthfulness of their own religious beliefs. Moreover, the Jews repudiate a Messianic mission of Jesus Christ and reject Christ himself, thus questioning legitimacy of Christianity (Karsavin, 1928: 76). Meanwhile, Russian Orthodoxy is considered by the Russian ethno-nationalists as the spiritual core of the Russian culture (Duncan, 1991: 325). This deep reason for hatred is combined by the contemporary Russian ethno-nationalists with charges that the Jewish people are linked with the Communist regime and the destruction of the Russian

culture. They treat the Semites, i.e. Jewish people, as everlasting enemies of humanity and, in particular, of the Russians.

It is this latter idea which is inherent in the neo-Pagan ideology. Skurlatov reminds us of 'the Russian-Semitic hostilities' in antiquity (1977a: 328). At the same time, he (Skurlatov, 1987: 215; Skurlatova, 1979: 56) and his followers (Shcherbakov, 1987: 178; Milov, 1991: 6; 1993) attempt to break the Phoenicians away from other Semitic peoples and argue that, originally, Palestine was inhabited by non-Semitic residents, most probably by proto-Slavs. Thus, the Jews are treated as brutal invaders who had no right to occupy Palestine. This concept is also deeply rooted in the Messianic 'Russian idea'. Although the neo-Pagans reject Christianity, they share with the Russian Orthodox nationalists the belief that the Sacred Land should belong the Russians, as to the chosen people, if only symbolically. It is worth remembering that during the wave of the Russian chauvinist campaign in the late 1940s, certain clergymen used to portray the Russians as 'the people of the Holy Land' and the Russian land as comparable to 'the Holy Land of Palestine' (Duncan, 1991: 317). On the other hand, the arguments in question also established intimate relationships between the Russian ethno-nationalists and the Palestinian ones (Kheifetz, 1981b: 168–169), whose newspaper 'Al-Kods' is one of the most militant opponents of 'Zionism' in contemporary Russia.

Until recently, a great many Russians were not affected by these ideas (Arutiunian, 1992: 399 ff.). Rather, they have only recently gained popularity as a response to the dramatic situation experienced by the Russians in the past few years (Dunlop, 1983: 152; Arutiunian, 1992: 407; Elliott, 1994). (This response was predicted by Barghoorn (1986: 640): an increase of intolerance towards the Russians in the non-Russian republics and regions, an emergence of the new Russian diaspora, discrimination against the Russians in the non-Russian environment, and finally, a mass repatriation of the Russians.) While considering themselves the builders of the mighty state, be it the Russian Empire or the USSR, which they treated as their Motherland (Arutiunian, 1992: 400), the Russians perceived its collapse as a heavy psychological trauma. This is why the extensive dispersion of the Slavs in the past, their civilizing mission and, at the same time, their return to the original homeland due to natural disaster or pressure from the enemy, is a constant trait characterizing the mythology in question. This is the origin of the Messianic belief that the misfortunes will vanish, and the Great Russian state will finally rise up like a phoenix.

In general, the ethnocentric mythology that was analysed has many common themes and structural similarities with the mythologies of this sort developed by ethnic minorities (Shnirelman, 1992; 1995; 1996; Smith, 1984: 100–105); in particular, calling upon a glorious past and an enormous exaggeration of that past in order to cure a psychological trauma caused by current hardships and disasters. The Russian case demonstrates that in certain environments a large dominant population, rather than an ethnic minority, may manifest an inferiority complex which expresses itself in a bizarre belief system. Historical claims use the latter, which upholds the common conservative view that 'legitimacy is the work of history and of traditions which go far beyond the resources of any single generation' (Nisbet, 1986: 23). A militant aspect of the ideology in question is worth mentioning: an ethnocentric world-view, super-patriotism, racial and ethnic prejudices and xenophobe set free aggression. Unfortunately, since the late 1980s, when the Russians began to feel uncomfortable, first in the borderland regions of the former USSR, and then in the newly established states, this set of attitudes began to spread among the Russians.

This is why the ideology in question is by no means innocent. This is especially true regarding the conclusions drawn by one of its founders, V. N. Bezverkhij, who advocates racial and anti-Semitic theories intended to exclude the offspring of mixed marriages, including Jews, Gypsies and mulattos. In addition, he is one of those who has forged an intellectual basis for contemporary Russian neo-Fascism (Solomenko, 1993).

The disintegration of the USSR and the emergence of the New Russian Diaspora are currently used in the rhetoric of the leaders of various factions of the Russian nationalists. For instance, Zhirinovskij warns Russians that without the Empire they themselves will become an ethnic minority, will be discriminated against and, finally, exterminated. He exploits in his politics the unhappy situation of the Russians who happened to live outside the Russian Federation and has already proved highly successful (Zubov, 1993: 174–175; Yanov, 1994: 223). A. Barkashov, a leader of the Russian National-Socialists, also uses this factor while stressing anti-Russian extremism, Russophobia and discrimination against the Russians in certain newly established states. He calls his own nationalism 'a defensive one' and insists on the militarization of the National-Patriotic parties in order to resist 'a pressure' from the non-Russians (Barkashov, 1994: 19–21, 28–29, 43, 54, 74). It goes without saying that contemporary Russian nationalists are very conservative in their political views: They advocate an authoritarian political structure and object to any democracy in order to establish a superior position for the ethnic Russians in the multicultural state. For thoughtful observers, it is obvious that an implementation of these politics may result in the further disintegration of the state (Zubov, 1993).

Acknowledgement

This chapter was completed at the Centre for the Studies of Nationalism, Central European University in Prague, where one of the authors was a Research Fellow from September 1994 to December 1995. We would like to gratefully acknowledge this institution.

Bibliography

Artemov, I. (1992), 'Rossija i Sredniaja Azija', *Nash Sovremennik*, 7, pp. 140–142.

Arutiunian, Yu. V. (ed.), (1992), *Russkije: etno-sotsiologicheskije ocherki*, Moscow: Nauka.

Barabash, V. I. (1993), 'Moloko giyeny', *Russkoje delo*, 5, pp. 1–2.

Barghoorn, F. C. (1986), 'Russian Nationalism and Soviet Politics: Official and Unofficial Perspectives', in R. Conquest (ed.), *The Last Empire: Nationality and the Soviet Future*, Stanford: Hoover Institution Press, pp. 30–77.

Barkashov, A. P. (1994), *Azbuka russkogo natsionalista*, Moscow: Slovo-1.

Beliakova, G. S. (1991), 'Puti – dorogi slavianskoj pis'mennosti', *Volkhv*, 1, pp. 3–8.

Bernstam, M. S. (1986), 'The Demography of Soviet Ethnic Groups in World Perspective', in R. Conquest (ed.), *The Last Empire: Nationality and the Soviet Future*, Stanford: Hoover Institution Press, pp. 314–368.

Bol'nye . . . (1995), 'Bol'nye zhiteli bol'nogo goroda', *Segodnya*, May 4, p. 9.

Dugin, A. (1993), *Giperborejskaja teorija (opyt ariosofskogo issledovanija)*, Moscow: Arktogeja.

Duncan, P. J. S. (1991), 'Orthodoxy and Russian Nationalism in the USSR, 1917–88', in G. A. Hosking (ed.), *Church, Nation and State in Russia and Ukraine*, London: Macmillan, pp. 312–332.

Dunlop, J. B. (1983), *The Faces of Contemporary Russian Nationalism*, Princeton: Princeton University Press.

Elliott, D. (1994), 'Revival of the Empire?', *Newsweek*, June 27, pp. 26–29.

Grinevich, G. C. (1993), *Praslavianskaja pis'mennost': rezul'taty deshifrovki*. T. 1, Moscow: Obshchestvennaja Pol'za.

Gusev, O. M. (1993), 'Russkaja ideja', *Rodnyje prostory*, 3, pp. 10–14.

Hobsbawm, E. (1983) 'Introduction: Inventing Traditions', in E. Hobsbawm and T. Ranger (eds), *The Invention of Tradition*, Cambridge: Cambridge University Press, pp. 1–14.

Iz glubiny . . . (1993), 'Iz glubiny vekov', *Russkoje delo*, 5, p. 2.

Kaganskaja, M. (1987), '"Vlesova kniga": istorija odnoj fal'shivki', *Yevrei i yevrejskaja tematika v sovietskikh i vostochnojevropejskikh publikatsijakh*, 3–4, pp. 3–19.

Karsavin, L. P. (1928), 'Rossija i yevrei', *Versty*, 3, pp. 65–86.

Kheifetz, M. (1981a), 'Russkij patriot Vladimir Osipov', *Kontinent*, 27, pp. 159–214.

——, (1981b), 'Russkij patriot Vladimir Osipov', *Kontinent*, 28, pp. 134–211.

Komarova, O. D. (1993), 'Sovremennaja dinamika etnicheskogo sostava naselenija Rossii (statisticheskij obzor)', *Rossijskij Etnograf*, 9, pp. 182–203.

Kozlov, V. I. (1992), 'Glavnyj natsional'nyj vopros v Rossii vchera i segodnia', *Etnopolis*, 2, pp. 97–109.

Kuz'min, A. G. (1993), *Kto v Pribaltike 'korennoj'?*, Moscow: Pisatel'skoje Aktsionernoje Obshchestvo.

Laqueur, W. (1993), *Black Hundred: The Rise of the Extreme Right in Russia*, New York: Harper Collins.

Lysenko, N. N. (1992), 'Nasha tsel' – sozdanije velikoj imperii', *Nash Sovremennik*, 9, pp. 122–130.

Mialo, K. (1992), 'Yest' li v Yevrazii mesto dlia Russkikh?', *Nash Sovremennik*, 9, pp. 102–105.

Milov, V. A. (1991), 'I vozroditsia Rossia . . . ', *Volkhv*, 2–3, pp. 5–6.

——, (1993), 'Kazhdyj iz nas v otvete za svoju istoriju', *Stranitsy Rossijskoj istorii*, 1, pp. 1–2.

Moroz, V. L. (1992), 'Bortsy za "Sviatuju Rus" i zashchitniki "Sovietskoj Rodiny"', in R. Sh. Ganelin (ed.), *Natsional'naja pravaja prezhde i teper'*. *Chast' 2, vyp. 1*, St. Peterburg: Institute of Sociology, RAN, pp. 68–96.

Morozova, G. F. (1994), 'Degradatsija natsii – mif ili real'nost'', *Sotsiologicheskije issledovanija*, 1, pp. 22–30.

Nisbet, R. (1986), *Conservatism: Dream and Reality*, Milton Keynes: Open University Press.

Ostapenko, L. V. and Subbotina, I. A. (1992), 'Russkije v blizhnem zarubezhije: migratsija, zaniatost', konflikty', *Puti k bezopasnosti*, 3(9).

Otkrytaja doktrina (1993), 'Otkrytaja doktrina (vidy na zavtrashnij den')', *Rodnyje prostory*, 3, p. 2.

Pribylovskij, V. V. (1992), 'Pamiat'', in R. Sh. Ganelin (ed.), *Natsional'naja pravaja prezhde i teper'*. *Chast' 2, vyp. 2*, St. Peterburg: Institute of Sociology, RAN, pp. 151–170.

Rybakovskij, L. and Zakharova, O. (1992), 'Demograficheskaja situatsija v Rossijskoj Federatsii: sostojanije i prognoz', *Etnopolis*, 2, pp. 87–96.

Savoskul, S. S. (1992), 'Sotsial'no-etnicheskije problemy Russkogo naroda', *Etnopolis*, 1, pp. 94–106.

——, (1994), 'Russkije novogo zarubezhija, *Obshchestvennyje nauki i sovremennost*', 5, pp. 90–101.

Shcherbakov, V. I. (1987), 'Tropoj Trojanovoj', in A. Smirnov (ed.), *Dorogami tysiacheletij, Kn. 1*, Moscow: Molodaja Gvardija, pp. 161–202.

——, (1988), 'Veka Trojanovy', in M. Kovalev (ed.), *Dorogami tysiacheletij, Kn. 2*, Moscow: Molodaja Gvardija, pp. 60–116.

——, (1990), *Vsio ob Atlantide*, Moscow: Obshchestvo po izucheniju tajn i zagadok Zemli, Large.

——, (1991), *Asgard – gorod bogov*, Moscow: Molodaja Gvardija.

Shnirelman, V. A. (1992), 'Nauka ob etnogeneze kak mifotvorchestvo'. A paper presented for the conference 'Myth and contemporary world' held in the Institute of High Humanitarian Researches, Russian National Humanitarian University, Moscow, December 8–10.

——, (1995), 'The Past as a Strategy for Ethnic Confrontation – Georgia', *hCa Quarterly*, 14(Summer), pp. 20–22.

——, (1996), *Who gets the Past*, Woodrow Wilson Press.

Simon, G. (1974), *Church, State and Opposition in the USSR*, London: C. Hurst & Company.

Skurlatov, V. I. (1977a), 'Sled svetonosnykh', in V. Sukhanov (ed.), *Tajny vekov. Kn. 1*, Moscow: Molodaja Gvardija, pp. 327–332.

——, (1977b), 'Uvidevshije vsio do kraja mira . . . ', in V. Sukhanov (ed.), *Tajny vekov. Kn. 1*, Moscow: Molodaja Gvardija, pp. 188–194.

——, (1987), 'Etnicheskij vulkan', in A. Smirnov (ed.), *Dorogami tysiacheletij, Kn. 1*, Moscow: Molodaja Gvardija, pp. 203–224.

——, and Nikolajev, N. (1976), 'Tainstvennaja letopis'. 'Vlesova kniga' – poddelka ili bestsennyj pamiatnik mirovoj kul'tury', *Nedelia*, Maj 3–9.

Skurlatova, O. (1979), 'Zagadki "Vlesovoj knigi"', *Tekhnika-molodiozhi*, 12, pp. 55–59.

Smith, A. D. (1984), 'National Identity and Myths of Ethnic Descent', *Research in Social Movements, Conflict and Change*, 7, pp. 95–130.

Solomenko, Ye. (1993), 'Adolf Hitler v Sankt-Peterburge', *Izvestija*, June 10.

Tishkov, V. A. (1993), 'Russkije ukhodiat (Migratsii i bezhentsy v SSSR: Russkije)', *Rossijskij Etnograf*, 3, pp. 5–20.

Tvorogov, O. V. (1990), 'Vlesova kniga', *Trudy Otdela Drevnerusskoj Literatury*, 43, pp. 170–254. Leningrad: Nauka.

Vedomysl, (1993), 'Pepel ottsov stuchit v moyom serdtse', *Russkoje delo*, 5, pp. 3–4.

A Word . . . (1971), 'A Word to the Nation', *Survey*, 17(3), pp. 191–199.

Yanov, A. (1987), *The Russian Challenge and the Year 2000*, Oxford: Basil Blackwell.

——, (1994), 'Veimarskaya Rossija', *Neva*, 4, pp. 215–259.

Zajonchkovskaja, Zh. A. (1995), 'Migratsii naselenija Rossii kak zerkalo sotsial'no-economicheskikh peremen', in T. I. Zaslavskaja (ed.), *Kuda id'jot Rossija? Al'ternativy obshchestvennogo razvitija, II*, Moskva: Aspect Press, pp. 41–53.

Zhukova, L. (1989), 'Pisali "chertami i rezami"', in A. F. Smirnov (ed.), *Dorogami tysiacheletij, Kn. 3*, Moscow: Molodaja Gvardija, pp. 159–166.

Zhuravskij, V. (1988), 'Azbuka neolita', in M. Kovalev (ed.), *Dorogami tysiacheletij, Kn. 2*, Moscow: Molodaja Gvardija, pp. 54–59.

Zubov, A. (1993), 'Tretij russkij natsionalism', *Znamia*, 1, pp. 146–178.

–12–

The Nationalist Game: State Dominance and Ethnic Nationalism

Jürg Helbling

In my discussion, I define an ethnic group as a cultural unit whose members conceive of themselves as different in language, descent, history, tradition, etc. from similar units within a state (Barth, 1969; Cohen, 1976). Thus, an ethnic unit is always defined in opposition to other units of its kind. It is defined primarily by language and descent; however, who exactly is a member of the grouping may vary according to specific situations of conflict (Keyes, 1976). In addition to ethnic identity a multitude of other cultural identities exist: racial units defined by physical attributes, religious units constituted on the basis of a common belief, regional-local units based on co-residence and interaction. All these groupings may overlap and enforce ethnic boundaries or may even supplant ethnic identities in the strict sense.[1] The members of all these units may claim common history and tradition, a common culture and descent.

Nationalist movements fight for ethno-national homogeneity within a territorial state and are a historically recent phenomena (Gellner, 1991; Hobsbawm, 1991). They first occurred as an expression of the resistance against the absolutist state in France and later of the European peoples against Napoleonic hegemony. Furthermore, they took the form of independence movements in the European colonial empires of South and North America. They also occurred in the multiethnic European empires of the nineteenth and twentieth century, namely the Habsburg monarchy, the Ottoman empire, and later, in the 1960s,

---

1. Serbs, Croatians and Bosnians speak approximately the same language. Croats are Catholics and were a part of the Habsburg Monarchy, the Serbs were Orthodox subjects of the Otoman Empire, and the Bosnians, who were Bogomiles, converted to Islam and had an elite status (Pfaff, 1994).

during the decolonization process in the former colonies and in Eastern Europe.

The historical study of nationalism has distinguished a Risorgimento- and an integral nationalism (Alter, 1985; Pomian, 1990). Risorgimento-nationalism (liberation nationalism) aims at the creation of a nation-state either by separating from a multinational empire (as the Soviet Union, etc.) or by uniting an ethnic population living in different states into one nation-state (Italy and Germany or the Kurds). The Risorgimento-nationalism characteristically opposes a ruling elite or an oppressive foreign power. On the other hand, integral nationalism is the defensive posture of an already existing nation-state. It aims at ethno-national homogenization of the state population and/or at a mobilization against an external or internal 'enemy'. This cultural and linguistic homogenization of the nation-state (Gellner, 1991; Senghaas, 1994) inevitably creates minorities. How these minorities are dealt with varies from a state sponsored multiculturalism and an assimil-ationist policy coupled with widespread popular hostility towards immigrants (Western Europe), to an outright oppression of ethnic minorities (Kurds in Turkey), to even 'ethnic cleansing' and ethnocide (Serbs in Bosnia). Thus, nationalism aims at the ethno-cultural homo-genization of a nation-state, an equation that has two solutions: either secession from a multinational state or the suppression, forced assimilation or the expulsion of ethnic minorities.

The state is the point of reference of ethnicity and nationalism and sets the framework for the formation of interest groups (Williams, 1989: 410, 421), ethnic identities and antagonism emerge only in the framework of a common political unit. Therefore, the ethnic compo-sition of the state is crucial. Besides ethnic groups and the state, classes, too, are part of the nationalist process. While classes are politico-economic strata ranked in a social hierarchy, ethnic groups are capable of organizing the members of a given society across a class hierarchy. Congruence of classes and ethnic groups is rather rare. Most states, especially those in the Third World, consist of a multitude of (ranked) ethnic groups and nationalities. Only approximately a dozen of 132 states had an ethnically homogeneous composition in the 1970s.

The following chapter centres on the idea that ethnic groups can be looked upon as collective actors. Each collective actor, then, has the choice between being part of a multinational state and fighting for a better, e.g. a dominant position within that state, on the one and, or striving for an independent state where it can improve its political and economic position, on the other hand. The option it ill chose, will be the one from which its members expect the most advantages or the least disadvantages.[2] To speak of 'expected gains and losses' means that these options are perceived as such by the actors: they cannot know for sure about the consequences of their actions; they do not have all the necessary information but rather must decide on the basis of subjective models tainted with ideology. Furthermore, 'expected' means that not only gains and losses must be taken into consideration. Instead, the actors must also take into account the probability of achieving certain benefits or of preventing costs, respectively. Therefore, not only the issue of benefits is at stake, but also whether these benefits are realizable. Both relative deprivation and the prospect of changing it successfully are relevant factors. A bad situation with no chance of improvement does not lead to action (Weede, 1986; Gurr, 1993; 1994). Hence, economic interests and status as well as political opportunities are most important here, whereas cultural resources are mobilized in order to achieve politico-economic goals.

It might be objected that nationalism is often a highly irrational phenomenon and that it is rather irrational to think of nationalists as rational actors. This may be true, but it is no more reasonable to deny 'good reasons' even to die-hard nationalists: we have to presume that even they strategically pursue self-defined goals – as absurd and illegitimate as they may appear. The damaging and destructive, thus, irrational effects nationalist movements have upon a society and sometimes even on their members, can be better explained by the recurrence of social and ideological constraints (path-dependence), i.e. the fact that a specific action restricts the alternatives available in the future (Banton, 1983: 104; North, 1990). More important are the unintended results of what nationalists and their opponents do in the aggregate. However, negative side-effects that cannot be accounted for by nationalist actors do not mean that actors behave irrationally.

Nevertheless, the model of an ethnic group as a collective actor that decides in favour of the policy with the highest expected gains and the lowest expected costs is too simple. First, an ethnic unit is not a homogeneous group but consists of classes, class factions and, in the last instance, of individuals with different interests and means to pursue these interests. Second, ethnic units are – and the same is true for classes – only latent groups that become political groups as a result of mobilization processes in political and ideological conflicts. Third, ethnic identity is only one among many politically relevant identities such as state, region, religion, class, etc. Which of these identities

2. I follow A. Cohen (1976) and M. Banton (1983) who propose an interest group theory concerning problems of ethnicity and the state (Williams, 1989).

become politically 'charged', i.e. relevant for groups and individuals depends on which of them is expected to yield the most advantages in a given constellation of power and resource distribution.

This argument may also be addressed from a different angle. Economic conditions and class relations determine the energy and direction of social change. Social interests are class dependent, but are not effective before being organized in parties and organizations, as Dahrendorf (1992) maintains. Parties and political entrepreneurs compete for votes and mass support in order to gain control over the state government. By means of appropriate programs and ideologies, they define themselves in opposition to their competitors and try to mobilize as many voters and supporters as possible (Downs, 1957). Both distinction from other parties and mobilization of supporters are aimed at a maximization of political capital. The extent to which nationalist parties are successful, therefore, also depends upon the political system and the actual distribution of power between the parties.

However, in order to mobilize popular support, a nationalist party or movement has to overcome a free rider problem, i.e. it has to convince people that advantages can only be achieved by actively participating in the movement or by working in the party (Hechter, Friedman and Appelbaum, 1982). For those working in the party, the advantages are immediate and obvious (jobs, income, status). As for the ordinary following, two conditions must be met. The first is a relative deprivation in the multiethnic state and/or the expectation to be better off in an independent nation-state. The nationalist rhetoric must present the current situation as a competition for resources between ethnic groups in a state. Competition means fighting for the same resources as a zero-sum-game. If resources are not limited, i.e. if their supply exceeds the demand, no competition will follow. If the amount of resources is limited and smaller than demand, two possible constellations may ensue: (1) competition between labour and capital or other factions of a population and the state, or (2) between ethnic groups, i.e. between national and 'foreign' populations. Second, low transaction (and opportunity) costs of political organization are also decisive for popular support: low repression, liberal atmosphere, and voting lowers the costs to express one's grievances, and indiscriminate repression leaves no other solution than to fight (North, 1990: 86). Thus, there are two alternative lines along which protest, opposition and aspirations may be expressed: class or nation, whereas costs and benefits of both options are influenced by economic situation as well as by political opportunity.

I will not propose a new theory of nationalism and ethnicity but will confine myself instead to developing an analytical model designed to study the multitude of different factors involved in every specific case of nationalism. I will illustrate the model outlined above by referring to several examples. In the first part of this chapter, I will deal with some aspects of the ethno-nationalist developments in the former Soviet Union and Yugoslavia. In the second part I will discuss some features of the anti-immigration nationalism in Switzerland which has parallels in other Western European countries.

Ethnic Nationalism in Eastern Europe

Ethnic Units as Interest Groups

The Soviet Union consisted not only of a multitude of ethnic groups among whom the Russians were by far the most important, but also of republics whose borders almost, as a rule, did not coincide with those between ethnic groups (Mellenthin, 1994: 33; Halbach, 1992: 84 ff.).[3] In order to deflect or neutralize nationalist separatism, the central state under Stalin's regime has tried to break up the ethno-national homogeneity of the republics by deportations, resettlements, immigration (of Russians) and/or by redrawing the borders of individual republics (Halbach, 1992: 83, 89). Multiethnic societies such as the former USSR remain rather stable as long as the central state disposes of the economic means to provide for an acceptable living standard, eases regional imbalances through transfer payments and as long as ethnic conflicts are contained politically through autonomy provisions, co-optation and participation or repression. The economic decline of the Soviet state owing to super-power competition (arms race) and the economic crises of the 1980s as well as its leaders' refusal of economic and political reforms led to a deterioration of living standards and, therefore, to an erosion of the elite's legitimization and, at the same time, to a reduction of the repressive potential of the central state (Reuter, 1992: 97).[4] High inflation rates, unemployment and staggering foreign debts as well as a decrease in living standards all contributed to the emergence of nationalist movements: Republics started to compete for the distribution of social wealth controlled by

3. Out of the 129 ethnic groups in the USSR, only 58 are titular nations, i.e. dominate a Soviet or an Autonomous republic. However, an important portion of titular nations are living in other republics, among them 18 per cent ethnic Russians (Halbach, 1992: 84–85, 87).

4. In the 1970s, Eastern European countries received cheap credits which, after the rise of interest rates in the 1980s, led them into an indebtedness crisis. They were forced to export according to world market conditions, even

the central state and complained that they contributed more than they got from the others, who free rode on them (Hubert, 1994: 97; Reuter, 1992; Gosztonyi, 1993; Snyder, 1993).

In this situation, some republics – most often dominated by, but not consisting of only one ethnic group – demanded a national state of their own in which they expected to be better off than in the multiethnic state. It seems that economic gains and costs have been the most important motive or catalysts for the emergence of ethno-nationalist separatism in the former USSR. The Soviet state was held responsible for the economic failure, and political independence was looked upon as a precondition for an improvement of the economic situation (Halbach, 1992: 75–76, 80–81). Newly founded parties promised that political independence would lead to economic growth, to a national control of its natural resources and to an economic policy in the interest of the nation, especially in regard to the regulation of immigration, a decision concerning industrial planning and sometimes an orientation towards the world market and the EU (Hofbauer, 1994a: 63; Halbach, 1992: 82, 91). Republics that were relatively well-off and contributed more than they received from the state expected to gain more by restricting access to their resources and by stopping the transfer payments to the central state. This is why the dissolution of the USSR started with the rich republics (the Baltic states and the Ukraine) and not with the poorer republics in Central Asia that opted for continued membership in the Soviet Union or, later, in the GUS (Halbach, 1992: 102). In Yugoslavia, too, the first to split off were wealthy Slovenia and then Croatia, whereas poorer Serbia wanted to uphold the central state where it controlled the army and the bureaucracy. This, of course, led to the tangled and explosive constellation which ultimately brought about the war in Bosnia.[5]

---

into the Soviet union, which in turn also began to sell goods to the other 'socialist brother countries' for world market prices (Hofbauer, 1994a: 66–67). This reorientation towards the world economy led to economic disintegration and 1991 to a dissolution of the RGW after the Soviet Union's monopoly of foreign trade had been abolished in 1988 (Hofbauer, 1994a: 60).

5. Many nationalist parties opted for integration into the EU for economic reasons. The competition among the applicant new nation-states for EU-affiliation led to a divide between the Western and the Eastern states and regions: Poles argued against 'uncivilized' White Russians, Ukrainians and Balts against the 'Asiatic' Russian, West Ukrainians in the Bukovina against the 'backward' Eastern Ukrainians (Hofbauer, 1994a: 62). 'Ungrateful' Slovenian and Croatia tried to approach the EU by differentiating between 'lazy' Serbs and their satellites, the Cheks (Reuter, 1992: 128), who had a competitive

However, not only jobs and housing are competed for but a restriction of access to the natural resources of the nation to be and to the revenues distributed by the state are also at stake. By excluding non-members of the ethno-national population from access to these resources, the number of available jobs in administration, army and industry available to the members of the new nation-state will increase. Ethno-national competition, then, is for economic and for political resources, i.e. positional goods (Weede, 1986: 11), and aims at the discrimination and exclusion of non-members of the national community. This can be observed in the newly created nation-states that are still ethnically heterogeneous. When Estonian and Latvian nationalists fought for independence, they were supported by the Russian minorities – a third of the population. The Russians expected a higher living standard in the Baltic states than in Russia and saw no advantage in opting for a continued membership in the USSR. The Estonians and Latvians, in turn, accepted the Russians as their allies in acquiring democratic legitimization for their secession from the USSR. It was only after independence that the latter were labelled as 'Russian immigrants' and their citizenship was curtailed (Halbach, 1992: 94–95; Hofbauer, 1994a: 74 ff.). In the poorer republics that gained independence only after the break-down of the USSR (e.g. Georgia, Moldavia), the dominant majorities, too, tried to exclude ethnic non-members from access to positional resources (jobs, housing, state revenues, etc.). Ethnic minorities could prevent a deterioration of their status only with the help of the central state or their titular republic. Therefore, if a strong nationalist movement of a majority population fights for secession from the central state, the minority group will oppose because they will loose in the new set-up. In turn, the minorities themselves are likely to demand a separate state or integration into their titular republic/state. The struggle for the 'national territory' and its resources will gain momentum and sometimes lead to war.[6] The same principle is effective here: an ethnic minority will opt to

---

economy and who were willing to join the EC against the Slovaks, who in turn had a heavy industry dependent on state subsidies which would not be able to survive on the world markets (Hofbauer, 1994b: 146, 149–150).

6. See the Abkhas, Azhars and Ossets in Georgia, the Armenians in Karabach which is a part of Azerbajdjan, the Gagaus, Russians and Ukrainians in Moldavia (Hofbauer, 1994a; Halbach, 1992). Bosnia is a special case because none of its main populations has a majority: Muslim constitute 43 per cent, Serbs 31 per cent and Croats 17 per cent of the total population. Serbs and Croats are fighting to secede from the Bosnian state and to join the Serbias or the Croation national state respectively.

separate from a newly constituted state when they expect higher advantages and lower disadvantages in a state of their own or under somebody else's control. In other words; each ethnic group will fight for membership in that state in which it constitutes a majority and is able to control or even to monopolize the political and economic resources.

In the meantime, the nationalist avalanche has also reached the Russian republic: provinces with rich deposits of natural resources such as Yakutia or provinces with a strategic position allowing control of the exploitation of natural resources (oil) such as Chechnia wish to separate from Russia, whereas Chechnia will have a better chance of separating due to its ethno-national territory at the border of Russia as well as because of its religious, cultural and historical unity and its ethnic homogeneity. However, a determined Russian leadership fights for the integrity of the Russian territory and tries to uphold control by military means. A more slawophil nationalism emerges opting for the separation from the Caucasian and the Muslim areas elsewhere and demands the unification of all republics and provinces where Russians are in the majority (Hofbauer, 1994a: 80–81; Halbach, 1992: 107–108).

A republic or an ethnic group will decide to separate from a multi-national state and form a national state of their own if the expected economic and political advantages outweigh those that tie it to the larger state. Not only the distribution of political and economic resources but, also the ethno-territorial unity, the relative size and political organization of an ethnic group and the central state's capacity to appease or to repress conflicts, are crucial dimensions in weighing up benefits and costs.

Classes and Ethnic Groups

In order to simplify things, we started from the assumption that ethnic groups are collective actors. However, ethnic groups are not homo-geneous actors but are rather hierarchically divided into classes with divergent interests. The 'decisions' made by ethnic groups, therefore, are the results of social and ideological conflicts as well as of the relative strength of classes both within the larger society and within each ethnic group. Each ethnic group consists of classes and class factions. In order to simplify things, elite, middle class and lower classes can be distin-guished. The 'behaviour' of classes and ethnic class factions depends largely on the constellations of conflict between ethnic groups or classes respectively and on their position in the 'social space' (Bourdieu, 1985). We shall use a simple model of a larger society consisting of classes, as well as a dominant and a subordinate ethnic group. Class and ethnic hierarchy do not coincide: both the dominant and the subordinate ethnic groups consist of different classes (Lenski, 1973).

Although a ruling elite will usually pursue a policy of national unity and seek to balance ethnic conflicts, it nevertheless will support 'its' lower classes in their competition with those of the subordinate ethnic group because the elite depends on popular support in their own group. The lower class of the ethnic majority is able to improve its material position by discriminating against its competitors from the ethnic minority. Distributive struggles and social conflicts do not evolve along class lines but along ethno-national cleavages, thus contributing to the vertical integration of the society along the interests of the ruling elite. The lower classes of the dominant ethnic group will opt for the nationalist alternative if they do not succeed in improving their situation against their own ruling elite – with the help of the lower class of the ethnic minority – and if they can improve themselves at lower costs and with a higher probability of success through a discrimination of the minority population (see below).[7]

The elite of the dominated ethnic group cannot realize its aspirations for a high position in the class hierarchy because of its low ethnic status, although some parts of it may be co-opted by the ruling elite. The remainder of the minority elite will found parties and organizations and will mobilize 'its' ethnic lower classes to fight either for the abolition of the ethnic hierarchy or for secession and an independent state (Smith, 1984). In order to gain nationalist leadership, they will also take on those collaborating with the ruling elite. Thus ethno-nationalist movements not only fight for a separate state by discriminating against ethnic 'others' in the competition for positional goods, but also, as the following example shows, exclude the collaborating factions of the minority elite. The educational policy of the former USSR aimed at enlarging the non-Russian faction of the elite. However, the rising expectations of these newcomers could not be matched. It were those non-Russian, frustrated elites (writers, teachers, journalists, civil servants, etc.) that formed the core of the nationalist movements that brought down the Soviet state. Since 1988, they

---

7. See the rise of Milosevic to power in 1987. He stands for an authoritarian-nationalist populism and aggressive expansionism that agitates against the 'atrocities' of the Kosovo-Muslims against the Serbs in the Kosovo, the 'treacherous ingratitude' of Slovenians and the 'rampant fascism' in Croatia (Reuter, 1992: 123 ff.). See the Russian nationalism taking up the cause of those 18 per cent Russians living in the neighbouring states (Halbach, 1992: 84 ff.).

supported the Perestrojka against the old bureaucracy but fought increasingly for national independence (Halbach, 1992: 66, 93). Their opposition against the old republic elites has led to conflicts since the early 1990s. In the Baltic states, in Georgia, and in Armenia, anti-Communist and nationalist politicians replaced the old communist and reform communist elites (e.g. Hubert, 1994: 94–95; Reuter, 1992: 128–129, 133 ff. for Yugoslavia), or former communists turned into nationalists, as in Kazakhstan and in the Ukraine (e.g. Halbach, 1992: 67, 95; for Serbia and Montenegro see Reuter, 1992: 130, 137 ff.; Gosztonyi, 1993).

While the nationalist elite will profit at any rate from an independent state (posts in the administration, industry and cultural sector, control over the army, etc.), they will only succeed if they receive support from the lower classes. The organized support of the popular classes depends on whether they expect to improve their social and economic situation in an independent state. They will support a nationalist movement if they expect that the repression costs will not be too high and the nationalist project achievable. The nationalist elite has to persuade its lower classes of the fact that they will not better their lot unless they actively engage in the independence movement, and that taking a free ride at the expense of others would lower their chances of participating in the distribution of a bigger cake among less people (Hechter, Freidman and Applebaum, 1982).

A common history makes ethnic mobilization easier: the memory of a former independent state (Baltic states) or of common suffering during terrible conflicts (Serbia, Croatia). The same holds true for discrimination or even suppression of the national culture and language in the school and the media (e.g. Halbach, 1992: 71 on the GUS; Hubert, 1994: 87–88 on Yugoslavia). However, histories can be recounted in very different ways depending on the actual conflicts and interests. Thus, Serbs stress the conflict between Croatian Ustasha and Serbian 'antifascists', while ignoring the opposition between (monarchist) Serbian Chetnics and (fascist) Croatian Ustashas on the one hand and (communist) Serbo-Croatians partisans on the other hand (Snyder, 1993: 5; Denich, 1994).

Ecological disasters – nuclear accidents, dried-up lakes and the degradation of soil by monoculture, industrial pollution, etc. – played a major role in ethno-nationalist mobilization in the former USSR. Ecological issues combined the love for the native soil of an ethnic community and the national territory of an independent state, and made plausible the nationalist program centring on the failed and destructive industrial policy and heteronomy of the central state. Instead, what is argued is a more reasonable regulation of the economy in the interest of the members of a smaller nation-state (Halbach, 1992: 75 ff.).

Ethno-nationalist separatism gains momentum to the extent that the capacity of repression by the central state decreases and the level of organization of the separatist movement rises.[8] This depends on (and enforces at the same time) the population's belief that the nationalist movement will be successful in achieving its goals. Ethno-territorial unity will both render the mobilization of the people easier and will heighten the probability of secession. If the ethno-nationalist movement is strong and successful, but territorial and ethnic boundaries do not coincide, then the ethno-territorial unity will be achieved by force as the ethnic cleansing by the Serbs in Bosnia and by Armenians in Karabach show (Halbach, 1992: 84–85, 87). These examples reveal that ethnic mobilization does not only proceed by propaganda but also by force: before the outbreak of the civil war, Muslims, Serbs and Croats lived more or less peacefully together in Bosnian villages, local-regional identity being more important than ethnic membership. The process of ethnic identification, conflict and mobilization began when (mostly) Serbian militias attacked and drove away the members of the two other groups. These sought the protection of their militias which, in turn, took revenge and forced the Serbian population to align with 'their' militias. The knowledge that they were being punished just for being Bosnians, Croatians or Serbs, seemed to lower the costs of engaging in a nationalist militias. No escape from the vicious circle of ethnic violence, hatred and ethnic antagonism was any longer possible (Denich, 1994).

Ethnic Units as Latent Groups

An ethnic group not only consists of different classes with diverging interests but also constitutes a latent group that only becomes a politically organized group through a process of mobilization and conflict (Bourdieu, 1985; for classes as latent groups). Different parties may

8. State repression may weaken a secessionist movement, although repression may sometimes lead to an intensification of the separatist process, as the examples of the Baltic states and Georgia show (Halbach, 1992: 94 ff.). However, if a liberalization policy leads to a rise of expectations that cannot be later matched, the repression of the national organizations then will accelerate rather than stop the nationalist movement. See the impact of the (failed) coup d'état in August 1991 in Moscow concerning the separatism of the Ukraine (Halbach, 1994: 71) and the aggressive policy by the Serbs in Kosovo and in Vojvodina on Slovenian and Croatian separatism (Reuter, 1992: 123 ff.)

propose socialist, liberal, nationalist and other programmes in a given moment, vying for the people's support (Gosztonyi, 1993: 633). The politicization of ethnic units can be seen as the result of individual decisions in the aggregate: actors dispose of a multitude of potential identities such as state, religious, ethnic, class membership, etc. Which social identity is being 'charged' politically by individual actors and groups depends from which identity they expect the highest gains or the least costs. Although there may be a semantic core of an ethnic identity defining its variation, the specific criteria of membership and exclusion are subjected to a conflictive bargaining process. Potential members and non-members always try to push through that definition of actual membership that best fits their interests and demands.

Which factors determine whether social conflicts and struggles of distribution are fought between ethnic groups rather than classes? Why is it that social actors tend to organize their demands along ethnic rather than class cleavages? To answer these questions is not an easy task. However, I think that the main reason seems to be that the political activation of ethnic units and classes as latent groups have different costs and probabilities of success. Although a central state will also try to suppress attempts of national separatism, the political mobilization of ethnic identity, nevertheless, is less costly than that of a class identity because ethnic units are already pre-existing units of communication (common language and culture). This cultural and linguistic common ground is experienced in everyday life by the members of an ethnic community and facilitates the co-ordination of their actions even before the intervention of state power.[9] As ethnic groups are already structured hierarchically, an emerging movement can rely on the well-established structures of control and leadership. The ethnic elite that leads an ethnonationalist organization usually belongs to the middle or the upper class. It has, therefore, an interest in improving its position by nationalist demands and in not changing the social hierarchy. Thus, both costs of organization and of repression

---

9. The same holds true for religious identity which can also be politically charged, i.e. to serve as a marker of social differences between groups (Catholics and Protestants in Northern Ireland, Hindu and Muslim in India) or to serve ideologically to fight against a secular but unsuccessful state (fundamentalism in the Maghreb states). In the Ukraine, the different options of groups are formulated in religious terms: The Russian population is oriented towards the Russian orthodox church in Moscow, the Eastern Ukrainians towards the Ukrainian orthodox church in Kiev, whereas the Western Ukrainian in the Bukovina are oriented towards the Greek-Catholic church (Hofbauer, 1994a: 69).

are low in the beginning of the movement. It could be assumed that a social conflict between ethnic groups is less costly and that the expected gains in the short run are higher than is the case with class struggle. This does not mean, however, that secession processes are without violence and victims. An ethno-national group with a compact territory may separate more easily than when settling in an intermixed manner with others (Bosnia); in a multiethnic state not willing or not able to repress (e.g. the former Soviet Union under Gorbachov, the Ottoman empire, etc.), secession will be much easier than in a strong and determined state such as Turkey, where Armenians have been massacred, Greeks driven out and where Kurds are now being oppressed by a nationalist state.

On the other hand the political activation of class identity seems to be much costlier because a state elite will fight a class movement from the beginning: a class-conscious lower class movement is very often aimed at a radical change of the social hierarchy at the expense of the elite. The costs of organizing are much higher since class membership entails a much lower level of commonness and its organization is more hampered by free riding, repression and by lack of leadership. Furthermore, the social situation after a social change might be worse than before because the radical transformation of institutions will produce chaos as well as military intervention or economic embargo from outside. A new elite may emerge, eager to install new privileges and thus reproduce a new class hierarchy (Weede, 1986). An underclass movement, nevertheless, can be neutralized in a reformist way, but this would require a state being able and willing to make political and economic concessions. Thus, the fact that social conflicts more often break out between ethnic groups than between classes can be explained by both higher costs of repression and lower chances of success concerning in the latter.[10]

A nationalist policy conducted by the elite of the majority population usually aims at integration of the society. This strategy of integral nationalism neutralizes the potentially dangerous conflicts between classes, especially in times of social and economic crises. The discrimination of an ethnic minority is aimed at improving the situation of the lower classes of the majority group and of thereby increasing their loyalty to the system and its elite. A majority nationalism, therefore, fosters the stability of the society. If an ethnic minority turns towards national separatism and against the state (or the ethnic majority,

10. It should be remembered that most of the successful revolutions in the Third world (China, Vietnam, Cuba, etc.) have been at the same time movements for national independence.

respectively), the state will try to repress or neutralize the secessionist movement. Nevertheless, the political activation of an ethnic identity often is less costly and has a higher chance of succeeding because it exists before being activated politically, whereas a class movement always tends to fight for a more or less radical change of society with higher costs and less prospects of succeeding.

Anti-Immigrant Nationalism in Western Europe

Similar features of nationalist politics as the ones observed in Eastern Europe can also be found in the industrial nations of Western Europe. Ethno-nationalist movements in Western Europe were predominant during the 1970s and 1980s, but declined in the 1990s. This might be explained by the emergence of a more closely integrated European Union taking over tasks from its member states. This eased the pressure exerted by the nation-states on their unsatisfied regions and minorities (Scotland, Bask, Flanders, Northern Ireland, e.g. Schulze-Marmeling, 1994). Many of their problems have been resolved by granting them more autonomy within the nation-states and money and support, not from their capitals, but from Brussels. In Eastern Europe, on the other hand, the process went in the opposite direction. The crumbling of the 'Russian empire' let to a disintegration of the former states: Yugoslavia, Chekoslovakia and especially the USSR. However, the newly independent states are forced by economic reasons to find new forms of co-operation. Thus, Georgia, Moldavia, Azerbaijan, etc. have rejoined the GUS and have eased off their nationalist refusal to cooperate with Russia.

Nationalism in Western Europe most often takes the form of anti-immigrationist movements, a form of majority nationalism against ethnic minorities we have already observed in the Baltic states, in Georgia and other Eastern European countries. We will not look at xenophobia (or racism) from a psychological angle, namely as a relation between manipulating demagogues and their disoriented and misguided victims.[11]

---

11. Very often, xenophobia and racism are misnomers: nationalists pursuing the discrimination or expulsion of immigrants are not necessarily afraid of foreigners and do not despise or hate them (Hoffman-Nowotny, 1973: 333). Although I do not deny the existence of either xenophobia or racism, I prefer the term nationalism because this concept opens a wider field of ethnosociological analysis and leads away from a psychological explanation of the phenomena being misleading on the whole both theoretically and politically (Windisch, 1978).

Such an approach would contradict an important principle of the social sciences, namely that all people have 'good reasons' (interests) to act and behave the way they do, even if we do not accept these reasons. The premise according to which actors decide for that alternative from which they expect the highest benefits and the lowest costs, refers to the necessity to analyse the socio-political interests, the pattern of resource distribution as well as the alternative options these actors have.[12]

The argument that the success of the anti-immigration parties and movements is a reaction to a threat of 'national identity' does not seem very plausible. Although nationalist circles repeatedly invoke a 'loss of values' and 'crises of national identity', this complaint does not explain why and who exactly has come into crisis: a crisis of national identity, if there is any, must itself be explained. I have assumed that actors have a multitude of identities at their disposal. However, it is not these identities, but rather the social well-being of social actors, that is 'in a crisis'. And actors will 'politically charge' their ethno-national identity when they expect the highest chance of improving their living standard and their status by doing so. The discourse of 'construction' and 'deconstruction of ethnic identity' in political conflicts is fashionable today. Indeed, it is important to take into account the historical formation and transformation of national identity (for Switzerland see Romano, 1995). However, without reference to economic conditions and class interests, a study of nationalism is not possible, despite the fact that economic analysis is somewhat out of fashion in present-day academia. The Hungarian case is a good example of my argument. The nationalist government (1990 until 1994) followed a policy of supporting the Hungarian minorities in neighbouring Slovakia, Yugoslavia and Romania. Many of these ethnic Hungarians, having a rather low economic and political status, expected to better their situation by migrating to Hungary. However, with the deterioration of the economic situation in Hungary, the lower classes developed a hostile stance towards immigrants, seeing them as co-

12. I think that even in a situation of crisis and fundamental insecurity, actors are able to assess these gains and losses – set aside path dependence and unintended side-effects in the aggregate – and that they decide on the basis of these expected advantages and disadvantages. This runs contrary to the position Siegenthaler seems to espouse. According to Siegenthaler (1994: 119 ff.), stable periods with confidence in rules and security of expectations are interrupted by periods of insecurity of rules and expectations. Therefore, action cannot be 'rational' in these periods of crisis. A new consent and new rules must first be worked out and the national (linguistic community) is the 'natural' unit of communication and becomes the political focus of orientation.

competitors for scarce jobs and accusing them of free-riding on limited welfare money at the expense of tax-paying citizens. Interestingly enough, even ethnic Hungarians from neighbouring countries were not welcomed, but discriminated against as immigrants, although less than other foreigners such as Gypsies, Arabs and others. Hence, economic considerations clearly overrode ethnic identity. Furthermore, this hostile attitude of Hungarian citizens towards fellow Hungarians and other immigrants could not be organized by rightist parties because these still followed a policy of greater Hungary uniting all Hungarians (Csepeli and Sik, 1995).

I will develop my argument along the following lines: In a situation of growing social inequality and ethnic heterogeneity, when the population is jurally segregated into national citizens and foreigners, when the state has only a limited capacity to deal with an economic crisis, and furthermore, when the organizations of the left are too weak to enforce an improvement in the living standards of the lower classes, then conflicts along ethno-national lines between the lower classes of the majority and the minority will be probable. The immigrant workers are interested in a liberal labour market (in order to earn more money than in their home countries), as are the entrepreneurs who favour a regulation of immigration according to their economic needs (low wages, low state expenditures). The lower classes of the national population, however, try to prevent a loss of income and a deterioration of their economic status (by fighting against a reduction of wages, rents, subsidies, welfare revenues and unemployment benefits) and therefore opt for a reduction of immigration. The government must take into account both the protectionist interests of the national electorate – especially the lower classes – and the interests of the entrepreneurs for a liberal labour market. The jural and political privileges of the national population enhance its position in the competition with immigrants who have no political rights, but hamper, at the same time, the prospect of organizing the interests of all workers – national and immigrant – against entrepreneurs (Hoffmann-Nowotny, 1973: 116). Thus, not only the relative deprivation of economic status but also the inability to improve the situation by placing pressure on government and entrepreneurs is responsible for the competition between the national and the immigrant population and for the discrimination of the latter. I will elaborate on this in the rest of this chapter by referring to the case of Switzerland. During the long post-war upturn of the economy, many labour migrants from the poorer countries came to the rich countries of Western Europe. In Switzerland, immigration increased from the 1950s until the crisis of 1974, after which it began to rise again, and totals almost a fifth of the population today (Dejung, 1984: 163; Hoffmann-Nowotny, 1973). Until the 1960s, both the government and the entrepreneurs thought of the economic upswing as being only of short duration. With the prospect of an economic crisis, the state stalled investments in the infrastructure such as housing, hospitals, schools, etc. (Dejung, 1984: 70). Until around 1963, economic growth has been mainly extensive, i.e. cheap labour was imported instead of investing in the modernization and rationalization of the economy (Dejung, 1984: 164). This development lasted until a rising demand for labour force and full employment caused pay rises and transition to a process of rationalization (Vuilleumier, 1989: 99). At the same time, the conviction gained ground that the Swiss economy was permanently dependent on foreign labour; the immigration policy had to be changed from a rotational to an assimilationist policy (Vuilleumier, 1989: 108; Dejung, 1984: 164): short-stay workers (*Saisonnier*) were allowed to stay longer, together with their families (*Aufenthalter mit Familiennachzug*). As a consequence, the foreign population grew faster than its working portion, which caused an increasing demand for housing, schools, hospitals and transportation facilities. In order to build up hitherto neglected infrastructures, more foreign labour was necessary (Vuilleumier, 1989: 167).

The foreign workers took over the unattractive, poorly paid jobs from the Swiss, who changed into the tertiary sector or were offered better-paid positions in the secondary sector. In the latter, one third of the labour force was foreign by 1965 (Dejung, 1984: 163; Hoffmann-Nowotny, 1973: 63). Especially Swiss workers in the labour-intensive and less profitable industry, with poor qualification and less prospect to move upward, had problems adapting to this new economic situation. They were afraid that immigrant workers would prevent them from getting higher wages and that they would be replaced by foreign workers in the next crises (Hoffmann-Nowotny, 1973: 71, 89, 91; Vuilleumier, 1989: 113–114). Therefore, the trade unions were the first to complain about these negative side-effects of immigration for Swiss workers (Dejung, 1984: 166). The lower classes of the national population perceived themselves as having to compete with immigrants for jobs and housing. Because neither state nor industry could be brought to create secure jobs, wages and cheap housing, etc., the conviction gained ground that jobs for Swiss could only be secured by reducing the number of foreign workers. *Familienachzug* and a high birth rate among the immigrant population (Dejung, 1984: 166; Vuilleumier, 1989: 114) led to the conviction among those who suffered most from the rent increase that cheap housing could be made available by expelling a portion of the foreign population.[13] Windisch (1978) has studied this popular argumentation of a nationalist zero-sum-game among those who adhere to anti-immigration positions.

For the anti-immigrationists, in addition to jobs and housing, the distribution of public expenditures was and is still at stake. In a globalized world economy dominated by transnational, high-tech and high-productivity trusts, the inequalities between nations, regions, economic sectors and between classes are increasing (Narr and Schubert, 1994). The nations enter into competition with each other for positional advantages by reducing wages, relaxing restrictions, investing in infrastructure, taking care of the stability of prices and currency, etc. (Borner, Brunetti and Straubhaar 1994). Because of the limitation of its power to regulate the economy (anticyclical intervention) and especially in times of economic crisis, national governments are less able to defuse social conflicts and even out material harshness through a general welfare policy (Narr and Schubert, 1994; Senghaas, 1994). In order to have a balanced budget, public spending has to be reduced. If an indebted state threatens to reduce its expenditures for retirement insurance, unemployment benefit and transfer payments to farmers, etc. a struggle for the distribution of public spending will commence. Nationalists and xenophobics will look upon the foreign population as parasites to Swiss wealth who put a strain on the welfare state with their families as well as when they are unemployed.[14] Even studies showing that immigrant workers contribute more than they profit financially from the national economy (Weber, 1994) cannot change these convictions. The fact that foreign workers lack political rights allows the most disfavoured classes of the national population to protect themselves against impending downward mobility or even to improve their living standard by advocating the discrimination and exclusion of foreigners (Linder, 1993: 158). Thus, there is not only a conviction of acute competition for jobs and housing but also for the distribution of public spending, which is especially sought after but also more limited in times of crises. It should be stressed, however, that the competition between the lower classes of the national and the immigrant population for jobs, housing, government spending, etc. is the result of the fact that the labour movement is weak and not able to

---

13. This also holds true for those seeking asylum in Switzerland, a group of people rising in number since 1985, even though they were usually denied the right to work (Linder, 1993: 150).

14. This argumentation particularly refers to those seeking asylum. The fact that they come from outside western Europe, are not allowed to work and that some of them are prominent in drug trafficking amplifies this view.

convince a sufficient portion of the lower classes to improve their living standard against entrepreneurs and the state. Therefore, anti-immigration and anti-Europe parties emerging since the end of the 1960s found support especially among the lower classes of the national population: unqualified workers, farmers and elderly people which were most severely affected and afflicted by the economic crisis (Hoffmann-Nowotny, 1973: 110). This is illustrated by the results of the relevant referendum votes.

In the first important plebiscite on this matter in 1970, 46 per cent of the electorate were in favour of curtailing the number of immigrant workers, especially the rural population in the central cantons and Berne, as well as the workers and the elderly in the north-eastern industrial cantons (Hoffmann-Nowotny, 1973: 138–152; Vuilleumier, 1989: 115). Linder (1993: 157) has examined the votes of 1981, 1982 and 1987. All liberalization of immigration had been rejected by the electorate, although xenophobic motives seemed to play a minor role.[15] It is no coincidence that the elderly and those with little education, i.e. the lower classes most threatened by downward mobility, voted in favour of the anti-immigrant policy (Linder, 1993: 158).[16]

Although we must rely on highly aggregated statistical data such as real wage, GNP etc., these data nevertheless show that in the middle of the 1960s (the beginning of the anti-immigration agitation), the growth of the GNP and of real wages were falling, while inflation and public deficit were rising (SBG, 1987), and that the inequality of the distribution of incomes between the upper and the lower 20 per

15. Linder states that not the fear of loosing one's jobs but rather of loosing one's national identity seems to account for the results in the first place. This can be explained by the fact that these plebiscites did not deal in particular with immigrant labour but rather with the issue of those seeking asylum who were not competitors for jobs. Those voting for a reduction of the immigration of foreign labour or asylum seekers or against a EEC-membership are the same. Linder (1993: 152) says that the alleged problems caused by immigrant workers and asylum seekers are treated the same in nationalist propaganda.

16. The 1988 plebiscite on a reduction of immigrant labour, as well as the plebiscites on the EEC-membership in 1992 and on the law against racial discrimination in 1994 showed that the same part of the population voted 'no' (Tagesanzeiger December 12, 1988 on Zurich; Kriesi, Longchamps, Passy and Sciarini 1993: 34–35; Schloeth, 1994: 9). When the EEC-membership was finally rejected in a plebiscite, economically-motivated fears were one of the most important factors. The second important factor – 'loss of national sovereignty' – may reflect the fear that the government may lose its capacity to intervene on economy issues in favour of the national population (Kriesi et al., 1993: 45, 49).

cent was growing (Hischier and Zwicki, 1992: 77 ff.).[17] However, it must be underlined again that not only the relative deprivation (perceived competition and threatening loss of position), but also the prospect of succeeding to improve one's own position, are crucial for the emergence of an *Anspruchsbewegung* (Weede, 1986). Action will not be taken when the threat of deprivation occurs with no prospect of avoiding it. Thus, economic and political factors are closely interlinked and must be taken into equal account. Economic conditions and class relations determine the energy and direction of social change. Social interests are class dependent, but are not effective before being organized into parties and organizations, as Dahrendorf (1992) maintains. Parties compete for votes in order to gain control over the government by mobilizing as many voters and supporters as possible. The extent to which nationalist and xenophobic parties are successful is therefore largely dependent upon the political system and the actual distribution of power between the parties.

The widespread loss of confidence in the electoral process and the turning away from the traditional parties can be explained partially by the fact that the most disfavoured classes do not have the means to participate in formal politics; either because of a lack of education or because of a lack of political rights, as in the case of the immigrant population. On the other hand, the more well-to-do, who do not believe that the distribution of income is unjustified, are heavily over-represented, both in voting and in political parties (Hischier and Zwicki, 1989: 120, 118). Furthermore, Swiss workers have enjoyed an improvement in their standard of living during the long post-war economic upswing (elevator effect). The *Unterschichtung* by cheap immigrant labour without political rights allowed Swiss workers to move upward in the social hierarchy (Hoffmann-Nowotny, 1973). Both developments accelerated the process of individualization, the retreat from party politics and the dissolution of traditional working class culture (Beck, 1986; Dahrendorf, 1992: 236). The most important reason, however, is the integration of the trade unions and the social democratic party in a system of liberal corporatism (Hischier and Zwicki, 1992: 86). Since the late 1950s, the social democratic party has been part of a largely bourgeois dominated 'permanent large coalition' and has thus been neutralized. Its left wing is dominated by middle-class academics

17. Siegenthaler (1994: 138) observes a close correlation between Kuznets-swings and nationalist movements that can also be observed in Switzerland. Although the emergence of an anti-immigration movement does not correlate with the proportion of immigrants in the resident population (Romano, 1995), its relative increase might be relevant (Linder, 1993: 150).

who entered the party in the late 1960s and influenced its political agenda accordingly, although without the support of the traditional working class electorate. Furthermore, the crisis of social democracy is largely the crisis of state-interventionist welfare-Keynesianism. This weakens the position of the left against the centre-right and right parties which have fought – 'more freedom, less state' – for a lean, liberal minimal state since the middle of the 1970s (Romano, 1995: 33). Many traditional lower class voters accordingly turned away from the social democrats in disappointment (Dejung, 1984: 172). Consequently, the pressure for change shifted from the political to the economic trade-union level (Hischier and Zwicki, 1992: 83). However, the trade unions are also integrated in the framework of co-operation with the entrepreneurs under the guidance of the welfare state. The compromise trade of employment and wage increase against renunciation of industrial action brought welfare but also ensured the loyalty of Swiss workers. This 'deal', however, is threatened by the forces of the world economy and internal economic adjustments processes (Hischier and Zwicki, 1992: 87), forces against which national trade unions cannot assert themselves. The influence of the trade unions is further reduced by the fact that foreign workers and – to a lesser extent – the most disfavoured Swiss workers, do not participate. The integration of the foreign labour force would boost trade unions' bargaining power, but would not fit the demands for privilege by the Swiss union members (Hischier and Zwicki, 1989: 119).

Thus, the lower classes' perception of both the inequality of income distribution and of the lack of any prospect of changing this politically within the given party constellation is quite accurate (Hischier and Zwicky, 1989; 1992). In times of economic crisis and when the left is weak and/or neutralized owing to a coalition of the main parties, popular discontent remains unarticulated. Consequently, the emergence of a nationalist-populist, anti-immigration party is highly probable in such a situation, both for economic and political reasons. In fact, nationalist parties – the 'Republikaner' and later the 'Nationale Aktion' – were founded and soon reached an organizational level demanding a plebiscite ('Referendum'). They increased their following and mobilized the growing discontent by stirring up the distrust between 'people' and 'classe politique', i.e. against all main parties forming one governmental block by demanding that immigration be stopped and by claiming to fight for Swiss workers against npatriotic left parties and even entrepreneurs.[18] They

18. The loss of confidence in the government was largely a result of the stepping out of line by the right wing of the great coalition (Schloeth, 1994: 5).

found and find their following primarily among the elderly, among farmers and among the middle-class in the countryside as well as among the urban lower class, who have the most to fear from the transformational economic crisis. The emergence of nationalist, anti-immigration parties created an organizational framework for the articulation of popular discontent and devised ways to take remedial action.

A well-established and widely accepted ideology of the 'Sonderfall Schweiz' supported a nationalist image of an armed, but neutral, independent and economically successful country with a separate history and culture, proud of its direct democracy. This ideology emerged at the end of the First World War and was strengthened during the time before and during the Second World War and later by the rising living standard and welfare after the war. It remained unchallenged until the 1990s (Romano, 1995). Its superior wealth compared to neighbouring countries, as well as the need to integrate a culturally heterogeneous nation, lend additional plausibility and necessity to this ideology, even if Switzerland was and still is heavily dependent on the world market. In opposition to the process of increasing integration of the European community since the 1960s, this nationalistic-patriotic ideology gained in strength and reached its peak in the plebiscite against Swiss membership in the EEC in 1992. The sudden change of position by the government and the main political parties in favour of a political and economic reorientation towards the EU threatened this long-standing national consent. The political vacuum had been filled by rightist parties (first by a few minor right-wing parties; later, in the 1980s, the 'Schweizerische Volkspartei' successfully took over the task of organizing the nationalist electorate). These parties mobilized and still mobilize – now up in arms against the political establishment – along these old positions, arguing against 'the politicians' who are said to betray national independence and identity by submitting to European bureaucracy, and demanding that the state be once again run in the interest of Swiss citizens and that the national wealth be distributed only to these citizens. Nationalist politics combine the demands of the lower classes with the interests of sections of the middle class and small industry, who are in need of being protected against foreign competition. The state elite is prompted to deal with the 'Überfremdungsproblem' and must try to negotiate between pressure from patriotic-national rightists and the adaptational pressure stemming from the highly competitive world economy of which Switzerland is a part.

Conclusion

If the state is no longer able to ease economic hardship by means of welfare policy in a situation of economic and social crisis, and if the political organizations and parties of the left are not able to organize public discontent along lower class demands (same status for foreign and native workers and solidarity against entrepreneurs) and to improve the living standard of these classes, nationalist parties of the right will emerge and promise the national population a larger slice of a bigger cake by discriminating against and excluding the immigrant portion of the resident population. A nationalist zero-sum-game follows that seeks to improve the material situation of the nation to the sole detriment of foreigners. Thus, we find the same integral nationalism – though in a much milder and less violent form – which we have already observed in the Baltic states, in Russia and elsewhere. However, it should be stressed that the competition between the disfavoured classes of the national and the immigrant population is already the result of a weakening of the labour movement, which has not been able to force entrepreneurs and the government to improve their living standards. The weakness of the left is mirrored by the emergence of rightist parties which profit from a pre-existing, well-established national ideology.

Two things should be emphasized: To follow a rational approach does not solely mean placing emphasis upon competition for jobs. Although people often argue about losing jobs to immigrants and of having their wages curtailed and therefore of wanting to limit immigration, national citizens also feel they must compete with immigrants for goods purveyed for by the state: welfare money, unemployment benefit, pensions, subsidies for farmers and cheap housing, etc. The poorer section of the national population views immigrants as free-riders on the 'national wealth' at the expense of tax paying citizens. The second point I would like to make is that it is not only economic competition between immigrants and national citizens which leads to nationalism and anti-immigrationism. In addition to the threat of losing economic status and the fear of deprivation, the existence of appropriate parties or organizations promising remedial action remains a second important factor. These parties have the power to lower the costs of organization to articulate one's claims and to increase the chance of achieving one's goals. This explains why a nationalist party can continue to exist or can even gain momentum, even when it is foreseen that the economic situation of its followers will ameliorate in an economic upturn.

Bibliography

Alter, P. (1985), *Nationalismus*, Frankfurt am Main: Suhrkamp.

Banton, M. (1983), *Racial and Ethnic Competition*, Cambridge: Cambridge University Press.

Barth, F. (1969), 'Introduction', in F. Barth (ed.), *Ethnic Groups and Boundaries*, Boston: Little, Brown, pp. 9–38.

Beck, U. (1986), *Risikogesellschaft*, Frankfurt am Main: Suhrkamp.

Borner, S., Brunetti, A. and Straubhaar, T. (1994), *Schweiz im Alleingang*, Zurich: NZZ-Verlag.

Bourdieu, P. (1985), *Sozialer Raum und 'Klassen'*, Frankfurt am Main: Suhrkamp.

Cohen, A. (1976), *Two-Dimensional Man: An Essay on the Anthropology of Power and Symbolism in Complex Societies*, Berkeley: University of California Press.

Csepeli, G. and Sik, E. (1995), 'Changing Content of Political Xenophobia in Hungary', Paper presented at the Cost A2 Workshop on Nationalism and Ethnicity, Berne, March 2–4.

Dahrendorf, R. (1992), *Der moderne soziale Konflikt*, München: dtv.

Dejung, C. (1984), *Schweizer Geschichte seit 1945*, Frauenfeld: Huber.

Denich, B. (1994), 'Dismembering Yugoslavia', *American Ethnologist*, 21, pp. 367–390.

Downs, A. (1957), *An Economic Theory of Democracy*, New York: Harper & Row.

Gellner, E. (1991), *Nationalismus und Moderne*, Berlin: Rotbuch.

Gosztonyi, K. (1993), Nationalitätenkonflikte in ehemals sozialistischen Ländern', *Osteuropa*, 43, pp. 630–640.

Gurr, T. (1993), 'Why Minorities Rebel', *International Political Review*, 14(2), pp. 161–201.

——, (1994), 'Peoples Against the State', *International Studies Quarterly*, 38, pp. 347–377.

Halbach, U. (1992), *Das sowjetische Vielvölkerimperium*, Mannheim: Meyer.

Hechter, M., Friedman, D. and Appelbaum, M. (1982), 'A Theory of Ethnic Collective Action', *International Migration Review*, 16(2), pp. 412–439.

Hischier, G. and Zwicki, H. (1989), 'Wahrnehmung der sozialen Ungleichheit in der Schweiz', *Widerspruch*, 17, pp. 109–122.

——, and Zwicki, H. (1992), 'Soziale Ungleichheit in der Schweiz', *Widerspruch*, 23, pp. 76–90.

Hobsbawm, E. (1991), *Nationen und Nationalismus*, Frankfurt am Main: Campus.

Hofbauer, H. (1994a), 'Ökonomische Krise, nationale Wiedergeburt, militärische Lösung. Zur Situation der ehemaligen Sowjetunion', in J. Elsässer, H. Hofbauer, H.-P. Hubert, W. Karl, A. Komlosy, K. Mellenthin, H. Möller, J. Renner, D. Schulze-Marmeling, R. Walther and S. Zimmermann (eds), *Krisenherd Europa: Nationalismus, Regionalismus, Krieg*, Göttingen: Verlag die Werkstatt, pp. 55–84.

——, (1994b), 'Tschechen und Slowaken: die Bindestrichnation', in J. Elsässer,

The Nationalist Game

H. Hofbauer, H.-P. Hubert, W. Karl, A. Komlosy, K. Mellenthin, H. Möller, J. Renner, D. Schulze-Marmeling, R. Walther and S. Zimmermann (eds), *Krisenherd Europa: Nationalismus, Regionalismus, Krieg*, Göttingen: Verlag die Werkstatt, pp. 137–170.

Hoffmann-Nowotny, H.-J. (1973), *Soziologie des Fremdarbeiterproblems*, Stuttgart: Enke Verlag.

Hubert, H.P. (1994), 'Minenfeld Balkan: Nationalismus im ehemaligen Jugoslawien', in J. Elsässer, H. Hofbauer, H.-P. Hubert, W. Karl, A. Komlosy, K. Mellenthin, H. Möller, J. Renner, D. Schulze-Marmeling, R. Walther and S. Zimmermann (eds), *Krisenherd Europa: Nationalismus, Regionalismus, Krieg*, Göttingen: Verlag die Werkstatt, pp. 85–110.

Keyes, C. (1976), 'Towards a New Formulation of the Concept of Ethnic Group', *Ethnicity* 3(3), pp. 202–213.

Kriesi, H.-P., Longchamps, C., Passy, F. and P. Sciarini (1993), 'Analyse de la votation fédérale du 6 Décembre 1992', *Vox*, No. 47, Adliswil.

Lenski, G. (1973), *Macht und Privileg*, Frankfurt am Main: Suhrkamp.

Linder, W. (1993), 'Migrationswirkung, institutionelle Politik und politische Öffentlichkeit', in W. Kälin and R. Moser (eds), *Migration aus der Dritten Welt*, Berne: Haupt Verlag, pp. 147–164.

Mellenthin, K. (1994), 'Nationalitätenkonflikte im Osteuropa. Ein Überblick', in J. Elsässer, H. Hofbauer, H.-P. Hubert, W. Karl, A. Komlosy, K. Mellenthin, H. Möller, J. Renner, D. Schulze-Marmeling, R. Walther and S. Zimmermann (eds), *Krisenherd Europa: Nationalismus, Regionalismus, Krieg*, Göttingen: Verlag die Werkstatt, pp. 23–42.

Narr, W.-D. and Schubert, A. (1994), *Weltökonomie: die Misere der Politik*, Frankfurt am Main: Suhrkamp.

North, D. (1990), *Institutions, Institutional Change and Economic Performance*, Cambridge: Cambridge University Press.

Pfaff, W. (1994), *Die Furien des Nationalismus*, Frankfurt am Main: Eichborn.

Pomian, K. (1990), *Europa und seine Nationen*, Berlin: Wagenbach.

Reuter, J. (1992), 'Jugoslawien: Zerfall des Bundesstaates, Systemwechsel und nationale Homogenisierung in den Teilrepubliken', in M. Mommsen (ed.), *Nationalismus in Osteuropa*, Munich: Beck, pp. 118–142.

Romano, G. (1995), 'Fremdenfeindlichkeit und Fremdenangst: Zur Semantik des Fremden im öffentlichen Diskurs', Manuskript.

SBG (1987), *Die Schweizer Wirtschaft 1946–1986*, Zurich: SBG.

Schloeth, D. (1994), 'Analyse der eidgenössischen Abstimungen vom 25. September 1994', *Vox*, No. 54, Adliswil.

Schulze-Marmeling, D. (1994), 'Nationalitätenkonflikte in Westeuropa', in J. Elsässer, H. Hofbauer, H.-P. Hubert, W. Karl, A. Komlosy, K. Mellenthin, H. Möller, J. Renner, D. Schulze-Marmeling, R. Walther and S. Zimmermann (eds), *Krisenherd Europa: Nationalismus, Regionalismus, Krieg*, Göttingen: Verlag die Werkstatt, pp. 43–53.

Senghaas, D. (1994), *Wohin driftet die Welt*, Frankfurt am Main: Suhrkamp.

Siegenthaler, H.-J. (1994), 'Supranationalität, Nationalismus und regionale Autonomie', *Traverse*, 3, pp. 117–142.

Smith, A. D. (1984), *The Ethnic Revival in Modern World*, Cambridge: Cambridge University Press.

Snyder, J. (1993), 'Nationalism and the Crisis of the Post-Soviet State', *Survival*, 35(1), pp. 5–26.

Vuilleumier, M. (1989), *Flüchtlinge und Immigranten in der der Schweiz*, Zurich: Pro Helvetia.

Weber, R. (1994), 'Wohlfahrtsgewinne durch Einwanderung', *Neue Zürcher Zeitung*, No. 305: 21.

Weede, E. (1986), *Konfliktforschung*, Opladen: Westdeutscher Verlag.

Williams, B. (1989), 'A Class Act: Anthropology and the Race to Nation Across Ethnic Terrain', *Annual Review of Anthropology*, 18, pp. 401–444.

Windisch, U. (1978), *Xénophobie? Logique de la pensée populaire*, Lausanne: l'âge d'homme.

–13–

Boundaries, Cohesion and Switching: On We-Groups in Ethnic National and Religious Forms

Georg Elwert

Research on nationalism, ethnicity, fundamentalism became – as it seems – an easy task. There are authors we all cite, and there are the objects of our study, which delineate themselves so clearly. This self-delineation, however, causes as this chapter shall argue, problems for social science, because it induces us to overlook: (1) processes of switching *between different* frames of reference; (2) processes of (physical) *reproduction* (namely the link to families), and (3) the *fuzziness* of limits, which may fulfil specific social functions. The first issue – the process of switching – is rarely used as a reference point in the study of we-groups, since the actors themselves insist rather on the eternalness and stability of their group. It seems to me, however, that it is precisely this odd phenomenon which can bring us new insights and may be used as a plough to work through the garden of ethnicity theory.

Some of the authors in the field, namely those representing the essentialist tendency, become victims of the discourse of the groups studied insofar as they believe in the primordiality of emotions and traditions as a basis for the creation and maintenance of we-groups.

So-called ethnic violence in Bosnia, Somalia and Turkey is explained in this way. This sounds plausible to us, because the suffering of the victims is expressed in emotions and creates strong emotions in us. But this is only a link of connotations and is not logical. Violence of the type reported from these countries, social (i.e. organized) violence, with weapons, the transport of actors to the field, the premeditation of ambushes, etc. requires logistics and a cool planning mind, not spontaneous emotions (nor the vagueness of historical references to traditions). There are central actors, such as warlords or political entrepreneurs, who need to be studied. In addition, it is necessary to see the role played by conflict-channelling institutions, by economic solidarity and by communication in order to understand the stabiliz-ation of we-groups. Switching becomes an important focus in this field of study not only insofar as it helps us to understand cases of failed stabilization and the conditions of stability, but also because it is a flagrant falsification of assumptions about 'deep-rooted traditions' which might condition a given we-group.

First, we shall try to understand what the usefulness might be of referring to the complicated concept of 'we-groups' instead of limiting ourselves to nationalism or to fundamentalism.

Processes Under the Appearance of Stable Entities

We-Groups

It is a common assumption that ethnicity is a case for anthropologists and that nationalism is a realm for political scientists. This is, however, an erroneous assumption. Both phenomena can be classified as we-group processes. They share with other we-group processes class movements and religious movements and the same driving forces and systemic patterns. Thus, there are no separate tools for their analysis, be it the hermeneutics of fieldwork or distanced systemic analysis.

Examples for motives underlying nationalism and other we-group processes are:

Mega-identities: migrants losing their frame of reference, which had provided them with a sense of prestige, are attracted by mega-identities, which compensate for the lost individual identity, e.g. Pan-Germany ('Groß-deutschland'), world revolution, etc.

Clientelism: when competing over new resources, it may be advantageous to create a clientelist network designed as a 'we-group'.

Moral ethnicity: if behaviour seen as antisocial is felt as a personal threat, one option may be to create a social form imagined as a community but framed as an organization which excludes immoral individuals and unites moral ones.

Social Construction

Two basic assumptions underlie this argumentation:

1. Neither ethnic groups nor nations constitute a 'natural' order. They compete in human history with other types of social organization

for a place in the central organizing structure. We can even find social structures where there is no we-group of the ethnic type (Elwert, 1989).

2. Nations and ethnic groups are social structures which have to be reproduced. That means, they have to be recreated by each successive generation. They may have to fulfil new functions and may use old plausibilities. But the transmission of plausibilities works only if the functions are satisfied.

Switching Between We-Group Identities

One remarkable feature of we-groups is the process we call *switching*. This means a rapid change from one frame of reference to the other. A class movement may become a nationalist one, a nationalist movement transforms itself into a religious mobilization, or a religious network redefines itself as a class movement. Switching processes easily escape scientific treatment because they 'change department' – from religious to social, to political studies and vice versa.

A series of examples illustrate this: Sri Lanka's Trotskytes turned their class movement into an ultra-nationalist militant organization. Iraq's secularist, nationalist Baath party redefined itself under Sadam Hussein as Islamic – and won international support. Hamas is about to gain political supremacy by restating the (beforehand secular nationalist) Palestinian cause as an Islamic one. Patrilineal descent groups in the tension field of Afghanistan reacted with identification or by stating difference to the religiously defined powers and thus turned into religious sects (Canfield, 1973).

We (Kristina Kehl and Georg Elwert) studied *Alevites* in Turkey (Kehl, 1992).[1] The first thing we were able to ascertain with some historical certainty, is that there were endogamous groups which wanted to distance themselves from Sunnite Ottoman rule. The Shiite facade and the rule of secrecy covered, in fact, a wide range of beliefs. Under Atatürk's Republic they became fervent republicans and were over-represented in the left of centre republican group and in socialist organizations. The installation of the holy men ('dedeler') who kept the oral traditions was discontinued. The holy books ('buyruk') were given away. However, since the Alevites' identity was also ascribed to them from the outside and was maintained by their social environment, they were forced to continue endogamy.

The new conjuncture of religious prestige symbols and boundary definitions and the self declared moral rearmament of fundamentalism

1. The project was financed by the *Deutsche Forschungs-Gemeinschaft*.

is precisely including them to re-create a religious 'identity'. They are very active in retrieving – with the help of foreign anthropologists – old religious folklore and are copying religious books; they are confronting the painful task of harmonizing the incompatible and some are directly moving forward to sheer invention of 'forgotten' beliefs (with some Iranian help). Nevertheless, none of these transformations could alleviate violence against this group. The readiness to hit – wrongly called 'hatred' – is conditioned by the internal dynamism of the dominant 'community', which, precisely in order to regain its self-image of community, longs for the symbolic affirmation of difference. Because of the heterogeneity of the dominant ones, the easiest option for the definition of the 'we' is the creation of foes represented as a negative print of the morality which one would like to use to describe oneself. The Alevites are easy targets for this, merely because they happen to be there and not because of this or that feature.[2]

The concept of switching refers: (1) to alternations between reference frames and (2) to moves between different more-or-less inclusive conceptions of the group's boundary. The switching may imply a redefinition of the group's boundaries, or these boundaries may be kept and reinterpreted.

Redefinition of boundaries: A strategically important minority may be included or an 'annoying' group of actors excluded (thus, Nazi Germany forged a concept of 'Volksdeutsche'/ethnic Germans, which included the Austrian origin 'Sudeten-Deutsche' and the Dutch origin Mennonites of Russia and Ukraine and excluded the Jewish population of East Europe, which had been the primary organizer of German schools and other cultural organizations in these countries and whose German ethnicity was hailed and instrumentalized by the German army's high command ('Oberkommando der Wehrmacht') in the first world war). A segment of a larger group may discover their 'real' identity or several groups may 're'-unite under one umbrella.

2. We can apply some of this paper's arguments to the Alevi case. The remarkable dynamism of a syncretistic group combining an overt and a hidden connotative identity may be caught in a trap if confronted with the rigidity of a modern state's structure. Double facades and integrative dynamism in the transformations of ritual and beliefs can be seen from the outside as falseness and confusion. The accusation is – in systemic terms – that of blurring boundaries and escaping clear categorization. The showing of unequivocal markers is imposed upon the community, and flexibility has to be given up in favour of a containment in restrictive conceived limits. This normalization into an ethnic or religious form, portrayed as modernization by the internal protagonists, may be seen in systemic terms – without any value judgement – as a 'trap'.

Redefinition of retained boundaries: In the case that the boundaries are kept, the change of reference level brings other actors or resources into play or pushes them to the background where they risk being forgotten. Sensible (or shrewd) political actors pre-empt changes; they take the lead.

Among the groups marginalized by dominating Christian and Islamic groups in the Horn of Africa emerged a label 'Galla' or 'Oromo' which was linked to a specific mode of cohesion.[3] A generation and age class system allowed for the integration of neighbours. The expansion of the very militant Oromo groups along with and against the Ethiopian empire was a constant historical undercurrent at the Horn of Africa – until they became, in the twentieth century, the most extended ethnic label of Abessinia. Modern civil war put them under a different stress. Although one can still observe 'Oromization' (Zitelmann, 1994) in refugee camps, in other situations 'identity' (belongingness) is redefined by using certain (patrilineal) kinship links, (Kushitic) multilinguality or Islam or Christian tainted laicism as a reference in order to become part of a Tigre kindred, a Somali clan, spearhead of an Islamic movement or Ethiopian nationalist.

The dynamics of maintaining or reshaping boundaries, of defining values and institutions as being core ones or as being odd, is the product of tensions within the socio-political context. This is valid whether the 'identity' sought for is the ideologized sentiment of value ascription or the definable characteristics of real or invented cultural traits. Similar contexts of tension will reproduce similar configurations of we-groups (Wimmer, 1995). When the crucial political categories are religious, the marginal populations tend to become 'heretics' (Canfield, 1973). When the crucial political categories are national or ethnic, those marginal populations which can only escape the dynamics of peripherization by marking their difference, show ethnic distinction.

In order to create difference or to reach incorporation, switching may be necessary. This follows a pattern which might be called the 'clarity imperative'. There is a need for both: an accepted code and clear markers.

Religion, ethnicity, local group and kinship are examples for codes. The code may even be narrowed down to a sub-code or may be expands. Consequently, 'religion' may be narrowed down to book religion, or book religion to Islam. So the Pashtoo nomads, who until the last century were Jews, had to mark their difference within the

---

3. Here I refer to a research project led by Thomas Zitelmann and myself; also financed by the Deutsche Forschungs-Gemeinschaft.

Islamic code when only it became accepted.[4] Inversely, the Christian Bogumil heresy on the Balkan increased the clarity of difference in reference to their Serb and Coat neighbours by switching to Islam when conquered by the Ottomans – thus, establishing the Bosnians. The codes of 'locality' and 'kinship', which are now presented as remnants from a past when human beings lived in accordance with nature, are neither natural nor banal. Like age, generation, gender and physical features, locality and kinship are means by which social order is given a natural appearance; 'to naturalize' it. Nevertheless, there is no natural law that made any of this a strictly observed organizing principle which could be found in every human group. 'Kinship' may also be an idiom expressing ties to neighbours, 'age' may mean rather generation, etc. The code of locality in the definition of we-groups may be a means of defining land rights – among the Mapuche in South-America as among the Gur speaking groups of northern Ghana, Togo and Benin, 'people of the earth' or 'people from here' are common self-given names. In other social environments, marriage rights and inheritance are the crucial issues; kinship (especially unilateral kinship) is the reference code defining the dominant we-group structure (not excluding locality, etc. as a secondary reference, to which one may switch).

Changes of shape or parameters of reference may occur with we-groups with amazing rapidity (which is conditioned by the volatility of power) (Wallerstein, 1980). This does not exclude the continuity of 'ethnic' names, which is instrumental for any claim of political inheritance rights.

Ethnic names, a specific type of music (e.g. Uzbekistan, see During, 1993), traditional norms and so forth constitute the *inventory* upon which a given group may draw in order to design its limits and its 'identity'. This inventory may be limited or it may be broad. It will be broad in situations of enhanced interregional communication. This inventory should be distinguished from a closet where one hangs a selection of one's coats, because these symbols are *not owned*. Some salient marker of distinction seen elsewhere else may as well be adopted as a sign familiar from childhood and onward. Inventories are shared with other collective actors. Thus, symbol use may overlap or may even alternate between enemy groups. The grasp of symbols is, how-ever, not random. Rather, it is conditioned by (1) the plausibility in regard to other markers of order and (2) by the communicative

4. Similarly, some Black Sea Christians in Turkey switched to Islam in this century dominated by 'ethnic exchanges', but maintained their difference by declaring themselves to be Alevites.

need to create salience and difference. An example of the first is the importance of all references which suggest collective rights of past generations in an environment where *inheritance* is a strong argument for claims. Examples which may be given of the second need are too obvious to be covered in detail here (national dress, orthographic reforms, racial ideologies, etc.).

Excursion on the Recurrence of Essentialism

The phenomenon of switching is an uncomfortable one in regard to essentialist theory. This is so because those 'primordial values', which presumably constitute by their very 'nature' the boundaries of ethnic groups, suddenly lose relevance. At this point, an excursion into the recurrence of essentialism might be appropriate. Since Max Weber's time, it was shown that those groups which call themselves 'ethnic' or 'national' use boundaries in respect to the criteria of functionality of the social structure aimed at, on the one hand, and criteria of plausibility, which 'went without saying' in their respective context, on the other hand. It is *society dressed as community* which produces the emotional cohesion of these we-groups.

Those who argued against Weber (or later against R. Thurnwald, W. Mühlmann, F. Barth, etc., who took up his ideas) that there were 'natural' forces binding all ethnic groups together – namely language, religion, culture – could be confronted with empirical examples of ethnic groups, recognized as such by all their neighbours, which lacked at least one of these criteria (see the latest demonstration by Thomas Höllmann (1992) on Southeast Asian examples, and for the history of ideas, Ernst W. Müller (1980)). Nevertheless, the reason why, in spite of all the proof supporting the formalist perspective, some authors come back to an essentialist view (or try to 'harmonize' these logically incompatible concepts), may be due to the fact that we are all working within an environment of common, popular ideas. Most ethnic groups try to present themselves as 'natural'; this induces a continuous stream of 'immigration of protoscientific ideas' into social science.

Multiple Options

Polytaxis – The Latent Multiplicity of Order and Identity

Groups and individuals may belong to different reference groups simultaneously; according to the opportunity of situations, they may stress one or another of these affiliations as being their 'real' one (Goody, 1956; Schlee, 1994; Zitelmann, 1994).

The switching process uses a characteristic of human society, which animal social structures, so popular in theories of in-group behaviour, do not share: the capacity to preserve, in latency, different orders. We are all multilingual. That is to say, at least in respect to language registers, we master different roles which we put into practice according to the situation, and we make consecutive use of several affiliations (several modes of belonging, or identities in the strict systemic sense). We may call this phenomenon *polytaxis* or polytactic potential.

Excursion on the Concept of Identity

At this point, we need to make an excursion into the concept of identity. There is currently a boom of essays treating this concept. However, it is not by accident that this term is almost never operationalized. Most common is a use whereby identity means, under the appearance of a scientific concept, an ideologized sentiment. A closer look, however, reveals three different meanings which sometimes are brought together:

1. Belongingness (membership, the binding *together* of different people, stemming from the original philosophical meaning; I will refer to identity in this sense, if not otherwise indicated). It is possible to belong to more than one category.
2. Self information (what people think which characterizes themselves).
3. Self-valuation/attribution of prestige (what are the parameters of esteem and where does one place one's own group in relation to others; a central field of research – as the foregoing one – which should not be confused with identity in the strict sense, but which should, rather, be seen in correlation to it).

Individual/Situational Switching

There is, however, a difference between the working of polytactic identities with closed and with open structures (in most cases identical with the opposition of ethnic groups and nations). For African ethnic structures, it is common that individuals claim several affiliations. Here we find *situational switching* (or ethnic conversion) as an individual process. It is quite rare that there is only one 'ethnic identity'. (In a famine, a Fulani herder in the West African Borgu might opt for the sedentary way of life of a Gando, if he were poor, or might become a Dendi trader, if he had some wealth.)

This remarkable freedom of option shall, however, not induce us to anthropological romanticism. The multiple opportunities of polytaxis also allow for involuntary situational switching. A person may be excluded, e.g. if it is 'discovered' by oracle that he or she belongs 'in reality' not to our we-group, but to the secret order of witches.

There are some configurations where individual switching is a common response to conjunctural ups and downs (Horn of Africa, the interior delta of the Niger). There are many others configurations whereby this is uncommon and may, ultimately, only be achieved at the point of burial, after having lived for a long period in the new community as the 'foreign' married wife or husband. The difference between these configurations seems to me to be created by the different (especially more or less elaborated) structure of the boundary zone and its 'import procedures', the liminality of social systems (see below).

Once open (ethnic) groups are transformed into 'para-national' bodies with established rights regarding the state, there begins a painful process of opting between these – quite convenient – multiplicity of options and of negating all but one of them by pseudo-historical text production. In regard to nationalities, it is rather the exception (and tolerated only with the idea of transition in mind) that multiple affiliations exist. Within the nation-state, ethnic options are rigidly welded onto the state structure and its formal procedures. Nationality and subnational entities with only singular options of belonging are such a case. Some countries even insist in a symbolically prominent manner on this singular subnationality by printing it onto identity cards (in Rwanda these were instrumental for the organized genocide of Tutsis).

This rigid coupling constitutes a major difference between identities referred to on an ethnic or on a national level. Individual switching in the national field tends to become a form of 'cheating'. Potential multiple belongings (identities) become something dangerous when agitators label them as potentially unloyal. Ethnic cleansing then becomes some nation-states' ultimate answer to polytaxis.

Political Entrepreneurs / Central Persons as Catalysators of Collective Switching

I said above that switching is a rather common – although rarely-noticed process (leaders tend to long for continuity and 'historical roots' and anthropologists are the natural prey for ideological leaders). This does not imply that a theory for collective switching exists. Individual situational switching (opportunistic switching in the descriptive sense) is one thing, but collective, co-ordinated and synchronized switching is another. Motives and boundaries must be redefined, new labels become markers for connection and old labels must be declared invalid currency. Therefore, a minimal consensus has to be sought. However, the social structure provides, in general, no routines or institutions for such negotiation processes. This requires a very specific type of social actor: political entrepreneurs or central persons.

My hypothesis is that switching processes are correlated with a process whereby the number of subjectively active actors in a given field (politics) is increased, whereas, paradoxically in the same process, the number of actors providing interpretation – especially of new phenomena – and implied in structurally relevant decisions declines. The subjective impression is that 'we are all getting politicized' – more people are entering the political arena. But after an initial ('chaotic') phase, the number of those who indicate (virtual) directions, leaders in the strict sense, decreases. If, subjectively, future chaos becomes a problem, if the 'creation of a future', the selection of paths for future events, becomes the desideratum, then the moment for a specific type of actor has come. These are people who can place a restriction on future options under the appearance of opening ways in a thicket. In other words, they can create power 'from nothing'; it is a power which emerges from beyond the established decision-making procedures. The ones who can produce this 'miracle' shall be called central persons. They are big men, warlords or adopted leaders (from the outside).

Big men and warlords both can convert prestige into power (i.e. big men) or wealth into power (i.e. warlords). They act in the resource triangle of power, wealth and prestige:

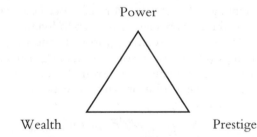

Power

Wealth   Prestige

Warlords turn the wheel clockwise. They create power with money for weapons and mercenaries and win prestige from power, which gives them credit for the acquisition of new wealth. Big men turn the wheel the other way around. They transform prestige into power. Power may create wealth, but wealth and labour power must be 'devoted' to the people in order to create prestige.

Power may also have its origin from outside of the we-group. These central persons can be referred to as 'adopted leaders'. One such case seems to me to be Kemal Atatürk when adopted by the Alevi-community. Another more recent example is the role chancellor Kohl played in the East-German transformation process (after the Protestant big men of the civil rights movement reached the limits of their mobilization capacity).

Nevertheless, the formal mechanism of importing power from the outside or of creating power from prestige or wealth is not sufficient. In order to be successful, central persons need a very specific personal quality: namely an interpretation capacity ('Deutungsmacht') linking them in a feed-back loop to the polytactic reference schemes of those they want to lead. Interpretation and orientation relieve one of the strain of complexity. The capacity to interpret with seeming clarity and to reduce the complexity of the future with intellectual tools is the personal attribute sought.

Political entrepreneurs may also switch individually from separatism to nationalism or vice versa. (Thus, the former separatist Konrad Adenauer later became a symbol of the moderate national feelings in Germany. Silvio Magnano left the Italian fascist student movement to become a successful leader of the (separatist) South-Tyrolians.) One is tempted to say that in the environment of nation-states, one must be a political entrepreneur in order to switch, since individual switching here is rather prohibited.

Ideologies for Switching

Switching is not a random process. It is not even 'normal'. For social scientists, the phenomenon of switching should of course be normal, but for the individual in most situations routine and continuity represent easier options. Switching has to refer, as formulated above, to established symbolic inventories and is limited by these; if, for example, religious we-groups have no historic precedence and if they do not constitute networks of communication or exchange nor provide institutions with conflict arbitrations, then there is no switching possible regarding this religious reference.

Central persons may have to add to the inventory and may have to alter the structure of relevances[5] (new goals must become more important than those stabilizing the routine) before they can operate

5. This necessary change in the structure of relevance assimilates switching we-groups to processes of individual conversion as described by Berger and Luckmann (1980).

the switching. In order to alter the structure of relevance, new fears and new hopes must be conceived.

Changes in the field of symbols which order perception andrender it concrete have a peculiar algorithm. They should be close to the routines of thinking and simultaneously should appear as innovations. An appropriate formula might read: '99 per cent accustomed concepts plus 99 per cent innovations'. The best solution is travesty! The innovations are presented as traditions (see, on the invention of tradition, Papstein, 1978; Hobsbawm and Ranger, 1983) and/or the conceptual limits keep their place and the appearance is altered.[6]

If deeper changes in the social structure are sought or if marginal persons want to occupy centre stage, then another algorithm might be more appropriate or might be used in combination: the creation of a co-ordinate system. Something is defined as a core norm and every behaviour is judged in terms of distance to this zero point. Belonging to a specific 'race' or belief in certain values or rather the practice of certain rituals are defined as 'the fundamentals' from which any other condition of well-being may be deduced. It does not seem convincing to me to accept the protagonists' self-made definition of the 'fundamentals' as being the doctrinal core of their religion. Whether the 'shador' or Trinitarianism, these beliefs are seldom those found in the holy books. Symbols are chosen which react to other symbols in the time of present action. Even a non-doctrinal religion such as Hinduism is attributed certain 'fundamentals' (Randeria, 1995). The leaders define their own place as 'zero'. This is the irony of fundamentalism.

Driving People into Otherness

It should not be forgotten that beyond ideologies used for active switching, people might be driven into another self-definition. Most of the Jews expatriated by Nazi-Germany relinquished their 'German' self-definition and kept their new American, Israeli, etc. identity, even after the war.

A paradigmatic case is that of the Alsatians (and Lothringians[7]), the inhabitants of the former German province Elsaß-Lothringen from 1872–1918, living on the left bank of the river Rhine (Jahr, 1995). In

6. This solution of changing the symbols and keeping the content can even be found in 'new' theories in the humanities.
7. In German 'Elsaß-Lothringer' or simplified 'Elsässer', though this only refers to the southern, Allemanian part of the population.

1914, at the start of the first world war, they were as engaged in the nationalist cause as any other German 'tribe' ('Stamm'). But since their 'Germanness' dated only from 1872 (when Germany annexed this part of France without permission from its inhabitants due to the fact that they spoke German), the military hierarchy was mistrustful. Thus, once the war started, they treated this territory as occupied land. When German troops accidentally fired upon one another, it was erroneously believed that the shots came from a guerrilla. Censorship was imposed upon newspapers and letters. If an Alsatian soldier did not return from the battlefield, it was immediately suspected that he was a deserter, although all others were assumed killed or taken prisoner. In spite of an absence of statistical support for this prejudice, the Alsatian recruits received special treatment. Civilians who called one anther names by making reference to the others' home region, faced imprisonment if the verbal aggressor was Alsatian and the other not – but not vice versa.[8] People felt given up on by Germany. With no underground pro-French movement, opinion completely changed until 1918. When the French entered the territory after the peace agreement, they were hailed, and everyone declared her- or himself as French, although the majority of the population had given up bilingualism during the German period and although for most people 'French' was only linked to the identity of their parents or grandparents. It would seem that the same procedure is used by the Turkish army 'in order to' drive all Turkish identity out of the Kurdish-speaking populations of its East. What is more, the Russian government probably 'succeeded' this year in driving out any remnant of Russian identity among the population of its province Chechnya.

Populations deprived of equal access to the social and material goods relevant to them tend to opt for another identity. The German proletariat of the nineteenth century which opted for the internationalist we-group of 'the working class' is, in my opinion, such a case. Such a phenomenon is strengthened if the people are ascribed a different identity by the majority – under such a condition, labelling and insult can become a material force. Certain Black American movements seem to me to illustrate such a case (Irek, 1992). A higher prestige status and the hope of a better associated material status make switching the best and easiest option.

---

8. The Suebian could call the Alsatian from the Vogese mountains 'Du Wackes!' but not the Alsatian the Suebian 'Du Schwob!' (one year prison).

Reproduction

Ethnicity/National Identity and Family Structures

Switching is more commonly linked to daily behaviour than our anthropological or political research indicates: the definition of belonging to a group is directly linked to the field of kinship and alliance structures. It depends upon the kinship structure, taking into account whether a person belongs to her/his father's, mother's, mother's brother's or spouse's ethnic group. Once ethnic groups or a nation are established, the production of kinship laws becomes one of their first preoccupations.

This brings us back to the classic definition of an ethnic group. Frederik Barth's (1969) definition, referring to ascription and to the self-ascription of boundaries, is too broad. This remained unnoticed for some time due to the fact that every reader had some preconception of what was meant. The definition also implies, if read strictly, political milieus and other subcultures. What was implicitly thought, as being a defining characteristic, although not written, is that these groups are a sub-set of those groups which transcend families and which integrate families as the central reproductive structures.

Definition

Ethnicity/national identity and family structures Ethnic groups are family-comprehending social categories, which ascribe themselves (or are ascribed by others) an (exclusive or multiple) identity.

To be born into a family identified with a given group produces the right to belong to this group according to the membership definition attached to this family. Switching implies the negotiation of identities, legal conflicts over the question as to whom someone belongs and the 'underliving' ('cheating') present in all human behaviour regarding norms. This is exposed in individual strategies dealing with ethnicity via kinship and alliance. People may be included by the initiation ritual required for marriage. They may opt for matrilineality instead of patrilineality. They may, in a virilocal environment, use uxorilocality as a means of integration. Endogamy as a group norm is no accident; it may be a strategically necessary element.

States are conscious of this. It is remarkable that even countries which claim – in simplification – that their citizenship is defined according to locality ('jus soli') and not according to descendance ('jus sanguinis'), such as is the case in France and the US, devote much attention to the difference between marriage and 'sham marriage' as well as to the marital status of their citizens' children born abroad.

This link between the dynamics of we-groups and reproduction has an impact upon demography when statistics are broken down to groups differentiated by social structure or culture. The mode of inclusion affects demographic growth or shrinking on different levels. That migration is linked to individual switching is obvious. Whether migrants who marry in the country are counted as locals or not depends upon the specific mode of inclusion. Neither the modes of inclusion nor the groups' limits are stable. The limits may meander within a generation.

In some groups (e.g. the Berba of northern Benin), women have no ethnic status at all. Their social integration is achieved through sons, who undergo the initiation ritual. To bear children is a primary social necessity for women in these or similar social conditions.

Finding Forms

Stabilizing We-Group Identities

Once we see switching as a normal process which reveals to us the universal polytactic potential, then we can have a fresh look at those groups which do not switch or who at least keep their boundaries.

What stabilizes ethnic groups and other we-groups? Current theory is primarily concerned with processes of splitting, of re-drawing boundaries and with the creation (invention) of legitimating ideology. Some hints may be found in how nations are built according to modernization theory. (Here, however, every conceivable factor is touched in such a way that the theories can never be wrong.)

It seems to me that two processes are of central importance:

1. Moral economy/practical solidarity: a distribution process of goods and services which, by many actors, is not viewed as being (market-) economy. Rather, the principles of distribution are that which economic anthropology calls generalized reciprocity or redistribution. This extends from help provided to anonymous persons belonging to the same we-group to redistribution through welfare and pension schemes (Elwert, 1987; Kohli, 1987).
2. Institutions of conflict resolution: an increase of the conflict processing capacities ('Konfliktfähigkeit'). This may be reached by the creation of institutions for arbitration or by the implementation of a normative system equally relevant for all the members of the

we-group (Hirschman, 1994). It was not 'common values' but the new 'B.G.B.' (common law) which made, at the end of the last century, German nationals out of citizens of German states. It is often stated that common values – at least a minimal core – are needed to create a we-group. Empirically, we have difficulty finding cases to illustrate this point; instead, what we have found, are institutions and mutually accepted procedures which forego the creation of common values.

As a German, I am supposed to bring language into the discussion (following Herder, who 'naturalized' nations by reference to language[9]). In order to retain some distance regarding this discourse, it should be seen that there are sufficient we-groups of ethnic form without a common language. We should, instead, draw attention to the fact that communities of discourse can also be interpreted or seen in relation to arbitration of conflict and economics of reciprocity. Arbitration requires a code, and this code has to have a linguistic form (a given language or two corresponding isomorphic registers of two languages). Norms about sharing knowledge or keeping it in secrecy – thus making it an economic good – constitute codes of communication, which make a language a relevant or an irrelevant tool for social action.

Not one language directly, but rather one network of communication combined with shared social norms, seems to be at the basis of all processes of we-group formation. Even in situations of seeming powerlessness, this combination allows for the attribution of honour and shame (the 'reputation sanction') as a means of social control.

Those features of community which strike us most – a common habitus (similarities in style and routines) – have been studied by Ralph Bohnsack and his group (Bohnsack and Çaglar, 1993) in their analysis of group formation among German youth. It was found that habitual community as a later development started by a mutual articulation of individual plans for activities, thus creating an interdependence, which one may call community of fate ('Schicksalsgemeinschaft'). Norm-breaking or violence which provokes revenge are a powerful but risky means of creating a community of fate in the emphatic sense; the weaker the groups' capacity to create a common code or habitus, the stronger is the inclination to produce collective risk or foes by means of violence.

---

9. See Diericks (1989) for a discussion of Herder and his followers.

Liminality

Social systems do not only exist in the self-limiting status of ethnic groups, although the mode of information storage in anthropology (arranged according to ethnic groups) may suggest this. There are two modes: one is characterized by opening up and networking with the imperative of including an optimal number of persons, who beforehand were strangers, into a network of reciprocal relations. The other is the restrictive closing up of we-group formation, addressed in this paper. But it is both forms, the bimodality of networking and group closure, which create the dynamism of mankind. Although we may conceive some historical processes as an alternation of both modes, I would like instead to draw attention to social arrangements which combine both – the definition of people as strangers and their inclusion.

The self-description of those features of we-groups which create their stability rarely mention the fact that all of these arrangements seldom produce unambiguous borderlines. Yet, the multiplicity of social subsystems produces rather complicated legal arrangements (e.g. differentiation between political and economic citizenship and civic rights for strangers as social or economic actors). Each of these boundaries are subject to a tidal movement whereby some actors are for some time in and some actors are for a short time out. This causes the social boundary – largely unnoticed by the major population – to become a broad *liminal zone*. This liminal zone fulfils important social functions. It is a field where new ideas and arrangements are tested out before they become adopted as 'ours'. This very adoption as 'ours', the 'nostrification', requires for some items social arrangements and institutions.

In order to find out what is accepted and what needs to be scrutinized, this liminal zone acts like ship locks. Due to their precarious positions, individuals in this field are highly sensitized. They may perceive in advance the usefulness of an upcoming new arrangement (because they saw earlier its functioning outside the system or in the liminal zone) and they may react more allergically to something as 'strange' (because they want to be 'in').

The 'Modernity' of Nationalism

The strength of the human race in respect to other animals is its great flexibility. Multiple identities and switching processes contribute considerably to this. The creation of nation-states (which was an 'evolutionary success', or more precisely, which proved to be instrumental for pattern expansion in other fields) produced, however, a set-back in respect to flexibility concerning an individual's polytactic social behaviour.

Rather complicated legal arrangements try to cope with this drawback (e.g. differentiation between political and economic citizenship, civic rights for strangers as social or economic actors). They contribute in such a way that social boundaries become broadened liminal zones and act as a surrogate for polytactic ethnic flexibility.

From the perspective of an individual actor who makes opportunistic use of his or her multiple affiliations in an ethnically defined environment, a national structure still looks 'underdeveloped'. We still have a long way before achieving the flexibility of we-group identity, which is the strength of ethnic systems.

Nationalism and other we-group mobilizations are, however, a product of 'modernization' in a restricted sense. If we understand 'formal modernization' as the concomitance of expanding market economies with expanding communication systems linked by a positive feedback, then nationalism and fundamentalism can clearly be understood as aspects of this modernization. We should, however, keep in mind that this definition of modernization does *not* make any reference to (civic) values or to social differentiation through institution-building.

In this perspective, warlord systems and genocides are part of modernization. Insofar as modernization increasingly creates links to anonymous people, and insofar as these links increasingly dominate the world as 'societal' ('gesellschaftliche') relations, there emerge *undercurrents* which reinterpret and reconstruct social links as built-upon emotions and or face to face relations (Frühwald, 1992). If, for example, marriage is less regulated by lineages, if selection of mating partners is opened to persons unknown to the heads of families and if the formal guarantees and rituals are handled more and more by state authorities, then 'love' becomes an attractive code which can be interpreted as being decisive in leading to marriage (Luhmann, 1982). I place this example in the foreground in order to underline the fact that nationalism is not the only 'undercurrent'. Nevertheless, it is a rather obvious case. Societal links are reinterpreted as community (Weber, 1922). The real process may be one of building institutions which link persons, who are, in most cases, anonymous to one another. The facade of self-descriptions dwells upon images of community, using metaphors of face-to-face groups and evoking emotions.

Nationalism and the related concept of 'Nation' have also contributed of course to our image of the modern world. It has contributed many ideological elements which go without saying today. It may be worth discussing them.

Modern politics can also be seen as a symbolic process, motivated and limited through sociohistorical dynamics. That modern nationalism is so intimately linked with war is not an obvious or even natural combination. For the masses, who had to be integrated as soldiers, war was a costly and risky enterprise. A reconstruction of the prestige system was necessary in order to alter this attitude. The 'Hero', particularly the dead one, needed to be constructed as a peak element in the prestige pyramid (removing from the soldiers the ridiculous image of Plautus' 'miles gloriosus') and even as an object of secular quasi-religious devotion. This ideologem was then artfully intertwined with oscillating metaphors of 'Freedom'. Freedom was seen, on the one side, as a controlled realm conceived of as 'own' – the own farm or workshop or family – and, on the other side, as an accessible realm – the freedom of movement for migrant traders and access to commodities. The oscillation of both aspects was responsible for the strength of this concept.

The more politics were associated with communication, the more it was plausible to link we-groups to languages. Thus, the idea that one nation should have one language – and later – that one language makes a nation, is incrementally gaining acceptance, although at the period when nationalism was formulated, the social reality was still that of multilingualism.

In its beginnings, nationalism was far from being a plausible concept. Now the combination of an 'obvious reality' (language) with strong sentiments of prestige (heroes) interwoven with equally strong sentiments of fear and hope (freedom) appears largely unchallenged and contributes to our image of the modern world. This combination, however, was acquired in a two-century long process of variation and selection which suggests that this is not the end of we-group -history; competing concepts may yet be in the process of evolving.

Acknowledgements

I would like to thank the following individuals for the useful hints they offered to me: Artur Bogner, Ayse Çaglar, Chris Gregory, Krisztina Kehl, Ute Luig, Rainer Münz, Günter Schlee, Andreas Wimmer and Thomas Zitelmann.

Georg Elwert

Bibliography

Barth, F. (1969), 'Introduction', in F. Barth (ed.), *Ethnic groups and boundaries*, Boston: Little, Brown, pp. 9–38.

Berger, P. and Luckmann, T. (1980 (1977)), *Die gesellschaftliche Konstruktion der Wirklichkeit*, Frankfurt am Main: Fischer.

Bohnsack, R. and Çaglar, A. (1993), *The Prison House of Culture in the Study of Turks in Germany*. Sozialanthropologisches Arbeitspapier, No. 31, Berlin: das arabische buch.

Canfield, R. L. (1973), *Faction and Conversion in a Plural Society: Religious Alignments in the Hindu Kush*. Anthropological Paper, No. 50, Ann Arbor: University of Michigan.

Diericks, L. (1989), *De Groene Idee, Mens en Natie*, Gent: Kritiek.

During, J. (1993), 'Nation et territoire en Asie Intérieure', *Yearbook for Traditional Music* 25, pp. 29–42.

Elwert, G. (1987), 'Ausdehnung der Käuflichkeit und Einbettung der Wirtschaft – Markt und Moralökonomie', in K. Heinemann (ed.), *Soziologie wirtschaftlichen Handelns, Sonderheft der Kölner Zeitschrift für Soziologie und Sozialpsychologie*, 28, pp. 300–321.

———, (1989), 'Nationalismus und Ethnizität – Über die Bildung von Wir-Gruppen', *Kölner Zeitschrift für Soziologie und Sozialpsychologie*, 3, pp. 440–464.

Frühwald, W. (1992), 'Romantik', in E. Fahlbusch et al. (eds), *Evangelisches Kirchenlexikon*, Göttingen: Vandenhoeck & Ruprecht, pp. 1667–1675.

Goody, J. (1956), *The Social Organization of the LoWiili*, London: H. M. Stationary Office.

Hirschman, A. (1994), 'Social Conflicts as Pillars of Democratic Market Society', *Political Theory*, 22(2), pp. 203–216.

Höllmann, T. (1992), 'Kritische Gedanken zum Ethnos-Begriff in der Völkerkunde – am Beispiel festländisch-südostasiatischer Bevölkerungsgruppen', *Tribus*, 41, pp. 177–186.

Hobsbawm, E. and Ranger, T. (eds), (1983), *The Invention of Tradition*, Oxford: Oxford University Press.

Irek, M. (1992), 'The European Roots of the Harlem Renaissance', Ph.D. dissertation, Freie Universität Berlin.

Jahr, C. (1995), 'Nationale Identitäten im Widerstreit: Elsässer und Lothringer im Ersten Weltkrieg', Paper read at the Graduiertenkolleg Gesellschaftsvergleich, Freie Universität Berlin, June 22.

Kehl, K. (1992), *Vom revolutionären Klassenkampf zum wahren Islam. Transformationsprozesse im Alevitum der Türkei nach 1980. Sozialanthropologisches Arbeitspapier*, No. 49, Berlin: das arabische buch.

Kohli, M. (1987), 'Ruhestand und Moralökonomie. Eine historische Skizze', in K. Heinemann (ed.), *Soziologie wirtschaftlichen Handelns, Sonderheft der Kölner Zeitschrift für Soziologie und Sozialpsychologie*, 28, pp. 393–416.

Luhmann, N. (1982), *Liebe als Passion*, Frankfurt am Main: Suhrkamp.

Müller, E. W. (1980), 'Der Begriff "Volk" in der Ethnologie', *Saeculum*, 40, pp. 237–252.

Papstein, R. (1978), 'The Upper Zambezi: A History of the Luvale Peoples', Ph.D. dissertation, University of California, Los Angeles.

Randeria, S. (1995), *'Hindu-Fundamentalismus': Zum Verhältnis von Religion, Politik und Geschichte im modernen Indien. Sozialanthropologisches Arbeitspapier*, No. 67, Berlin: das arabische buch.

Schlee, G. (1994), *Identities on the Move: Clanship and Pastoralism in Northern Kenya*, Kisumu, Kenya: Gideon S. Were Press.

Wallerstein, I. (1980), *The Capitalist World-Economy*, Cambridge: Cambridge University Press.

Weber, M. (1922), *Wirtschaft und Gesellschaft*, Tübingen: Mohr.

Wimmer, A. (1995), 'Stämme für den Staat – Tribale Politik und die kurdische Nationalbewegung im Irak', *Kölner Zeitschrift für Soziologie und Sozialpsychologie*, 47(1), pp. 95–113.

Zitelmann, T. (1994), *Nation der Oromo. Kollektive Identitäten, nationale Konflikte und Wir-Gruppenbildungen*, Berlin: das arabische buch.

-14-

Italy's Northern League: Between Ethnic Citizenship and a Federal State

Gianni D'Amato and Siegfried Schieder

Introduction

When the *Leghe* first appeared in the region of Veneto and unexpectedly gained 4 per cent in political elections, the dominant rhetoric of the time explained this event as a preindustrial residual and nostalgic holdover resisting modernity. The wave of modernism experienced in the 1980s did not appreciate localism. The new anthropology was represented at its best by Bettino Craxi, prime minister from 1983 to 1987 of the most durable government in the history of the Republic, and secretary of the Socialist Party from 1976 until 1993 (for which socialism was no more than a tribal memory). Aspiring for an Italy in fifth place among industrialized nations, Craxi and other leading political figures predicted an imminent reabsorption of the *Leghe*.

A more detailed look at the political landscape would have shown how wrong this assessment was. The localities in which the *Leghe* succeeded were not marginal, but rather, since the 1970s, distinguished themselves by being exceptionally socially and economically dynamic. The provinces of Veneto and Lombardy invested a large amount of their resources (Tuscany and Emilia-Romagna) in the flexible reorganization of their industries and enforced a set of social innovations. Known as the 'third Italy', a multitude of little and medium-large enterprises settled in these prospering towns and provinces (for a brief introduction see Bagnasco, 1977; Trigilia, 1981; 1986; Piore and Sabel, 1984). The protest of the *Leghe* in these areas signified more than a simple longing for the past: it signified anticipation of the future.

The *Lega Nord*, an umbrella organization covering six regional leagues and led by Umberto Bossi, manoeuvred itself into the centre of Italian politics. This new political actor has risen on a vague platform of federalism by appealing to northern dislike of anything and anyone farther south than Rome. Their demands for a tri-partition of Italy in 'macro-regions' would allow connecting citizenship (Kleger, 1995a) with an ethnically regulated territory (Rusconi, 1993).

The 'southern question' – i.e. the economic and cultural gap between northern and southern Italy – represented an important analytical and theoretical framework since unification in 1861. This tradition was vital for the nation-building, although one of the results was the creation of a stereotyped self-image of the north as holder of all economic and social advantages and of a backwards south. This interpretation, which is not completely wrong, impeded a reflection on problems concerning the north and an interrogation of the 'northern question'.[1] The current paradox is constituted by the fact that it is not the weakest parts of the country which are threatening by rebellion and secession, but rather the developed areas of the north.[2] Historically in the last century, grown solidarities and institutions have been challenged in regions which command unification and have announced their hegemony to the entire territory. Nevertheless, the foundations of unity have turned: a large part of the northern population expresses its resentments concerning southerners, immigrants and the state, and wants to cut them off in order to prevent endangerment of further social and economic development.

The formation and spread of the *Leghe* is symptomatic of the cultural and political change Italian society has experienced in the past fifteen years. Therefore, reconstructing the rise of the Northern League should allow us to understand the basis of this reversal that prompted many northern Italians to cut their traditional bonds to the south and to support a movement promoting localism, autonomy and ethnicity. By referring to the *Resource Mobilization Theory* (McCarthy and Zald, 1977), we will depict *Lega Nord* as a political entrepreneur which does not only react to popular demands but which is also able to construct identities and offer new mobilizing supplies which distinguishes it from other traditional parties.

The Lega Nord as a Political Entrepreneur of Crisis

Comparative international studies have shown that in western societies conventional forms of political participation are diminishing (Tarrow, Klandermans and Kriesi, 1986). Traditional politics seem to be insuf-

1. See the special issue in *Meridiana: Revista di Storia e Scienze Sociali*, 1993 (January), No. 16.
2. Hobsbawm (1959) offers an accurate history of Italian rebellious movements.

ficient to better educate and politicize active citizens. For this reason, unconventional politics and forms of civil disobedience have received growing attention (Kleger, 1993). Social movements and new parties undertake problems neglected by traditional organizations. What is more, increasing alienation from traditional politics and the decreasing importance of left-right categories are not exclusively an Italian phenomenon; they abound in all western societies. The Italian case is marked by the fact that many of its citizens are closely connected to a party, even if they do not feel represented (Biorcio, 1991: 43–46). More than in any other country, this gap between old politics and the population has created a demand for new political parties.

Since the 1970s, different groups and movements have coped on the political market but none as successfully as the Northern League. Its leaders acted as political entrepreneurs – to use a metaphor from the *Resource Mobilization Theory* – and responded exceptionally well to changing realities. They chose their resources skilfully and succeeded in enlarging their influence and in mobilizing an increasing number of citizens.

The rise of the Northern League with its threats of ethnic secession, has inspired a series of reflections in the press and among intellectuals and scholars concerning the historic weakness of Italy's national identity, its causes and consequences. In the absence of any strong attachment to the institutions of the nation-state, the decline of consolidated political identities provoked a crisis. The proceeding secularization of the 'white' Catholic subculture[3] in the north-eastern part of the country weakened long existing solidarities. Economic tensions in the new industrialized areas, growing dissatisfaction among the new entrepreneurial elite, and the dividing contrasts between an economically strong, but politically weak periphery and Rome created a growing demand which traditional parties could not satisfy.

The Northern League provided an answer to this disorientation by reinventing the identities of territorial communities, by reconstructing solidarity bonds through a strong appeal to the common *ethnos*, and by successfully challenging other political parties. What is more, the *Lega Nord* proved to be a capable competing political actor which deeply questioned the qualifications of traditional parties to satisfy demands concerning political identity. *Lega Nord* seems to be an entrepreneur well experienced in strategically utilizing the crisis of the political regime to its own profit. Although their symbols are not new, their direct communication and language is markedly different

---

3. 'Political subculture' refers to the work of Milton Yinger (1960). For the Italian discussion see Galli (1966) and Trigilia (1981).

and represents an innovation in Italian politics (Allieri, 1992). Although at times their techniques recalled the beginning of the ecological movement, *Lega Nord* does not support post-materialist values. Their resentment concerning taxes and their appeal for a new tax legislation are indicators of a neo-materialist perspective (Diamanti, 1993a: 105). Even their field of action is not extra-parliamentary but, on the contrary, focuses upon the parliamentary arena where they defend and promote their values and identities. Further difference between it and new parties lies in its organizational structure which is based on a tri-partition between the core (*militanti*), the members (*appartenenti*), and the constituency (*simpatizzanti*).

The Four Periods of Development

The development of the autonomist movement in Italy has been divided into four periods by the renowned *Lega* scholar Ilvio Diamanti: the constituent period (1983–1987), the constructive period (1987–1990), the affirmative period (1990–1992) and the present period of consolidation (Diamanti, 1993b; 1994). The concept of territory and the disenchantment of the traditional political system remain the main reference when measuring the success of the Northern League during these stages. Long before the Northern League appeared, territorial commitment was a significant pattern of political mobilization. Its importance lies in its ability to construct historic and cultural identities (Melucci and Diani, 1992). Retaining distance from the political system was not only a way of limiting the power of the state, the parties, the unions, and the administration, but it was also an expression of dissatisfaction with the degeneration in Italy today. The demands of the citizens in the northern regions concerning these two dimensions were better registered, formulated, and represented by the *Lega Nord* than by any other party and became the specific content of a new political identity. Consequently, the ductility of these concepts are particularly adequate in reconstructing the phenomenon of the Northern League.

The Constituent Period (1983–1987)

The constituent period was influenced by the first appearance of the *Liga Veneta*[4], an autonomist movement in the region of Veneto which

---

4. The 'mother of all Leagues' according to its former leader and later president of the Northern League Franco Rocchetta.

received in the most industrialized areas nearly 8 per cent of the vote (1983). Their success, however, was mainly determined by the political environment. One explanation refers to the widespread crisis of the 'white' subculture in north-east Italy, which formerly depended on a tight relationship between the Christian Democrat Party (DC) and the civil society mediated by the Catholic Church and its associations. This regional society experienced a strong process of secularization beginning in the 1960s to which the Christian Democrats responded by lowering their catholic profile. Since a relation to politics was no longer a matter of religious commitment but rather one of materialistic exchange, new orientations towards local affairs and against the nation-state expanded; namely attitudes which had been formerly integrated into the common sense of the universalist and national church.

To many commentators, it was the sensation of relative deprivation in Veneto which favoured the rise of the autonomist movement. There was a common feeling in the beginning of the 1980s of living in a prosperous but politically peripheral region experiencing heavy economic percussions. Being politically powerless in such promising provinces enhanced the sense of frustration; the *Liga Veneta* represented the possibility to express of expressing this dissatisfaction in times of insecurity. Thus, the *Liga Veneta* was a result of a secularized society and of the fear of losing control over territory in times of radical change (Diamanti, 1993a: 115). According to this view, it becomes clear why the autonomist did not penetrate into the 'red zones' (Tuscany, Emilia-Romagna, Umbria), the central regions of the peninsula led by the Communist Party (PCI). This subculture was not affected by the libertarian values of the *Leghe* and went through a crisis only after the fall of the Berlin Wall and the break-down of the Soviet myth.

Although the extraordinary performance of the *Liga Veneta* had demobilizing effects on the old parties (Corbetta and Parisi, 1985), the needs promoted by the autonomists should not be underestimated. With graffiti slogans such as *Veneto ai Veneti*, *Roma KanKaro d'Italia* and *Forza Etna*, they advocated a strong territorial identity against all transformations that might endanger local integration. A vote for them was a vote against Rome, against the state and the south – symbols and projections of all Italian deficiencies.

By using the concept of 'ethno-regionalism', the *Liga Veneta* defended the idea of the territory based on ethnicity. The request for autonomy and self-comprehension as a 'nation' united by cultural, historical and anthropological peculiarities was legitimated in the name of the 'people' (Diamanti, 1993a: 135). This understanding, however, was not entirely shared by their electors, who were mainly interested in defending their material interests. This asymmetrical relation between electorate and leadership was the origin of decreasing support of the *Liga Veneta* in later elections.

The Constructive Period (1987–1990)

The second stage – the constructive period – was determined by the *Lega Lombarda* and the leadership of Umberto Bossi. Although, in the beginning, Bossi's concept coincided with that of the *Liga Veneta*, and although he tried to construct a Lombard identity through the public use of the dialect, he was soon forced to review his politics (Biorcio, 1991: 68). Bossi's distinction of the jargon of the political class (*politichese*) was often incomprehensible to ordinary people. The language of left-wing intellectual discourse (*sinistrese*) was often even more impenetrable. In contrast to Veneto, Lombardy has many dialects, and in urban areas of Milan, Italian became the language of most of the habitants. Consequently, speaking dialect did not prove to be a successful political support for the *Lega Lombarda*. To prevent marginalization in pure folklorism, Bossi had to create new territorial categories. Instead of appealing to an ethnic identity and to Lombardy as a 'nation', the 'community of interest' was defined as being the new common ground. Cohesion to this new solidarity was enforced by the notion of a 'shared enemy', illustrated by the inefficiency of the state, the abuse of power by the parties, high taxes and the 'southern mentality' (*mentalità terrone*).[5] This rhetoric confronted the apparently industrious and productive 'Lombard people' with the state, and the south accused the wastefulness of resources produced in the north. As the intolerance and impatience of the corruption and inefficiency of the political class increased, the *Lega Lombarda* succeeded in supplying explanations for the state of the nation.

With a 'neo-regionalist' identity, the *Lega Lombarda* not only mobilized the discontented citizens, but also offered a new *frame alignment* with which to interpret reality. This construction diverged completely from that of the traditional parties. For the first time in many years, a party spoke a language that corresponded with the feelings and the imagination of ordinary people. This affinity strengthened the social and territorial acceptance of the *Lega Lombarda* and in 1987 they succeeded (Diamanti, 1993b: 120) – as had the *Liga Veneta* some years before – in those industrialized areas in Lombardy that were formerly dominated by the Christian Democrats and the Socialist Party.

5. 'Terrone' is pejoratively used to indicate southerners in Italy. For a short account of intra-Italian racism see Lepsius (1990).

For a long period, the phenomenon of the Leagues was not under-stood by the traditional parties. They did not confront the problems the Leagues pointed out, but instead concentrated upon the political language the Lega Lombarda used, thus enhancing the antagonistic legitimization of the new political actor. Bossi's crude and often vulgar lexicon was a substitute for the impossible utilization of dialect and an indispensable part of his populist appeal to many northern voters. Sexual innuendo was also a part of his repertory ('La lega ce l'ha duro') and helped create an effective political language that reflected the break with habits, practices and the forms of organization of the post-war Republic (Biorcio, 1991: 70). This style of communication and its constant appeal to the 'people' were the elements at the end of the 1980s which constituted the success of the northern populist movement and its position on the political market. Even the profile of *Lega Lombarda*'s voters had changed: in the first period uncultured, elderly men living in little cities voted significantly more than did others for the League. At the end of the last decade, this difference significantly decreased. The *Lega Lombarda* started expanding in cities such as Brescia, Como, Varese, Mantova and Milan eliminating other Leagues and strengthening its central position among the autonomist movement.

The Affirmative Period (1990–1992)

Of all of the Leagues, only the *Lega Lombarda* challenged the Christian Democrat strongholds in northern Italy in the beginning of the 1990s, although the Leagues in Piedmont and Veneto celebrated successes here as well (Macke, 1990: 688). Nevertheless, they could not compete with the dominance the *Lega Lombarda* reached in Lombardy, which won more than 20 per cent of the votes in an administrative election and which became the second political force in the regional parliament.[6]

Hence, one of the targets of the *Lega Lombarda*'s leadership was unification of the Leagues' protest to win strategic importance in northern Italy. According to this aim, *Lega Lombarda* and other auto-nomist movements such as *Liga Veneta*, *Piemont Autonomista* and leagues from Liguria, Emilia-Romagna and Tuscany unified themselves as confederation called *Lega Nord*, led by the Lombard leader Umberto Bossi, after defeating Franco Rocchetta (*Liga Veneta*) and Gipo Farassino (*Piemont Autonomista*) in the beginning of the 1990s. This unification became of fundamental importance to the rise of *Lega*

6. See *La Repubblica*, 9 May, 1990.

Nord and prevented the leagues from continually struggling against one another for influence in the north of the country.

During its first congress in February 1991, the Northern League expressed doubts about the persistence of the Italian nation. This policy was apparently confirmed by an increasing impatience among large sections of the north-Italian population concerning state-institutions and traditional parties. The lack of *alternanza* (taking turn) in post-war Italian government resulted from an electoral system, under which proportional representation virtually guaranteed that centrist alliances would rule eternally and which made the state a stronghold of the Socialist-Christian Democrat coalition. Because of the persistent asymmetry between north and south, huge amounts of tax money flowed southward, via Rome, in the name of economic development. Although this policy strengthened consent in the south, the so-called *assistenzialismo*, the spending money for social purposes, increased the budget deficit, which is currently at an annual rate equalling approximately 10 per cent of the GDP. The wastefulness and corruption of the public sector have been fostered by the enduring system of *lotizzazione* (dividing up power among the main political parties), which reinforced distrust in the traditional parties. The national debt, regarded by some economists as unsustainable, presented the DC government with difficult choices: it lifted taxes and investigated tax evasions more thoroughly. In particular, small entrepreneurs and artisans – the potential electorate of the Northern League – experienced a restraint of their sphere of action. Growing dissent towards such politics and towards the state made the *Lega Nord* a successful 'anti-party'-party (Diamante, 1993a: 123).

However, not only economic and social problems have favoured the rise of the Northern League; events of international importance, such as the fall of the Berlin Wall and the perestroika process in USSR, have also contributed in dissolving the blocked party-system in post-war Italy. There was no longer a reason to continue anti-Communist rhetoric after 1989, and its absence had devastating effects on the legitimization of cold war parties such as the DC and their allies (Allum, 1993).

While *Lega Lombarda* was still promoting a defensive ethno-regionalism during the 1980s which considered the region a 'nation', in the 1990s *Lega Nord* backed a radical federalism which defined democratic participation in terms of an ethnically determined, inter-regional territory. Gianfranco Miglio, an expert in constitutional matters and a former 'ideologue' of the *Lega Nord* (who in years past dabbled unsuccessfully in Christian Democrat politics), divided Italy into three financial and cultural autonomous 'macro-regions', namely

Padania in the north, *Etruria* in the centre of the country, and the *Repubblica del Sud.*[7] In order to enforce this constitutional change, Bossi threatened secession of the northern regions and discontinuations of all alignments of solidarity between north and south by boycotting taxation. *Padania*, a construct which, in the beginning, did not have a common identity, gained, through the threat of secession, an identification platform enlarged symbolically by flags and bills.

A further reason for promoting a radical federalism (which was more a confederation than a federation) was based upon the assumption of an existing economic and social homogeneity in northern Italy. *Lega Nord* was able to explain the gap between north and south by the use of anthropological patterns. An important category was the discovery of a so-called 'entrepreneurial culture' which – according to Bossi – was particularly diffused in the northern regions of the country. By merging ethnic and economic contents, the leadership of *Lega Nord* created the foundations of their existence and identity.[8]

Federalism was conducive to the strategy of the Northern League because it was able to evoke different emotions and ideas. One aspect of federalism which proved important to the *Lega Nord* was its functionality in overcoming the Unitarian-centralist structure of the Italian state and its 'parasitarian bureaucracy' as a way of defeating the diffused patronage system of the parties. Another important aspect of federalism was its political opportunity structure which gave northern regions sovereignty in economic and fiscal policy. These instruments would have enlarged and cemented the northern hegemony over the country.

The success *Lega Nord* experienced was based on developments it had implemented itself. *Lega Nord* reacted earlier than other political actors to shifting realities. In addition to this awareness, Umberto Bossi succeeded as a political entrepreneur in directly communicating to his audience, in intervening in political processes and in addressing new political themes. In the beginning of the 1990s, *Lega Nord* presented itself as an entrepreneur of the political crisis wishing to be at the forefront of the institutional renewal of Italy.

The Consolidated Period (1992–1995)

It is a common belief in political science that electoral results are indicators by which one can analyse the quantitative and territorial

7. See his contribution to *Il Mondo economico*, 1990. Miglio was a professor in constitutional law at the Cattolica University of Milan.

8. See Diamanti (1993b: 90). Miglio (1994: 11) offers an anthropology of Lombards as businessmen.

expansion of parties and movements. Hence, shifting successes refer to a change in power between political forces. Against this background, the parliamentary elections of 5 April, 1992 can be considered a breakthrough in the history of the Italian republic. *Lega Nord* won 18 per cent of the votes in the north of the country and became the second strongest political force in the region.[9] Nevertheless, in central and southern Italy, *Lega Nord* was not able to gather consent, and its importance remained marginal. As of May 1992, Italy was characterized by an electoral tri-partition with different geographical representations: the *Lega Lombarda* ruled in the North, the renewed post-Communist PDS in central Italy, and the Christian Democrats, the Socialists and their allies in the South.

Why did so many former DC and PSI voters change their mind and promote the rise of the Northern League in northern Italy? The reasons are very complex and are primarily based on three events that shook public opinion: the anti-corruption operation of Milan prosecutors Antonio Di Pietro and his chief Francesco Saverio Borelli which placed more than three thousand political figures, businessmen, and senior government officials under criminal investigation for a wide-spread series of corrupt acts known collectively as *Tangentopoli* (Bribesville). Another reason was the killing in May 1992 of two Mafia prosecutors, Giovanni Falcone and Paolo Borsellino, which revealed the terrorist combat force of organized crime and awoke public resistance against criminal infiltration into civil society. Last but not least, the devaluation of the lira in September 1992 forced Italy out of the European Currency System and provoked serious irritations in the business world.

Due to the fact that the traditional party system was completely delegitimatized, the Northern League procured a strategic position in the political market. Its credibility was honoured in conjunction with further successes in the northern regions. In local elections in June 1993, a candidate of the *Lega Nord* was elected mayor of the financial capital Milan and the party established its presence in Lombardy, Veneto and Piedmont. Its leading political figures tried to consolidate their power, avoiding promoting too explicitly the former attitude of the antisystem-movement and presenting themselves as the only credible force able to renew the institutions of the peninsula. Although their new outfit propagated, they experienced their first set-back at the end of 1993 when the *Lega Nord* failed to win in Genova, Trieste or Venice. The League was not able to rid itself of its 'northern' identity

9. DC received 24 per cent of the popular consent, the new PDS 12.2 per cent, the Socialists 11 per cent (Visentini, 1993: 114–117).

in such a short time span, and the elections proved that *Leghismo* could scarcely be exported to other parts of the country (Diamanti, 1994: 671–677). Furthermore, the electoral reform approved by a referendum in April 1993, under which a single candidate wins the entire constituency, turned out to be disadvantageous for minor parties running without allies. In order to defeat the left coalition, which had showed its capability in Rome, Naples, and other major towns in central Italy, *Lega Nord* was forced during the political elections of 1994, to accept an alliance with *Forza Italia*, the movement run by media tycoon Silvio Berlusconi (who agreed not to fight for the same electorate in the north of the country, reducing his activity in central and southern Italy). Today, the electoral structure of *Lega Nord* is similar to that of other parties. Nevertheless, intolerance against immigrants and southerners remains a particularity of *Lega Nord* voters. Racism is still a dominant source of *Leghista* feeling.[10]

What Kind of Federalism for Italy?

Using a *trial-and-error* procedure, *Lega Nord* has tested various strategies and communication styles during its evolution. At the same time, the old parties were not able to react adequately to shifting realities. Three central resources enabled *Lega Nord* to use the political vacuum in Italy in entrepreneurial fashion for its own purpose. First, the autonomist party had a clear agenda made up of a flexible content. Federalism was one of these categories. A second important resource was its differentiated language and its direct communication. Finally, the *Lega Nord* distinguished itself from other movement parties by its hierarchical structure, capillary and operational flexibility (Diamanti, 1993b: 118).

Its most innovative resource was, without doubt, federalism. Nevertheless, by instrumentalizing this concept, it denigrated a potential principle of organization in Italy. As a frame alignment, it was useful to cover the economic strength of the North and to exclude the South and the immigrants of third world countries. But beyond the Northern League, what significance could federalism have in Italy? Is the request of a late federalization of the peninsula an anachronism or a possible option for the future?

The Italian case has shown evidence that concepts such as federalism and autonomy can also be used in societies with small internal integration, where this process has been interrupted by deep political

10. For an account on racism in the Lega Nord (Moioli, 1991).

divisions. Nevertheless, federalism becomes potentially dangerous when right wing populist movements adopt it to strengthen an ethnic particularity and to reduce concern about the nation as a social democracy.

Nevertheless, it is not necessary that federal projects exclusively refer to ethnic patterns and that they dismiss long grown solidarities between different parts of the country. Federalism should not be understood as an exclusionist policy, but rather as a functional multi-level structure able to combine centralized and decentralized decision-making, and able to compensate in the area of resource mobilization (Mayntz, 1990: 235). Seen from an evolutionary perspective, the advantage of federalism lies not in its decentralized structure, but in its contemporary decision-making on various levels.[11]

In the meantime, federalism has experienced a renaissance in Italy, although it has primarily been used in a pejorative manner. The *Lega Nord* contributed to this negative accentuation, although it portrayed it as a project of institutional and political innovation on the agenda.[12] Such reflections, however, were not considered in traditional parties. Nevertheless, it should be remarked that there are democratic concepts of federalism that surpass the early century theorist Carlo Cattaneo (to whom *Lega Nord* is referring, see Cattaneo, 1991) which should be reconsidered in current Italian political thought. It is worth mentioning Altiero Spinelli at this point, the former European Community Commissioner and member of the European Parliament, who was banished to a prison island during Fascism and who wrote, in 1941 together with Ernesto Rossi (Spinelli, 1991) the famous 'Manifesto di Ventotene', one of the most important Italian commitments to federalism. It is to this tradition that the collected papers edited by Nadia Urbinati and Marco Sabella (1994) and Massimo Luciani (1994) refer.

Federalism, understood as a functional and democratic concept, could help Italy to overcome its chronic incapacity at decision-making and at allowing vertical power-structures to recede. Federalizing a former Unitarian and centralist state is not meant to be a form of political conservatism and romanticism, but rather the efficient reaction of a nation-state weakened in its autonomy by a world-wide globalization process. In opposition to *Lega Nord*, we do not believe in a federalism which depends upon the traditional evocation of regionalism, nor do we believe that its functionality can be reduced to mere social or ethnic identification.

11. A profound theoretical reasoning can be found in Simon (1967) and Kleger (1995b).

12. The Agnelli Foundation proposed a reduction of the 20 regions to 12. See *Il Sole-24 Ore*, 3–4 December, 1992.

Bibliography

Allieri, S. (1992), *Le parole della Lega*, Milan: Garzanti.

Allum, P. (1993), 'Cronaca di una morte annunciata: La prima Repubblica Italiana', *Teoria Politica*, IX(1), pp. 31–55.

Bagnasco, A. (1977), *Tre Italie: La problematica territoriale dello sviluppo italiano*, Bologna: Il Mulino.

Biorcio, R. (1991), 'La Lega come attore politico: dal federalismo al populismo regionalista', in R. Mannheimer (ed.), *La Lega Lombarda*, Milan: Feltrinelli, pp. 34–82.

Cattaneo, C. (1991), *Stati Uniti d'Italia, il federalismo, le Leghe*, Milan: Edizioni SugaCo.

Corbetta, P. and Parisi, A. (1985), 'Struttura e tipologia delle elezioni politiche in Italia (1946–1983)', in G. Pasquino (ed.), *Il sistema politico italiano*, Bari: Laterza, pp. 33–73.

Diamanti, I. (1993a), 'La Lega come imprenditore politico della crisi italiana', *Meridiana, Rivista di Storia e Scienze Sociali*, 16, pp. 99–133.

——, (1993b), *La Lega: Geografia, storia e sociologia di un nuovo soggetto politico*, Rome: Donzelli Editore.

——, (1994), 'Lega Nord: un partito per le periferie', in P. Ginsborg (ed.), *Stato dell'Italia*, Milan: Il Saggiatore, pp. 671–676.

Galli, G. (1966), *Il bipartismo imperfetto*, Bologna: Il Mulino.

Hobsbawm, E. (1959), *Primitive Rebels: Studies in Archaic Forms of Social Movement in the 19th and 20th Centuries*, Manchester: Manchester University Press.

Kleger, H. (1993), *Der neue Ungehorsam: Widerstände und politische Verpflichtung in einer lernfähigen Demokratie*, Frankfurt am Main: Campus Verlag.

——, (1995a), 'Transnationale Staatsbürgerschaft – oder: lässt sich Staatsbürgerschaft entnationalisieren?', *Archiv für Rechts- und Sozialphilosophie*, Supplement 62.

——, (1995b), 'Verhandlungsdemokratie. Zur alten und neuen Theorie des kooperativen Staates', in R. Voigt (ed.), *Der kooperative Staat*, Baden-Baden: Nomos.

Lepsius, R. M. (1990), 'Immobilismus: das System der sozialen Stagnation in Süditalien', in R. M. Lepsius (ed.), *Interessen, Ideen und Institutionen*, Opladen: Westdeutscher Verlag, pp. 170–210.

Luciani, M. (1994), *La Democrazia alla Fine del Secolo*, Bari: Laterza.

Macke, C.-W. (1990), 'Der Aufstieg der Ligen in Italien', *Die Neue Gesellschaft/ Frankfurter Hefte*, 37, pp. 688–690.

Mayntz, R. (1990), 'Föderalismus und die Gesellschaft der Gegenwart', *Archiv des Öffentlichen Rechts*, 115(2), pp. 232–244.

McCarthy, J. D. and Zald, M. N. (1977), 'Resource Mobilization and Social Movements: A Partial Theory', *American Journal of Sociology*, 6, pp. 1212–1241.

Melucci, A. and Diani, M. (1992), *Nazioni senza stato*, Milan: Feltrinelli.

Miglio, G. (1994), *Io, Bossi e la Lega*, Milan: Mondadori.

Moioli, V. (1991), *I nuovi razzismi. Miserie e fortune della Lega Lombarda*, Rome: Edizioni Associate.

Piore, M. J. and Sabel, C. F. (1984), *The Second Industrial Divide: Possibilities for Prosperity*, New York: Basic Books.

Rusconi, G. E. (1993), *Se cessiamo di essere una nazione*, Bologna: Il Mulino.

Simon, H. A. (1967), 'The Architecture of Complexity', *Kommunikation*, III(2), pp. 55–83.

Spinelli, A. (1991), *Il Manifesto di Ventotene*, Bologna: Il Mulino.

Tarrow, S., Klandermans, B. and Kriesi, H. P. (1986), *New Social Movements in USA and Europe*, New York: Cornell University Press.

Triglia, C. (1981), *Le subculture politiche territoriali*, Milan: Feltrinelli.

——, (1986), *Grandi partiti e piccole imprese*, Bologna: Il Mulino.

Urbinati, N. and Sabella, M. (1994), *Quale federalismo?*, Milan: Vallecchi Editore.

Visentini, T. (1993), *La Lega. Italia a pezzi?*, Bolzano/Bozen: Edition Raetia.

Yinger, M. J. (1960), 'Counterculture and Subculture', *American Sociological Review*, 25, pp. 625–635.

–15–

The Dilemma of Separation Versus Union: The New Dynamic of Nationalist Politics in Belgium[1]

Marco Martiniello

Introduction

Théo Lefèvre, a former Prime Minister of Belgium, used to say that 'Belgium is a happy country composed of three oppressed minorities' (Covell, 1985: 230). As a matter of fact, since its creation in 1830, Belgium has been a divided country in which national unity has remained problematic. The opposition between the Flemings and the Walloons has been almost perennial, reaching peaks on several occasions, as for example the 'Royal issue' in 1945, the 'educational issue' resolved in 1958 and the 'Fourons-Voeren issue' which, while currently in state of slumber (Ubac, 1993), regularly reasserts itself into the forefront of Belgian political life like, as was the case, in the end of 1994. Despite these conflicts, there was implicit consensus between the major political forces in the country to keep the Belgian unitary state working. In this context, a set of institutional devices was constructed in order to control the centrifugal forces towards separation and to lead, when necessary, to what is usually called *un pacte à la belge* (a pact the Belgian way). When critical issues were at stake, conflicting groups rarely opposed one another beyond a point considered to be critical for the survival of the state. Instead, they engaged in extraordinary negotiations aimed at re-establishing harmony between the groups and in establishing a climate of moderation. There was thus a general willingness to prevent divisions and to control conflicts which might have led to the dissolution of the state. In other words, Belgium was 'sufficiently concerned with its potentiality for

1. A Spanish version of an earlier version of this chapter has been published in *Antropologia* (1995) 9, pp. 65–80.

internal conflicts and with its intrinsic risk of self-demolition to establish and maintain permanent pacts between the various actors about social issues considered to be critical' (Martiniello, 1993: 251).

Claims for autonomy have always existed both in Flanders and in Wallonia. Such claims led to the 'linguistic laws' of 1962, which divided the country into two unilingual areas: a Flemish speaking zone in the north and a French speaking zone in the south. Other threats to the unitary state linked to the Femings-Walloons divide were given a legal basis when, in 1970, crucial amendments to the Constitution were passed which began the slow process of federalization of the state (Witte and Craeybeckx, 1987). This 'top-down' process of gradual acknowledgement of regional and communitarian autonomies took more than twenty years to complete. Belgium itself has been a federal state since 1993. It is important to note that Belgian federalism does not at all consist of the 'down-top' integration of small entities into a larger federation. Rather, precisely the opposite process has progressively taken place.

The aim of this chapter is to show that the existence of a broad consensus, which once warranted the unity of the state, requires serious questioning. The recent evolution towards completion of the federalization of the state has been accompanied by a rise in ethno-nationalism in Flanders which has been primarily stimulated by the extreme-right-wing party, the *Vlaams Blok (VB)*, by a rebirth of regionalism in Wallonia and by a resistance of Belgian patriotism, above all in the newest region, namely Brussels, and in the Eastern German-speaking Belgian community. Consequently, the debates about separatism are no longer taboo. The mere existence of a Belgian state in the twenty-first century is less taken for granted than ever before in the short history of the Belgian Kingdom. It will be shown that the process of federalization and the evolution of the domestic ethnic conflict in Belgium have led to the ideological and political re-assertion of different conceptions of the nation in Flanders and in Wallonia. Furthermore, federalization has brought about some degree of *de facto* separation between the various ethno-linguistic groups. Consequently, the hypotheses of separation and secession are worth examining due to the fact that they constitute one realistic scenario, amongst others, for the future of Belgium.

The Politics of Nationalism and the Federalization Process

In 1992, the Belgian Constitution was modified for the fourth time in twenty-two years. Since 8 May, 1993, Article 1 of the 'new'

Constitution states that Belgium is a federal state composed of Communities and Regions.[2] There are three linguistic and cultural entities: the Flemish community, the French community and the German community. There are three social and economic entities: the Flemish region, the Walloon region and the region of Brussels–Capital. In the case of Flanders, the community and the region were merged into one single institution. As a result, the long-standing domestic ethnic conflict between the Flemings and the Walloons eventually led to an end to the original unitary state.

The main features of the latest restructuring of the state[3] include an end to the traditional parliamentary system along with its principle of equality between the *chambre* and the *sénat*. In the new system, the *chambre* is actually granted exclusive powers in certain fields. The size of the *sénat* is dramatically reduced, from 184 senators to 71, as are its powers. The new *sénat* will merely serve as an 'arena for discussion and reflection'. Furthermore, the members of Parliament of the new federal entities, namely the Communities and the Regions, will be directly elected. Another noticeable change is the erosion of Royal powers in the 'new Constitution'. The King's freedom to choose and appoint Ministers is significantly reduced by Article 65. As far as the judiciary system is concerned, it is crucial to underscore that it has not been hitherto altered.

The new division of powers between the various levels of the Belgian federation may be summarized as follows: A detailed list of the powers of the federal state has been agreed upon. This list includes monetary policy, foreign affairs, defence and security, social security (pensions, unemployment benefits, family allowance), public health, national, cultural and scientific institutions and certain aspects of those powers which have been federalized. All other competencies are devoluted to either Regions or Communities. Among the main powers of the Regions, one finds economic policy, employment policy, public transport, housing policy, environment policy, agriculture, urban planning and external trade. The Communities are responsible for most of the cultural matters (television, radio, sport), education, social aid and health policy, familial policy, etc. It must be added that clashes of competencies and shared powers between the various levels of the state have not entirely disappeared. This further increases the great complexity of the Belgian federal setting.

2. *Moniteur belge*, Saturday 8 May, 1993, no. 91, page 10,506.

3. For a clear introduction see *La Belgique fédérale en 1993*, *Le Soir*, 15 December, 1993 (free supplement).

In the beginning, the federalization process was seen as a response to the opposition between the Flemings and the Walloons in the framework of a unitary state. In other words, it was seen as a means of preserving the central cohesion of the state by giving limited autonomy to both parts. Partial federalism was not merely an attempt to struggle against separatism, but above all a strategy to reinforce the unitary state. It progressively became clear that the process could not be totally controlled and that separatist tensions were far from being removed, especially in the context of deep recession, growing unemployment and economic divide between Flanders and Wallonia with the advantage going to the former.

The politicization of separatism took on a new dimension after the legislative elections of 1991. The success of the *VB*, whose main objective is an independent Flanders free of immigrants, marked a new phase concerning the national question: debates about separatism were no longer taboo in Flanders and in Wallonia. The reasons behind the emergence of these debates, however, are to be found elsewhere. Here it is useful to distinguish external political factors and internal economic factors.

The evolution of the political situation in Eastern Europe after the fall of the Berlin Wall has, in all probability, had an impact on the conceptions of the future of the state in Belgium. The examples of separation, secession and ethnic conflict in Central and Eastern Europe show that, as Hobsbawm has put it (Martiniello, 1995: 2), we have undoubtedly entered a period of creation of new states. This newly perceived situation has, to a certain extent, increased the doubts that many Belgians traditionally had about the durability of the state. If a mega power such as the USSR could collapse in a few months, why could the same, at least theoretically, not occur in Belgium? In other words, issues concerning the partition of existing states and the creation of new states forced their way onto the international political agenda, and debates concerning these phenomena quite logically emerged in Belgium and in many other countries.

The bloodless partition of Czechoslovakia, for example, gave the idea to some separatists that a peaceful Belgian divorce was possible and even desirable. In his speech on 30 August, 1992, Lionel Vandenberghe, the former president of the yearly Flemish pilgrimage of the 'Ijserbedevaart', explicitly invited the Walloons to a pacific discussion with the view of sharing Belgian goods and of organizing a partition as soon as possible.[4] Belgian Unitarists, on the other hand, saw the

4. *Le Soir*, Monday 31 August, 1992.

violent break-up of Yugoslavia as proof of the validity of the Belgian pluralist model, despite its imperfections and problems.

As far as internal factors are concerned, the growing economic divide between Flanders and Wallonia has been politically mobilized to invigorate the debates concerning separatism. Contrary to the past, the Flemings are now not only demographically, but economically and politically dominant as well. In this context, the idea of solidarity with the Walloons, especially under the form of monetary transfers within the framework of a federal social security system, raises doubts and growing opposition amongst the Flemish political class and to a lesser extent amongst the Flemish population. Certain politicians try to profit from the situation by stimulating independentist ideas. On the Walloon side, solidarity is seen as a sacred principle, whereas, paradoxically, the relative Flemish economic success is often viewed negatively.

Furthermore, the importance of the separatist tendency should not be overestimated. On the Belgian scale, it is still a minority phenomenon in the entire political spectrum. The only Flemish party openly considering federalism as a transitory phase towards separatism as well as the total independence of Flanders is the aforementioned *VB* (Gijsels, 1993). In Wallonia, the marginal *Mouvement Wallon pour le Retour à la France* (Movement for the Return to France) states its main objective in its name. Nevertheless, the quantitative weakness of the separatists does not mean that their influence on the political process is unimportant.

At the opposite extremity of the political spectrum, the extreme anti-separatists – the defenders of a unitary pre-federal Belgium – are even less numerous and less politically significant. They are thought to be primarily found in catholic-monarchist circles in Brussels.

Nevertheless, a majority of political actors are both openly in favour of federalism and openly against separatism. In other words, federalism is seen as a means of preserving a certain degree of cohesion in the state through the acknowledgement of the need of a certain degree of autonomy for Flanders, Wallonia and Brussels. This is, by and large, the official position of the *Parti Socialiste (PS)*, the *Socialistische Partij (SP)*, the *Parti Social Chrétien (PSC)*, the *Christelijke Volkspartij (CVP)*, the two ecologist parties (*ECOLO* and *AGALEV*) and the two main Unions.

The latest tendency of the debate is to rally together single and collective political actors who adopt an ambiguous position towards separatism and federalism oscillating alternatively between one side and the other. Such is the case of the *Vlaamse Liberalen en Democraten (VLD)*, the *Volksunie (VU)* and of certain *CVP* politicians such as

Minister Luc Van den Brande, the head of the Flemish government, with his recurrent project of a confederation between two sovereign entities, Flanders and Wallonia, Brussels being the capital of the former.[5]

The previous classification of separatism and federalism is based on the manifest statements in the media or in public documents of various political actors. Therefore, it can only account for part of the reality. Effectively, in politics, what is not said is often more important than what is. Thus, the role of the political scientist is, precisely, to try to uncover the hidden agenda of the political actors as well as the hidden social logic behind political statements.

Beyond the debates on separatism, the federalization process and the restructuration of the state have produced some degree of *de facto* separation of the Belgian population, both on an institutional level and also on a collective identity level. This point can be illustrated by taking a look at four examples.

Firstly, the federalization of the public media, especially television, has had an impact on collective identity and public opinion formation. In this field, a scientific analysis of the programmes of the various Flemish and francophone channels would probably confirm the following empirical observations. Firstly, in each region, the information concerning the other regions of the country is quantitatively poor. Secondly, when this type of information does exist, it is very simplistic and tends to offer a negative image of the other region. For example, the Flemish public television might emphasize the financial scandals in the Walloon city of Liège. Conversely, the francophone public television might pay attention to any expression of racism in Flanders. How can a spectator maintain a global Belgian identification in circumstances in which he or she is only somewhat correctly informed about what is happening in his or her region and in which, simultaneously, he or she is misinformed about other regions' reality? In other words, how can he or she remain conscious of the fact that the other regions are part of the same country? Although answering these questions requires further development, they nevertheless underline the fact that federalization of television may contribute to the *de facto* separation of the country in the spectator's mind.

The case of education goes somewhat in the same direction. After federalization of education, the Flemish and Walloons pupils and students, including those in the public education system, no longer follow the same curriculum. The communitarian Flemish and Walloon authorities are free to create the content of their curriculum. Further-

5. *Le Soir*, 2 March, 1993.

more, the Flemish and Walloon pupils are sometimes allowed different holiday regimes. It is well-known that the educational system has been one of the cementing factors of the nation-states through the creation of a fictive ethnicity, a national community of belonging (Balibar, 1989). It is doubtful whether or not it will still be able to play this role as far as a Belgian national identity is concerned.

The third example, suppression of the compulsory conscription and the professionalization of the Belgian army, is not directly linked to the federalization process. Until recently, every young Belgian was obliged to spend nearly one year of his life in a military service. Although the soldiers were separated into linguistically homogeneous divisions, Flemish and Walloons youngsters nevertheless had the opportunity to meet and to get to know one another. Young Flemings were usually sent to Wallonia and vice versa. In this sense, the army represented a component of the fragile Belgian national identity, and suppression of the conscription had the power to underline the separation of the Flemish and Walloon youth. This reform was initiated by Léo Delcroix during the period when he was Minister of Defence. Delcroix, a *CVP* politician, closely held Van den Brande's view concerning the future of Belgium. One can make the hypothesis that, in his view, Belgian patriotism, as expressed in the past by compulsory conscription, should be a matter of personal choice. In the Belgium context, this decision testifies to the minimal importance given to the Belgium state in certain fractions of the *CVP*. Belgium is worth only optional loyalty.

The last example is drawn from a study concerning the movements of the population since 1963 across the 'linguistic border' separating Flanders and Wallonia, that is soon after the creation of this linguistic border. The author of this research shows that very few Walloons migrate to Flanders and vice versa due to the administrative problems and the hostility they expect to encounter.[6] He concludes that the 'linguistic border' is real in the sense that it impedes Belgians from moving across it.

The growing *de facto* separation within Belgium and the reduction of contacts and reciprocal knowledge between Flemings and Walloons is an expression of a decrease of national Belgian identity, although not necessarily of Belgian patriotism. At this point of the discussion, the distinction made by Walker Connor (1993) between nationalism, understood as loyalty towards one's national group, and patriotism, defined as loyalty towards one's state, helps us to understand the

---

6. *Le Soir*, 10 September, 1993. The author of the study, Jean-Pierre Grimeau, works at the Université Libre de Bruxelles.

aforementioned feature of the Belgian situation. Both the anti-separatist demonstration of April 1993 and the various manifestations of intense collective emotion following the death of King Baudouin could be interpreted more as an expression of Belgian patriotism than as proof of the force of Belgian nationalism. These events do not challenge the view of *de facto* separation. Therefore, it is not surprising that even though the political debate on separatism was interrupted by the death of King Baudouin in August 1993, it has since re-emerged on several occasions in relation to three recurrent issues: the federalization of the social security system, the federalization of the public debt and the status of bilingual Brussels.

Is the decrease of a national Belgian identity compensated for by the emergence of sub-Belgian national affiliations facilitated by the aforementioned *de facto* growing separation? Besides the official loyalty towards federalism claimed by the majority of the political forces, are there more or less hidden projects, strategies or merely social dynamics inspired by one form or the other of Flemish or Walloon nationalism?

Alter is perfectly right when he states that nationalism 'is one of the most ambiguous concepts in the present-day vocabulary of political and analytical thought' (Alter, 1992: 4). Nevertheless, this is not a sufficient reason to reject the concept since many others used in the social sciences, such as culture, ethnicity or class, suffer an analogous ambiguity. It is, however, a concept which should be 'handled with care'. The same author observes that 'nationalism does not exist as such, but a multitude of manifestations of nationalism do. In other words, it is more appropriate to speak of nationalisms in the plural than of nationalism in the singular' (Alter, 1992: 5). The various forms of nationalisms in Belgium will now be discussed by taking these two considerations into account.

In recent years, any account of nationalisms in Flanders inevitably started with a reference to the spectacular manifestation of the *VB*, particularly during the 1991 legislative elections.[7] Even though the *Vlaams Blok* is undoubtedly the historical inheritor of the Flemish collaborators with the Nazis during World War II, many of its activists, including the two young leaders Philip Dewinter and Gerolf Annemans did not know the war. Consequently, the *Vlaams Blok* represents much more than a group of nostalgics for the Third Reich.

In the 'manifesto' of the *VB* published in 1979, emphasis was strongly placed on Flemish nationalism, whereas immigration and racism were explicitly minor themes (Govaert, 1992: 24). Nationalism

---

7. The *VB* obtained its best results in Antwerp with more than 25 per cent of the votes (Gijsels, 1993: 80).

according to the *VB* refers to the defence of the Flemish popular community, which is considered to be a natural community made up of language, customs, historical traditions (Gijsels, 1993) and, I should add, blood. In other words, the existence of an ethnically pure Flemish people and nation is viewed as an objective fact on the basis of which a Flemish independent state should be developed. In this sense, it is reasonable to state that the *VB* advocates a sort of popular ethnic nationalism (Smith, 1991) or ethnonationalism (Shu Yun, 1990). Furthermore, the project to create a large Flemish federation – *Groot-Dietse federatie* – including the Belgian Flanders, the French Flanders and the Netherlands (Gijsels, 1993: 127) stresses the hidden expansionist ambitions of some 'Blokkers' tempted by what Alter calls integral nationalism (Alter, 1992).

Progressively, the *VB* gave more space to the struggle against immigration and multicultural society, in an attempt to make racism overt in its political rhetoric. Since the sixth congress of the party in 1984, these themes have become its favourite topics, to which they owe a large part of their growing electoral success. In 1989, the *VB* officer for immigration, Philip Dewinter, presented his 'ideas' in a book, the title of which is very explicit (Gijsels, 1993): *Eigen volk eerst* ('own people first'). In 1992, the *VB* published seventy propositions to solve the immigration problem, a few months after an analogous initiative made in France by the number two of the *Front National* at the time, Bruno Mégret. Among other 'solutions', the *VB* proposed repatriation of all illegal immigrants in order to restore integral *jus sanguinis* in Belgian nationality law, the creation of a separate social security system for foreigners, the prohibition of intercultural education and the creation of a separate school system for young foreigners, etc. In March 1993, the *Vlaams Blok Jongeren (VBJ)* circulated a letter addressed to the second and third generation Moroccans and Turks in Brussels. The letter stressed the impossibility of them becoming real Flemings as well as the absurdity of a multicultural society. Therefore, the best solution for young Moroccans and Turks – most of them who were born and who grew up in Belgium! – would be to return to their homeland to take part in its development. 'Marokko aan de Marokkanen – Vlaanderen aan de Vlamingen' ('Morocco to Moroccans, Flanders to Flemings') was the last sentence of this letter. Furthermore, several members of the *VB*, above all in Antwerp, have been suspected of racial attacks against immigrants.

In addition to the *VB*, there are other forms of nationalism in Flanders which are less extremist and more democratic. Flemish nationalism was, in the beginning, essentially a movement toward Flemish cultural emancipation. In the context of a state dominated by the Francophones, the Flemings were denied any cultural and linguistic autonomy. One such example is exemplified by the fact that all official activities at the Flemish universities were carried out in French. It was not until 1930 that the university of Ghent began to teach in Flemish (Witte and Craeybeckx, 1987). Flemish nationalism was pacific and quite liberal. It was a movement of resistance against the 'Francophone oppressor' and an assertion of a denied Flemish identity. Obviously, World War II and the collaboration with the Nazis marked a dramatic change for the Flemish movement. Nevertheless, what is called democratic Flemish nationalism basically refers to the original Flemish movement and is to be found in the traditional parties, especially the *CVP*. Some of the 'ideas' defended by the *VB* are, nevertheless, also penetrating these traditional parties.

In order to summarize the points made at this stage, it is important to underline that, firstly, nationalisms are an important dimension of Belgian and Flemish politics. Secondly, a distinction should be made between the extreme ethnic nationalism and racism of the *VB* on the one hand and, on the other hand, more democratic and liberal forms of nationalism which are partially rooted in the memory of the resistance against the Francophones and the struggle for the assertion of a Flemish identity in Belgium. Thirdly, and this is the primary dimension of this discussion, the various forms of Flemish nationalism seem to share a common feature, namely the tendency to believe in the objective existence of a Flemish ethnic group holding specific characteristics inherited from the past. Different forms of Flemish nationalism appeal to different inherited characteristics (collective memory of resistance and oppression, language, culture, blood, etc.), but they all appeal to some kind of common heritage rather than to a mere social project for the future. Furthermore, according to Jan Blommaert and Jeff Verschueren (1991; 1993), two Flemish researchers whose work has been largely contested in Flanders and is unknown in Wallonia, there is, in Flanders, 'a collective psyche profoundly troubled by the very idea of diversity in society (linguistic or otherwise)' (Blommaert and Verschueren, 1991: 503). In other words, according to these authors, there is in Flanders a widely shared belief, a common nucleus, that defines ethnic and cultural diversity as a problem and homogeneity as the most preferable situation. The imposition of this common belief may then be considered as being in large part responsible for the major success of the *VB*. For all of these reasons, it seems that Flemish nationalisms refer predominantly and in different ways to some sort of Flemish 'Kulturnation' (Alter, 1992), which appears to be not far from the notion of ethnic nationalisms (Smith, 1991).

In Wallonia, things are apparently somewhat different. In comparison to Flanders, the region has a longer conscious history of immigration and assimilation. Since the end of last century, poor Flemish workers were recruited to work in the coal mines of rich Wallonia and, until quite recently, many of them were employed in the Walloon metal industry. Historians have shown how Flemish immigrants were forced to assimilate (Quairiaux, 1990). Consequently, it is only partially surprising to find many politicians of 'Flemish descent' in the contemporary Walloon socialist movement (Onkelinckx, Van Cauwenberg, etc.). The former Minister murdered in Liège in 1991, André Cools, probably the last popular Walloon leader of the industrial era, was, for example, the son of a Flemish mineworker who had emigrated to Liège. Wallonia also seems to have quite a vivid memory of past working class struggle. Nowadays, the *PS* is still largely dominant in most areas of Wallonia.

These two features, namely a subjective history of assimilation and pregnant socialist rhetoric, help to explain the neglect of the cultural and ethnic dimensions of politics. As a former Minister-President of the Walloon Region once put it:

> In Wallonia, there is no nationalism if the term supposes aggression towards another ethnic or linguistic group. There are far more foreigners here than in Flanders, and this situation has never created any major problem: there is no discrimination, either towards those who come from Italy, Portugal and from more distant countries, or towards those who come from Flanders and are quite numerous in certain areas.[8]

In other words, nationalism, racism and ethnic problems are seen exclusively in the official Walloon rhetoric as Flemish problems. This approach is undoubtedly to be understood as an attempt to mobilize the non-nationalist, non-racist factions in the framework of the Belgian domestic ethnic conflict between the Flemings and the Walloons.

Logically, an official political discourse appeals more often to the concept of 'Staatsnation', (Alter, 1992) which obviously draws upon the French model of citizenship and national identity. Guy Spitaels, a former Minister-President of the Walloon government, was very clear concerning this topic when interviewed:

> I agree strongly with the French philosopher Ernest Renan for whom the national identity is not based on a language, and certainly not on an ethnic belonging, but on a way and on a willingness to live together . . . I think

8. *La Wallonie*, 28 January, 1993 (free translation).

that identity is that plebiscite that raises constantly the following question: do we want to live together and do we have things to share?[9]

This conception of a Walloon nation 'à la française', of a Walloon political community of destiny, is clearly a political construction, a political project which became significant when the Walloon Region was created approximately fifteen years ago in the middle of a period of economic decline in Wallonia. It represents the official philosophy of the Walloon government, although not the only form of nationalism in Wallonia.

A form of Walloon ethnic nationalism has, historically, also existed. At the turn of the century, a professor of the University of Liège turned to anthropology in his attempt to define the differences between the Flemish and Walloon ethnic types (Kesteloot, 1993). Certain historians, such as Félix Rousseau and other intellectuals, attempted to uncover the ethnic origins of Walloons as well as the common ancestor of the contemporary Walloons, namely the Celtic tribe of the Walhas (Destatte, 1990). This search for the 'original Walloon' could, nevertheless, not ignore the fact that Wallonia has always been an immigration country. However, external migration was considered as secondary when compared with the importance of the original Walloon nucleus.

Nevertheless, it seems that ethnic nationalism in Wallonia is bound to be irremediably superseded by territorial nationalism. After World War II, even the movement *Wallonie Libre* explained that the slogan 'la Wallonie appartient aux Wallons et à eux seuls' ('Wallonia to Walloons and only to them') was not at all the mark of an ethno-racial conception of the Walloon identity: it was the Walloon affirmation which was important and not the ethnic origin (Kesteloot, 1993). Nowadays, not even all of the small, extreme right-wing parties active in Wallonia are represented by a Wallon ethnic group, even though racism and a strong anti-immigrant attitude remain two of their most fundamental characteristics. Certain of these groups, such as the Belgian *Front National (FN)*, present themselves as Belgian nationalists, while others such as the small Liège-based party *Agir* advocate the defence of the Walloon people.

Brussels and its periphery, the traditional battleground of the Flemings and the Walloons, is most likely the shelter of Belgian patriotism. Belgium is still seen as the most comfortable representative of this small bilingual and cosmopolitan region. The conception of a Brussels nation has not yet emerged.

9. *La Wallonie*, 28 January, 1993 (free translation).

If Flanders is characterized by a relative predominance of ethnic nationalism, if Wallonia officially copies the French model of national identity and citizenship, if Brussels speaks in favour of a Belgian patriotism, the question must be posed as to the impact of these different conceptions of the nation on the debates concerning the future of the Belgian state: Are the two 'nations' still interested in living under a common Belgian roof? What place does Belgium have in contemporary Europe? What are the prospects of separation, partition and secession?

The Future of Belgium: No Easy Solution, No Easy Prediction

According to Eric Hobsbawm (1995), in the new world disorder, one thing is certain: a status quo is impossible. Nobody knows exactly how many new states will be created in the near future. In this context, the future of Belgium should not be taken for granted. Effectively, Belgium appears even more artificial than do the surrounding states. The role of the great powers of the post-napoleonic era was very important in the creation of the Belgian state. Afraid that France would rise once again, Belgium created a buffer state on its border. In another international situation, the Belgian revolution would probably not have succeeded.

The future of Belgium will most likely depend upon the evolution of both external and internal factors. As far as the former are concerned, no European state seems to be in favour of a Belgian split. Due to the fact that Brussels is the capital city of the European Union, the member states are undoubtedly concerned about maintaining peace. Nevertheless, as Brussels is the crux of the opposition between the Flemings and the Walloons, an escalation is not totally improbable. Brussels is officially the capital city of the Belgian federation, of Flanders, of the Brussels region and of the European Union. It is therefore an ideal symbolic battleground for various interests. In the case of escalation to such a battleground, the European Union would probably intervene in one way or another in order to restore peace. In the case of a Belgian divorce, certain European circles advocate giving Brussels a specific status in the form of a District of Europe similar to that of Washington D.C.

In Belgium, it is usually said that the new federal arrangement certainly has a chance of functioning but that the next ten years will prove crucial. This period is presented as a test for the validity of the Belgian federation. Nevertheless, certain elements impede exaggerated optimism. Firstly, while the extreme right-wing appears to have settled in Flanders, it is starting to emerge in Wallonia and in Brussels as well. The *Front National* has a Belgian nationalist platform whereas *Agir*, a small party now represented in a few city councils, displays Walloon nationalism. A further increase of this party would certainly be a step towards separation. Secondly, the past years and months have witnessed a nationalist radicalization of the Flemish government as well as of some sections of the Walloon socialist party. Thirdly, the political expression of unitarism is increasingly marginal. Fourthly, the *de facto* separation is certainly increasing and separatist and secessionist ideas are multiplying among the population. Even certain intellectuals have become tempted to legitimize these ideas.

It would therefore seem reasonable to state that, as far as internal factors are concerned, the future of Belgium as a state will depend upon the emergence of a federal political culture, a sort of 'constitutional patriotism'. Unfortunately, in the new world disorder, nobody can tell whether or not this will occur. The only thing that can be claimed, is that nothing would seem impossible.

Bibliography

Alter, P. (1992), *Nationalism*, London: Edward Arnold.

Balibar, E. (1989), 'Racism as Universalism', *New Political Science*, 16–17, pp. 9–22.

Blommaert, J. and Verschueren, J. (1991), 'The Pragmatics of Minority Politics in Belgium', *Language in Society*, 20, pp. 503–531.

———, and Verschueren, J. (1993), 'The Rhetoric of Tolerance or, What Police Officers are Taught about Migrants', *Journal of Intercultural Studies*, 14, pp. 49–63.

Connor, W. (1993), 'Beyond Reason: The Nature of the Ethnonational Bond', *Ethnic and Racial Studies*, 16, pp. 373–389.

Covell, M. (1985), 'Ethnic Conflict, Representation, and the state in Belgium', in P. Brass (ed.), *Ethnic Groups and the State*, London: Croom Helm.

Destatte, P. (1990), *L'identité wallonne*, Namur: Présidence de l'Exécutif Régional Wallon.

Gijsels, H. (1993), *Le Vlaams Blok*, Bruxelles: Ed. Luc Pire.

Govaert, S. (1992), *Le Vlaams Blok et ses dissidences*, Bruxelles: Courrier Hebdomadaire du CRISP, no. 1365.

Hobsbawm, E. (1995), 'The New World Disorder', Paper presented at the

International Conference 'Dialogues Européens', Brussels, U.L.B., February 24–25.

Kesteloot, C. (1993), *Mouvement wallon et identité nationale*, Bruxelles: Courrier Hebdomadaire du CRISP, no. 1392.

Martiniello, M. (1993), 'Ethnic Leadership, Ethnic Communities' Political Powerlessness and the State in Belgium', *Ethnic and Racial Studies*, 16, pp. 236–255.

——, (ed.), (1995), *Migration, Citizenship and Ethno-National Identities in the European Union*, Aldershot: Avebury.

Quairiaux, Y. (1990), 'L'immigration flamande en Wallonie (1880–1914). Problèmes d'intégration', Paper presented at the Conference 'Second Generation Immigrants in Europe', Florence, European University Insitute.

Smith, A. D. (1991), *National Identity*, London: Penguin Books.

Shu Yun, Ma (1990), 'Ethnonationalism, Ethnic Nationalism, and Mini-Nationalism: A Comparison of Connor, Smith and Snyder', *Ethnic and Racial Studies*, 13, pp. 527–541.

Ubac, P. (collective penname) (1993), *Génération Fourons*, Bruxelles: De Boeck Université, Pol-His.

Witte, E. and Craeybeckx, J. (1987), *La Belgique politique de 1830 à nos jours. Les tensions d'une démocratie bourgeoise*, Bruxelles: Labor.

Ethnicity and National Educational Systems in Western Europe

Cristina Allemann-Ghionda

Ethnicity Used as a Dividing Criterion in Education

In the framework of a research project,[1] one of the issues is the treatment of ethnicity in the educational systems of nation-states made up of culturally and linguistically mixed school populations. The project is a cross-national comparison of how ethnicity is referred to in educational policy-making papers and in teachers' and school principals' statements collected within six case studies, and what consequences this particular perception of ethnicity has on the organization and contents of education. The educational systems addressed are those of Germany, France, Italy, and Switzerland (in the latter, three cantons in the German, French and Italian-speaking areas are particularly considered).

In this text, the term 'ethnicity' is used in a slightly more comprehensive sense than is the case in, for example, the definition of Christina Bratt Paulston; according to her, an ethnic movement is an unconscious source of identity, while ethnicity is a conscious strategy used to obtain certain advantages, a distinction based upon Royce's definition of 'ethnic group' (Bratt Paulston, 1987: 296, 294). The concept of ethnicity in this chapter includes phenomena related to attribution by others and self-attribution of individuals to an ethnic group, ranging between more or less structured, explicit, and assertive strategies. Autochthonous minorities as well as migrants are included. Giving

1. The project 'Migration and Education in a Multicultural Perspective: European Strategies in Transition. A Comparative Analysis' was financed by the Swiss National Science Foundation (1993–96). It was granted further contributions by the Federal Office for Education and Science and the Uarda-Frutiger Fonds, Basle.

'ethnicity' a broader connotation seems to make sense in the Western European situation, especially when the minorities concerned are migrants. One of the differences between the ethnicity of minorities in North America or Canada and that of migrants in Western Europe seems to be the degree of elaboration and the type of strategies used to demonstrate ethnic identity. This difference becomes immediately apparent in a comparison between what ethnic minorities have attained in the educational system in the United States in terms of space gained (quota) and influence on the objectives and contents of curricula, and the changes which they have or have not achieved in the educational systems of Western Europe. This different status has to do with the very origin of the United States and Canada as modern nations and with the role played by and assigned to migration and minorities in these two nations and in immigration countries in Western Europe. The status of ethnic minorities varies according to the citizenship laws of the immigration countries, i.e. depending on whether they apply *jus soli* or *jus sanguinis*.[2] It makes a difference whether the host countries grant migrants political rights or not. Further factors are the different migration projects of persons and groups, the size of each community in absolute and relative terms and, finally, the intellectual, political and economic climate of each country at a particular time, which may or may not favour the rise of an ethnic movement and/or of different kinds of strategies of ethnicity. Most migrant groups in the four countries considered in this research do not actually develop ethnicity in the sense of a visible and conscious strategy to obtain certain advantages (for example in education), or, if so, they do it in a very modest way that does not affect the core of the educational systems. In Italy, this lack of influence especially affects those non-EU migrants who have only recently migrated from Poland, ex-Yugoslavia, China, Iran, Morocco and other African countries. However, other migrants do appear as organized groups with strong interests and demands related to their ethnicity. This is the case for example with Italians in Switzerland. Nevertheless, even those groups which show little apparent structured action appear to identify them-selves with norms, values, and customs clearly related to their ethnic groups of origin, and are perceived in this way by the institutions (e.g. schools) of the immigration society. It is in this sense that Payet

2. In this choice of countries, only France applies *jus soli*, although with some restrictions introduced recently to inhibit the naturalization of second and third generation migrants. Italy's law on citizenship is based on *jus sanguinis*, but was changed (law no. 91 of 5 February, 1992) and now partially extends the application of *jus soli*.

claims that 'the question of ethnicity is at the heart of this redefinition of the school's relationship with its users in school buildings at the periphery' (Payet, 1994: 7).[3]

Two groups of linguistic and cultural minorities which the majority perceives as being different and which are designated (with, however, differing degrees of officiality) as ethnic minorities are included in the analysis of how educational systems manage their integration or separation:

(1) Persons who identify with and are perceived as belonging to a national (regional) linguistic and cultural minority (e.g. German-speaking minorities in South Tyrol, North-East Italy, and Alsace, East of France; see European Bureau, 1993). These are citizens of the nation who belong to a minority, which is sometimes recognized and provided with or concentrated in a certain territory, and which sometimes is not. They may also be called minorities with a territory (Giordan, 1992).

(2) Persons who identify with and are perceived as belonging to a non-national linguistic and cultural minority (e.g. migrants and their children in any of the four immigration countries involved in this project). These persons are not citizens of the nation in which they are part of a minority nor do they live in their territory of origin; some of them are denied a territory (e.g. Kurdish people) or are nomads.

In this chapter, I shall concentrate on how education relates to non-national, regional linguistic and cultural minorities (i.e. migrants) and their ethnicity. Some comparisons with the situation of national minorities will however be made in order to highlight similarities and differences.

National educational systems use the concept of ethnicity as a particularly significant, dividing criterion in education (Fase, 1994). When a population is mixed due to migration or due to historical events such as the annexation of a territory of a neighbouring country (as Italy did with Austria in 1919 by incorporating South Tyrol with the treaty of St. Germain), policy-makers take measures in order to deal with the coexistence in the educational system of the majority and of the ethnic minority or minorities. Such measures may be more or less integrating or separating, depending on the pressure of separatist movements and on the decisions of the mainstream educational system. Ethnic differences are usually implicitly considered to be more crucial than socio-economic differences, in spite of the fact that the present theoretical and empirical knowledge concerning the mechanisms of

3. This quotation, as well as the following, was translated by the author.

the construction of the 'ethnic factor' and of its consequences (for example, school achievement in combination or not in combination with socio-economic background) is rather scant (Fase, 1994: 155). If policy-makers, school principals and teachers do not draw their ethnic criterion of division from the results of scientific results, what is it, then, that supports this kind of discrimination? Policy documents suggest that ethnicity is used for two purposes:

(1) To define and strengthen national and autochthonous identity by encouraging an opposition in ethnic terms (Heckmann, 1994).
(2) To relieve the mainstream educational system of additional tasks and responsibility in the event of dysfunctions in the system and in poor student achievement.

As for purpose (1), the following quotation from a document of the Italian Ministry of Education will illustrate the issue:

Anyway there is an essential difference between the rights and the needs of these traditionally resident minorities and the situation of pupils who only recently entered the Italian schools after their families immigrated into Italy . . ., they represent cultural backgrounds very different from ours. The traditionally resident minorities, whether they be recognized or not, are full Italian citizens . . . It would be absurd if the Italian school . . . tried to study, understand, take into account, customs, histories, spiritualities that are very remote, instead of those realities that are close and so similar to us . . . such as the linguistic minorities. (Ministero, 1993)

Purpose (2) appears in the following example: 'the variety of ethnic groups characterizing migration' (Ministero, 1989) is considered as being one of the elements a school must face in order to guarantee the right to study, a basic principle in the Italian constitution. A double interpretation is possible: 'we have to understand the background of ethnic groups in order to grant them equal opportunities'; or 'ethnic groups with their different backgrounds may make the task of school more difficult and may damage autochthonous pupils'. Educational systems claim equal opportunities. Differences in the socio-economic situation and their effects on school achievement are an embarrassment in societies based on democratic principles. The ethnic variable is expedient in explaining failures of the system or poor student achievement.

In the four educational systems involved in this project, schools with ethnically mixed populations take into account the ethnic factor (or are asked to do so by the authorities) on the following levels:

(1) Schools may organize special teaching for newly arrived children. 'Fremdsprachenklassen' in the Swiss-German canton of Basle-Urban ('Basel-Stadt')[4] remedial teaching in Italian as a second language (L_2) in Italy or in the Italian-speaking canton Ticino, 'Classes d'initiation' (*CLIN*) in France and similar measures in Germany. Models in which newcomers are directly integrated for most lessons instead of being taught separately are the rule in Italy and in the canton Ticino, and are being increasingly discussed and implemented in other parts of Switzerland, for example in the cantons of Geneva, Zurich and Basle-Urban. Italy abolished the segregation of children with learning or behavioural problems in 1977. Thus, the Italian school system does not have 'special classes'. Similarly, the canton Ticino has only a very small percentage of children in such classes. This supports the hypothesis that a school system based on the principle of inclusion is also less likely to segregate pupils following an ethnic criterion.

(2) Teaching materials provide information about 'foreign cultures' and correspond with what the cultures of origin of the children in a particular school are thought to be. Despite the criticism of researchers, this particular approach is still very popular among teachers who have to teach heterogeneous classes. Examples of it are found in every country, including Italy, a new immigration country. This pedagogical approach to the ethnicity of migrant children is not necessarily negative, as long as the teaching materials convey correct information and up-to-date elements of both the migrant and the host culture (Cercenà, Codignola and Faglia, 1992). Generally speaking, in textbooks the risk of Eurocentrism seems to be greater than the risk of an uninformed exotism and culturalism.

(3) An in-depth reform of curricula is implemented in order to include the topic of migration, or to introduce a variety of perspectives of different cultural areas in the teaching of all subjects, or to eradicate messages suggesting ethnocentrism from the point of view of the host country, xenophobia or racism. A close look at curricula reveals that they are usually less ethnocentric and nation-orientated than they are reputed to be, and that they do not unduly stress the ethnicity of migrant pupils (for an analysis of German curricula of primary schools, see Luchtenberg, 1995). Curricula are generally at least vague enough to allow space for any type of activity. In some cases, curricula recommend considering the dimension of diversity and/or of migration. This is the case for the primary school curriculum in Italy and in some Swiss cantons. The French curriculum, however, does not

---

4. Classes for newly arrived children; this rather clumsy term literally translates as 'classes of' or 'classes for foreign languages'.

mention these topics at all. Unlike the curricula mentioned above, it stresses the importance that pupils learn about the national flag, anthem, etc.

(4) Guidelines may recommend a general openness towards the different linguistic, cultural and religious characteristics of ethnic groups present in schools. This general openness does not go so far as to radically change the monolingual habitus (Gogolin, 1994) of multilingual and multicultural schools. However, teachers and school principals are forced to face variety, and, to some extent, official policy documents encourage them to do this. For example, an official directive of the Italian Ministry of Education encourages schools to 'appreciate and enhance the resources of different cultures for the sake of co-operation between peoples, totally respecting the ethnic origins' (Ministero, 1989). On the contrary, it appears that France is revising its conception of openness towards the variety of cultures in education. While in the 1980s the migrants' cultures were said to enrich the national culture (Berque, 1985: 46) the official policy of the nineties once again emphasizes the objective of 'intégration à la Française' (Haut Conseil, 1991) according to which the universalist principles of the French Republic are to inhibit cultural particularism.

(5) Strategies of the teachers for coping with intercultural misunderstandings which may disturb social interaction in school. Teachers appear to be often unprepared to accomplish this task. The consequences may be that misunderstandings are interpreted as cultural, intercultural, ethnic, or interethnic, even when their meaning is of another nature (i.e. different behaviour due to a different socio-economic background). Different behaviours may be seen as bad manners or lack of discipline instead of expressions of culturally determined customs or as symptoms of cultural shock, which the teacher does not recognize as such. Teacher training programmes in Western Europe only seldom deal with the acquisition of skills in the field of intercultural communication, despite the fact that this issue is increasingly being recognized as important (Luchtenberg, 1994).

(6) Institutions may develop strategies in the case of value conflicts due to the behaviour of ethnic groups, especially in religious matters; or institutions may refrain from doing so and leave their personnel free to decide how to act. Such strategies have not yet been developed in the four countries dealt with in this project, although the statements of teachers and school principals suggest that this may be one of the important issues which will need to be tackled in the coming years.

Specific National Means of Managing Ethnicity

National Means Despite European Policies

Each national educational system (whether federal, as in Switzerland and Germany, or central, as in France and Italy) develops its own, and partly highly characteristic way of dealing with ethnicity, although the use of the ethnic factor as a dividing criterion is a feature common to all four of the systems. The diversified management of ethnicity is occurring despite the European endeavours, subscribed by the countries involved, to build a common educational policy for management of linguistic and cultural variety (European Parliament, 1993; Allemann-Ghionda, 1994b). Some differences between the four countries involved here become apparent when one compares the attitudes and reactions of the school authorities towards the following core issues considered to be important markers of ethnic identity.

The first issue concerns the teaching of the language of origin (L_1), and the second is the extent to which non-dominant (in practice: non-Christian and non-Jewish) religious symbols, actions and behaviours are or are not tolerated in school.

The teaching of L_1 to migrant children is regulated by an EC-directive (EC, 1977) in the EU-member states and applies to the languages of those countries. In Switzerland, the recommendations of the CDIP (1995) have a similar meaning and function. L_1 is taught in very different organizational frameworks ranging from a poor to a fairly high degree of integration into the mainstream educational system of the host country. A hierarchy of languages is implicitly established. Languages of EU-member states which are also languages of migrants (Italian, Portuguese, Spanish, Greek) range at the top of this hierarchy in all countries. Turkish and Arab are also quite well considered in Germany and in France, where they are included in several ways in the choice of foreign language teaching, in bilingual curricula or as subjects for high school certificates. This relatively high consideration is based on the high number of migrants, on the potential entry of Turkey into the EU, and, in the case of Arab in France, on this country's ties with the ex-colonial territories in North-Africa. In the four countries considered here, other languages apart from those mentioned are either not taught at all in state schools (Italy, France) or kept in a more or less marginal position (Germany, Switzerland). In some cases, ethnic groups organize private tuition in their own language, culture and sometimes religion; this is the case, for example, for the large Chinese community in Florence and its surroundings, as well as in Milan. The attitude and reaction of the host countries towards this form of ethnicity vary from country to country. France is the most reticent on account of its constitution, which does not allow the concept of minority. Italy, also a centralist State, declares in its constitution that minorities are to be protected, thereby referring to the national linguistic minorities; although this principle may be extended to other minorities as well, in practice it is not applied, but nevertheless allows a liberal attitude. Switzerland and Germany, both federal states, have differentiated and quite flexible solutions. Language policy applied to migrant languages either proves to be a tool for ethnic segregation when based on a pattern of separation or, on the contrary, an instrument for respecting ethnicity as a facet of plurality when ruled by the principle of integration.

A further issue is that of religious symbols, actions and behaviours as aspects of ethnic identity and of ethnicity. Here, too, the host countries' reactions vary. France has increasingly developed a hard-line policy against the use of a *foulard* or headscarf (Le Monde, 21 September, 1994); the rights of minorities to live according to their customs and to express their beliefs are limited to the private domain and have to give way to the equality and laicism principles of the Republic. Although the following quotation represents an extreme, it is nevertheless a typical and eloquent example of this problem:

There is a provisional respect for Muslim tradition on this issue . . . it is going to evolve, they have to evolve . . . This respect (which is provisional, I insist on this) . . . means that we don't eat any pork at the canteen anymore . . . as a Frenchman I like pork and I would like this to be taken into account . . . And then, for example, on Fridays we eat fish, which I find as shocking as not to serve any pork, since I am an atheist. I think it is outrageous to eat fish on purpose on Fridays . . . For example, when we go together to a vacation camp in the country, then we have a food problem . . . there are children who are not particularly religious . . . they are going to protest they don't want any pork. We give them a double answer: 'Listen, you are in France, you are going to stay here. Eventually you will have to tackle the pork problem.' Second part of the answer: 'All right, you don't eat any pork, but today there is sausage. If you want your own food, we'll help you to make your own food, but you organize it yourself. You are not going to wait for someone to bring this food from Heaven and that everything will be done for you. You have to assume this task. If you have chosen not to eat any pork and to respect a certain tradition, which I regard as obsolete, well, it's your right, but it's your duty to organize things so that we shall be able to fix you something else to eat' . . . There is a necessary evolution about the pork issue that has to come from them, same thing as for the headscarf, by the way . . . It is an extreme minority, only the media make a noisy minority of them. Food is managed by the local authority. So they prepare meals which are respectful of these religious whims . . ., and on the other hand fish on Fridays. This, as a laicist in a laicist school of the Republic, which has imposed laicism in its principles, I think something is contradictory here. There is a respect for differences which disturbs us . . . If there has to be respect for a certain religious prohibition, then we have to manage it, tackle it . . . Some will act as imams, they will dictate others the Islam lesson. There, also, we intervene very strongly, very severely. In other words, respecting cultural difference has nothing to do with the respect for religion. There is a clear difference in our practice. (Interview with Mr. George, principal of the primary school Lily, 1994)[5]

This interview was recorded in a primary school in a popular district of the city of Paris, in which the inhabitants have been confronted with different waves of immigration for decades and have developed a habit, as the school principal puts it, of living in an ethnically mixed environment. It is a school known for its reform orientated bias. The school principal's views reflect his rather strong identification with, but also his most personal interpretation of, the present government's policy about cultural variety and ethnicity in school. It also shows that general universalist principles of *égalité* and *laïcité* are not enough to provide a methodology which would enable the school personnel to negotiate the solution of conflicts in a clear, professional way. However, in the other countries, a policy of flexibility is observed, as the 'bathing suit dispute' in Switzerland demonstrates. In this case, according to a judgement by the Federal Court (18 June, 1993), an Islamic father was granted the right to forbid his daughter to take swimming classes in school. The same kind of decision about a similar conflict was made in Germany in the same year. Episodes such as the *affaire du foulard* have not, thus, been frequent in Germany, Italy and Switzerland. The increasing proportion of non-EU and non-Christian migrants, the subsequent discussions and choices concerning migration policies, as well as the increasing strength of fundamentalist movements, suggest that this kind of issue might become relevant in these countries as well. Increasing ethnic variety is often perceived by authorities and by school personnel as a new situation which can no longer be mastered by improvisation. Institutions, and in particular schools and university teacher-training institutes, should consider a rational management of ethnicity as opposed to a radical particularism or to universalist policies which, in fact, turn out to be assimilationist (Allemann-Ghionda, 1995a).

5. Fictitious name used here to preserve the anonymity of the respondent.

Cristina Allemann-Ghionda

National Backlash in Education Counteracts European Policies for Linguistic and Cultural Variety

National means of dealing with ethnicity in education are negotiated within the space existing between two contrary poles. One pole of this tension is the renaissance of national or sometimes nationalistic discourses; the other pole is the emergence of regionalistic and particularistic demands. An increase in national or even nationalistic perspectives, which is to be expected in the present situation, has not become noticeable in those politico-educational documents which explicitly deal with the subject of cultural variety. Some signs, however, indicate that the evolution in daily life may be faster than and contrary to official policies. Autochthonous families tend to move away from areas with a high concentration of migrants. Such reactions are well-known in old immigration countries and have begun to appear in Italy as well. What takes place is a process of 'territorialization of school' (Payet, 1994: 9) on socio-economic grounds, but with a strong ethnic component since the most segregated pupils and families happen to be migrants, many of them with a darker skin and a religion different from the majority. Official policies developed in a tendencially pro-national climate will certainly not stop this process.

The general educational policies of some countries are, in fact, once again placing the national languages as pillars of identity into the centre of programmes and guidelines. For example, the French Government has launched an educational reform summarized in the *Nouveau Contrat pour l'Ecole* (Ministère, 1994), according to which the French language has an absolute priority and must, therefore, be given more space in the timetable. This trend to renationalize education is reinforced by the language-purifying law which has recently been introduced. As far as the ethnicity of minorities is concerned, the pole of regionalistic and particularistic movements appears in the demands of national (regional) language minorities such as German-speaking or Occitan-speaking citizens in France, Sorb-speakers in Germany, Romansh-speakers in Switzerland, Furlan-speakers in Italy, etc. European and international organizations support this particular form of ethnic revival (Giordan, 1992: Annexes). In general, this form of ethnicity of national, regional minorities presently seems to be growing stronger and more apparent in both Western and Eastern Europe. Some results have been achieved in education in terms of more respect and recognition of minority or lesser used languages. The European Commission and the European Parliament, as well as the Council of Europe, foster linguistic and cultural variety as a resource and in particular enhance the linguistic potential migrants represent.

Educational developments in a pro-national direction could counter-act the process of the legitimization of cultural and linguistic minorities, the European policy of fostering linguistic and cultural variety, as well as negatively influence the way in which educational authorities and schools react to linguistic and cultural variety and outline their strategies of dealing with ethnicity. The result would be a national (in some cases nationalist) backlash in education. An evolution of this type seems to be taking place in France. In this case, dealing with linguistic and cultural variety and with ethnicity may mean reverting back to a pattern of assimilation to the dominant culture in the name of integration and of 'universal' principles.

Italy and Germany seem to be reticent in developing such an explicit policy of protection of the national language. To do so would mean to reproduce the protectionist and excluding policies of the Fascist and National-Socialist regimes. It is not by chance that, after the second World War, these two countries unlike France, included principles and norms to protect national minorities in their democratic consti-tutions and laws. However, the boundary between national and non-national minorities, if not defined on a normative level, is illustrated by the unequal status which national and non-national minorities are assigned in education.

Switzerland's management of languages is built upon a principle of territoriality. The language policy promotes the four national languages: German, French, Italian and Romansh. These do not have equal status and weight in practice. Consequently, the discussion about the protection of minority languages (especially Romansh and Italian) is heated. The principle 'one language, one territory' and the polarity between national and non-national languages are constants in the Swiss language policy. However, there is an evolution and progressive opening of this four-fold monolingualism towards the plurilingualism of the population. In the cantonal educational systems, there are several pilot projects under way which endeavour to implement forms of bilingual and multilingual education and which tend to make the boundary between national and non-national minorities more perm-eable. Official recommendations support this evolution (CDIP, 1993; CDIP, 1995).

When simultaneously comparing how languages of migrants and those of national, regional minorities are transmitted in schools, one recognizes the following four basic patterns: hierarchic separation, equal separation, hierarchic integration, equal integration. Moreover, a deeper observation of each country's management of language minorities in education reveals that in each country and society there are specific cultural and political traditions behind the attitudes and patterns which appear on the surface. A hypothesis according to which federal systems are more likely than central ones to accept and foster linguistic and cultural variety (including that of non-national minorities) cannot be confirmed, as is exemplified in Switzerland. One would expect a federal organization of the educational system which is used to dealing with the problems of a national four-fold monolingualism, with many bilingual and plurilingual individuals and with internal intercultural interactions, to be extraordinarily open to the additional variety brought in by migration. The opposite is true. The ethnic criterion of division is actually applied to mark the boundary between national and non-national language varieties and to protect national and regional interests in education. The French and the Italian examples demonstrate that central states can develop totally opposing policies concerning linguistic and cultural minorities.

An interesting attempt to grasp the origin of the more separating and the more integrating patterns of dealing with minority languages and cultures and other expressions of ethnicity, and also of diversity in general, has been made by Emmanuel Todd (1994). In his comparative historical and anthropological analysis, he concludes that two basic approaches to diversity are found in immigration countries: the universalist approach (e.g. France, Italy) and the differentialist approach (e.g. Germany, German-speaking Switzerland, as well as countries of Anglo-Saxon culture). According to Todd, France's universalism, which implies a policy of cultural assimilation both of national (regional) and non-national minorities, proves to be a better way of coping with diversity than the differentialist mode, which in his opinion results in racism and physical destruction.

The historical cross-national approach, supported by empirical evidence, makes clear, however, that in the long run assimilationistic options lead to more disadvantages than to advantages. Even Todd admits that the social marginalization and identity problems of many migrant youths of the second and third generation in France are due to an assimilation which takes place too rapidly and which cannot be absorbed by the individual (Todd, 1994: 369). Inter-ethnic conflicts and extreme forms of ethnicity can also be seen as a reaction to the assimilationistic pressure of the host societies, which are poorly supported by an efficient and humane integration policy. On the contrary, respect for linguistic and cultural plurality demonstrated by structural and curricular planning in education may contribute to the avoidance of severe inter-ethnic tensions. Successful examples of this are found in bilingual and trilingual territories in the Region of South Tyrol in Northern Italy (Baur, Carli and Larcher, 1995) and in the canton of Grisons in Switzerland (Fried-Turnes, 1994). The same principle, with the necessary accommodations, should apply to non-national minorities. Several pilot-projects in different parts of Europe prove that this is possible.

Conclusion

A radical change in the manner of analysing migration and minorities occurred with increased research regarding the ethnicity paradigm (Bratt Paulston, 1987: 291) during the 1970s in the USA. This approach was taken up and developed in some European immigration countries, but not in France, the cultural and scientific traditions of this country being characterized by a widespread 'répugnance à l'interethnique et au minoritaire' (de Certeau, 1987: 191n) or, put more positively, by a high consciousness of the dangers of particularism. Under the ethnicity paradigm, the basic concepts of integration and assimilation of previous migration research are reconsidered from a new perspective. The cultures of minorities become a core value in research. The educational and pedagogical counterpart of the ethnicity approach is the idea that the cultures of origin of the migrants or members of minorities or, in a more developed version, the variety of cultures, should be taken into account in education. Different interpretations of this principle are possible, as the development of intercultural education in Europe in the last twenty years demonstrates.

With this change of perspective, certain shifts from old to new patterns in dealing with language and culture variety and with ethnicity in education take place and generate innovations (Allemann-Ghionda, 1995b). Taken from this point of view of ethnicity, the common features of such innovations are:

(1) Cultural, linguistic, religious and social variety are better managed in education. In a balanced approach conscious of the risks of culturalism and of ethnicism, ethnicity is not used to describe phenomena that are everything but ethnic. The usual ethnic criterion, which splits education into a mainstream structure for the majority and subordinate structures for minorities, becomes meaningless.

(2) The teaching of languages is reorganized in such a way that a barrier between national and non-national languages, autochthonous and 'foreign' speakers is no longer necessary.

(3) The intercultural idea was first developed in Western Europe as a pedagogical reaction to migration. Therefore, it has, for a long time, retained a strong connotation of 'pedagogy of the poor', and has been related to ethnically defined groups of migrants. Parallel to this, European, bilingual and international schools were created for a

privileged population. These two conceptions can be seen as complementary. Both imply changes in the organization of education and in the priorities and contents of curricula and teaching materials, from ethnocentric, Eurocentric or parochial, to multiperspective thinking and teaching. Schools associated with this type of innovation in Germany, prove that it is possible to extend both an intercultural methodology and a European orientation to a broad range of state school types, from the 'Realschule' (school which precedes vocational training), 'Gesamtschule' (comprehensive school) to the 'Gymnasium' (grammar or high school). For example, a project called 'Lernen für Europa' was officially supported by the authorities of the 'Bundesland Nordrhein-Westfalen' from 1991 to 1994 (Landesinstitut, 1995). In this conception, the use of ethnicity for pedagogical purposes gives way to the inclusion of linguistic and cultural variety on a higher level.

Intercultural approaches are far from having thoroughly transformed the nationally orientated, monolingual and monocultural educational systems. The ethnic factor is not only used as an instrument of division in education, but in all social structures and in politics. Therefore, in order to remain realistic, the influence of education should not be overestimated. Nevertheless, considering the role education has played in history to form and strengthen national identities (Mitter, 1993), it would not be wise to underestimate the devastating effects which can be produced by an irrational relationship between education and ethnicity.

Bibliography

Allemann-Ghionda, C. (1994a), 'Die Schweiz und ihr Bildungswesen: von Babylonia zu MultiKulti', *Zeitschrift für Pädagogik* 1, pp. 127–145.
——, (ed.), (1994b), *Multiculture et éducation en Europe*, Berne: Lang.
——, (1995a), 'Interkulturelle Bildung zwischen Universalität und Partikularität. Überlegungen im Rahmen eines europäischen Vergleichs', *Tertium comparationis* I(2), pp. 96–111.
——, (1995b), 'Implementing European Strategies for Language and Culture Diversity. A Cross-National Comparison Based on Six Case-Studies', *EERA Bulletin* I(3), pp. 12–22.
Baur, S., Carli, A. and Larcher, D. (eds), (1995), *Interkulturelles Handeln. Neue Perspektiven des Zweitsprachunterrichts/Agire interculturale. Nuove prospettive per l'apprendimento delle lingue seconde*, Meran/Merano: Alpha & Beta.

Berque, J. (1985), *L'immigration à l'école de la République*, Rapport au Ministère de l'Education Nationale, Paris: La documentation française.

Bratt Paulston, C. (1987), 'Conséquences linguistiques de l'ethnicité et du nationalisme dans des contextes plurilingues', in OCDE (ed.), *L'éducation multiculturelle*, Paris: OCDE, CERI, pp. 280–317.

Cercenà, V., Codignola, N. and Faglia, M. (eds), (1992), *Ci vieni a casa mia? I bambini italiani e i bambini cinesi si incontrano*, Florence: Fatatrac.

CDIP (1991), *Recommandations concernant la scolarisation des enfants de langue étrangère*, Berne: Conférence suisse des directeurs cantonaux de l'instruction publique.

———, (1993), *Recommandations de la CDIP sur la dimension européenne de l'éducation*, Berne: Conférence suisse des directeurs cantonaux de l'instruction publique.

———, (1995), *Promotion de l'enseignement bilingue en Suisse. Déclaration de la CDIP et des directeurs cantonaux de l'économie publique responsables de la formation professionnelle*, Berne: Conférence suisse des directeurs cantonaux de l'instruction publique.

de Certeau, M. (1987), 'Economies ethniques: pour une école de la diversité', in OECD (ed.), *L'éducation multiculturelle*, Paris: OCDE, CERI, pp. 170–196.

EC (1977), 'Council Directive 77/486/EEC of 25 July 1977 on the education of the children of migrant workers'.

European Bureau (1993), *Mini-Guide to the Lesser Used Languages of the EC. Baile Atha Cliath*, Brussels: The European Bureau for Lesser Used Languages.

European Parliament (1993), 'Resolution on cultural plurality and the problems of school education for children of immigrants in the European Community. No. A3–0399/92', *Official Journal of the European Communities*, February 15.

Fase, W. (1994), *Ethnic Divisions in Western European Education*, Münster and New York: Waxmann.

Fried-Turnes, U. (1994), 'Ein Modell zweisprachiger Schulung: die Rätoromania', in C. Allemann-Ghionda (ed.), *Multiculture et éducation en Europe*, Berne: Lang, pp. 355–369.

Giordan, H. (ed.), (1992), *Les immigrés en Europe. Droits linguistiques et droits de l'homme*, Paris: Kimé.

Gogolin, I. (1994), *Der monolinguale Habitus der multilingualen Schule*, Munster and New York: Waxmann.

Haut Conseil (1991), *Pour un modèle français d'intégration. Premier rapport annuel*, Paris: La documentation française.

Heckmann, F. (1994), 'Politik, Staat und ethnische Minderheiten', in I. Gogolin (ed.), *Das nationale Selbstverständnis der Bildung*, Munster and New York: Waxmann, pp. 13–45.

Landesinstitut (1995), *Lernen für Europa: Abschlussbericht*, Soest: Landesinstitut für Schule und Weiterbildung.

Le Monde, 21 September, 1994.

Luchtenberg, S. (1994), 'Überlegungen zur interkulturellen Kompetenz', in S. Luchtenberg and W. Nieke (eds), *Interkulturelle Pädagogik und interkulturelle Dimension*, Munster and New York: Waxmann, pp. 49–66.

——, (1995), *Interkulturelle Sprachliche Bildung*, Münster and New York: Waxmann.

Ministero (1989), *Inserimento degli stranieri nella scuola dell'obbligo: promozione e coordinamento delle iniziative per l'esercizio del diritto allo studio*, Rome: Ministero della Pubblica Istruzione (September 8).

——, (1993), *Pronuncia, di propria iniziativa, in merito alla tutela delle minoranze linguistiche*, Rome: Ministero della Pubblica Istruzione, Consiglio Nazionale della Pubblica Istruzione (June 26).

Ministère (1994), *Le nouveau contrat pour l'école. 158 décisions*, Paris: Ministère de l'éducation nationale.

Mitter, W. (1993), 'Nationalism, Regionalism and Internationalism in Europe', in K. Schleicher (ed.), *Nationalism in Education*, Berne: Lang, pp. 107–131.

Payet, J.-P. (1994), 'L'école à l'épreuve de la réparation sociale: la relation professionnels/public dans les établissements scolaires de banlieue', *Revue Française de Pédagogie*, 109, pp. 7–17.

Todd, E. (1994), *Le destin des immigrés. Assimilation et ségrégation dans les démocraties occidentales*, Paris: Seuil.

Notes on Contributors

Cristina Allemann-Ghionda studied German, English, Romance philologies, and social sciences at the Universities of Basle and Torino. Her publications address language and culture variety issues in educational policies, curricular arrangements and pedagogical theories; comparative education; women and migration. She is a leader of research projects funded by the Swiss National Science Foundation. Currently she is a senior lecturer at the University of Berne.

Aleksandra Ålund is a professor at the Department of Sociology, Umeå University, and DAMES (The Danish Centre for Migration and Ethnic Studies), Denmark. She has published a number of articles and books on ethnicity in multicultural societies focusing on issues of class, gender, power, and youth culture. Books in English are *Will they Still be Dancing: Integration and Ethnic Transformation* (1987), and, together with C.-U. Schierup, *Paradoxes of Multiculturalism* (1991).

Gianni D'Amato, born in 1963 Paternopoli (AV)/Italy, is currently writing his dissertation on *Immigrant Politics and Citizenship* at the University of Potsdam (Germany). He completed his studies in Sociology, Social and Economic History and Political Science in 1992 at the University of Zurich (Switzerland) with a thesis on *Industrial Transformations in Western Societies*. Together with Siegfried Schieder he recently published 'Die europapolitische Diskussion in Italien im Vorfeld der Regierungskonferenz 1996', in R. Erne, A. Gross, H. Kleger, B. Kaufmann (eds), *Transnationale Demokratie. Impulse für ein demokratisch verfasstes Europa*, Zurich, 1995.

Georg Elwert, born 1947, is professor of social anthropology and sociology at the Freie Universität Berlin. He did fieldwork on oral history of the Ayizo and Fon of 'Danxome' (Dahomey) and on the peasant economy of southern Benin (former Dahomey). He earned a Ph.D. from the University of Heidelberg (1973) and the 'Habilitation' from Bielefeld (1980). His second field of research is Turkey and Isbekistan (migration, ethnicity and land rights). He has published *Bauern und Staat in Westafrika* (Frankfurt am Main, 1983), *Entwicklungshilfe und ihre Folgen* (together with Thomas Bierschenk, Frankfurt am Main, 1993). Recent articles include: 'Changing Certainties and the move to a "Global" Religion – Medical Knowledge and Islamization among Anii in the Republic of Benin', in J. Weny *The Pursuit of Certainty*. *Religious and Cultural Formulations* (London, 1995) and 'The Longterm Effects of Development Aid: Empirical Studies in Rural West Africa', *Economics* 47 (together with Thomas Bierschenk and Dirk Kohnert).

Matteo Gianni is lecturer assistant at the Department of Political Science at the University of Geneva, where he is completing a Ph.D. in Political Theory. Supported by the Swiss Nation Science Foundation, he was a 1995–96 Visiting Fellow at the Walt Whitman Centre for the Culture and Politics of Democracy at Rutgers University.

Christian Giordano, born October 27, 1945, has been full Professor and Head of the Department of the Institute of Ethnology of the University of Fribourg (Switzerland) since 1989. He has held academic positions at the University of Basel, Frankfurt am Main and Munich; guest professorship in Torun (Poland), Asuncion (Paraguay), Berlin Humboldt University (Germany). His main interests are: Mediterranean societies, socio-political transformations in Central and Eastern Europe, ethno-nationalism in former socialist societies. Among his publications is: *Die Betrogenen der Geschichte. Ueberlagerungsmentalität und Ueberlagerungsrationalität in mediterranen Gesellschaften* (Frankfurt am Main 1992).

Donna M. Goldstein is professor of Anthropology at the University of Colorado at Boulder. Her research interests within the fields of cultural and medical anthropology include AIDS, gender, sexuality, nationalism and cultural citizenship. She has carried out field research in Mexico, Ecuador, Brazil, and most recently in Hungary.

Montserrat Guibernau (M.Phil., Ph.D., University of Cambridge) is a Research Fellow at the Centre for Research in Ethnic Relations, University of Warwick. Her latest publications include: *Nationalisms: The Nation State and Nationalism in the Twentieth Century* (1995); 'Spain: A Federation in the Making?' in *Federalism: The Multiethnic Challenge*, G. Smith, London (1995) and 'Identidad nacional y cultura: un análisis crítico de la teoría del nacionalismo de Ernest Gellner' *Antropología*, 9, 1995, Madrid.

Natividad Gutiérrez (MSc, Ph.D., The London School of Economics) is a founder of the Association for the Study of Ethnicity and Nationalism and teaches 'Theories and Problems of Nationalism' at the London School of Economics. Her recent publications include 'Miscegenation for Nation-Building: Indigenous and Immigrant Women in Mexico' in *Unsettling Settler Societies*, D. Stasiulius and N. Yuval-Davis N. (1995) and 'Ethnic Intellectuals and National Identity', *Bulletin, Société Suisse des Americanistes* (1995).

Jürg Helbling is professor at the Department of Anthropology at the University of Zurich. He has conducted field research among the Alangan-Mangyan in Mindoro (Philippines). His main interests are ecology and economy (resource management in tribal societies), politics (war in tribal, traditional and modern societies, ethnicity and nationalism), as well as the application of game theory in anthropology.

Kurt Imhof, born in 1956, is Lecturer in Sociology and Social History at the University of Zurich and Director of the Institute of Sociology's Research Sector for Public Sociology and Public History. Moreover, he is Director of the National Research Programme 'Migration and Intercultural Relations'. His fields of interest are public sociology, religious sociology, minority and migration sociology. Among his publications are 'Zur Diskontinuität des sozialen Wandels' (Frankfurt am Main, 1990), 'Migration, Ethnizität und Staat. Das Fremde in der Gesellschaft' (Zurich, 1996), 'Die Diskontinuität der Moderne. Zur Theorie des sozialen Wandels', in A. Honneth, H. Joas and C. Offe (eds), *Theorie und Gesellschaft* (Frankfurt am Main, 1996) and he is editor of the series *Krise und sozialer Wandel* (Zurich, 1993; 1996; 1997), *Medien-Symposium Luzern* (Zurich, 1995; 1996; 1997).

Galina A. Komarova, Candidate in History, Senior researcher of the Center for the Study of Interethnic Relationships, Institute of Ethnology and Anthropology, Russian Academy of Sciences, Moscow. She is an author and editor of several books on contemporary ethnopolitical processes in Russia and in Estonia. Recently she has completed an extensive study of various ethnic groups living in the heavily radioactive polluted area in the Southern Ural. The study was supported by the McArthur Foundation.

Josep R. Llobera is Visiting Professor of Anthropology at the University College London and at the Universitat Pompeu Fabra of Barcelona. He has published extensively on Western European nationalism, with particular reference to Catalonia and France. His recent writings include: *The God of Modernity: The Development of Nationalism in Western Europe* (1994) and *The Role of Historical Memory in (Ethno)-nation Building* (1996).

Marco Martiniello (Ph.D in social and political sciences, European University Institute, Florence) is research fellow of the Belgian National Fund for Scientific Research (FNRS) and lecturer in political science at the University of Liège. He was either visiting professor or visiting scholar in the following institutions: Cornell University, University of Warwick, European University Institute, Institut d'Etudes Politiques de Paris. He has recently published *L'ethnicité dans les sciences sociales contemporaines* (1995) and edited *Migration, Citizenship and Ethno-National Identities in the European Union* (1995).

Siegfried Schieder, born in 1968 in Kastelruth (BZ)/Italy, graduated in Political Science at the Free University of Berlin (Germany) with a thesis on *The Logic of Multi-level Governance in the European Union*. He is now Research Assistant at the International Politics Department at the University of Dresden and Member of the Graduiertenkolleg in Berlin.

Carl-Ulrik Schierup (Ph.D. in Social Anthropology / Ph.D. in Sociology) is a professor of ethnic studies, at present director for the Centre for Studies on Migration, Ethnic Relations, and Globalization at the University of Umeå, Sweden. Schierup has written numerous articles and books on topics of international migration, multiculturalism, nationalism and ethnicity. Among the author's publications in English are *Migration, Socialism, and the International Division of Labour: The Yugoslavian Experience* (1990) and *Paradoxes of Multiculturalism: Essays on Swedish Society* (1991, with Aleksandra Ålund).

Victor A. Shnirelman, Doctor in History, Leading Researcher in the Institute of Ethnology and Anthropology, Russian Academy of Sciences, Moscow. An author of about 160 publications, including several books on archaeology, social anthropology, history, modern ethnopolitics. The most recent book is *Who gets the past? Competition for Ancestors among non-Russian Intellectuals in Russia* (1996). Now his interests are focused on ethnopolitics and ethnonationalist ideologies. He was one of the contributors to the volumes: M. Diaz-Andreu and

T.C.Champion (eds), *Nationalism and Archaeology in Europe* (1996) and P.Kohl and C. Fawcett (eds), *Nationalism, Politics and Practice of Archaeology* (1995).

Hans-Rudolf Wicker is Professor of Anthropology at the University of Berne, Switzerland, where he received his Ph.D. in Social Anthropology. He is the author of numerous articles and books including a recent co-edited volume, *Das Fremde in der Gesellschaft: Migration, Ethnizität und Staat* (Zurich, 1996) and 'Flexible Cultures, Hybrid Identities and Reflexive Capital', *Anthropological Journal of European Cultures* 5 (1996). He has conducted fieldwork on St Lawrence Island, Alaska, in rural Paraguay and in Switzerland, and writes on issues of anthropological theory, applied anthropology, migration and medical anthropology.

Index

Index

nationalists 218–19; capitalist image 197–8; closeted identity 198–9, 207–8; current situation in Hungary 193–5, 203–9, 208–9; exclusion from Nazi Germany's identity 254; identified with Communists in the Hungarian 1956 uprising 201–3; linguistic assimilation in Hungary 195–7; members of Communist Party in Hungary 198–200; in Soviet Union 182, 183; unassimilated group in Hungary 200
justice: state as an agent of 82

Kallen, Horace 112; crisis in the 'symphony of civilization' 113–14
Das Kapital (Marx) 73–4
Karady, V. 197, 198
Karadzic, Vuk S. 189
Kemal Atatürk, Mustafa 261
Keynesianism 9; state intervention 16
King Jr, Martin Luther see multiculturalism
kinship: defining ethnic groups 264–5; we-groups 256
Kleisthenes 8
Kohl, Helmut 261
Kymlicka, W.: citizenship 128–9; no formula for rights 138; The Rights of Minority Cultures 129; societal culture 130; three types of actors 136–7

labour: anti-immigration tensions 240–7; concern of Marx's social model 88; importing cheap and docile workers 120; the proletariat of Marxism and nationalism 75–9; stratifying effect of multiculturalism 116

language: education 309; minorities in education 312–15; stabilization of we-groups 266; Swiss ethnicity 148–9
Latvia see Baltic states
League of Nations 187–9
Lefevre, Théo 287
Lenin, V. I.: question of nationality 181–2
Levy, J.: assistance rights 139–40
liminal zone 267
List, Friedrich 9, 74
Lithuania see Baltic states
Llobera, Josep R. 35–6
Lucco (rap artist) 106
Luciani, Massimo 284
Luhmann, N. 67
Lyotard, Jean-François: death of grand theories 17–18

Macedonia: territorial disputes 189
Marable, Manning 118–19
Marcus, G. E.: Writing Culture (with Clifford) 3
Marshall, T. H. 28, 118
Martin, D. 6
Martiniello, Marco 25, 36
Marx, Karl: The Communist Manifesto 73, 75, 77; Contribution to the Critique of Hegel's Philosophy of Right 74; Critique of List 74; Critique of the Gotha Programme 77; The German Ideology 75; German nationality and bourgeoisie 73–5; history of society in class struggle 87–9; Das Kapital 73–4; nationalism 26–7, 75–9; production and the social sphere 157–8
Marxism: in communist countries 16; in context of globalization 16–18
Mauss, Marcel: defining nations 45
McCarthy, J. D.: resource mobilization theory 274
Mead, Margaret 12
media: identity formation and public opinion 292
Mégret, Bruno 295
methodology: ethnography of immigrant communities 96–7
Mexico: composed of many groups 168, 170
Miglio, Gianfranco 280
migration see immigrants and emigrants
Miladinov, Dimiter and Konstantin 189
Miller, D. 136
Milov, V. A. 217
modernity: Gellner's approach to nationalism 164–7; nationalism 267–9; three pillars of nation, republicanism and capitalism 8–10
Moroccan immigrants 295
Mouffe, C. 208–9
Moynihan, D. P.: Beyond the Melting Pot 65
Mühlmann, W. E. 183
Müller, Ernst W. 257
multiculturalism: ascriptive and chosen 130–3; defining 111; differentiated citizenship 127–9; identity politics and liberal citizenship 133–8; ideological battleground 112–13; increasing use as institutional framework 111–12; Los Angeles inter-ethnic feuding 118–20; more than choice between particularism and universalism 117–18; political fragmentation and cultural divisions

Index

113–14; separation into cultural
products 91–3; social fact of cultural
differences 129–33; in spheres and
domains models 147–8, 153–4, 159–60;
Switzerland 150–2; three types of actors
136–7

Myrdal, Gunnar 108; *American Dilemma*
121

myth and folklore: Eastern Europe 189;
Hungary rebuilds identity 206; neo-
Pagan ethno-nationalists in Russia
215–21; Smith's myth-symbol complex
167

Naïr, Sami 178
Narin, Tom 47
nation and state *see also* citizenship:
boundaries of cultural groups 44–5; and
capitalism 8–10; collective action and
we-constructions 23; and colonialism
27–8; community 63; deconstructivist
approach 3–4; defining 45–7, 79–80;
democracy 82–3; economic equality
and inequality 13–15; 'ethnic discourse'
175–6; formed by culture 11–12;
French citizenship 176–8; German Volk
179–81; and identity 5; immigration
and emigration 10–13; individual within
80–1; internal and external actions
81–2; Italian federalism 283–4;
Keynesian state intervention 16; lean
and just-in-time production 15; linking
nation with state 59–62; Marx's critique
of bourgeoisie 73–5; open only partly to
outside 175; religious identity 83–4;
republican ideals 7–8; sociological self-
criticism and Weber's theory 58–9;
Soviet citizenship and nationality 181–5;
totality of national idea 10; transnational
organizations 15

nationalism: defining the state 59–60;
differences and similarities to Marxism
79; as distinguished from patriotism
293–4; Durkheim's theory of patriotism
84–7; evaluative labels 53–4; Gellner's
modernist approach 164–7; historical
rise 225–6; homogenization and
multiculturalism 28–34; liberation or
integral 226; Marxist struggle of
oppressed 75–9; modernity of 267–9;
negative assessment of we-constructions
23; political parties 228; Smith's
historical-cultural approach 164, 166–9;
theories of Marx and Durkheim

compared 87–9
natural disasters 234
Norman, W.: citizenship 128–9; three
types of actors 136–7
Northern Ireland: state identity 47–9

Orientalism (Said) 3

Panitch, L.: transnational organizations 15
Park, Robert E. 11
Parsons, Talcott 64; ethnonationalistic
exclusion 65
Payet, J.-P. 304–5
Pizzorno, A. 130
Poland: minority groups 186, 187; national
identity without state 85
politics: Belgian constitutional
restructuring 289–92; charismatic and
tradition power 60; democracy in
Durkheim's theory 82–3; East–West
dichotomies 64–5; EU's forms of power
52–3; Lega Nord as political
entrepreneur of crisis 274–6; modernity
of nationalism 267–9; parties and
political entrepreneurs 228; political
entrepreneurs and collective switching
259–61; separatism in Belgium 294–9
The Politics of Recognition (Taylor) 25
polytaxis 257–8
Popper, Karl: open society 2
postmodernism: and modernism 21–2;
social power and inferiority 135; and
social sciences 1–2
poststructuralism: essentialism and
primordialism 2–4, 20–2
primordialism: deconstructive approach
6–7; examined by poststructuralism 2–4;
poststructuralist approach 20–2
privacy: model of three spheres 146–8
production: lean and just-in-time 15
public sphere: model of three spheres
146–8

Qui a voulu la guerre? (Durkheim) 86

racism: experience in Sweden 105–6;
'new' 101
Ragozin, D. A. 218
Rákosi, Mátyás 201
Rawls, John: reasonableness 132–3
religion *see also* Islam; Jews: Catholic
Church and Italian autonomous
movement 277; discouraged by
Communist Party 200; Durkheim on

Index

60, 83–4; essentialism 24; frame of reference for identity 254–6; identity and Russian Orthodox Church 212, 218–19; individuals as social and cultural actors 136–7; reductionist explanations of fundamentalism 145; Weber's religious economics 60

resource mobilization theory 274, 275

Rex, John 33; model of two domains 148–53; multicultural society 115, 117; two domain theory 159–60

Ricoeur, Paul 18

rights *see* citizenship

The Rights of Minority Cultures (Kymlicka) 129

Robespierre, Maximilien de 176

Romania 187; Hungarians within 204, 206; territorial controversy 189

Romans: foreigners 8

Rosaldo, R. 195

Rossi, Ernesto 284

Rousseau, Félix 298

Russia *see also* Soviet Union: anti-Semitism 218–19; Baltic state Russian community 91; 'Book of Vles' 215–16; demographic trend of Russians Soviet era to present 211–13; development of Slavic ethnogenesis 214–15; neo-Pagan ethno-nationalists 215–21; Orthodox Church 212, 218–19; war with Chechnya 232, 263

Rwanda: reductionist explanations of war 145

Sabella, Marco 284

Said, Edward: *Orientalism* 3

Sanjek, R. 4–5

Schieder, Siegfried 36

Schierup, Carl-Ulrik 33, 34

Schlesinger Jr, Arthur M.: *Disuniting America* 120

Schnapper, D. 45, 182–3

Schutz, Alfred 26; the stranger 93, 95–7

Schwartz, Jonathan: *The Cultural Construction of the 'Stranger' in Social Scientific Thought* 95–7

Scotland. Independence in Europe 52–3; state identity 47–9

separatism *see* politics

Serbia 189; ethnic cleansing 235; mixed fascist and communist history 234; poorer than Croatia 230

Serres, M. 155

Shcherbakov, V. I. 217–18

Shils, E. 2, 24

Simmel, Georg 26; *Bridge and Door* 92, 93–5

Skurlatov, V.I. 216–17, 219

Slovakia: territorial controversy 189, 204

Smith, Anthony D. 26; historical-culturalist approach 164; myth-symbol complex 167–70; recreating ethnicity 214

social sciences: Arendt's three spheres model 146–8, 153–9; Chicago school 11–12; fuzziness of limits 251; ideology 20; modernization 64–8; processes of reproduction 251; processes over systems 6–7, 17–18, 19–22; reviewing classical sociology 26–8; Rex's model of two domains 148–53, 159–60; and science 12–13; self-criticism and debate about macrotheory 57–8; switching frame of reference 251–2; Western model of society 64–5

social sphere 146–8; economic production 157–8

socialism 185–6

Sollors, Werner 105

Soviet Union 189–90 *see also* Russia: anti-ethnic policies 229; citizenship and nationality 191–5; demographic trends of Russians in Soviet republics 211–13; disintegration of empire leads to disintegration of states 238; republics as ethnic interest groups 229–32; results of collapse 52

Spain: state identity 49–50

Spinelli, Altiero 284

Spitaels, Guy 297–8

Stalin, Joseph: ethnic policies 229; question of nationality 181–2

state *see* nation and state

structuralism 7; process-based thinking negates 21

Sweden: crisis of multiculturalism 115–16; ethnic boundaries 92; identity-building in polyethnic settings 103–4; multiculturalism 98

switching frame of reference 251–2; ideologies 261–2; individuals and situational switching 258–9; political and collective switching 259–61; polytaxis 257–8; stabilizing we-groups 265–6; we-group identities 253–7

Switzerland: and the EU 246; immigration and emigration 11; labour and anti-immigration tensions 241–6; national